CICS/6000
Application Development

J. Ranade Workstation Series

CICS/6000
Application Development

Neil Kolban

McGraw-Hill

New York San Francisco Washington, D.C. Auckland Bogotá
Caracas Lisbon London Madrid Mexico City Milan
Montreal New Delhi San Juan Singapore
Sydney Tokyo Toronto

Library of Congress Cataloging-in-Publication Data

Kolban, Neil.
    CICS/6000 application development / Neil Kolban.
        p.   cm.—(J. Ranade workstation series)
    Includes bibliographical references and index.
    ISBN 0-07-036023-5 (pc)
        1. CICS (Computer system)   2. IBM RS/6000 Workstation.
    3. Application software—Development.   I. Title.   II. Series.
    QA76.76.063K645   1996
    005.2—dc20   96-4966
                                                         CIP

McGraw-Hill

A Division of The McGraw-Hill Companies

1 2 3 4 5 6 7 8 9 0   DOC/DOC   9 0 1 0 9 8 7 6

ISBN 0-07-036023-5

*The sponsoring editor for this book was Steve Chapman, the editing supervisor
was Fred Bernardi, and the production supervisor was Suzanne Rapcavage. It
was set in Century Schoolbook by Don Feldman of McGraw-Hill's Professional
Book Group composition unit.*

Printed and bound by R. R. Donnelley & Sons Company.

McGraw-Hill books are available at special quantity discounts to use as premi-
ums and sales promotions, or for use in corporate training programs. For more
information, please write to the Director of Special Sales, McGraw-Hill, 11 West
19th Street, New York, NY 10011. Or contact your local bookstore.

Contents

Preface

The purpose of this book is to describe the operation and use of the CICS/6000 product, including the features not found in any other CICS family product member. CICS/6000 provides a rich and full implementation of the IBM CICS on-line transaction processing environment previously available on other IBM platforms including VSE, MVS OS/400, and OS/2. The CICS/6000 product extends the CICS environment onto the AIX operating system for the IBM RISC System/6000 range of machines.

This book covers the major topics of using, administrating, and developing applications for CICS/6000. A knowledge of CICS, AIX, and C or COBOL programming is assumed for many topics.

AIX skills assumed by this text include

- Concepts of AIX heirarchical directories
- Basic AIX shell commands including **cd, ls, pwd**, and others.

Sample and example programs are written in the C language as opposed to the more CICS-familiar COBOL language both to show the power of the language and to provide a base on which UNIX-literate readers, who are more familiar with C, will better appreciate the power of CICS.

The book contains chapters on the following topics:

Product overview   This chapter provides an overview of the CICS/6000 product and identifies some of the prerequisite products required for CICS's operation. The internal architecture of CICS/6000 is also explained.

Application servers   The CICS/6000 application server is introduced and explained in depth. Understanding CICS application servers is key to understanding CICS/6000's operation.

Configuring CICS/6000   CICS installation and configuration are described from installing the product from supplied media all the way through to starting up and connecting to a running CICS region.

CICS/6000 clients   The CICS/6000 client components are introduced and explained with illustrations of their operation and use. The client components provide users with multiple connectivity option to communicate with a CICS region.

Resource definition   The definition of CICS resources is explained, and each of the different resource types is discussed. CICS resources are used to describe the programs, transactions, and other CICS managed objects.

Programming language   The CICS/6000 programming language is described, with each CICS command available in CICS/6000 being described in turn. Examples of how these commands differ from the same command available on other CICS platforms is provided.

Developing applications   Tools and techniques for developing CICS applications are described, including CICS command translation, program compilation, and debugging. The CICS user-interface technologies are described.

CICS/6000 data resources   Descriptions of each of the CICS data resources are provided, including files, queues, and journals. Creation and access examples for CICS/6000 files are shown.

User exits   The user exits available with CICS/6000 are explained. These exits allow CICS to take alternative actions during its execution. These actions are controlled by user-supplied programs that are defined to CICS.

Communications   One of the key functions of CICS/6000 is its ability to communicate with other CICS platforms to access their data or to allow others to access CICS/6000 data. The key concepts of communication are explained, and the new connectivity options available with CICS/6000 are described.

Client programming   The client programming techniques available to access CICS data and programs are described. These include the external call interface (ECI), the external presentation interface (EPI), and the TCP/IP programming interface called *sockets*. Development of graphic interfaces to CICS transactions is also described with working examples that use the different client programming techniques.

Performance   Performance tuning and information gathering are described, including CICS statistics and monitoring data.

Database   CICS access to databases is described and includes the use of the X/Open XA interface.

Troubleshooting   Some techniques for problem determination are provided to assist with those times when things do not go exactly according to plan.

There are currently two versions of CICS/6000 supported by IBM; these are CICS/6000 V1.2 and CICS for AIX V2.1. With the release of V2.1, the name of the product was changed. For brevity, CICS/6000 will continue to be used throughout this book. The primary difference between these two versions is the underlying level of the AIX operating system on which each has been designed to operate. CICS/6000 V1.2 requires AIX V3.2.5 for its operation, whereas the newer CICS for AIX V2.1 requires AIX V4.1.3. IBM's AIX V4 provides support for symmetric multiprocessing. This book was written using the CICS/6000 V1.2 level of the product but has been reviewed in conjunction with the newer version. The majority of information contained within this book is applicable to both versions.

Neil Kolban

Acknowledgments

I would like to acknowledge my friends and colleagues who reviewed this book and contributed good ideas, many of which are included in these pages. Specifically, I would like to thank my friends at the IBM Dallas System Center for their encouragement and support, particularly Fred Spulecki, Dennis Weiand, Thea Hygh, and Wes Poteet. I would also like to acknowledge the excellent suggestions and ideas shared by the many users of CICS/6000 whom I have met and talked with throughout the United States. Also, I would like to thank the developers, planners, and managers of the CICS/6000 product at IBM's UK Hursley development laboratory with whom I share fond memories are am proud to have once been a collaborator. Finally, and most importantly, I would like to thank my wife Stephanie for her patience, support, and love during the many months it took to write this book.

Foreword

Today, businesses both small and large are becoming increasingly dependent on computer-based information resources and systems. As such, the availability of reliable, scalable, and manageable computing environments with the flexibility to adapt to evolving requirements is crucial for these businesses, and indeed, their very survival often depends on them. On-line Transaction Processing systems are primarily intended to address these most stringent requirements.

Customer Information Control System (CICS) is IBM's premier, and also the most widely used distributed On-line Transaction Processing monitor in the industry today. It is a unique product developed to assist in the most challenging of Information Technology endeavors—to protect the integrity of an organization's resources and to provide an optimal execution environment in which to develop and deploy critical "running the business" applications. No other software technology can offer the same breadth of services and support for such critical applications—integrity of the databases, continuous availability of the application service, performance tuning and load balancing, integration of various resource managers (databases, queue managers, network communications), wide-ranging scalability, and cost savings achieved through efficient resource utilization.

CICS has a long history, having been first developed for the mainframe environment some 20 years ago. However, the CICS brand and products have evolved and remained vital through a process of constant innovation and re-engineering. The team who have responsibility for its development at the IBM development laboratories in Hursley, England, have always responded in a timely fashion to changes in the Information Technology industry and to changing customer requirments, ensuring that the product remains a leading edge environment and a reference for the deployment of "run the business" applications. Another key factor in its success and longevity is the particular attention paid to carrying the installed customer base along with this evolution of the product as well as growing the customer base. The development of the UNIX-based product, CICS/6000, is a good example of this ongoing evolution through innovation.

The key motivating driver for implementing a version of CICS on the RS/6000 and IBM's UNIX operating system, AIX, is the belief that modern transaction processing technology is an important intersecting technology and architectural linchpin for a modern approach to distributed and client/server computing that would facilitate the deployment of business-critical applications. A key design objective was to provide an "open" implementation of CICS. Also it was important that in addition to providing an environment that addressed the deployment of new modern client/server applications, customers could also leverage any existing investment in applications and data either through interoperation with their CICS systems or by easy migration of the applications and data to CICS/6000, and in both cases, leverage their application programming skills and infrastructures. Another objective was to ensure that the very large third-party market for CICS applications, development, and support tools could also exploit this new environment.

The goals for CICS/6000 were achieved via layered and extensible architecture and engineering that fits as a natural extension to the operating system rather than creating a specialized operating system-like environment, as is the case with the mainframe version of CICS. Additionally, CICS/6000 supports and incorporates most of the important industry standards and standard technologies, such as support and integration of XPG and POSIX services, X/OPEN transaction processing, integration and use of OSF/DCE, TCP/IP, and SNA networking services, and SQL for data access. Another major goal for the product in support of its open objective was its availability on non-IBM hardware/software platforms. The engineering was done with this portability requirement in mind and versions of CICS/6000 are now available on Digital, Hewlett Packard, Siemens/Nixdorf, and Sun UNIX-based platforms, through licensing of the code to these vendors.

At this time, the product has been in the field for some two years and is being used very successfully in diverse application scenarios. It is reliably supporting and running some of the largest and most challenging commercial distributed transaction processing applications known to be running on the UNIX operating system today. During this time it has been complemented with extensive and sophisticated systems management software (CICS/SM). The design and engineering has demonstrated its flexibility and scalability through its deployment on IBM's RS/6000 SP2 parallel processing system delivering mainframe class performance, demonstrating its suitability as a scalable network application processor in the emerging world of network-centric computing and electronic commerce.

Neil Kolban was one of the founder members of the CICS/6000 team. His book will provide a very complete and comprehensive coverage of the product which will be invaluable to those people who currently are, or are thinking of, deploying CICS/6000. It also more generally provides a very practical insight into the architecture and engineering involved in the construction of a modern distributed On-line Transaction Processing System.

Tony Storey
IBM (UK) Laboratories
Hursley, England

The CICS/6000 Product

This chapter introduces the CICS/6000 product and provides an overview of its architecture and operation. The prerequisites for CICS's operation are explained, including the Distributed Computing Environment (DCE) and Encina components.

CICS/6000 is the most recent member of the CICS product family. CICS has been available for over 25 years and has become the leading transaction processing environment, allowing applications to be written significantly simpler without having to be concerned with actions to be taken in the event of program or system errors. Thousands of CICS programs, millions of lines of code, and hundreds of company employees skilled in CICS make CICS popular today and into the future.

With the onset of open systems and the growing popularity of the UNIX operating system, IBM developed an implementation of CICS on its own UNIX operating system implementation called *AIX*.

Overview of CICS

This section briefly outlines some of the many features provided by a CICS environment. Discussion of the CICS/6000 product specifics will be covered in subsequent sections.

Transactional services

The function of CICS is to provide a transactional environment for business applications. A *transactional environment* is one in which changes to information made by an application program must all succeed or fail together. It is unacceptable for a transactional application to modify the contents of a file and later fail, resulting in the changes made to the file remaining. Undoing changes made to the file is known as *backing out* the changes. CICS provides an environment in which the modification of file records and other data items is managed such that those changes are automatically undone (backed out) when a transaction or program failure occurs. The application programmer need not explicitly code for failure; CICS implicitly knows about changes made to data by an application and will back out those changes in the event of a failure. A significant benefit of the CICS environment is the knowledge that CICS will provide the data integrity without requiring any explicit logic in the applications. Programs utilizing the CICS environment are considerably smaller and more likely to be correct than those which would otherwise have to contain explicit recovery logic.

In many modern software systems, an application may need to access or update data being managed by a remote system. CICS provides an environment in which two or more CICS systems can cooperate to transactionally perform a single task. Changes made to local file records and to remote file records by the same application will be committed or backed out together. The functions that allow these CICS systems to communicate are called *Inter-System Communication* (ISC).

CICS allows transaction programs to be executed by many users simultaneously without the transactions interfering with each other. An example of interference would be one user updating a record in a file while another user attempts to update the same record. CICS provides locking techniques to prevent uncommitted records in such files from being accessed until those records have committed. This provides another key component of transactional programming known as *consistency*.

Presentation services

Interacting with a user is accomplished by requesting and presenting information and questions to the user. In many environments, the development of the presentation code may be complex and time-consuming, often having to be recoded for each new application. CICS provides a higher-level interface to user interaction by providing a wealth of presentation services. Screens can be described in a high-level language called *Basic Mapping Support* (BMS) that can contain areas of input and output which have names associated with them. The applications can refer to areas on the screens by name and thus disassociate themselves from the actual location of where data are on the screen.

Management services

The definitions of new programs, transactions, maps (screens), and users are also provided by high-level CICS management services. CICS keeps track of all the different types of information related to the successful operation of a CICS environment. This also includes security attributes to prevent unauthorized access to files and other data items that only certain users should be allowed to access.

CICS benefits

The benefits of developing applications within a CICS environment quickly become apparent when considering the task of providing services similar to those provided by CICS. The resultant smaller programs can concentrate on the business logic and rules for the task being undertaken. The complex but necessary task of maintaining data integrity and consistency across all types of unexpected failures is provided implicitly by the CICS environment.

CICS also provides job or task scheduling capabilities not found in the native AIX operating system environment.

Introduction to CICS/6000

CICS/6000 is a new implementation of the CICS transaction processing environment. It was designed and implemented to take advantage of the functions available on the AIX environment to perform identical services to those found on other CICS platforms. It also was designed to exploit the services of the AIX operating system and other prerequisite products to achieve high performance coupled with high reliability.

Functionally, it was designed to allow applications that contain CICS statements and commands written in either the C or COBOL programming language to execute within a transactional environment. The CICS models of file control, queue management, communications, and presentation services all were provided. Programs that currently execute on other CICS platforms can be ported or migrated to CICS/6000 with relative ease. Little or no program changes are required. Users with current skills in CICS can exploit their skills in the CICS/6000 environment without requiring a substantial retraining effort.

The transactions supplied with other CICS systems are also present on CICS/6000; these include CECI, CEMT, CEDF, and CEBR. New transactions are also included to provide easier migration and management and additional functions not found on other CICS platforms.

Architecture

CICS/6000 was designed to use the services of the Encina toolkit developed by Transarc Corporation. The Encina toolkit is comprised of services to allow the development of an on-line transaction processing (OLTP) transaction monitor. Since any OLTP environment requires services such as those provided by Encina for operation, the decision to not have CICS duplicate Encina functions allowed the CICS product designers to concentrate their efforts on just the CICS functions. The following services are provided by the Encina toolkit:

- Logging
- Transaction management

- Recoverable files
- Volume management
- Transactional communications
- XA database integration

The Encina toolkit utilizes the services of yet another product called *Distributed Computing Environment* (DCE). DCE provides services to allow applications to be written that may execute in a distributed environment. A distributed application is one in which, during the course of its execution, some of its task may be processed in multiple machines. The functions provided by DCE include

- Remote Procedure Calls (RPC)
- Security
- Multithreading
- Name services

Encina utilizes the services of DCE to allow many of its constituent components to execute in multiple machines. CICS/6000 also uses the DCE services to allow a single instance of CICS to execute distributed to take advantage of multiple machines with different characteristics.

CICS/6000 and AIX

The AIX operating system has an architecture consistent with other implementations of the UNIX operating system. Included in this architecture are many concepts that are confusing to anyone new to UNIX. Readers who are not familiar with UNIX or AIX are encouraged to review some fundamental UNIX books. The following section describes some of the key UNIX concepts used in the remainder of this book.

AIX processes

Whenever a new AIX program is started, usually at the request of the user, AIX creates an environment in which that program may execute. This environment is known as a *process*. An AIX process can be considered an address space that includes program code and program data as well as other program execution characteristics such as open files, user information, and priority. An AIX process provides isolation between one executing program and another. Any attempt to access machine memory outside that allocated to the process is trapped, disallowing a badly behaved program from corrupting other programs. The abstract concept of a process also may be used for administration, allowing lists of currently running processes (programs) to be generated and accounting information such as CPU utilization to be gathered and providing a means to terminate a program that otherwise will not end. AIX processes are assigned unique numeric identifiers called *processids* when created.

The list of currently running processes may be determined by the AIX command **ps,** which has a rich set of options to produce many different types of report.

AIX file systems

AIX files are stored on disk as flat, unstructured arrays of bytes. These files have names associated with them. Files may be grouped together usually because they have a common purpose in a construct known as a *directory*. An AIX directory contains both files and other directories that may themselves contain both files and directories. The organization of directories creates a treelike structure that is hierarchical in nature. A directory that contains another directory is said to be the *parent* of the subdirectory, while the subdirectory is termed the *child*. Every directory has a parent except the topmost directory, which has no parent. Like the tree analogy, this topmost directory is called the *root* directory.

Files and directories are stored on disk. For administration reasons, related files and directories may be stored on the same areas of disk to allow backup and restoration of those files as a whole. Additionally, space allocated for files and directories may wish to be bounded to prevent all the available disk space to be consumed by one set of files, preventing others from growing. AIX provides the concept of a *file system* to partition groups of files and directories onto the same area of disk. File systems are of configurable and modifiable sizes and are mapped onto the AIX hierarchical directory structures. From an end user's perspective, file systems are not normally visible. When changing from one directory to another, it is not noticeable that the underlying file system has changed.

AIX shells and commands

The AIX operating system provides primitive functions to perform tasks. These tasks include opening files, writing data, starting new processes, getting input from the user, and many others. These operating system services may be invoked by a program making requests. The program requests services by performing a system call to the operating system. When the operating system receives the request, the request is processed, and a response is returned to the caller. All these tasks are executed at a low level.

To allow higher-level activities to be performed, AIX provides a set of programs known as *shells* or *command interpreters* that prompt the user for input and execute commands based on the user's response. Shells are commonly used to invoke other programs and commands. When a user enters a command name at the shell prompt, the shell looks in the AIX file systems for a file of the command name entered and creates a new process containing the program contained in the file. The shell normally suspends its execution until the program started by the command has completed. Programs may be started optionally from shells such that the shell immediately prompts for another command before the preceding one has completed. This is known as running a program in the *background.*

Shells also provide a simple interpreted language known as *shell script.* Commands entered that correspond to files containing shell script are executed by the shell without starting a new program. The shell scripts may in turn start other programs, the output of which may be used to control the operation of the script.

CICS and AIX processes

CICS/6000 exploits many features of the AIX operating system for its execution and management. AIX provides process control and multitasking control to allow multiple processes to seemingly execute simultaneously. CICS/6000 allows AIX to handle the dispatching of AIX processes. The AIX process scheduler controls the concurrent execution of CICS transactions.

CICS/6000 executes as a set of AIX processes. These processes execute user-written programs in a transactional environment.

Each user program contains EXEC CICS statements that are translated by a CICS-provided utility called the *CICS translator.* The output of the translator is a source file that has had the CICS statements replaced with native C or COBOL statements. Once the program has been translated, it is compiled by a C or COBOL compiler. The CICS statements are replaced by calls to the CICS runtime. These programs are executed within the CICS environment; they may not be executed directly from the AIX shells. When a user submits a request to execute a transaction, CICS loads the compiled program into an AIX process that CICS calls an *application server.* The loaded program is then given control within the process. When the program ends, the application server process is again available to execute other programs on behalf of the user. Since the application server processes are constantly running, the overhead of starting a new AIX process is not required for each new transaction request. Application servers may be managed within a CICS environment. A minimum and maximum number of application servers may be configured.

When a CICS statement is executed, an area of AIX memory containing both code and data is attached to the process to access CICS code and internal control structures. The ability to dynamically attach memory to an AIX process is an AIX feature called *shared memory.* Once the command has completed, the shared memory is detached. This prevents accidental modification of critical data structures within CICS. This feature prevents one CICS transaction from accidentally damaging the operation of another.

A CICS-provided transaction scheduler process accepts incoming transaction requests. The scheduler will schedule the transaction on the first available application server process. If no application server is currently available, the scheduler will queue the transaction until an application server becomes available. The scheduler also prioritizes queued transactions.

CICS and AIX file systems

The AIX file systems are hierarchical file structures holding files and directories. CICS/6000 uses the AIX file systems to hold CICS resource definition files, extrapartition transient data queues, programs, and maps. With the AIX file system, a user can create, copy, or delete files. CICS allows access to AIX files using the Extrapartition Transient Data API commands. Native AIX file commands also may be used in CICS transactions under certain circumstances. CICS/6000 uses the services of an Encina component called the *Structured File Server* (SFS) for management of CICS recoverable and nonrecoverable files. These files can be accessed using the EXEC CICS READ, WRITE, DELETE API. Additionally, CICS uses files to manage auxiliary temporary storage and intrapartition transient data. These files are stored and managed by the SFS. When CICS/6000 is installed, the AIX programs that comprise the CICS product are stored in the /usr file system in the /usr/lpp/cics directory. AIX products are stored in the /usr/lpp directory by convention.

AIX SMIT management

AIX provides a powerful utility called the *Systems Management Interface Tool,* or SMIT. SMIT allows the user to administer many AIX and application-related tasks through a series of menus and panels. Each entry on a panel allows the user to select and modify options relating to the task being attempted. In many instances, SMIT will allow the user to select from a series of choices. Once a panel has been completed, SMIT will execute an AIX command to perform the specified task. Each of the commands executed by SMIT could have been executed from the AIX command line, but through SMIT, the administrator need not remember as many commands and options.

When CICS/6000 is installed, it adds a set of additional panels and menus into the SMIT database. These new SMIT panels and menus provide the administrator with a simpler interface to manage CICS/6000. Almost all CICS administration and definition tasks may be accomplished through SMIT. CICS/6000 does not provide the CEDA administration transaction. Resource definition and activation are performed through the SMIT interface instead.

AIX Subsystem Resource Controller

The AIX Subsystem Resource Controller, or SRC, is a mechanism to control the start-up and shutdown of groups of AIX processes. SRC allows the definition of subsystems such as TCP/IP, mail, SNA, and others. Through SRC, an administer can request the start-up of a subsystem by name. SRC will know the correct start-up commands and destination of output. Once SRC has started a specified subsystem, its operation can be monitored and controlled through a set of SRC commands. When termination of a subsystem is required, SRC can again be requested to stop that subsystem. Detailed knowledge of start-up and shutdown commands is not required. SRC provides a consistent interface to the start-up and shutdown tasks.

CICS/6000 utilizes the AIX SRC to start and stop CICS/6000-related servers and processes. Specifically, SRC is used to control

- The Encina SFSs
- The Encina PPC Gateways
- The CICS/6000 regions

All these tasks may be accomplished through CICS/6000-supplied scripts and commands or through the AIX SMIT panels for CICS/6000. Figure 1.1 shows the SRC and the CICS/6000-related servers.

AIX tracing

AIX provides a high-function trace-collection mechanism. CICS/6000 integrates with this trace strategy by allowing CICS/6000 trace items to be merged with other AIX-generated trace entries produced by the operating system or other products also utilizing the AIX trace mechanism.

CICS/6000 and DCE

The Distributed Computing Environment (DCE) is a set of services that simplifies the development of distributed applications. The goal of DCE is to provide a set of services on heterogeneous environments that will allow applications on one machine to make use of services from another machine.

Not all the features available from DCE are utilized by CICS/6000. Only those which pertain to CICS/6000 will be discussed, and these are

- Remote Procedure Calls (RPC)

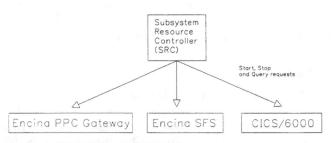

Figure 1.1 AIX SRC and CICS/6000.

- Cell Directory Services (CDS)
- Security services
- Threading support

Remote Procedure Call

The Remote Procedure Call (RPC) is a mechanism that allows a client application to make a request for services to a server application. From a programmer's perspective, the RPC call looks like a normal function call. The RPC runtime makes the network connection to the provider of the service, and the server provides the service. When the server completes the service, the caller of the RPC is informed of the result. From the client's point of view, the function call may have been a local function call, and the client program is unaware that the service was provided remotely. The RPC is integrated with the other components of DCE to provide security for the remote call and lookup services for finding the provider of the service.

Cell Directory Services

Machines that participate in DCE activities, such as an application on one machine utilizing RPC to communicate with a server application on another, must be defined within a group of machines known as a *cell*. The concept of a cell is used only for administrative purposes; the machines that comprise a cell may be on the same local area network or distributed over a wider area. Cells are named entities, and an application executing in a machine in one cell may make a call to a server application in another cell, providing there is a communication path between the two cells.

Cell Directory Services (CDS) provides a network-wide naming scheme to locate other DCE services by name. When a client application wishes to utilize the services of a server application, CDS may be consulted to determine the location of the server by name.

CDS maintains a hierarchical naming structure containing directories and objects (servers). When the SFS and other DCE servers start, they advertise themselves in CDS name space. When CICS/6000 wishes to utilize these servers, their actual location is obtained by querying the CDS name space for the name of the machine on which the server is executing or available.

When the CICS/6000 regions are started, the locations of the regions are also advertised within CDS name space. This allows CICS/6000 clients (users of CICS/6000) to locate CICS/6000 regions without having to be explicitly configured with their locations.

A CDS name usually begins with the sequence / . : /. This signifies that the local "cell" of DCE machines will be used rather than attempting to contact a remote DCE cell. CICS/6000 creates a directory called / . : /cics/ once it has been configured. CICS/6000 regions will advertise themselves in this directory when they start.

Security services

DCE provides a security service for verifying that a user of a service is actually allowed to make use of that service. To achieve this, DCE maintains a concept of a user identity known as a *principal*. A principal may be thought of as a userid. Principals have attributes that include a password. To access a DCE server, a user must be authenticated as a DCE principal that has sufficient permissions to access the service in the desired way.

The DCE security service provides both authentication and authorization access control. *Authentication* is used to verify that the user making the request is really the user that is claimed. *Authorization* controls whether the user has access to the requested service.

The SFS and other DCE servers provide authorization control and thus prevent unwanted or accidental modification. CICS/6000 also utilizes authorization control to restrict the set of users who can access the region. CICS/6000 userids and passwords are also mapped to DCE principals and passwords.

DCE authentication.   The process of *authentication* means proving to the system that you are who you claim to be. In most computer systems, this is achieved by supplying a user name (who I claim to be) and a password (proof that I am who I claim to be). In a distributed environment such as that provided by DCE, this task becomes more complex. Since DCE allows multiple machines to be members of a cell, a user should be allowed to authenticate from any one of those machines. To achieve this, DCE provides a concept known as the *registry*. The registry is a DCE-maintained database of DCE principals, passwords, accounts, and other principal and security information. The registry is itself a special DCE application, and communication with the registry is achieved by means of DCE RPCs. On the machine(s) running the registry service, a DCE server application executes that has a process name called **secd**. Machines that wish to access the registry contain a client access process called **sec_clientd.**

DCE provides a programmable API to access the registry and validate principals and passwords. A set of commands that use the DCE security API is also provided to work and authenticate with the registry.

When a request is made to the registry to authenticate a principal, the principal and password are supplied. If the registry accepts that the principal is who it claims to be, a ticket is granted to allow that principal to perform security services. The environment in which the principal can perform authenticated work is known as the *login context.*

From a user's perspective, a login context is created by executing the DCE-supplied command **dce_login.** This command takes a principal name and a password as parameters and performs authentication with the DCE security services and the registry. If successful, a login context is created. Specifically, a new AIX shell is created. Any commands executed in this shell are authenticated with DCE with the principal specified. If the shell is exited, the login context for that shell is destroyed.

When a DCE login context is obtained from the DCE security service, an authorization ticket is created that allows the user to execute DCE applications and commands in the secure context.

The ticket that is granted by the security service has a specified lifetime. After the lifetime of the ticket has passed, the login context is invalidated until the user reauthenticates with DCE by supplying the principal and password again. The lifetime of a login context can be configured on a per-principal basis and queried with the DCE **klist** command.

DCE server application authentication.   The DCE security API requires that a principal and password be supplied when authenticating with the security service. A user may create a secure login context by specifying a principal name and password. For applications that are designed to execute without user interaction, the creation of a login context is more complex. When a server application wishes to authenticate with security, it too must supply a principal name and password. It would be self-defeating to have a password hardcoded or kept in an AIX file in plain text. The principal could be easily undermined by scanning the executable for strings or reading a file containing the password. The DCE security API allows for such circumstances by providing a mechanism known as *password* or *key caching*. In DCE documentation, a key is identical to a password.

DCE provides a set of API calls for storing and retrieving DCE keys from AIX files. The keys themselves are stored in the files as unreadable strings of bytes. It is not possible to work back to the actual password for a principal given the encrypted key in a file. The file contains both the passwords and the principal names associated with these passwords. The files that contain DCE keys are known as *keytab* files.

CICS/6000 and Encina make extensive use of keytab files. The following CICS and Encina servers authenticate themselves with DCE using keytab files:

- Each CICS/6000 region

- Encina SFSs

- Encina PPC Gateways

- CICS cicsteld telnet servers

DCE authorization.   Once a principal has authenticated with DCE, it still may only be able to perform a limited set of tasks. It would be meaningless if each DCE principal could perform exactly the same set of tasks. Each DCE server application may utilize DCE API to provide authorization to its functions based on the DCE principal making the request. The set of functions that may be performed by a specific principal is controlled by a DCE server's *Access Control List* (ACL). These ACLs specify which principals may perform which tasks. The actual tasks that may be performed by a specific DCE server are governed by that DCE server.

ACL access is governed by the following principal and account parameters:

- Principal name
- DCE groups to which the principal belongs
- Default access if the user is not authenticated with DCE security

CICS/6000 utilizes DCE authorization to provide a high level of security access to each of the CICS- and Encina-related servers. To access a CICS function, the principal attempting access must belong to a set of predefined DCE groups. These DCE groups include

`cics_admin`   Allowed to perform administrative CICS tasks (includes cics_users and all other CICS/DCE groups)

`cics_users`   Allowed to access the CICS region as a client (e.g., cicsterm)

`cics_regions`   The DCE group of which all CICS region principals must be a member

`cics_sfs`   The DCE group of which all SFS server principals must be a member

`cics_ppcgwy`   The DCE group of which all PPC Gateway server principals must be a member

Threading support

DCE provides a model of multithreading that may be utilized by DCE applications. Multithreading allows an application to create multiple threads of control within a single application. This allows a program to continue doing additional work while one or more of its threads are blocked awaiting additional work or response to previous work. In a DCE RPC server, each incoming RPC call will cause a new thread to be created to handle that request. This allows a single RPC server to handle multiple RPC requests simultaneously.

CICS/6000 makes extensive use of DCE multithreading support. Today's uniprocessor machines allow only one thread to really have CPU control at any one point in time. With Symmetric Multi-Processing (SMP), multiple processors exist in a machine. CICS/6000 will take advantage of this new technology by allowing multiple CICS tasks and threads to execute simultaneously on the multiple processors.

CICS/6000 and Encina

CICS/6000 utilizes the services of the Encina OLTP toolkit. Some services are utilized internally, while others are exposed externally. A design goal of CICS/6000 was to present both a usage and administrative interface that had a strong CICS feel. The majority of the underlying Encina technology has been hidden from the CICS/6000 user.

The services that are used internally include

- Client log services
- XA database support
- Transaction management
- Transactional RPC
- Peer to Peer Executive

The services that are used externally are

- Structured File Server (SFS)
- Peer to Peer Gateway

The Structured File Server

This section describes the Encina Structured File Server, including its operation and how it is utilized by CICS.

Operation of the SFS.   The Encina Structured File Server (the SFS) provides the services of a record-oriented recoverable file system. The AIX operating system, like other UNIX operating systems, maintains files as a stream of contiguously accessible bytes of data. The model of CICS programming, however, is that of record-oriented files with indices and various modes of access. The modes of access that CICS requires are keyed, sequential, and relative record access. These correspond with KSDS, ESDS, and RRDS in the mainframe VSAM terminology. The SFS provides both the record-oriented view of files and modes of access that are comparable with those required by CICS.

The SFS also provides the model of recoverable files. The addition, deletion, or modification of records within an SFS file can be accomplished within a transactional context. The changes to the file are not made permanent until the transaction has been committed. If the transaction aborts, the changes made to the file are undone. The process of undoing these changes is termed *rollback*. The SFS is able to achieve the rollback by recording information required to undo the changes. The information logged may be "before images" or "inverse operations." The actual data logged are not important to understanding the operation of the SFS. The SFS is an instance of an Encina toolkit application. It utilizes the other Encina server capabilities, including logging, volume management, and transaction management. The SFS utilizes the log services to record the information required to undo a particular transactional request.

The SFS executes as a single AIX process that registers itself as a DCE server in the DCE CDS name space. A client application of the SFS may send requests to be processed. The requests usually will consist of file open, read, write, update, and other file-related activities. The requests made by a client would be coded in the client as C language function calls that will be resolved by an Encina-supplied library. Within the library, DCE RPC calls will be made to the server to process the request. These RPC calls will be authenticated by the DCE security service to ensure that the client making the request has appropriate authority and privileges. A client may make a request to the SFS in either transactional or nontransactional mode. In the nontransactional mode, when a request modifies the contents of a file, the changes are made permanent immediately. In a transactional request, the changes are not made permanent until the transaction explicitly commits.

The Encina SFS, like other DCE servers, can be contacted by client applications using the DCE RPC. Because of the SFS's integration with DCE, the server need not execute on the same machine as a client that requires access. Any client who has DCE RPC access to the server and appropriate security can issue requests against the server. When the SFS starts, it advertises its availability within the DCE CDS name space. This allows clients to locate the SFS server without having to know explicitly on which machine it is currently operating. The SFS may be located on a separate machine from any CICS regions. A single SFS also may be utilized by multiple CICS regions simultaneously and with data integrity maintained.

CICS utilization of the SFS.   CICS/6000 is itself a client of the SFS, internally making requests to the server. The requests that are made correspond to the CICS file control commands such as EXEC CICS READ, EXEC CICS WRITE, EXEC CICS UPDATE, and others. CICS also maps certain other CICS constructs such as transient data and temporary storage queues onto predefined SFS files. Within a CICS transaction, the updates made to a recoverable file cause transactional requests to be made to the SFS. When the transaction ends or an EXEC CICS SYNCPOINT command is issued, the SFS will commit all changes made to the file up to that point in the transaction. If the transaction abends, the SFS will undo recoverable changes made to the file. In the event that the SFS loses contact with a CICS region and recoverable work is still in progress, the changes made to the SFS file will be backed out automatically or may be forced by administrator intervention.

CICS/6000 administration of the SFS.   The creation of the DCE principals, CDS directories, and ACLs is performed through CICS administration commands. A design intent for CICS/6000 was to minimize the amount of Encina administration knowledge required by a CICS/6000 administrator. Administration of SFS includes

- Creation of DCE entries
- SFS start-up
- SFS shutdown
- SFS file creation

Even with all these CICS/6000-related administration options, knowledge of SFS administration and commands will still be required. CICS commands are not provided for

- Backing up SFS files
- Monitoring free file space on SFS volumes
- Providing access control to SFS files
- Forcing the outcome of "hung" transactions
- Controlling trace during problem determination

Each of these tasks will be discussed in later chapters. SFS instance creation includes the creation of the DCE server principal, caching the password of the principal in a DCE keytab file, creating DCE CDS directory entries, and setting appropriate ACLs for the server. The first time the server is started, it should be started *cold*. This is actually an artificial term, since the SFS is always started the same way. A cold start is a start of the SFS followed by the deletion of any SFS files it may be managing. Subsequent starts of the SFS usually will be in *warm* mode. If the SFS is restarted cold, any files will be lost. This may be disastrous if recent SFS file backups are not available.

The PPC Executive and the PPC Gateway

Encina provides an implementation of the SNA LU6.2 CPI-C API over the TCP/IP protocol. This component of Encina is called the *Peer-to-Peer Executive*. An Encina-based application can interoperate with another Encina-based transaction using this API. Both partners in the communication can perform transactional work with full integrity.

A companion Encina product to the PPC Executive is the PPC Gateway. This is a server application that accepts incoming PPC Executive TCP/IP flows and converts these requests into SNA flows onto an SNA network. The PPC Gateway also can accept incoming SNA flows and direct these to a PPC Executive listening application.

CICS/6000 utilizes the PPC Executive as the underlying transmission protocol for CICS/6000-to-CICS/6000 intercommunication. If CICS/MVS connectivity is required, the Encina PPC Executive also may be utilized as the interface to a PPC Gateway for SNA connection. The PPC Gateway need only be used if full synclevel 2 communication is required. If synclevels 0 and 1 are acceptable, CICS/6000 can make direct SNA calls to have SNA flows take place.

CICS/6000 and Encina: Summary

In summary,

- The Encina SFS provides a recoverable, record-oriented file model for client applications.

■ The SFS is used to manage files used by CICS internally to hold such data items as recoverable storage queues and CICS terminals that have connected. The SFS also holds files that may be modified by programs via EXEC CICS file control commands. Figure 1.2 shows the logical relationship between these servers.

CICS/6000 and Communications

CICS/6000 provides connectivity to other CICS systems. The connectivity used may be either TCP/IP to another CICS/6000 system or SNA to a CICS system on a different platform. Full CICS ISC is supported, including

■ Transaction routing
■ Function shipping
■ Distributed program link
■ Asynchronous processing
■ Distributed transaction processing

Communication from CICS/6000 to an SNA-connected CICS system is provided via the AIX SNA server or services product and the Encina Peer to Peer Gateway.

CICS/6000 Architecture Summary

The diagram shown in Fig. 1.3 illustrates the relationship between the various AIX, DCE, Encina, and CICS components. As can be seen, CICS attempts

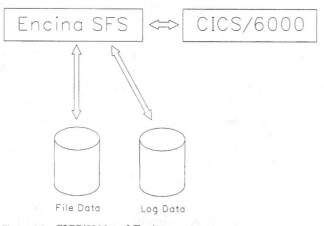

Figure 1.2 CICS/6000 and Encina servers.

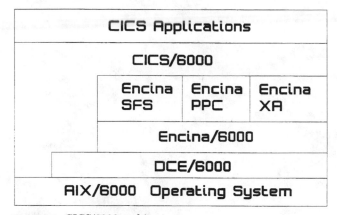

Figure 1.3 CICS/6000 architecture.

to mask as much of its underlying implementation on top of other components as possible. Only the administrator of a CICS/6000 environment should need to be concerned with DCE, Encina, and other related technologies. CICS programmers and end users may utilize CICS without knowledge of its base technologies.

The CICS/6000
Application Server

When CICS is requested to execute a transaction, a program associated with the transaction is started in one of the CICS/6000 processes known as *application servers*. These AIX processes are the key to CICS/6000 program execution. The CPU cost of creating an AIX process is relatively high. Because of this, CICS creates a set or pool of these processes when CICS is started initially. Application servers may be reused by subsequent transactions when the preceding transaction completes. This optimization significantly reduces the execution cost of running a CICS transaction by effectively removing the cost of creating a new AIX process.

The number of application server processes started at CICS region start-up is configurable. CICS also allows dynamic creation of additional application servers when the pool of available processes is exhausted and additional concurrent transaction requests arrive. Each application server is utilized by a CICS transaction until the transaction fully completes; only then is the process freed for utilization by another CICS transaction. As a result, if CICS programs are relatively long running, the utilization of the application servers may be high. A minimum and maximum number of server processes may be configured. CICS creates a new application server process only if the configured maximum number of processes has not been reached. Requests to start new CICS programs received after the maximum number of processes has been reached are queued in the transaction scheduler component of CICS. Associated with application servers is an attribute known as the *server idle period*. This is a time interval specified in seconds. If an application server does not receive additional requests to execute programs within the idle time-out period, the application server shuts down if doing so would not cause the number of servers to fall below the minimum. Although application servers can be stopped to release resources owned by those processes, the idle time-out period should not be set too low. The default idle time-out value of 5 minutes should be increased to 15 minutes. The cost of starting and stopping application server processes themselves is not insignificant. CICS internally executes transactions periodically. These internal transactions are short-lived but do consume an application server for the duration of their execution.

Since an application server is reused between transaction executions, the state of the process must be maintained. An AIX process's state includes

- AIX open-file descriptors
- TCP/IP socket descriptors
- Environment variables
- Shared memory
- Dynamically allocated memory
- Current working directory
- Process priority

Care must be taken to clean up the state of an application server should a CICS program modify any of these attributes. A CICS program that opens an AIX file directly and fails to close the file before the program ends would result in the file remaining open until the end of the application server. If this continued, a subsequent execution of the program within the same application server might result in failure, since AIX allows only a finite number of files to be open concurrently within a single AIX process.

It is possible to utilize the state of a process for functional or performance enhancements. If a TCP/IP socket connection is opened to a remote server, the socket could be reused by subsequent CICS programs without having to remake the connection. Such programming practices should be avoided. The architecture of CICS may change, and utilization of such a function is not portable to other non-UNIX-based CICS platforms.

CICS database applications that utilize the XA interface form connections to the databases through connections maintained by the application servers. This is addressed further in Chap. 28, "Database restrictions with XA."

The AIX processid of the application server executing a CICS application may be obtained programmatically or from the output of the CEMT INQUIRE TASK transaction. This attribute may be used to log transaction output or to utilize AIX-based applications to inquire on the state of a process. AIX commands such as **ps, svmon,** and **kill** each require AIX process IDs as parameters. It is not advised to use **kill** against an application server unless a complete CICS stall has occurred (and only as a *very* last resort).

The Region Definition (RD) attributes that affect application server creation are

- **MinServer**   Minimum number of application servers
- **MaxServer**   Maximum number of application servers

- **ServerIdleLimit**   Number of seconds that an idle application server will remain

The **MinServer** and **MaxServer** attributes may be changed dynamically during the execution of a CICS region using the CEMT INQUIRE TCLASS command. Changing these values may result in an immediate increase in the number of application servers if the minimum is increased or an immediate stop of idle application servers if the maximum is reduced.

Program Caching

When an application server loads a CICS program for execution, the code and data of the program may be cached in the application server's storage. This allows the program to be reexecuted without a corresponding read of the code from disk. Effectively, the program remains in memory as long as the application server is available. Programs are cached in particular application servers, and the same program may be cached in more than one. CICS does not keep track of which application servers have cached which programs but simply allocates tasks to first-available application servers. Program caching behaves differently based on the language in which the programs are written.

C program caching

C programs that are cached do not have their static storage reinitialized at reinvocation of the program. C programs that are to be cached must ensure that they explicitly initialize statics, not assume that variables are initialized to zero, and ensure that sensitive data are not left in variables at program termination.

Program symbolic maps also should be reinitialized to zero or else previous data may be redisplayed when the map is sent to the display.

CICS and C language programs are not cached by default. To enable a C program to be cached, two attributes must be set. The first is specified in the Region Definition (RD) in the **CProgramCacheSize** attribute. This attribute controls the number of concurrent programs that may be held dynamically within an application server's memory. The default value for this attribute is zero, meaning no programs will be cached. Changing this attribute to a nonzero value potentially allows that number of programs to be held in memory by one server. The second attribute is the **Resident** value in the Program Definition (PD) for an individual program. For C language programs, this may have a value of yes or no, stating whether the program is eligible for caching or not. Programs defined as eligible will only be cached if the **CProgramCacheSize** is nonzero. Programs held in an application server's cache are removed from the cache whenever

- A SET PROGRAM NEWCOPY command is issued against the program.

- The Program Definition for a program is dynamically changed to **Resident = no.**

- The number of programs specified by the Region Definition **CProgramCacheSize** has been reached, in which case the least recently used program will be purged from the cache.

Care must be taken with C program caching because modifying the underlying executable in the file system corresponding to the CICS program will not necessarily cause that program to be used at next reference. A SET PROGRAM NEWCOPY command should be issued against the program to ensure that the latest version of the program as found on disk will be used.

The program shown in Fig. 2.1 was used to test C language program caching. The program performs a CICS LINK to a second CICS program 1000 times. With caching disabled, the 1000 links executed in 40 seconds, whereas with program caching for the called program enabled, the 1000 links took only 4 seconds to execute. This shows that for this short application, the bulk of the time was spent continually loading a new copy of the program into memory.

```
/* Source of CACHE program.   This program performs a 1000 EXEC CICS */
/* LINK statements to call the TIME2 program.                        */

#include <stdio.h>
#include <time.h>

main()
{
    time_t          timeStart, timeEnd;
    int             i;

    time(&timeStart);
    fprintf(stderr, "Time at start: %s", ctime(&timeStart));

    for (i=0; i<1000; i++)
    {
        EXEC CICS LINK PROGRAM("TIME2");
    }

    time(&timeEnd);
    fprintf(stderr, "Time at end: %s", ctime(&timeEnd));

    EXEC CICS RETURN;
}




/* Source of the TIME2 program */

main()
{
    EXEC CICS RETURN;
}
```

Figure 2.1   C language samples for caching timings.

COBOL program caching

CICS programs written in the COBOL language are also cached by CICS application servers. These programs are loaded into memory by the COBOL runtime. Whenever CICS loads a new program, it first checks to see if that program has been loaded previously. If it has, the runtime need not be reloaded with the program. COBOL runtime modules are loaded into each instance of an application server. If a new version of the COBOL program is generated by recompiling a modified source program, CICS must be informed that it should use the new COBOL program as opposed to using one that may have been cached previously. The **CEMT SET PROGRAM(name) NEW-COPY** transaction should be used to flag that a new copy of the program is required.

The caching of COBOL programs by the COBOL runtime can be disabled by switching on a COBOL runtime flag using the **COBSW** environment variable in the CICS region environment file. Setting this variable to the value **−l0** (note that this is a lowercase letter L) disables COBOL program caching. This may be a good idea during application testing to ensure that the very latest version of the program is read from disk whenever referenced.

Transaction Scheduler

Priorities

When a CICS client such as cicsterm, cicsteld, ECI, or EPI submits a transaction start request or a request from a remote CICS region is received, the request is first handled by the CICS/6000 transaction-scheduling logic. Since an application server is required to execute a transaction, if too few application servers are configured or the load is too high, transactions may have to be queued by the scheduler until application servers complete their current tasks. When an application server becomes available, the transaction scheduler must decide which of the queued transactions should be next executed. To assist the scheduler, transactions, users, and terminals each have a priority associated with them. When a user submits a transaction start request, the user's priority, the transaction priority, and the terminal priority on which the transaction was started are added together. This combined priority value is used to determine which transaction should be started next. The higher the value, the higher is the priority.

User, transaction, and terminal priorities are specified by the **Priority** attribute in each of the resource definition classes of user, transaction, and terminal. The attribute may be assigned a decimal number ranging from 0 to 255. If the combined value of all the priorities is greater than 255, 255 is used.

Transaction start requests of equal priority will be processed in the order in which they were received.

Transaction classes

CICS/6000 provides a mechanism to restrict the number of transactions of specified types from executing concurrently. This can be used to provide a load-balancing scheme to prevent too many CPU-intensive transactions from monopolizing the application servers. CICS defines 10 different groups or classes. Individual transactions may be associated with one or none of these classes. When a transaction is submitted that belongs to a transaction class, if the maximum number of transactions for that class are already running, the transaction will be queued by the scheduler until the number of executing transactions in the class falls below the maximum. Different transactions can be associated with the same transaction class, so the scheduler works on classes and not transaction names. If two transactions belonging to the same class are queued, the one with the higher priority or the one received first will be scheduled when the number of transactions running in that class is reduced.

The number of transactions allowed to execute for a specific class is specified in the **ClassMaxTask** attribute in the Region Definition (RD). This attribute specifies the number of transactions concurrently executable for each of the 10 classes by specifying 10 numbers that are separated by commas. The position of the number associates with that class. For example, the value

```
ClassMaxTask = 1,1,4,10,1,10,1,1,1,1
```

specifies that for classes 1, 2, 5, 7, 8, 9, and 10, only 1 transaction at a time is allowed to execute. For class 3, 4 transactions are allowed, and for classes 4 and 6, 10 concurrent transactions of those classes may execute.

Associated with the classes is another attribute called **ClassMaxTaskLim** that is also held in the Region Definition (RD). This attribute specifies the maximum number of transactions of the specified class that may be running or queued at one time. If the maximum number of transactions of a class are queued or running, the arrival of another transaction of that class will cause the new transaction to be purged with a message indicating the transaction is disabled be returned to the CICS transaction invoker. This resource attribute is specified as 10 positional numbers corresponding to the classes. The numbers must be separated by commas. A value of 0 specifies that there is no limit to the number of transactions for the class that may be queued.

By default, a transaction is not associated with a particular class. To associate a transaction with a class, the class number must be defined in the **TClass** attribute in the transaction's resource definition (TD). A value of 1 through 10 specifies the associated class, while a value of **none** specifies that the transaction is not associated with any particular class.

Chapter

3

Configuring CICS/6000

This chapter describes installing and configuring the CICS/6000 product. This chapter covers the following topics:

- Installing CICS/6000
- Using the Encina Structured File Server
- Defining a CICS region
- Starting and stopping a CICS region
- Distributing CICS

Installing CICS/6000

Installing CICS/6000 is achieved by following a series of steps, each of which is simple, but when taken as a whole, the process appears to be complicated. As experience with CICS/6000 grows, the steps used to install and configure CICS/6000 become clearer, but the first time may seem confusing. This chapter will list the major tasks and explain the purpose behind each task.

The first task of installation is to load the CICS/6000 software from the IBM-supplied media on which it was delivered onto the file system on the target machine. The data format of the CICS/6000 product on the tape is known as the **installp** format after the name of the command that is used to load the software. When any AIX product is installed by installp, its installation is marked in a database called the *Object Data Manager* (ODM). The database allows AIX administrators to determine what software is installed and at what levels. Additionally, the ODM holds the names and locations of files created during installation of a product.

AIX products have prerequisite products. These prerequisites are automatically checked during the installation of a new product. If any of the prerequisites are not present, the installation will be stopped, and the list of missing products will be displayed.

When CICS/6000 is installed, its product files will be located in the /usr/lpp/cics directory. Sufficient space must exist or be available for these files in the /usr file system.

The process of installing CICS/6000 is illustrated in Fig. 3.1. The diagram illustrates the relationship between the AIX install commands, the ODM database, and the AIX file systems. At completion of the installation, the AIX file systems will have the CICS/6000 product installed in the /usr/lpp/cics directory, and the AIX ODM database will reflect the fact that CICS is installed.

CICS/6000 has prerequisites including the Encina and DCE products. If these are not installed at the correct level, the CICS installation will fail. Before installing CICS/6000, ensure that the listed prerequisites are present on the machine or on the same media as the CICS/6000 product.

Occasionally, CICS, Encina, or DCE requires that Program Temporary Fixes (PTFs) be installed. These also should be located and installed prior to or concurrently with the installation.

Prior to the installation taking place, an option is presented to COMMIT the software or to only APPLY the software. If the software is committed, it

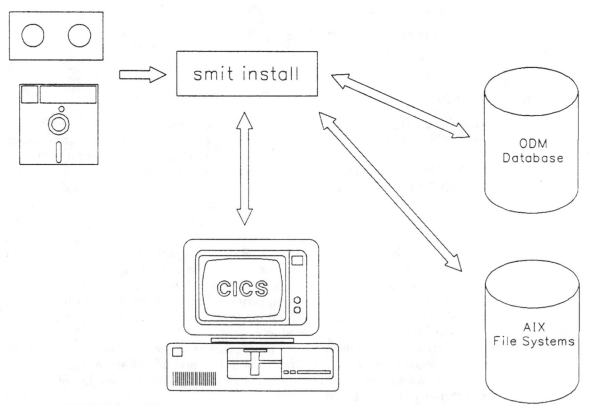

Figure 3.1 CICS/6000 installation.

may not be removed subsequently. If it is applied, it may be removed at a later time. It is not possible to commit a product that depends on a product which is itself not committed. If this were allowed, inconsistencies could arise if a dependent software component were left while its dependencies were removed.

Before installing CICS/6000, AIX groups and userids must be created. Following the transfer of the CICS product files from the install media to disk, the CICS files are associated with these groups and userids. These include

- An AIX group called *cics*
- An AIX group called *cicsterm*
- An AIX userid called *cics* which is a member of the AIX group called *cics*

These groups and userid are used to become the owners of the CICS files retrieved from the media and stored on disk. Once the product is installed, these groups and userids should not have their AIX uid or gid numbers changed. If changed, the files installed and used by CICS must be reowned. Care should be taken in an AIX NIS environment to ensure that the userids and groupids are set up correctly initially.

The creation of AIX groups and users is achieved through the SMIT tool. To create users and groups, root permissions are required. The SMIT path to group creation is

```
smit security
     Groups
          Add a Group
```

The resulting panel is illustrated in Fig. 3.2. The panel shows the addition of the cics group. This command must be reexecuted for the cicsterm group.

```
                          Add Group

Type or select values in entry fields.
Press Enter AFTER making all desired changes.

                                          [Entry Fields]
   Group NAME                             [cics]
   ADMINISTRATIVE group?                  false                +



F1=Help            F2=Refresh        F3=Cancel        F4=List
F5=Reset           F6=Command        F7=Edit          F8=Image
F9=Shell           F10=Exit          Enter=Do
```

Figure 3.2 AIX group panel.

Once the cics and cicsterm groups are created, it is recommended that the root user be made a member of these groups. This is not required for installation but allows root to execute the CICS administration commands and tools at a later step.

To define an AIX userid, follow the SMIT path:

```
smit security
      Users
            Add a User
```

The resulting panel is shown in Fig. 3.3, which adds the AIX "cics" user. Note that the primary group for cics is the AIX group also called *cics*.

To install the CICS/6000 product, the installer must be logged into AIX as the root user. The AIX SMIT utility should be used for the installation. The following path should be used to navigate to the product installation panels:

```
smit install
      Install / Update Software
            Install / Update Selectable Software (Custom Install)
                  Install Software Products at Latest Available Level
```

```
                              Create User

Type or select values in entry fields.
Press Enter AFTER making all desired changes.

[TOP]                                           [Entry Fields]
* User NAME                                     [cics]
  ADMINISTRATIVE User?                           false                    +
  User ID                                       []                        #
  LOGIN User?                                    true                     +
  PRIMARY Group                                 [cics]                    +
  Group set                                     []                        +
  ADMINISTRATIVE Groups                         []                        +
  SU Groups                                     [ALL]                     +
  HOME Directory                                []
  Initial PROGRAM                               []
  User information                              []
  Another user CAN SU to user?                   true                     +
  User CAN RLOGIN?                               true                     +
  Trusted path?                                  nosak                    +
[MORE...12]

F1=Help           F2=Refresh        F3=Cancel          F4=List
F5=Reset          F6=Command        F7=Edit            F8=Image
F9=Shell          F10=Exit          Enter=Do
```

Figure 3.3 AIX user panel.

```
╭─────────────────────────────────────────────────────────────────────────╮
│              Install Software Products at Latest Available Level          │
│                                                                           │
│                                                                           │
│  Type or select values in entry fields.                                   │
│  Press Enter AFTER making all desired changes.                            │
│                                                                           │
│                                                       [Entry Fields]      │
│  * INPUT device / directory for software              /dev/rmt0.1         │
│  * SOFTWARE to install                                [all]            +   │
│    Automatically install PREREQUISITE software?       yes             +   │
│    COMMIT software?                                   no              +   │
│    SAVE replaced files?                               yes             +   │
│    VERIFY Software?                                   no              +   │
│    EXTEND file systems if space needed?               yes             +   │
│    REMOVE input file after installation?              no              +   │
│    OVERWRITE existing version?                        no              +   │
│    ALTERNATE save directory                           []                  │
│                                                                           │
│                                                                           │
│  F1=Help            F2=Refresh         F3=Cancel         F4=List           │
│  F5=Reset           F6=Command         F7=Edit          F8=Image           │
│  F9=Shell           F10=Exit           Enter=Do                           │
╰─────────────────────────────────────────────────────────────────────────╯
```

Figure 3.4 Install panel.

Once executed, a prompt will be displayed to allow selection of the media device on which CICS/6000 is contained. Pressing the F4 function key will generate a list. The panel illustrated in Fig. 3.4 shows the settings for installing without committing which will leave CICS/6000 in the applied state. If the software is installed without committing, the save replaced files flag on the panel also must be set to yes.

The installation may take some time depending on the other AIX products already installed on the machine. Perquisite checking takes some time to complete because all products and PTFs may have to be scanned.

CICS Files and Directories

The result of installing CICS on the target machine will be the creation of CICS files and directories on the target AIX file systems. The majority of CICS files are installed under the /usr/lpp/cics directory structure, with some others being created under the /var directory. The diagram shown in Fig. 3.5 illustrates the major CICS directories installed.

Each of the directories installed holds a different set of CICS files used for separate purposes. This grouping of product files allows the location of files quickly by meaning. The meanings of the separate directories are shown below:

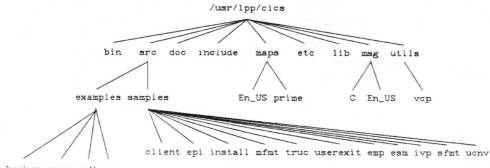

Figure 3.5 CICS directories.

/usr/lpp/cics   The root of the CICS product file tree. Files below this directory are not to be changed by users or administrators, with the exception of the CICS COBOL runtime called **cicsprCOBOL.** Application of later levels of CICS or PTFs may change individual files.

/usr/lpp/cics/bin   The location of all CICS executables. These executables include the commands intended for user invocation and those used internally by CICS. This directory should be added into the AIX PATH environment variable for every user who wishes to access CICS. It is recommended that this path be added into the AIX default PATH setting in the /etc/environment file. Following a change to /etc/environment, a machine reboot is advised to ensure that each process, especially those which had been running before the change, is restarted and picks up the changes made to the environment.

/usr/lpp/cics/lib   The location of all CICS library files. CICS is implemented as many millions of lines of code which, when compiled, produce many megabytes of object code and executables. Since much of the code executed by one CICS command may be the same code executed by another, CICS utilizes an advanced AIX facility known as *shared libraries.* An individual compiled executable does not necessarily contain all the code it requires to execute. When it is invoked, AIX arranges for portions of code known as *libraries* to be dynamically bound to the executable. This technique has many advantages, including reducing the size of executables on disk, since they do not all need to contain the same compiled code. Additionally, this technique saves on memory usage when a program runs because AIX need only load a given library once and provides shared access to the executable text of the library. This AIX directory holds all the libraries used by CICS/6000. The majority of these libraries are used internally by the CICS region, but some libraries are provided to be linked directly with user-written CICS programs, user exits, and client applications.

`/usr/lpp/cics/include` The location of CICS C language include files and COBOL language copybooks. When a user-written CICS program is translated by the CICS translator, the generated code includes constants and function calls that must be resolved. Included in the generated code are `COPY` statements in COBOL programs and `#include` statements in translated C programs. The files that are to be included in the code during compilation are located in this directory. For user exits and client applications, certain files must be explicitly included. The compiler must be directed to search this directory for these files.

`/usr/lpp/cics/etc` CICS miscellaneous files. This directory holds data files used by CICS/6000 that do not fit into other categories. Included in this directory are keyboard mapping definitions, trace and dump format files, templates for SFS, and others.

`/usr/lpp/cics/doc` Additional documentation. If additional instructions are provided for CICS after the manuals have been printed, ASCII text files with those instructions will be included in this directory.

`/usr/lpp/cics/maps` Physical BMS maps used by CICS-supplied transactions. These maps are stored in subdirectories below this directory. The subdirectory names are based on AIX locales. This allows language-specific maps to be created.

`/usr/lpp/cics/msg` Message catalogs for CICS. Subdirectories below this directory contain CICS message catalogs in directories named after AIX locales. The message catalogs allow CICS-displayed messages to be language-specific.

`/usr/lpp/cics/util` This directory holds utilities supplied with CICS/6000 that users may find useful. These utilities are not formal parts of CICS/6000, and support and testing may be limited.

`/usr/lpp/cics/src` This directory contains subdirectories for both sample and example CICS programs and tools.

`/usr/lpp/cics/src/examples/backup` Example backup scripts for taking backups of SFS and CICS data.

`/usr/lpp/cics/src/examples/sdt` Example conversion templates for the **cicssdt** tool.

`/usr/lpp/cics/src/examples/xa` Example configuration files for integrating CICS/6000 with many of the major databases via an XA interface.

`/usr/lpp/cics/src/examples/nonxa` Example configuration files for integrating CICS/6000 with many of the major databases without using an XA interface.

`/usr/lpp/cics/src/samples/client` Sample CICS client autoinstall user program.

`/usr/lpp/cics/src/samples/epi`   Sample CICS EPI programs.

`/usr/lpp/cics/src/samples/install`   Sample terminal autoinstall user program.

`/usr/lpp/cics/src/samples/mfmt`   Sample CICS monitoring data formatter.

`/usr/lpp/cics/src/samples/truc`   Sample transaction routing user conversion program.

`/usr/lpp/cics/src/samples/userexit`   Sample user exits.

`/usr/lpp/cics/src/samples/emp`   Sample CICS event-monitoring program.

`/usr/lpp/cics/src/samples/esm`   Sample external security manager program.

`/usr/lpp/cics/src/samples/ivp`   Sample installation verification programs.

`/usr/lpp/cics/src/samples/sfmt`   Sample CICS statistics data formatter.

`/usr/lpp/cics/src/samples/ucnv`   Sample DFHCNV conversion programs.

Configuring DCE for CICS

Before CICS can be configured for operation, the DCE product must itself be configured. Configuration tasks for DCE include defining a DCE Security Server and a DCE Cell Directory Server. The Security Server is used to provide secure access to CICS/6000, define passwords for CICS users, and provide authorization for access to Encina resources. The Cell Directory Server allows CICS to locate distributed components of the CICS product, including

- CICS clients locating a CICS server
- CICS locating an SFS
- CICS locating a PPC Gateway

During the operation of DCE, files will be created and destroyed under the DCE-owned directory `/var/dce`. It is strongly advised that a separate AIX file system be created for `/var/dce`. Since CICS and other products create files under the `/var` file system, if `/var/dce` is itself part of the `/var` file system, filling the file system may result in DCE not being able to create new files or update old files. This can result in DCE failing or becoming permanently broken.

If DCE has already been installed and the `/var/dce` directory is part of the `/var` file system, it can be copied into a separate `/var/dce` file system later. To accomplish this, the following tasks may be done:

- Ensure that DCE has been completely stopped by executing the **/etc/dce.clean** command as root.

- Back up the /var/dce directories using the AIX **tar** command:

```
tar -cvf /tmp/dce.backup /var/dce
```

This will create an AIX file containing the complete backup of DCE.

- Remove the /var/dce directories using the AIX **rm** command:

```
rm -rf /var/dce
```

- Create a new AIX file system called /var/dce:

```
mount /var/dce
```

A size of 4 megabytes should be sufficient. Ensure that the file system is mounted once it has been created.

- Restore the contents of the backed up DCE directories:

```
cd /var/dce
tar -xvf /tmp/dce.backup
```

- Reset the permissions on the /var/dce/security/creds and /var /dce/rpc/socket directories. These directories need read/write permission for everyone, but only the users who create files can delete those files.

```
chmod 1777 /var/dce/security/creds
chmod 1777 /var/dce/rpc/socket
```

These permissions must be reset explicitly because they were not saved in the **tar** backup.

- Restart DCE with the **rc.dce** command.

The configuration of a DCE environment consists of the configuration of a DCE Security Server and a DCE Cell Directory Server.

Configuring a DCE Security Server

The configuration of a DCE Security Server creates the DCE registry database used to securely hold the DCE principals and accounts used by Encina and CICS. During configuration of the Security Server, the symbolic name of the DCE cell must be chosen. This name is used to refer to servers within the cell from DCE environments outside the cell. The name of the cell need not be known from within the cell because the directory prefix / . : can be used to specify the local cell.

A recommended name for the cell is the full TCP/IP domain name on which the DCE security server will execute.

To configure a DCE Security Server, the following SMIT path may be followed:

```
smit dce
      Configure DCE/DFS
            Configure DCE/DFS Servers
                  SECURITY Server
                  1 primary
```

The following panel will be presented:

```
                         SECURITY Server
◄Type or select values in entry fields.
Press Enter AFTER making all desired changes.

                                              [Entry Fields]
* CELL name                                   [host.name]
* Cell ADMINISTRATOR's account                [cell_admin]
  Machine's DCE HOSTNAME                       []
  PRINCIPALS Lowest possible UNIX ID           [100]
  GROUPS Lowest possible UNIX ID               [100]
  ORGANIZATION Lowest possible UNIX ID         [100]
  MAXIMUM possible UNIX ID                     [32767]



F1=Help          F2=Refresh        F3=Cancel          F4=List
F5=Reset         F6=Command        F7=Edit            F8=Image
F9=Shell         F10=Exit          Enter=Do
```

The name of the DCE cell must be entered. Executing the command generated by the panel will configure the DCE Security Server. The password for the **cell_admin** DCE principal will be requested. Once the Security Server has been configured, the DCE Cell Directory Server also must be configured.

Configuring a DCE Cell Directory Server

The configuration of a DCE CDS initializes the CDS database in which the locations of DCE servers will be registered. The following SMIT panel can be used to configure a DCE CDS server.

```
smit dce
      Configure DCE/DFS
            Configure DCE/DFS Servers
                  CDS (Cell Directory Service) Server
                  1 initial
```

The following panel will be presented. The default options will create a suitable DCE CDS.

```
                    CDS (Cell Directory Service) Server
Type or select values in entry fields.
Press Enter AFTER making all desired changes.


                                              [Entry Fields]
* CELL name                                   [/.../host.name]
* SECURITY Server                             [hostname]
* Cell ADMINISTRATOR's account                [cell_admin]
* LAN PROFILE                                 [/.:/lan-profile]
  Machine's DCE HOSTNAME                       []




F1=Help           F2=Refresh        F3=Cancel         F4=List
F5=Reset          F6=Command        F7=Edit           F8=Image
F9=Shell          F10=Exit          Enter=Do
```

Configuring DCE for CICS

Once DCE has been configured, a CICS-supplied command must be executed to create DCE groups in the Security Server and DCE directories in the Cell Directory Server. To execute this command, the administrator must be logged into AIX as root and authenticated to DCE as the **cell_admin** DCE principal. The command to be executed is

```
cicssetupdce -v
```

Using the Encina Structured File Server

The Encina SFS is used by CICS/6000 to manage CICS user files as well as a number of CICS internal files such as intrapartition transient data queues and auxiliary main storage queues. The SFS must be defined, started, and configured before a CICS region may be used. The tasks involved in the definition of an SFS for CICS/6000 usage include

- Choosing a name and short name for the SFS
- Creating an AIX userid for the SFS
- Defining an SFS through the SMIT panels
- Creating AIX logical volumes for the SFS use
- Cold starting the SFS

Naming an SFS

In a subsequent step a CICS region will be created. This region has many attributes associated with it, including the name of the SFS on which certain CICS files should be located. The name of an SFS is its full DCE CDS name, which usually will be `/.:/cics/sfs/<name>`. When a CICS region is created, the name of the SFS to be used defaults to the name of the AIX host on which the CICS region is running. This is specified in the CICS region definitions with the `%H` characters. When CICS starts up, the `%H` characters are expanded to the host name of the AIX box. To determine the AIX host name, the AIX command **hostname** may be used.

For simplicity and during the first tests of CICS/6000, the SFS name should include the host name (i.e., `/.:/cics/sfs/<hostname>`).

When using SMIT panels to work with SFSs, if no SFS name is supplied during a configuration or start, the name of the SFS will be taken from the **CICS_SFS_SERVER** environment variable. It is recommended that this environment variable be set after the name has been selected. A good place to define this value is in the AIX system-wide environment file called `/etc/environment`.

When an SFS is defined, besides specifying the name of the SFS in terms of its DCE CDS name, a second name must be supplied. This name is termed the *short name* and is used to associate other AIX attributes with the SFS. The attributes associated with the short name include

- The AIX userid under which the SFS will execute
- The names of the logical volumes which the SFS will use
- The name of the AIX Subsystem Resource Controller subsystem

Both the SFS name and its corresponding short name must be unique within a CICS environment. The default short name used by an SFS, when configuring with AIX SMIT, is **SFS_SERV.**

Creating the SFS definitions file

When an instance of an SFS is defined, its specific attributes are saved in an AIX file. This file is read whenever the SFS is started, and the file is updated whenever SFS definition changes are made. Before the SFS definitions can be saved in the file, a template for the file must be created. This is achieved by executing the following command as root:

```
cicsdefaultservers
```

The template file for SFS definitions will be created in the `/var/cics_servers/SSD` directory. The file itself is called `SSD.stanza`, which stands for SFS definitions.

Defining an SFS AIX userid

When the SFS executes, it will execute as an AIX userid. The default userid it will execute has the same name as the short name chosen for the server. This may be changed in the SFS definition panels. The creation of the SFS definition does not create this userid; it must be created prior to configuring an SFS. The userid for the SFS must have a primary group of cics. The AIX userid for SFS may be created by following the SMIT path:

```
smit users
    Add a User
```

The following panel will be presented:

```
                            Create User

Type or select values in entry fields.
Press Enter AFTER making all desired changes.

[TOP]                                       [Entry Fields]
* User NAME                                 [SFS_SERV]
  ADMINISTRATIVE User?                       false                  +
  User ID                                   []
  LOGIN User?                                true                   +
  PRIMARY Group                             [cics]                  +
  Group set                                 []                      +
  ADMINISTRATIVE Groups                     []                      +
  SU Groups                                 [ALL]                   +
  HOME Directory                            []
  Initial PROGRAM                           []
  User information                          []
  Another user CAN SU to user?               true                   +
  User CAN RLOGIN?                           true                   +
  Trusted path?                              nosak                  +
[MORE...12]

F1=Help           F2=Refresh        F3=Cancel        F4=List
F5=Reset          F6=Command        F7=Edit          F8=Image
F9=Shell          F10=Exit          Enter=Do
```

The **User NAME** and **PRIMARY Group** attributes should be completed with the AIX userid name and the cics group. If a default SFS configuration is required, create the user as **SFS_SERV,** which is the default SFS short name.

Defining an SFS

The SFS is configured through a CICS set of panels. To reach the panels used for SFS configuration, follow the path shown below.

```
smit cics
     Manage Encina SFS Servers
```

These panels allow for the creation, deletion, start-up, and shutdown of SFSs. The first task in getting CICS operational is to define an SFS. This task creates a set of definitions for starting the SFS that include its name and the AIX logical volumes it is to use.

To create an SFS definition, the following SMIT path should be followed:

```
smit cics
     Manage Encina SFS Servers
          Define Encina SFS Servers
               Create
```

A panel will be displayed to allow the selection of a predefined SFS on which to base the definition of the new server. Pressing the enter key at this point will use the default. The following panel will be displayed, allowing the SFS to be defined. The name of the SFS should be entered as a full DCE CDS name (e.g., /.:/cics/sfs/<hostname>).

```
                         Create Encina SFS Server

Type or select values in entry fields.
Press Enter AFTER making all desired changes.


                                              [Entry Fields]
* SFS Server Identifier                   [/.:/cics/sfs/cicsaix7]
* Model SFS Server Identifier               ""
  Ignore errors on creation?                no                        +
  Resource description                    [SFS Server Definition]
* Number of updates                         0
  Protect resource from modification?       no                        +
  Protection level                          none                      +
  Enable MRA Archiving?                      no                        +
  Buffer pool size in Kbytes              [1000]                      #
  Idle timeout                            [300]                       #
  Number of Log writes per checkpoint interval  [5000]                #
  Number of threads devoted to normal operations   [12]               #
  Number of threads devoted to resource operations  [3]               #
  Collating language                      [C]
  Short name used for SRC                 [SFS_SERV]
  AIX user ID for server                  [%S]
  AIX logical volume for data             [sfs_%S]
  AIX logical volume for logging          [log_%S]
  Log File Name                           [logfile]



F1=Help          F2=Refresh          F3=Cancel          F4=List
F5=Reset         F6=Command          F7=Edit            F8=Image
F9=Shell         F10=Exit            Enter=Do
```

Defining the SFS logical volumes

Before the SFS may be started, two AIX logical volumes must be created for its use. These volumes are used to hold recoverable log information and SFS file data. The log volume is used to hold the "before" images of changes made to an SFS file. If the transaction that makes changes to the file abends, the original contents of the file will have to be restored to return the file to its exact state prior to the start of the abended transaction. The SFS data volume holds the current contents of SFS files. This volume should be sized according to the amount of data expected to be managed by the SFS. These file data correspond to the amount of data expected to be manipulated through CICS file control.

The names of the AIX logical volumes to be used are specified in the definition of the SFS illustrated in the preceding step. By default, the names used will be sfs_<short name> and log_<short name>. The string %S, when encountered in an SFS definition, expands to the short name value. These logical volumes may be created through AIX SMIT panels by following the path:

```
smit lv
     Add a Logical Volume
```

A prompt will be displayed asking for the AIX volume group on which the logical volumes are to be created. Using **rootvg** is a good default. Following this, the following panel will be displayed:

```
                          Add a Logical Volume

Type or select values in entry fields.
Press Enter AFTER making all desired changes.

[TOP]                                              [Entry Fields]
   Logical volume NAME                            []
 * VOLUME GROUP name                              rootvg
 * Number of LOGICAL PARTITIONS                   []
   PHYSICAL VOLUME names                          []                    +
   Logical volume TYPE                            []
   POSITION on physical volume                    midway               +
   RANGE of physical volumes                      minimum              +
   MAXIMUM NUMBER of PHYSICAL VOLUMES             []
       to use for allocation
   Number of COPIES of each logical               1                    +
       partition
   Mirror Write Consistency?                      yes                  +
   Allocate each logical partition copy           yes                  +
       on a SEPARATE physical volume?
[MORE...9]

F1=Help           F2=Refresh        F3=Cancel        F4=List
F5=Reset          F6=Command        F7=Edit          F8=Image
F9=Shell          F10=Exit          Enter=Do
```

The **Logical volume NAME** and **Number of LOGICAL PARTITIONS** fields should be entered. This command needs to be executed twice, once for the logging logical volume and once for the SFS file data volume. The following table illustrates suggested names and sizes. The size of a partition of AIX volume storage is 4 megabytes.

Volume name	Volume size (partitions)
log_SFS_SERV	16
sfs_SFS_SERV	16

Once the volumes have been created, they must have their attributes changed to allow the SFS to access them. Since the volumes were created by the AIX userid root, they will not be accessible by the AIX userid under which the SFS will execute. To change the attributes, the AIX **chown** command may be used. For example, if the defaults were chosen, the following commands will set the attributes correctly:

```
chown SFS_SERV.cics /dev/*log_SFS_SERV
chown SFS_SERV.cics /dev/*sfs_SFS_SERV
```

Starting an SFS

The first time an SFS is started, it must be cold started. Cold starting an SFS results in a low-level reset of all its attributes and logical volumes. Cold starting a previously started SFS results in all files managed by that server being lost.

```
smit cics
    Manage Encina SFS Servers
        Cold Start and Encina SFS Server
```

If the **CICS_SFS_SERVER** environment variable has been set correctly, the **SFS Server Name** attribute on the top of the presented panel should match that of the SFS to be started. To prevent accidental cold starting of the server and hence loss of all SFS file data for that server, the invoker is asked to enter "continue" to proceed with the cold start.

Completing this command will result in an executing SFS with no files defined in it. Subsequent tasks will define CICS and user files. On a machine restart, the SFS must be autostarted or all SFS files will be lost.

The diagram shown in Fig. 3.6 illustrates the interaction between the various tasks performed to create an SFS.

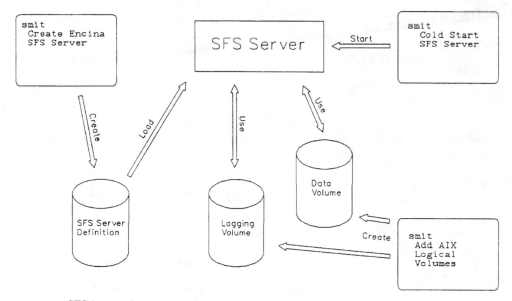

Figure 3.6 SFS interactions.

Defining a CICS Region

Once the SFS has been defined and started, a CICS region may be defined. A *CICS region* is an instance of all the definitions of a CICS system. Each region has its own copy of Region Definitions, including programs, transactions, maps, users, queues, and files. The creation of a region results in a new instance of the default region being created. This new region can then be modified to hold all the new programs, transactions, maps, and other Resource Definitions. Before a region can be created, it must be named. The name of a region is a string of one to eight characters in length. The region name is used to stop, start, and modify the parameters of the region and is used as the name of the CICS region provided to clients which wish to connect. Once the name is chosen, it may be set in the **CICSREGION** environment variable for default selection in future CICS SMIT panels and menus against the region. To define a CICS region, the administrator must be both the AIX root user and authenticated as the DCE **cell_admin** principal. The SMIT path to create a CICS region is

```
smit cics
    Manage CICS/6000 Regions
        Create (Import) a CICS/6000 Region
```

The following panel will be displayed:

```
                    Create (Import) a CICS/6000 Region

Type or select values in entry fields.
Press Enter AFTER making all desired changes.

                                                [Entry Fields]
* Name of Region to be Created                  [cicstest]
  Action to be Taken for Resolving Links         mandatory              +
  Force redefinition of region?                  no                     +
  Group Id. for Region Data                      []
* Input file                                    [/usr/lpp/cics/DEFAULT]



F1=Help              F2=Refresh         F3=Cancel         F4=List
F5=Reset             F6=Command         F7=Edit           F8=Image
F9=Shell             F10=Exit           Enter=Do
```

This field contains the name of the new CICS region to be created. The "Name of Region to be Created" attribute will be taken from the CICSRE-GION environment variable if set or else may be entered in the panel.

The creation of a new CICS region performs the following tasks:

- Creates a new directory structure named after the CICS region created under the /var/cics_regions directory.

- Creates a new entry in the AIX Subsystem Resource Controller definitions for start-up and shutdown of the region.

- Creates a new DCE principal called **cics/<region>** in the DCE security registry allowing the CICS region to operate as a DCE authenticated server.

Creating a CICS/6000 region is a much simpler process than that found on other CICS platforms. When a region is not running, it consumes no AIX resources other than that of the resource definitions held on the AIX file system. Regions may be created and destroyed at will and used for testing purposes by different users. Later in this book it will be shown that creating a new region is a specific case of restoring (importing) a previously saved (exported) region. New regions can be created quickly from already existing regions by first exporting an old region and then reimporting the exported region with a new name. The default region is an IBM-supplied instance of an exported region.

Defining CICS region files onto the SFS

When the CICS region has been defined, the SFS used to hold the files need-ed for CICS operation must have those files defined to it. These file-definition steps result in the SFS files being created and appropriate SFS access permissions set. The following SMIT access path may be followed to configure an SFS with CICS required files. The invoker should be logged into AIX as root and DCE authenticated as the DCE principal **cell_admin.**

```
smit cics
    Manage CICS/6000 Regions
        Configure CICS/6000 Resources on an Encina SFS Server
            Configure an Encina SFS Server Without
            Changing Any Region Definition Values
```

The following panel will be presented:

```
  Configure Encina Servers Without Changing Any Region Definition Values


Type or select values in entry fields.
Press Enter AFTER making all desired changes.

[TOP]                                          [Entry Fields]
* Region Name                                  cicstest
  Ignore errors on configuration?              no                      +
* Number of updates                            5
  SFS server storing CICS Queue Data           /.:/cics/sfs/%H
  Recoverable Auxiliary TSQ Volume Name        sfs_%S
  Number of pages to preallocate for RecTSQFile  5
  Maximum number of records for Recoverable Auxiliar  1000000
  y TSQs
  Non-recoverable TSQ Volume Name              sfs_%S
  Number of pages to preallocate for NonRecTSQFile  5
  Maximum number of records for Non-recoverable TSQs  1000000
  Logically Recoverable TDQ Volume Name        sfs_%S
  Number of pages to preallocate for LogicalTDQFile  5
[MORE...17]

F1=Help          F2=Refresh        F3=Cancel       F4=List
F5=Reset         F6=Command        F7=Edit         F8=Image
F9=Shell         F10=Exit          Enter=Do
```

If the CICSREGION variable was not set, the region will have to be selected from the region selection SMIT panel.

The files created on the SFS all begin with the name of the CICS region for which they are intended for use. The files can be shown with the Encina **sfsadmin** command by executing

```
sfsadmin list files -server ).:/cics/sfs/<host name>
```

The following files should be listed:

```
<region>cicsnlqfile        Locally queued unprotected STARTS
<region>cicsnrectsqfil     Nonrecoverable TS auxiliary queues
<region>cicsplqfile        Locally queued protected STARTS
<region>cicsrectsqfile     Recoverable TS auxiliary queues
<region>cicstdqlgfile      Logically receoverable TD queues
<region>cicstdqnofile      Nonrecoverable TD queues
<region>cicstdqphfile      Physically recoverable TD queues
```

Once this command has been completed, the region may be started. The first time a region is started it must be cold started, subsequent starts may be either cold starts or autostarts.

Multiple regions may share the same SFS. Unless the SFS is lost due to a software or hardware failure without a backup, there should be no need to recreate an SFS. New regions may be created at any time, but each new region requires the addition of SFS files for that region's operation by performing the preceding step.

Starting, Stopping, and Using a CICS Region

CICS regions are started by sending a request to the AIX SRC demon. The SRC demon has the names and locations of the programs that are to be started defined to it. When a CICS region is created, a new entry is added to the AIX SRC configuration specifying the details of the new region. The AIX SRC entry is called **cics.<region>.** To use SRC, the AIX user must have a primary group of **system.** There are two modes of CICS region start-up. These are termed *auto* and *cold*. The first time a region is started, it must be started cold. The cold start of a region does not attempt any recovery of transactions that may have been executing the last time a region was shut down or terminated.

An autostart of a region will cause recovery processing to occur when the region starts; this includes

- Recovery of files
- Recovery of recoverable queues
- Recovery of region-wide modifications made with CEMT and other system configuration APIs

To start a CICS region, the following SMIT path may be followed:

```
smit cics
    Manage CICS/6000 Regions
        Cold Start a CICS/6000 Region
```

The following panel will be displayed:

```
                    Cold Start CICS/6000 Region

Type or select values in entry fields.
Press Enter AFTER making all desired changes.

[TOP]                                         [Entry Fields]
* Region identifier                           cicstest
  Resource description                        [Region Definition]
  Startup groups                              []
  Programs to execute at startup              []
  Programs to execute at phase 1 of shutdown  []
  Programs to execute at phase 2 of shutdown  []
  Name of the default user identifier         [CICSUSER]
  Type of RSL checking for Files              external              +
  Type of RSL checking for TDQs               external        .     +
  Type of RSL checking for TSQs               external              +
  Type of RSL checking for Journals           external              +
  Type of RSL checking for Programs           external              +
  Type of RSL checking for Transactions       external              +
  Do you want to use an External Security Manager?  no              +
[MORE...63]

F1=Help          F2=Refresh       F3=Cancel        F4=List
F5=Reset         F6=Command       F7=Edit          F8=Image
F9=Shell         F10=Exit         Enter=Do
```

A CICS/6000 region can be started from the AIX command line by issuing the AIX command **startsrc.** This command requests that the AIX SRC demon start the specified subsystem. The syntax of the **startsrc** command is as follows:

```
startsrc -s <subsystem> -a "parameters"
```

The subsystem to be started should be **cics.<region>** where *region* is the name of the CICS region to be started. The start-up mode of the region (cold or auto) is specified in the CICS/6000 Region resource definitions. To override this attribute, specify **StartType** = **cold** or **StartType** = **auto** after the -a parameter. Care must be taken that a cold start is not used when an autostart is required; it is good practice to always specify the **StartType** when using the AIX command line mechanism to start a region.

When the request to start a CICS/6000 region has been made, the region will begin to log messages to two AIX files. These files are /var/ cics_regions/<region>/console.msg and /var/cics_regions/ <region>/data/CSMT.out. The console.msg file is the CICS console message output. The file should always be monitored during CICS region start-up. Included in this file will be informational, warning, and error messages issued by the CICS system. The most important message in this file is the

CICS start-up is complete message. Only when this message is written is CICS fully up and available.

The message is

```
ERZ010020I *** CICS/6000 startup is complete ***
```

As CICS writes these files, they should be examined. The best way of examining these files is to execute the AIX **tail** command with the -f flag against these files. The **tail** command displays the last few lines of an AIX file to the terminal. With the -f flag, the **tail** command does not terminate but waits for new messages to be added to the file. When the messages are added, the **tail** command will display these new messages and continue to wait for new messages. The **tail** command may be interrupted with the CTRL + C interrupt. The AIX shell script in Fig. 3.7 may be used to follow both the console.msg and CSMT.out logs in the same window. Entering CTRL + C will stop both of these and return to the AIX command prompt.

The program functions by executing one **tail** command in the background and one in the foreground. When a CTRL + C interrupt is received, the **tail** command in the foreground is terminated, and a trap function is executed that terminates the **tail** command in the background.

The cicscp Command

The **cicscp** command allows many CICS administration commands to be performed from the command line. This command can start and stop DCE, Encina servers, and CICS regions. This command may be incorporated into AIX shell scripts to automate start-up and shut down of the controllable resources. Use of this command may be appropriate once the underlying function of these services is understood. The underlying commands that are executed by **cicscp** are the same as those executed by using the AIX-provided SMIT panels and interface. The **cicscp** command can create, destroy, start, and stop the following items:

- *COBOL: create, destroy*   Build the CICS/6000-integrated COBOL language runtime. This runtime image is stored in the cicsprCOBOL file in the CICS bin directory.

- *DCE: create, destroy, start, and stop*   Configure, unconfigure, start up, and shutdown the DCE environment and DCE servers.

- *SFSs: create, destroy, start, and stop*   Define, destroy, start, and stop an SFS used by CICS regions.

- *PPC Gateway server: create, destroy, start, and stop*   Define, destroy, start, and stop the Encina PPC Gateway used for synclevel 2 communications. Creation of the PPC Gateway results in DCE creating necessary DCE principals and keytable files. The environment variables CICS_PPCGWY_VG, CICS_PPCGWY_SIZE, and cics_admin_pw are used by this command.

```ksh
#!/bin/ksh
#
# Program: tailcics
# Version: 1.0
#
# Function:
# This program follows the output of the two main CICS output files:
#
# /var/cics_regions/<region>/console.msg
# /var/cics_regions/<region>/data/CSMT.out
#
#
#
# Function to be called for an INT signal
#
EndTail()
{
   kill -9 $backtail
   print
   print "***************************"
   print "***** End of tailcics *****"
   print "***************************"
}


#
# Check that the CICSREGION variable is set
#
if [ -z "$CICSREGION" ]
then
   echo "tailcics: Error: CICSREGION not set"
   exit 1
fi

cd /var/cics_regions/${CICSREGION}
if [ ! -r console.msg ]
then
   echo "tailcics: console.msg does not exist or is not readable"
   exit 1
fi
if [ ! -r data/CSMT.out ]
then
   echo "tailcics: CSMT.out does not exist or is not readable"
   exit 1
fi
tail -f console.msg &
#
# Capture the PID of the last background task
#
backtail=$!

#
# Trap an interrupt
#
trap EndTail INT
tail -f data/CSMT.out
```

Figure 3.7 tailcics program.

- *CICS regions: create, destroy, start, and stop a CICS a CICS region instance* Required DCE principals will be created. The cics_admin_pw environment variable can be used to indicate the **cell_admin** password.

Using the **cicscp create region <region>** command combines the creation of the CICS region and configuration of the SFS files on the SFS for the CICS region.

- *SNA and SNA links*
- *The cicsteld telnet server: create and destroy* Create and destroy a cicsteld telnet server allowing telnet 3270 clients to connect with CICS/6000 as CICS terminals over TCP/IP.

Starting CICS/6000 at Machine Boot Time

The AIX shell script shown in Fig. 3.8 can be defined to the AIX inittab file to be started at machine boot time. This shell script will start DCE, the Encina SFS, and the CICS region named by the CICSREGION environment variable.

The **cicscp** command must be executed as the root AIX user and authenticated to DCE as the **cell_admin** principal. If the user is not authenticated as **cell_admin,** if the cell_admin_pw variable is set to the **cell_admin** password, **cicscp** will authenticate as **cell_admin** on the user's behalf.

A suitable addition to the /etc/inittab file to cause the shell script to be executed at boot time and hence start DCE, SFS, and CICS is

```
cicsstrt:2:wait:/etc/rc.cicsstart > /dev/console 2>&1
```

```
#!/bin/su root
{
    print "**** Starting CICS ****"
    date
    cell_admin_pw=-dce-
    cicscp -v start dce
    cicscp -v start sfs_server all StartType=auto
    if [ -z "$CICSREGION" ]
    then
        print "No region specified in CICSREGION variable, not starting any region".
    else
        cicscp -v start region ${CICSREGION} StartType=cold
    fi
    date
} > /tmp/cicsstart.log 2>&1
```

Figure 3.8 Shell script to start CICS at machine boot.

Configuring CICS/6000 Clients

Once CICS/6000 is operational, a terminal may be attached to the region to submit requests to start transactions. Before a terminal can be started, the machine and userids on which the CICS/6000 clients are to be executed must be configured. CICS provides a command to configure any machine on which the clients are to be executed. This command need only be executed once per machine. The command creates a DCE principal that identifies the machine as a valid CICS client machine. To execute the command, the administrator must be logged into AIX as root and authenticated to DCE as **cell_admin.** The following command configures a machine as a CICS client:

```
cicssetupclients -v
```

To execute a CICS client, the AIX user that attempts to run a client must be a member of the "cicsterm" AIX group and be DCE authenticated as a DCE user that is a member of the DCE cics_users group. When a CICS client starts, it expects to communicate with a CICS region. The location of the CICS region is determined by querying the DCE Cell Directory Service. When a CICS region starts, it advertises itself in DCE Cell Directory Service. The diagram in Fig. 3.9 illustrates the relationship between a CICS client (cicsterm), DCE Cell Directory Service, and the CICS region. If cicsterm is invoked without having specified a region name, CDS is queried, and a list of available CICS regions is displayed. Selecting a CICS region will then connect the client with the region.

Configuring CICS with COBOL

If CICS applications written in COBOL are to be developed or used with the MicroFocus COBOL compiler, an instance of the COBOL runtime must be built that includes links to CICS code. This new runtime will be loaded into CICS application servers when COBOL programs are to be executed. The runtime allows the CICS COBOL applications to make calls using the COBOL CALL statement, which cause CICS-integrated code to be executed. Code fragments other than CICS also may be included in the COBOL runtime such as C language programs and database access routines.

To build the new COBOL runtime, the user must be logged into AIX as root and be in the /usr/lpp/cics/bin directory. The following command should be executed:

```
cicsmkcobol
```

Distributing CICS

As a result of CICS/6000 utilizing the facilities of DCE, it is a simple matter to distribute the functions of CICS/6000 across more than one machine.

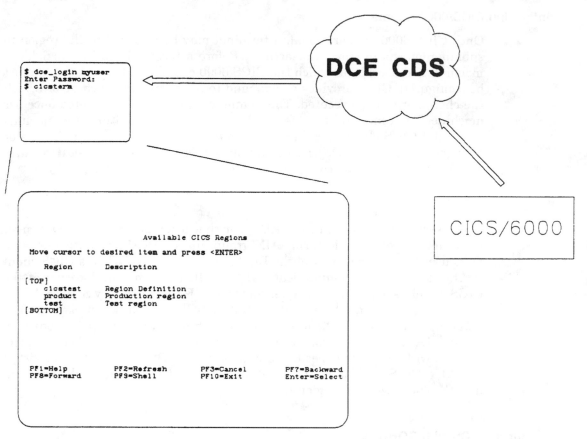

Figure 3.9 CICS/6000 clients.

CICS/6000 locates servers and can itself be located by the use of the DCE Cell Directory Service. Each of the CICS/6000 components that are distributable advertise themselves in DCE CDS. When CICS wishes to utilize one or more of these services, it locates the physical machine on which they reside by querying DCE CDS. Security between the components is achieved by means of the DCE security service, allowing authentication of transmissions all the way up to data packet encryption.

The components of CICS/6000 that are eligible for distribution include

- The SFSs
- CICS clients, which include cicsterm, cicsteld, cicstermp, and ECI/EPI clients
- Encina PPC Gateways
- Databases

The SFSs used by CICS/6000 are all configured to CICS by SFS name and SFS file name. Individual files either used internally by CICS or defined as files to CICS programs may be defined on separate SFSs. A single SFS may be shared by multiple CICS regions. For file-intensive applications, distributing the SFS to a second machine will reduce the CPU and IO consumption on the machine executing the CICS region. Additionally, the machine executing the SFS may need larger disk capacity, possibly involving disk mirroring, which may improve reliability and availability. An SFS machine may be part of a High Availability Cluster Multi-Processing (HACMP) configuration, allowing a second machine to take over the functionality of the SFS machine in the event of a machine failure.

The CICS clients connect to CICS/6000 by querying DCE in the case of the UNIX-based clients or by being configured with the TCP/IP address in the case of the PC and Macintosh clients. If the cicsteld telnet server is configured, telnet 3270 clients may be used to provide terminal access to a CICS region from remote TCP/IP-accessible workstations and mainframes.

If synclevel 2 connectivity to a CICS host is required, the PPC Gateway component of Encina may be used. Like the SFS, the PPC Gateway may be located on a machine other than the one executing the CICS region. This machine may have sole access to the SNA network for enhanced security and administration. The PPC Gateway can be utilized by multiple CICS regions concurrently.

Most of the major database servers available allow client access to the database from a machine other than the one executing the database server itself. The client access of database can be used from a CICS region to access a remote database. If the database is either CPU- or IO-intensive, the separation of the CICS region and database may increase throughput of both systems.

There is a tradeoff between distributing components and having them locally available on the same machine as their clients. When a client and server are located on the same machine, optimized interprocess communication techniques can be utilized to more efficiently pass requests between them. This may involve techniques such as shared memory access or interprocess sockets. In many cases, if a client and server communicate on the same machine, they will automatically determine the most efficient communication path.

When components are distributed, points of failure increase. A failure in one component or a network failure may cause more than one system to fail in a greater cascade effect. Distributed components also require additional administration as more environments are involved. Since start-up ordering is important, additional care must be taken to ensure that remote servers are indeed operating and available.

On a positive side, the CPU or IO requirements of a server may significantly outweigh the latency in communication of transmitting a request from a local client to a remote server. In this event, if a combined environment would produce a shortage of one or more resources, distributing the components may have a dramatic performance improvement.

Using the CICS/6000 Clients

CICS/6000 Clients Overview

CICS/6000, like the other CICS product family members, generates 3270 data stream as output to terminals. The 3270 data stream is an IBM protocol that describes the format of data sent and received from 3270 devices. The data include control orders to position the cursor, create a field on the display, and change the color of a field and other formatting controls. The destination of these data is usually a 3270 device capable of interpreting the 3270 data stream. Historically, these have been dedicated hardware devices connected via special communication controllers.

The 3270 data stream and the 3270 terminals are ideal for high-performance application systems. Each character entered at a keyboard is interpreted by the 3270 device itself, unlike the AIX terminal interaction model, where each keystroke results in an interrupt to the operating system kernel, which takes valuable cycles away from other processing work.

Unfortunately, AIX provides no mechanism to attach 3270 terminals directly to RISC System/6000s. Additionally, 3270 support has to be provided for users at ASCII terminals or X-terminal windows. To meet these requirements, 3270 terminal emulators are provided for CICS/6000.

To provide the ability to obtain hard-copy output from a CICS/6000 application, an interface to the AIX standard print spooling mechanism is provided. A CICS/6000 client application called *cicstermp* is provided to enable this interface.

Each of the client applications described is a distributed application capable of executing on a machine other than the one running the CICS/6000 region. The communication between the client and the CICS/6000 server is serviced by DCE RPC calls. DCE is required for the operation of the CICS/6000 clients. The machine that will execute the CICS/6000 clients may be in the same DCE cell as the CICS/6000 server or reachable via global directory services (GDS). The clients also may execute on the same machine as the CICS/6000 server.

The Cicsterm Program

AIX applications normally interact with users via ASCII terminals. These may be real ASCII terminals such as IBM 3151s or DEC VT100s, they may be *aixterm* or *xterm* windows in an X-Windows environment, or they may be remote network terminals such as telnet or rlogin clients. Unfortunately, there is no standard describing the mechanisms for controlling these terminals. Each terminal type understands a different set of control characters necessary to drive the terminal. On one terminal type, one control sequence may be used to clear the screen or position the cursor, whereas on a different terminal type, a different control sequence is required to achieve the same results. AIX applications that wish to control a terminal could hard code the control sequence necessary to control the terminal into the programs, but then these programs would only work with specific terminal types and would be useless against others. To solve this problem, a database was created called *terminfo*. This database contains the control sequences necessary to control the screen for particular common operations. When an application wishes to clear the screen, for example, it would access the database keyed on the terminal type and retrieve the control sequence necessary to clear the screen. To ease the access to this database, a set of callable functions is provided by AIX to access the database from an application. This library of functions is called *curses* and provides functions to move the cursor, clear the screen, display text, and retrieve keystrokes from the user.

A CICS/6000 client called *cicsterm* provides a 3270 emulation that utilizes the AIX curses functions to control the screen. The cicsterm program receives 3270 data stream from the CICS/6000 region via RPC and makes appropriate curses calls by interpreting the data. The result is a screen display that corresponds to the visual appearance had the data been sent to a real 3270 device. Cicsterm supports the majority of 3270 data stream commands and orders including color, highlighting, inverse, and hidden.

The syntax of the cicsterm command is as follows:

```
cicsterm [-r region] [-t transaction] [-n netname]
[-m model] [-A animator_TTY] [-T animator_TERM]
```

-r region   The name of the CICS/6000 region that is the target for the terminal install. If no region name is supplied, a menu of available regions located within the local DCE cell is displayed. Upon the user selecting a region, the client connects to the region.

-t transaction   The name of an initial transaction may be specified by this parameter. Upon successful installation of the terminal into the CICS/6000 region, the transaction will be started. If no transaction is specified, the user is presented with a blank screen, and the user must enter a transaction name to initiate a transaction. A common use for this parameter is to specify the CESN sign-on transaction.

`-n netname`   Specifies an optional netname used by the autoinstall algorithm. If no netname is specified, a unique netname will be generated internally by CICS/6000.

`-m model`   Specifies the model used for terminal autoinstall selection. If the flag is not specified, the contents of the environment variables CICSTERM and TERM are used.

`-A animator_TTY`   This flag enables the use of the Micro Focus COBOL Animator to perform debugging services for CICS/6000 applications started on this terminal. The parameter specified is the AIX location for a terminal on which to display the Animator screen and output.

`-T animator_TERM`   If the `-A` flag is specified, this parameter specifies the AIX TERM type of the AIX terminal specified by the `-A` parameter. Since CICS/6000 starts and controls the Animator application, CICS/6000 must be informed of the terminal type, since it has no mechanism to deduce this programmatically. The default value for this parameter is aixterm.

Before executing cicsterm, the user must be explicitly authenticated as a DCE principal with sufficient authorization to access the target CICS/6000 region. This principal must be a member of the DCE group cics_users that is created during configuration. The principal is used both to provide access control to the CICS region and to decide which CICS user the terminal will be associated with following autoinstall. If the user is not matched in the region, the default CICS user is specified by the **DefaultUser** attribute in the Region Definition resource definitions on the target region.

The Cicsteld Program

TCP/IP specifies a set of protocols known as *telnet*. Telnet is a client/server protocol that allows a user at a TCP/IP-connected workstation to invoke a telnet client to connect to a telnet server and login to the operating system on which the telnet server is executing. The telnet client communicates with the telnet server over the TCP/IP protocol. The telnet client has the responsibility for presenting information to the user and handling all keystrokes from that user. Many different telnet client implementations exist, emulating different types of terminal. The telnet server is able to determine which terminal types a client is capable of emulating and passing that information to the underlying operating system during login. Since the telnet server knows the type of terminal the telnet client is emulating, the telnet server and operating system will send appropriate control characters over the connection such that the telnet client will honor the requests and display appropriate information. For the majority of telnet clients, each keystroke entered is flowed over the connection and is handled by the telnet server and the operating system.

Certain telnet clients have the capability of emulating 3270-style terminals. AIX supplies just such a telnet client called *tn3270*. Telnet servers with which these clients work are commonly found on IBM mainframe and midrange systems such as MVS, VM, and OS/400.

Telnet clients that are capable of emulating 3270 terminals can be found on the majority of common TCP/IP implementations for most operating systems, including

- Windows
- DOS
- AIX
- OS/2
- VM
- MVS

CICS/6000 provides a suitable telnet server that is capable of working with telnet clients that support 3270 datastream. The telnet server is known as *cicsteld*. Instead of connecting the user to the operating system, cicsteld connects incoming telnet clients directly to CICS/6000.

Like cicsterm, cicsteld requires that it be executed as a DCE authenticated server. A single cicsteld server will handle one connection between a telnet client and CICS/6000. The cicsteld command may be executed from the AIX command line or be automatically started when an incoming telnet client request is received.

Configuring cicsteld to inetd

Since a new instance of cicsteld is required for each telnet client that wishes to connect to CICS/6000, a mechanism to start a new instance of cicsteld as needed is required. AIX has a demon program that provides such a service. An AIX demon program is one that executes in the background without a terminal. The AIX demon called *inetd* can be configured to listen on multiple TCP/IP ports simultaneously for incoming connections. On receipt of a connection request, inetd will start a new child process and pass the connection request to the newly started task. Cicsteld may be defined as a service to inetd that will then listen for incoming telnet client connection requests and create a new instance of cicsteld when a request arrives. Since cicsteld must execute as a DCE authenticated server, a DCE principal must be defined for the server and its password cached in a DCE keytab file. Both the name of the DCE principal and the location of the keytab file must be specified as start-up parameters for the cicsteld server started by inetd. The start-up flows are shown in Fig. 4.1.

Before configuring cicsteld, the following items must be chosen:

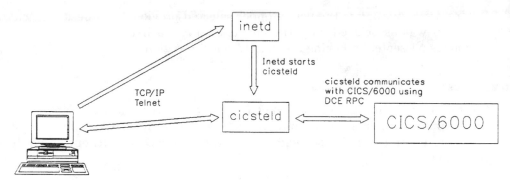

Figure 4.1 Cicsteld start-up flows.

TCP/IP port number The port number is a TCP/IP port that will be used by a telnet client when connecting to cicsteld. The port number may be any number between 1 and 65535 that is not currently used by any other TCP/IP service.

TCP/IP service name Inetd requires that a TCP/IP service name be associated with the port number. The service name is a sequence of ASCII characters that will be associated with the port.

DCE principal name This is name of the DCE principal that the cicsteld server will use for authentication. This principal must be made a member of the cics_users DCE group.

DCE keytab file name This is the name of a file that will contain the encrypted password for the DCE principal which the cicsteld server will authenticate as. Cicsteld must have read permission for this file.

Executable path name This is the full AIX path name to the executable that will be executed when the telnet client connection request is received. This usually will be the path name to the cicsteld executable itself but may be the path name to an AIX shell script which will in turn start cicsteld.

Executable parameters The parameters that are used to control cicsteld also should be specified. These will include the DCE principal name and the path name to the keytab file holding the password for the DCE principal.

The creation of the DCE principal may be achieved by following the SMIT panels for DCE principal and account creation. The principal should be made a member of the DCE group cics_users.

The actual configuration of inetd may be accomplished through SMIT panels or through the AIX command **inetserv.**

Once defined, the cicsteld server may be tested by executing

```
tn3270 <hostname> <port-number>
```

Where port-number is the port number selected previously. Unless a specific region was associated with the cicsteld server, a list of available CICS regions is presented, allowing the user to select a region for use.

Configuring with cicscp

Cicsteld may be configured with the CICS-provided *cicscp* utility. The following command will create and configure a telnet server for CICS/6000. It must be executed as the AIX root user and while being DCE authenticated as cell_admin.

```
# cicscp create telnet_server <server name> <-P port_number>
```

The DCE principal and keytab file creation and inetd update are all accomplished in one step with this command.

Printing from CICS/6000: Cicstermp

CICS/6000 provides printer support through a CICS provided server called *cicstermp.* This server connects to the CICS/6000 region and installs itself as a printer terminal. Once installed, any output from transactions scheduled against this terminal have their output sent to the cicstermp server. When the task ends or a request to print is issued, the cicstermp server builds an AIX file containing a representation of the screen as it would have appeared on the terminal. Once the file is written, cicstermp will execute an AIX program with the file as input. Typically, this will be the AIX print spool command, which will cause the file to be sent to the printer. Once the command has completed, the file will be removed. The relationship between a CICS region, cicstermp, and the AIX print program is illustrated in Fig. 4.2.

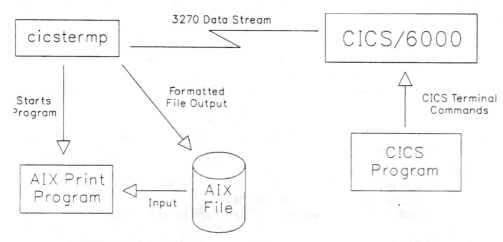

Figure 4.2 CICS/6000 and cicstermp.

To define a suitable terminal definition, the following attributes must be set within the Terminal Definitions (WD).

■ The terminal model size for a CICS/6000 printer must be 64 lines by 132 columns (**NumLines** and **NumColumns**).

■ A one- to eight-character netname that will match the name specified on the cicstermp command must be used to locate the terminal entry (**NetName**).

■ Flags must designate the terminal model entry as being for a printer (**IsPrinter**).

If the terminal printer is to allow transactions asynchronously scheduled against it, the **CanStartATIs** attribute must be set to **yes** in the terminal definitions. By default, this attribute is set to **no** and thus will not accept asynchronously started transactions via the EXEC CICS START command request.

Only some visual attributes are honored in the output; specifically, the following are ignored:

■ Highlight

■ Underline

■ High intensity

■ Color

The cicstermp command has the following syntax:

```
cicstermp -r region -n netname [-t transaction] [-P command]
```

-r region   This required parameter specifies the name of the CICS/6000 region into which the printer terminal will be installed.

-n netname   This required parameter specifies the one- to eight-character netname used to select the terminal model to install.

-t transaction   This parameter specifies an initial transaction to be initiated against the terminal once it has been installed.

-P command   Specifies the name of an AIX executable that will be executed by cicstermp when a request to print is issued. If no command is specified, the AIX command **lp** will be used. **lp** spools a file to the default printer spool queue.

The name of the executable passed with the -P parameter may be any supplied AIX executable or user-written shell script. When invoked, the last parameter passed to the program will be the name of the AIX file containing the screen output. When the command completes, cicstermp will erase the temporary file used to hold the output.

To execute cicstermp, the user must be authenticated as a DCE principal with authorization to attach a terminal to a CICS/6000 region. Since the cicstermp server is not interactive, it must be started with a principal matching the name of the CICS/6000 user it is to execute as. If the DCE principal name does not match any known CICS/6000 user, the CICS/6000 default user will be used. There is no mechanism to install a terminal and have the user associated with the terminal changed during its operation.

Using cicstermp

This section illustrates use of cicstermp and includes an example. Before a cicstermp printer server can be attached to CICS/6000, an appropriate terminal definition must be defined to CICS. This definition will include the *TermId* that a program will use when referring to the printer and a *NetName* that will be used by cicstermp to associate itself with the TermId. The following command illustrates resource definitions for such a terminal:

```
cicsadd -c wd -r ${CICSREGION} P001 \
    NetName = PRNT0001 \
    NumLines = 64 \
    NumColumns = 132 \
    CanStartATIs = yes \
    IsPrinter = yes
```

This command defines a terminal with a TermId of P001 with an associated NetName of PRNT0001. When the cicstermp server is started and connects to CICS/6000, it will specify the NetName and be installed into CICS/6000 with a TermId of P001. Any transactions now started against this terminal either by asynchronous starts (EXEC CICS START) or by triggered transient data queues directed to the terminal will have the terminal as their principal facility. Any terminal output generated by the program will be directed to the cicstermp server. If the application also includes the 3270 datastream print command, the cicstermp server will execute the specified AIX program, passing a copy of the output sent by the CICS program to the newly started AIX program in a file. During development of CICS/6000 applications that generate printer output, it is a good idea to have the printer output captured in an AIX file or sent to a display. This saves the generation of reams of paper and helps to isolate problems that may not be application-related but are due to AIX printer definitions. This may be achieved by starting cicstermp with the following command:

```
cicstermp -r <Region> -n <NetName> -P"cat >> /tmp/cicstermp.out <"
```

This -P command causes the screens destined for the printer to be appended into the file /tmp/cicstermp.out. If the file does not exist initially, it will be created upon first data write.

The following messages will be produced by cicstermp during start-up:

```
ERZ011062I/3714: Connecting to region '<region>'.
ERZ011083I/3721: Installed as printer 'P001', netname 'PRNT0001'.
```

To stop a cicstermp server, set the terminal definition associated with the cicstermp demon out of service. This can be achieved through the CEMT INQUIRE TERMINAL transaction and changing the **Ins** attribute (inservice) to **Out** (outservice). Alternatively, the terminal may be deinstalled through the EXEC CICS SET TERM(<termid>) OUTSERVICE command from within a program. If the region is shutdown, the cicstermp printer servers are automatically stopped. If the cicstermp server is stopped by setting the terminal outservice, the terminal must be set back in service before attempting to reconnect cicstermp with the same netname.

When the cicstermp is set outservice, the following message will be produced from cicstermp before it ends:

```
ERZ011071I/3906: cicsterm/cicstermp terminated (terminal out of service)
```

Although designed to allow output from CICS to be sent to an AIX-attached printer, the cicstermp server may be used as a general-purpose tool for off-line processing of CICS originated data. The AIX program defined to be executed when a printer request is issued by a CICS program may be any AIX application, including shell scripts. The shell script could utilize the data received by processing the data as shell script input, effectively allowing CICS to execute arbitrary AIX shell commands.

Terminal Autoinstall

When a terminal attach request arrives at CICS/6000 either from cicsterm, cicstermp, or cicsteld, CICS internally makes note that the terminal is being installed. If the terminal supplied a netname, the CICS/6000 Workstation Definitions (WD) resource class is searched for a matching netname. If found, the terminal will be installed with all the attributes associated with that definition, including the specified TermId. All clients that attempt to connect with a netname must have a corresponding terminal definition. Specifying a netname allows special characteristics to be associated with the terminal as well as guaranteeing a constant TermId.

In most cases, a CICS client will not supply a netname, and CICS will internally generate a TermId for the installing client. CICS generates this netname and selects the attributes for the terminal being installed based on an autoinstall program that may be customized within the region. The autoinstall program is discussed in Chap. 13, "Terminal Installation."

5

CICS/6000 Resource Definitions

Once CICS/6000 is ready for operation, it may be configured with definitions relating to the programs, transactions, users, and other resources required for its specific use. These definitions are known as *resource definitions* and differentiate one CICS region from another. Each implementation of CICS on different operating system platforms has its own mechanism for defining resources. These range from adding entries into tables to defining the resources from within CICS. With CICS/6000, resource definition is accomplished by the execution of AIX command line programs. Since these commands can be extensive, AIX SMIT panels have been developed to allow ease of entry of the different parameters for the definitions.

The resource definitions themselves are split into groups of related definitions. The following is a list of the different types of CICS resource groups:

Communication Definitions (CD)   This resource class defines the connections from one CICS system to another. The remote CICS system identifier is used as the key in these resources.

File Definitions (FD)   This resource group defines the CICS files accessible under CICS/6000. These files may be defined remotely on other CICS systems or specified as being available on a local CICS/6000 file manager.

Gateway Definitions (GD)   This resource group defines available Encina PPC Gateways for use by CICS/6000 to communicate with a CICS host using synclevel 2 over SNA. The gateways defined here are referenced in the Communication Definitions (CD) entries if nonlocal SNA is to be used.

Gateway Server Definitions (GSD)   This resource group defines the characteristics of Encina PPC Gateways, allowing them to be started and stopped through CICS commands.

Journal Definitions (JD)   This resource group defines the characteristics of CICS journal files. Journals are a CICS construct used for logging information.

Listener Definitions (LD)   This resource group defines the different CICS components that listen for incoming requests to start transactions on behalf of remote systems. Two types of listeners may be defined, TCP/IP listeners and SNA listeners. SNA listeners are required for local SNA.

Monitoring Definition (MD)   This resource group contains one entry that controls CICS/6000's ability to capture monitoring data.

XA Database Product Definitions   This resource group defines databases that support XA data commitment protocol.

Program Definitions (PD)   This resource group defines CICS programs, maps, and tables.

Region Definition (RD)   This resource group contains one entry that defines CICS region-wide characteristics such as security, amount of memory to be used, number of application servers, and many others.

Schema File Definitions (SCD)   This resource group is used to describe the layout of CICS files as managed by an Encina SFS.

Structured File Server Definitions (SSD)   This resource group describes the characteristics of Encina SFSs, allowing them to be started and stopped through CICS commands.

Temporary Storage Definitions (TSD)   This resource group defines temporary storage queue definitions that are not dynamically created by programs.

Terminal Definitions (WD)   This resource group contains models for both CICS terminal autoinstalls and predefined hard-installed terminals.

Transaction Definitions (TD)   This resource class defines CICS transactions available to be started from the region.

Transient Data Definitions (TDD)   This resource group defines both intra- and extrapartition transient data queues to the CICS region.

User Definitions (UD)   This resource group describes the CICS user names locally defined to the region as well as their characteristics such as security.

Permanent and Runtime Resources

CICS/6000 maintains its resource definitions in human-readable files within the AIX file system. These files are known as *stanza* files because of their nature of defining a resource entry as a set of stanzas within the file. A separate stanza file exists for each of the different resource types. The stanza files are located in the region database directory in subdirectories named after the resource classes they define. For example, the Program Definitions (PD) stanza file is located in `/var/cics_regions/<region>/database/PD/PD.stanza`. Although these files may be edited with an AIX editor, great caution should be used. Errors in typing can result in difficult to diagnose problems when a region is restarted. The files are properly modified with the rich set of CICS-supplied commands.

When a region is started, it reads each of the stanza files into memory, parsing the **name** = **value** attribute pairs from their human-readable character representations into a more compact and usable machine format. Once the files have been read, an in-memory representation of the resource definitions exists. This is termed the *runtime database*. Changes made to the runtime database by CICS system management commands such as EXEC CICS SET and changes made by supplied transactions such as CEMT will be lost during the next CICS start. If permanent changes are desired, they should be made to both the permanent definitions (stanza files) and in the runtime. When changes are added to the runtime or resources removed from the runtime, CICS reflects these changes in new stanza files called the *autostart stanza files*. These files are identical to the permanent stanza files except that they reflect the resources defined in the running region. For example, if a transaction is removed from a running region, the autostart stanza is rewritten with the transaction removed. If a CICS region is cold started, the permanent stanza files are used, if it is autostarted, the autostart stanza files are used. By keeping two copies of the stanza files, one for cold starts and one for autostarts, CICS is able to start up in a mode that better reflects its definitions at the time it was last stopped. Changes made to individual attributes within a resource do not cause the autostart stanza files to be rewritten, only additions and deletions. An autostart stanza file is located in a subdirectory below the permanent stanza file directory in a directory called <Resource Name>.<Region Name>, where the resource name is PD for Program Definitions, TD for Transaction Definitions, and so on. The actual file is called <Resource Name>.auto. Again, these may be manipulated by an editor with great care.

CICS/6000 Resource Group Details

The following subsections detail some of the more important attributes of the CICS resources. The attribute of a given resource is described in terms of its attribute name as opposed to the English description shown in the SMIT panels. Familiarity with the attribute names becomes more important in detailed CICS configuration.

Listener Definitions (LD)

This resource type defines individual CICS listener servers that will listen for incoming requests to start transactions on the local CICS region. Two types of listeners may be defined. The first type of listener consists of those which listen for incoming TCP/IP start requests from CICS clients on PCs or Macintosh systems. The other type specifies SNA connections if a local SNA server component is available on the CICS region machine.

<**Listener Name**>   This attribute is the key field to name the instance of the listener being defined. It may be from 1 to 12 characters in length. It is not referenced by any other CICS resources.

Protocol   This is the type of listener being defined. This may be either **TCP** for TCP/IP incoming requests from PC or Macintosh clients or **SNA** for incoming requests from other CICS regions over a local SNA connection. The SNA entry must be specified if local SNA is used as opposed to the PPC Gateway method of communicating with an SNA connected host.

TCPAddress   This is the TCP/IP network adapter IP address if incoming TCP/IP connections are to be accepted from only one network interface if multiple are available. The default value of "" specifies that all TCP/IP network interfaces on the CICS region machine may be used.

TCPService   This attribute specifies a TCP/IP service name used to determine the TCP/IP port on which the listener is going to accept incoming requests. The name specified in this attribute should be defined in the AIX /etc/services file with a corresponding TCP port number. If the default "" value is used, the CICS architected port of 1435 will be used.

Name	Default	Summary
<**Listener Name**>	N/A	Name of this listener instance
Protocol	**TCP**	Type of listener being defined
TCPAddress	""	Network interface for TCP requests
TCPService	""	Port number for TCP requests.

Communication Definitions (CD)

This resource class defines the communication attributes to remote CICS regions and partner APPC applications used for DTP. Included in these definitions are the methods of communicating between this region and the remote system. This may be over TCP/IP or SNA through local SNA connection or through a PPC Gateway if synclevel 2 is required. Additionally, communication security attributes may be specified, allowing userids to be sent to the remote system. If the remote system is not an ASCII character set environment, a character-translation attribute may be set to allow transaction routing requests to be converted correctly.

<**SYSID**>   This key attribute specifies the CICS SYSID of the remote CICS system.

RemoteSysType   This attribute specifies whether the connection is made over TCP/IP or over SNA. For TCP/IP connections, **TCP** should be specified; for SNA connections, **SNA** should be specified. The **GatewayName** attribute specifies whether local SNA or a PPC Gateway will be used if the connection type is SNA.

RemoteNetworkName   The SNA network name on which the remote CICS system is SNA connected.

RemoteLUName   The SNA LU name, which when combined with the network name, specifies the SNA LU name of the remote CICS region. For TCP/IP connections to other CICS/6000 regions, this attribute should be set to the remote CICS region name.

RemoteCodePageTR   The AIX codepage of the remote CICS region used to convert transaction routed requests. For an EBCDIC mainframe, the codepage of **IBM-037** should be specified. The default for an ASCII system is **IBM-850.**

GatewayName   If the **RemoteSysType** is specified as SNA, this attribute specifies whether local SNA will be used to communicate with the remote CICS system ("") or if a PPC Gateway should be used to communicate with the remote system. If a PPC Gateway is to be used, the name of the gateway should be specified here.

Name	Default	Summary
AllocateTimeout	0	Seconds before a back-end DTP request times out
DCECell	""	Cell name of remote CICS/6000 region or PPC Gateway
GatewayName	""	Name of PPC Gateway
InService	yes	Availability of remote system
LinkUserId	""	Userid for link security
OutboundUserIds	sent	Should userids be sent on outbound requests
RemoteCodePageTR	IBM-850	Code page for transaction routing data conversion
RemoteLUName	""	Name of remote CICS region
RemoteNetworkName	""	Name of remote network
RemoteSysSecurity	local	Inbound authorization checking type
RemoteSysType	TCP	Type of connection
RSLKeyMask	none	Link security RSL keys
TSLKeyMask	none	Transaction security TSL keys

File Definitions (FD)

The File Definitions resource group specifies files accessible through CICS commands. Both local and remote files may be defined in this group. For locally defined files, the SFS name, SFS file name, and index name must be specified, and for remote files, the remote CICS server name and its remote file name must be supplied. Access control and capabilities for the file, as well as any conversion templates used, may be defined. Among the access controls available for a file are

- Whether the file may have records added to it (addable)
- Whether the file may have records deleted from it (deletable)
- Whether the file may have records read from it (readable)

- Whether the file may be emptied (emptyable)
- Whether the file may be browsed (browsable)
- Whether the file may be updated (updatable)

<**File Name**>   This key attribute specifies the name of the file as known to CICS. This need not be the same as the actual file name managed by the SFS or the file defined on the remote CICS system.

BaseName   The name of the file held on the SFS.

FileServer   The CDS name of the SFS holding the file.

IndexName   The name of the SFS file index used to organize the file.

RemoteName   Name of the file on a remote CICS region.

RemoteSysid   Name of a remote CICS region. If this is specified, a matching SYSID must be defined in the Communication Definitions (CD).

KeyLength   Length of the key field in a CICS file if the file is defined as remote.

OpenStatus   Initial status of the file when the region is started. This may be specified as **open** or **closed.** If the file is closed, no access will be allowed on the file until it is opened.

EnableStatus   Specifies whether the file is enabled or disabled.

RecoverStatus   This attributed describes whether the file is recoverable or nonrecoverable. For nonrecoverable files, changes made to the file are permanent immediately. For recoverable files, changes made to the file will be undone if the transaction fails.

Name	Default	Summary
AddOpt	addable	Can records be added to the file
BaseName	""	SFS file name
BrowseOpt	browseable	Can the file be browsed
DeleteOpt	deletable	Can records be deleted from the file
EnableStatus	enabled	Is the file enabled or disabled
ErrorIsolation	on	Error control with an SFS
FileProtection	none	DCE RPC security between CICS and an SFS
FileServer	""	Name of an SFS on which the file is located
IndexName	""	Name of an SFS file index
KeyLen	0	Length of a remotely defined file key
OpenStatus	closed	Is the file open or closed
ReadOpt	readable	Can records be read from the file
RecordSize	0	Length of a record when the file is defined as remote
RecoverStatus	recoverable	Is the file recoverable or nonrecoverable
RemoteName	""	Name of the file on a remote CICS region
RemoteSysid	""	Name of a remote CICS system if the file is remote
TemplateDefined	no	Is a conversion template available for function shipping
UpdateOpt	updateable	Can records be modified within the file

Gateway Definitions (GD)

This resource class specifies Encina PPC Gateways that may be used for CICS intersystem communication. The gateways defined here may be referenced in Communication Definitions (CD). A Gateway Definition is not required for all SNA communications, only those which require synclevel 2 connectivity. A Gateway Definition is named by a one- to four-character name that may be specified in the **GatewayName** attribute of a communication definition. A Gateway may have an LU name associated with it that differs from that of the local CICS region; this allows remote CICS systems to access the region by multiple names. These definitions are usually associated with a Gateway Server Definition, and many of the attributes must match. The attributes of a Gateway Definition specify its DCE CDS name, DCE cell name, and the DCE principal under which the gateway is operating to authorize incoming requests.

<**Gateway Name**>   This key field is one- to four-character string naming the Gateway as known to CICS. This is associated with the **GatewayName** entry in a communication definition.

DCECell   This is a DCE cell name in which the Gateway server may be located.

GatewayCDSName   This attribute defines the name of the PPC Gateway within the DCE CDS name space. It may be specified as a single name, in which case the prefix `/.:/cics/ppc/gateway/` will be added. This entry usually pairs with a Gateway Server Definition (GSD).

GatewayLUName   This attribute allows the PPC Gateway to know the CICS region by a different LU name than that defined in the CICS Region Definition (RD). If left blank ("*"), the Region Definition LU name value will be used.

GatewayPrincipal   This attribute specifies the DCE principal name if secure incoming DCE RPCs are required from the PPC Gateway. The principal name specified here must match that under which the gateway itself is authenticated. This is normally of the form `cics/ppc/gateway/ <name>`.

Name	Default	Summary
DCECell	/.:/	DCE cell in which PPC Gateway is located
GatewayCDSName	""	DCE CDS name at which the PPC Gateway will advertise its location
GatewayLUName	""	SNA LU name that the PPC Gateway will be known on the SNA network
GatewayPrincipal	""	DCE principal under which the PPC Gateway executes. Used for incoming request authorization.

Gateway Server Definitions (GSD)

This resource class defines the attributes of an Encina PPC Gateway Server. These resources allow CICS commands to be used to execute underlying Encina commands to start, stop, and configure a PPC Gateway. The attributes defined here include the name that the PPC Gateway will register for itself within DCE CDS. An AIX logical volume is defined to allow the PPC Gateway to log recoverable information and configuration.

Entries in this resource class are created and deleted by CICS commands that create PPC Gateways.

<Gateway CDS Name>   This key attribute specifies the DCE CDS name of the PPC Gateway. It will usually be of the form `/.:/cics/ppc/gateway/<name>`. When the Gateway is started, it will use this attribute to advertise itself within DCE CDS name space, allowing CICS to locate and utilize it. This attribute is usually defined in CICS Gateway Definition (GD) resource entries in the **GatewayCDSName** attribute.

ShortName   This attribute defines the AIX short name of the resource used to build an AIX SRC entry for starting the Gateway. Short names for Gateways must be distinct from any other Gateway short name on any one machine.

StartType   This attribute specifies how the Gateway processing should be performed when it is started.

ThreadPoolSize   This attribute defines the number of concurrent requests that the PPC Gateway can process concurrently from the CICS region.

UserId   This attribute defines the AIX userid that the PPC Gateway will execute as when started by the AIX SRC.

Name	Default	Summary
LogVolume	**log_%S**	AIX logical volume name used for logging
ProtectionLevel	**none**	DCE authentication level for RPCs
ShortName	**PPCGWY**	Short name of gateway and value of %S macro
ThreadPoolSize	**10**	Number of concurrent RPC requests
UserId	**%S**	AIX userid for gateway

Journal Definitions (JD)

This attribute group defines the CICS journals available for CICS program use. A CICS journal allows a CICS program to write arbitrary information to AIX files for off-line processing. A CICS journal has two different AIX files defined to it; these files have the journal data written to them. Only one of the files will be in use by CICS at any one time, allowing the other to be processed or emptied. If a journal write error occurs, a journal can be configured to cause the region to terminate instead of returning an error. This allows guaranteed audit and logging information to be collected.

<Journal Id>   This key attribute specifies the journal being defined. Journals are identified as two-digit names with values from 01 to 99. Journal 01 is reserved for CICS usage on other CICS environments and should not be used by applications.

CruicalFlag   If an unrecoverable write error occurs while writing a journal record, this flag specifies whether the region should be allowed to continue.

DiskA   This attribute specifies an AIX file name to hold the journal data. If no name is specified, the AIX file name is set to `Cjrnlxx`A, where xx is the journal identifier. If a name is specified, the file will be created in the region data directory.

DiskAStatus   This attribute specifies whether the "A" file should be used for logging. If so, the attribute should be set to **current** and the **DiskBStatus** set to **ready.** If the "B" file should be first, then the preceding attributes should be swapped.

DiskB   See **DiskA** attribute.

DiskBStatus   See **DiskAStatus** attribute.

InitialOpenFlag   This yes/no attribute specifies whether the journal is defined as being initially available for use.

Name	Default	Summary
CrucialFlag	no	Action on journal I/O error
DiskA	""	Journal file "A" name
DiskAStatus	current	Journal in use flag
DiskB	""	Journal file "B" name
DiskBStatus	ready	Journal in use flag
InitialOpenFlag	yes	Is journal available flag

XA Database Product Definitions (XAD)

This resource class defines the database products that CICS should work with using the X/Open XA protocol. This protocol allows CICS-managed resources and database resources to keep their data in synchronization. Database products that provide an XA interface supply a module that can be compiled or link-edited with CICS-provided code. The result of this is a file called the *Switch Load File* that contains both CICS and database code. This code allows CICS to make requests to the database server to allow the XA protocol to flow. Detailed information on this resource class is given in Chap. 28, "Resource Definition with XA databases."

<XA Interface Name>   This key field is used to name a specific XA interface. It is not referenced by any other CICS attribute.

SwitchLoadFile   This attributes specifies the AIX file name of the Switch Load File built in conjunction with CICS and the database. If an absolute AIX path is not specified, the file is first searched for in the region's bin directory and, if not found, in the CICS product bin directory.

XAOpen   This attribute specifies a set of parameters passed to the Switch Load File and hence onto the database code when an internal XA Open command is issued to form a connection with the database. The parameters passed depend on the different database implementations but may include database names, database userids, and other information.

XAClose   This attribute, like the **XAOpen** attribute is used to pass database-specific commands to the database when an XA Close command is issued internally.

Name	Default	Summary
SwitchLoadFile	""	Name of AIX Switch Load File
XAOpen	""	XA Open parameters
XAClose	""	XA Close parameters
XA Serialize	**all_operations**	Database serialization controls

Program Definitions (PD)

This resource group defines CICS programs, BMS maps, and tables that may be executed under CICS. The type of the resource, whether it is a program, a map, or a table, must be specified. For all types, the underlying AIX file name of the file containing the program, map, or table also must be supplied. If the program is defined as remote, the remote CICS SYSID and program name also may be specified.

<**Program Name**>   This key field defines the name of the CICS program, mapset, or table as accessed by CICS. This may be a one- to eight-character name and must be unique within the region.

ProgType   This resource defines the type of the resource entry. Valid types are **program, map,** and **table.**

PathName   This attribute specifies the AIX path name to the program, map, or table that is used when the resource is referenced. If an absolute path name is supplied, the file should be defined at that location. For COBOL programs, no suffix such as **.gnt** or **.int** should be used. If a relative name is supplied, the search varies based on the type of resource. For programs, the file is searched for first in the region bin directory, followed by the region product bin directory. For mapsets, the file is searched for in the region maps/locale directory followed by the region maps/prime directory. If not located there, the CICS product maps/locale and maps/prime directories are searched. For tables, the region data directory is first referenced, followed by the CICS product data directory.

EnableStatus   Programs may be disabled, preventing them from being used. Setting this attribute to **disabled** prevents the program from being executed until it is reenabled.

Resident   For C language programs, setting this attribute to **yes** flags it as eligible for program caching within an application server.

TemplateDefined   Setting this flag to **yes** states that a data-conversion template exists for incoming function-shipping requests. The template allows conversion from one machine data format to another if the machine making the request has different data representations from the target.

UserExitNumber   This attribute defines the program as a CICS user exit and calls the program associated with this resource whenever the exit is encountered.

Name	Default	Summary
EnableStatus	enabled	Enable status of the program
PathName	""	AIX path name to the program, mapset, or table
ProgType	program	Type of resource
RemoteName	""	Name of program on remote system
RemoteSysid	""	Name of remote CICS system
Resident	no	Program eligible for caching
TemplateDefined	no	Conversion template defined
TransId	""	Mirror transaction name associated with program when an incoming distributed program link request arrives
UserExitNumber	0	User exit defined

Region Definitions (RD)

This resource type has only one entry for the CICS region as a whole. There are many attributes for this resource that specify many of the operational characteristics of the region.

CheckpointInterval   This attribute specifies how often CICS checkpoints its state to the log.

ClassMaxTasks   This attribute defines the maximum number of transactions that can execute concurrently for each of the 10 CICS defined classes. Transactions do not have to be associated with a class, but if they are, this attribute defines the maximum number of running transactions for that class. The value of this attribute is 10 comma-separated integers, one for each of the classes. The position of the integer is the count for class associated with that integer. The **TClass** attribute within the transaction definition defines the class with which a transaction is associated.

ClassMaxTaskLim   This attribute defines the maximum number of queued and running transactions for a given class that should be allowed before rejecting transaction start requests for transactions of the class. The value of this attribute is 10 comma-separated integers stating the task limits for each of the 10 CICS-defined classes. A task limit value of 0 indicates that there is no limit for transactions for that class.

CProgramCacheSize   This attribute specifies how many C language CICS programs may be cached in an application server. Caching improves performance of a CICS region by allowing an application to remain in memory once it has completed. If invoked again, it need not be reloaded from disk. Programs that are eligible for caching have their **Resident** attribute set to **yes** within their Program Definitions (PD).

CWASize   This attribute defines the size of the CICS Common Work Area in bytes. This is an area of CICS-maintained storage that is available for application use. This storage is visible to all CICS applications. The maximum size of this storage is 3584 bytes.

DefaultUserid   This attribute specifies the CICS user to be used when a user has not signed on or otherwise identified itself to CICS.

ESMLoad   This yes/no flag controls whether an external security manager application should be invoked to handle CICS security.

ESMModule   This attribute specifies the path name of an AIX application that will be invoked by CICS to handle external CICS security.

ExternalTrace   This yes/no attribute specifies whether CICS trace will be written directly to files or whether it will be sent to the AIX trace facility.

IntrospectInterval   This attribute specifies the number of minutes between internal CICS consistency checking.

LocalLUName   This attribute specifies the local LU name by which the CICS region is known for ISC communications definitions. If not specified, the LU name will be the name of the CICS region.

LocalNetworkName   This attribute specifies the network name to which the CICS region is attached.

MaxRegionPool   This attribute specifies the maximum size of the region pool of storage. This storage is used to maintain CICS internal data such as program names, transaction names, users, etc.

MaxTSHPool   This attribute specifies the amount of storage allocated for task shared storage. This storage holds data that are accessible by multiple CICS tasks. Included in this storage are

- COMMAREAs
- The Common Work Area (CWA)
- TIOAs
- TCTUAs
- Main temporary storage
- Mapsets and tables

- Conversion templates
- Temporary storage for unprotected STARTs

MaxServer   This attribute specifies the maximum number of application servers that the region can start when the load on the system is high.

MinServer   This attribute specifies the minimum number of application servers that the region will maintain when the load is light.

ServerIdleLimit   This attribute specifies the number of seconds after which an idle application server will be ended. If ending an application server would result in fewer than **MinServer** application servers remaining, it is not ended.

StatFile   This is an AIX file name used to hold the output of CICS statistics information. If a nonabsolute path is specified, the file is written relative to the region data directory.

TSQAgeLimit   This attribute specifies the number of days that an idle or unaccessed temporary storage queue should be deleted automatically by CICS. Since these queues can be created dynamically by an application, this mechanism prevents accidental use of resources.

Name	Default	Summary
CheckpointInterval	1000	Interval between checkpoints
ClassMaxTasks	1,1,1,...,1,1	Maximum tasks for class
ClassMaxTaskLim	0,0,0,...,0,0	Class task limit
CProgramCacheSize	0	Programs to cache
CWASize	512	Size of CWA
DateForm	ddmmyy	Format of CICS dates
DefaultUserid	CICSUSER	Default CICS user
ESMLoad	no	Should an external security program be used
ESMModule	""	Name of external security program
LocalLUName	""	CICS system LU name
LocalNetworkName	""	Name of local network
MaxServer	5	Maximum number of application servers
MinServer	1	Minimum number of application servers
MaxTSHPool	1048576	Task shared memory pool size
MaxRegionPool	2097152	Region memory pool size
ServerIdleLimit	300	Number of seconds until idle application server ended
TSQAge	20	Days until unaccessed TS queue is deleted

SFS Schema Definitions (SCD)

This resource class defines the structure, names, and indices of SFS files. These resources can be applied to an SFS to create the files. This resource type allows CICS commands to be used to define files on an SFS without having to know the underlying Encina SFS commands.

<**File Name**>   This key attribute defines the name of an SFS file. No SFS prefix should be specified.

FileType   This attribute defines the type of SFS file being created. Choices include **clustered** for CICS KSDS files, **relative** for CICS RRDS files, and **sequential** for CICS ESDS files.

VolumeName   This attribute specifies the AIX logical volume being used by an SFS on which the files will be stored.

MaxRecords   This attribute defines the maximum number of records that the file is allowed to store.

PreallocatePages   This attribute defines the number of SFS pages that are preallocated to an SFS file. Preallocating pages guarantees that the file has sufficient space to hold data.

FieldName1-20   These attributes define individual field names within an SFS file record. These field names are unknown to CICS but are required when defining an SFS file.

FiledType1-20   These attributes define the SFS field type of the fields within an SFS file record. The field types are defined as Encina SFS field types but are almost always defined as **byteArray.**

FieldLength1-20   These attributes define the length of an SFS field type if the field has a variable size such as **byteArray.**

PrimaryIndexName   Name of the SFS primary index for the file being defined. Every SFS file requires a primary index.

PrimaryIndexFields   This attribute specifies the field names that comprise the primary index.

PrimaryIndexUnique   This yes/no attribute defines whether or not the file can contain records with duplicate entries keyed on the primary index.

Name	Default	Summary
FileType	**sequential**	Type of SFS file
VolumeName	**sfs_%S**	Name of AIX logical volume for SFS data
PrimaryIndexName	**""**	Name of SFS file primary index
PrimaryIndexFields	**""**	Name of fields comprising the primary index
PrimaryIndexUnique	**yes**	Allow duplicate records in file
MaxRecords	**10000**	Maximum number of records in file
PreallocatePages	**100**	Number of preallocated SFS file pages
FieldName1-20	**""**	Names of SFS records fields
FieldType1-20	**none**	Type of SFS field
FieldLength1-20	**0**	Length of SFS field

SFS Server Definitions (SSD)

This resource class defines the definitions for Encina SFSs, allowing them to be configured, started, and stopped by CICS commands. The resources specified here mirror the underlying Encina options for the SFS itself. Detailed descriptions of the SFS commands may be found in relevant Encina manuals.

\<SFS Server Name\>   This key attribute names the Encina SFS in terms of its DCE CDS name. This attribute normally should be specified as `/.:/cics/sfs/<name>`. When the SFS is started, it uses this attribute to advertise itself to DCE CDS, allowing it to be located by SFS commands and by CICS

ShortName   This attribute defines the name of the SFS as known to the AIX SRC. It must be eight characters or less and unique within the definitions of all SFSs on this machine. This value is also expanded by the **%S** macro in other attribute settings.

BufferPoolSize   This attribute defines the size of internal storage that the SFS allocates for itself to buffer file records.

Checkpoint   This attribute defines the amount of time before the SFS checkpoints its own status to its log.

DataVolume   This attribute defines the AIX logical volume name used to hold the SFS file data.

LogVolume   This attribute defines the AIX logical volume name used to hold SFS logging data used for recovery.

IdleTimeout   This attribute specifies the time in seconds after which a lock held on an SFS file will be released when there is contention on the lock and the original acquirer of the lock has been idle.

MRAArchivingEnabled   This attribute defines whether SFS Encina data volume backup is enabled.

OpThreadPoolSize   This attribute defines the number of threads available within the SFS to handle concurrent file requests. The number of threads directly contributes to the concurrent requests available from CICS.

UserId   This attribute defines the AIX userid used to execute the SFS. The value of this attribute directly affects the permissions of the AIX logical volumes specified in the **DataVolume** and **LogVolume** attributes.

Name	Default	Summary
BufferPoolSize	**1000**	Size of SFS buffer pool
Checkpoint	**5000**	Checkpoint interval
DataVolume	**sfs_%S**	AIX volume name used to hold SFS file data
LogVolume	**log_%S**	AIX volume name used to hold SFS log data
IdleTimeout	**300**	Time to release contended, idle locks
MRAArchivingEnabled	**no**	Allow SFS volume backups
OpThreadPoolSize	**12**	Number of threads for concurrent operations
ShortName	**S%H**	Unique short name for SFS
UserID	**%S**	AIX userid under which SFS executes

Temporary Storage Definitions (TSD)

These attributes define characteristics of CICS temporary storage queues. Although temporary storage queues need not be defined prior to use, defining them allows additional attributes to be assigned to them.

<**Queue Name**>   This key field defines the one- to eight-character name of the temporary storage queue described.

RecoverFlag   This attribute defines whether the queue is recoverable. Only auxiliary queues may be defined as recoverable. Main storage queues are not recoverable.

TemplateDefined   This attribute defines whether a data conversion template exists for remote communications for this queue.

RemoteName   This attribute allows the name of the queue to be defined as something other than the key queue name if the queue is defined as remote.

RemoteSysid   This attribute specifies the name of a remote CICS system on which the queue actually resides.

Name	Default	Summary
RecoverFlag	no	Is the queue recoverable
TemplateDefined	no	Has a user conversion template been defined
RemoteName	""	Name of queue on remote CICS system
RemoteSysid	""	Name of remote CICS region

Terminal Definitions (WD)

This resource class defines models for terminal installations and predefined terminals that attach with specified network names. When a CICS client terminal attaches to CICS/6000, the attributes associated with that terminal are derived from the definitions defined in this resource class. A terminal attached to CICS can either be autoinstalled or hard-installed. An *autoinstalled terminal* is one that has no corresponding or supplied netname defined. A *hard-installed terminal* is one that supplied a netname during the connect with CICS/6000.

The attributes associated with all terminals include

CanStartATIs   Can asynchronous transactions be started against this terminal by running an EXEC CICS START command? If no, an attempt to start a transaction asynchronously will fail.

CanStartTTIs   Can transactions be started by entering a transaction identifier at the terminal? If no, transaction codes entered at the terminal do not result in those transactions being started.

NumColumns   The number of columns that the terminal supports. This value can be inquired from a CICS program with the EXEC CICS ASSIGN SCRNWD command.

NumLines The number of rows that the terminal supports. This value can be inquired from a CICS program with the EXEC CICS ASSIGN SCRNHT command.

Priority This attribute, in conjunction with the transaction and user priority values, specifies the overall priority for a transaction when there is contention for which transaction will start next.

TCTUALen This attribute defines the length of the Terminal Control Table User Area (TCTUA), which is an area of storage associated with the terminal that applications can use to store data.

TSLKeyList List of TSL keys given to a user from this terminal.

Name	Default	Summary
CanStartATIs	no	Can asynchronous starts be issued against the terminal
CanStartTTIs	yes	Can transactions be started from the terminal from user input
DevType	""	?
ERRColor	no	Default color for error messages
ERRHilight	no	Default hilighting for error messages
ERRIntensify	yes	Should error messages be displayed intensified
ERRLastLine	yes	Should the error message be displayed on the last line
ExtDS	no	Does the terminal support extended datastream
Foreground	no	Does the terminal support foreground color changes
Hilight	no	Does the terminal support hilighting
IsPrinter	no	Does the terminal represent a CICS printer
IsShippable	yes	Can the terminal be shipped to a remote CICS
ModelId	""	Terminal model identifier
NetName		Netname of terminal
NumColumns	80	Number of columns on the terminal
NumLines	24	Number of rows on the terminal
Outline	no	Does the terminal support outlining
Priority	0	Terminal priority
TCTUALen	0	Size of the terminal TCTUA
UCTranFlag	no	Should CICS translate data to uppercase

Transaction Definitions (TD)

This resource class defines the transactions that may be started on the CICS region. Transactions are identified by one to four characters. The attributes of a transaction identify its operational nature such as the program to be invoked when the transaction is submitted. The program must be defined in the Program Definitions (PD) if the transaction is local.

<Transaction Name> This key attribute defines the one- to four-character name for the transaction.

ProgName This attribute defines the name of the CICS program that is to be started when a request to start the transaction is processed. The program name must be defined in the Program Definitions (PD). If the transaction is defined as remote in the **RemoteSysId** attribute, this entry is ignored.

EnableStatus   This attribute defines whether the transaction is enabled or disabled. Disabled transactions cannot be started until they are reenabled. Transactions can be enabled or disabled at CICS runtime through the EXEC CICS SET/INQUIRE TRANSACTION API or through the CEMT transaction.

Dynamic   This attribute defines whether the transaction will be sent to a dynamic transaction routing user exit when a request to start the transaction is processed.

DeadLockTimeout   This attribute defines how long the transaction should wait before being abended in the event that CICS detects a potential deadlock situation involving this transaction. If the value is set to **0,** the transaction will not be abended in such cases.

Priority   This attribute defines the priority of the transaction in the transaction scheduler if there are multiple transactions waiting to start. The higher the priority value, the better is the chance that the transaction will be scheduled next.

TClass   This attribute defines the transaction class that is to be associated with the transaction. The value may be specified as an integer in the range **1** to **10** relating to the 10 defined CICS classes or may have a value of **none** indicating that the transaction is not associated with any CICS task class.

TSLCheck   This attribute defines how Transaction Security Level checking should be performed. This may be set to **internal** for CICS internal security checking or **external** to specify that external security checking via an external security manager should be used.

RSLCheck   This attribute defines how Resource Security Level checking should be performed. Values include **internal** to specify that CICS internal security should be used, **external** to specify that an external security manager should be used, or **none** to specify that no security checking should be used for any resource access.

Name	Default	Summary
DeadLockTimeout	**0**	Time till deadlock abend
Dynamic	**no**	Is transaction eligible for dynamic transaction routing
EnableStatus	**enabled**	Is transaction enabled or disabled
InDoubt	**wait_backout**	Purge effect during syncpoint
InvokationMode	**any_facility** **any_start** **at_normal_running**	When transaction can start
IsBackEndDTP	**no**	Can transaction be started through DTP
Priority	**0**	Priority to start
ProgName	**""**	Name of program to start
Purgeability	**purgeable**	Can transaction be purged
RemoteSysId	**""**	Name of remote CICS system

Name	Default	Summary
RemoteName	""	Name of transaction on remote CICS system
RSLCheck	none	Type of resource security checking
TWASize	0	Size of task work area
Timeout	0	Conversational timeout
TSLCheck	internal	Type of transaction security checking
UCTranFlag	no	Convert output to upper case

Transient Data Definitions (TDD)

This attribute defines the transient data queues available within the CICS region. Unlike temporary storage queues, which may be used without definition, transient data queues must be defined before use. Two types of transient data queues may be defined: intrapartition and extrapartition. Not all resource attributes apply to both types of queue. For *intrapartition* queues, the attributes that apply include

- **FacilityId**
- **FacilityType**
- **RecoveryType**
- **TriggeredTransId**
- **TriggerLevel**

For *extrapartition* queues, the attributes that apply include

- **ExtrapartitionFile**
- **IOMode**
- **OpenMode**
- **RecordLen**
- **RecordTerminator**
- **RecordType**
- **WhenOpened**

All other attributes in this resource class apply to both types of queues. A description of transient data queues under CICS/6000 is discussed in Chap. 10, "Transient Data Queues."

<**Queue Name**> This key field defines the one- to four-character queue name.

DestType This attribute defines the type of transient data queue being defined. Valid values include *intrapartition* for intrapartition queues, *extra-*

partition for extrapartition queues, *indirect* for indirect queues, and *remote* if the queue requests are to be function shipped to a different CICS region.

ExtrapartitionFile   This attribute defines the AIX file name used for a queue that is defined as **extrapartition** in the **DestType** attribute. If no absolute path name is specified, a path relative to the CICS region data directory is used.

FacilityId   This attribute identifies the terminal identifier or communication connection against which a transaction is to be executed if the intrapartition queue is triggered and the **FacilityType** is not **file.**

FacilityType   This attribute defines the type of facility to be used for triggered intrapartition queues. The values specified here may be **terminal** if the transaction is to be started against a terminal, **system** if an ISC link is to be used, and **file** if neither a terminal nor an ISC link is to be used.

IOMode   This attribute defines whether the queue is **input** or **output** for **extrapartition** queues.

OpenMode   This attribute defines whether extrapartition transient data queues that are defined as output should be emptied when opened or should new data be appended on the end.

RecordLen   This attribute defines the length of records in an extrapartition transient data queue defined as having a **fixed_length** record format.

RecordType   This attribute defines the record format of an extrapartition transient data queue. It may have one of the following values:

- **fixed_length**
- **variable_length**
- **byte_terminated**
- **line_oriented**
- **null_terminated**

RecordLen   If the queue is extrapartition and has a **RecordType** of **fixed_length,** this attribute defines the length of each record.

RecordTerminator   If the queue is extrapartition and has a **RecordType** of **byte_terminated,** this attribute defines the byte terminator value. It is specified in integer format.

TriggerLevel   This attribute defines the number of records added to the queue that will cause the transaction specified in the **TriggeredTransId** attribute to be started. If this value is **0,** no trigger is in effect.

TriggeredTransId   This attribute defines a transaction name to be started when a trigger level has been reached on the queue.

Name	Default	Summary
DestType	intrapartition	Type of queue
ExtrapartitionFile	""	AIX file name for extrapartition queue
FacilityId	""	**TerminalId** or **SysId** for triggered transaction
FacilityType	file	Type of facility for triggered transaction
IOMode	output	Direction of data for extrapartition queue
OpenMode	truncate	How the file is opened
RecordLen	1024	Length of fixed-length extrapratition record
RecordTerminator	0	Terminator value for byte-terminated extrapartition record
RecordType	fixed_length	Type of records in an extrapartition queue
RecoveryType	logical	Recoverability of intrapartition queue
RemoteSysId	""	Name of remote CICS system
RemoteName	""	Name of queue on remote CICS system
TemplateDefined	no	Data conversion template defined
TriggeredTransId	""	Transaction to be started if triggered
TriggerLevel	0	Number of items in queue until triggered
WhenOpened	at_startup	When is the queue opened

User Definitions (UD)

This resource defines users to a CICS region. The CICS definition of users is different from that of AIX and that of DCE principals. A CICS user has attributes associated with it, including a password to allow a user to prove that it is authorized for that userid. Additional CICS attributes for a user include **Priority** used to determine whether a transaction should be executed before another if there is a conflict, a set of security permissions defining the capabilities of the user, and a relationship between the CICS user and a DCE principal. A DCE principal must be associated with a CICS user. The DCE principal is used to associate a password and other attributes with the CICS user. CICS does not maintain passwords but relies on the DCE Security Server for password verification and password maintenance. Changing a CICS user's password may be achieved through DCE commands such as the **rgy_edit** command or the DCE SMIT panels. Additionally, the CICS-supplied transaction **CESN,** which is used to authenticate a user, also may be used to change the password.

The DCE user defined for the principal may be created as part of the definition of the CICS user when the SMIT interface is used to add the user. The password for the user is also set at that point. If a preexisting DCE principal is to be used, it must be made a member of the DCE group cics_users. The DCE principal may be created using the DCE command **rgy_edit** or through the DCE SMIT panels. The following commands illustrate the creation of a suitable principal.

To create a new DCE principal suitable to be associated with a CICS user, the creator must be DCE authenticated as **cell_admin.** The following SMIT path may be followed to create the principal:

```
smit dce
    DCE Security & Users Administration
        Principals and Aliases
            Add a Principal
```

```
                            Add a Principal

Type or select values in entry fields.
Press Enter AFTER making all desired changes.

                                                [Entry Fields]
* Principal NAME                            []
  Principal ID                              []
  FULL name                                 []
  Registry object QUOTA                     []




F1=Help           F2=Refresh      F3=Cancel       F4=List
F5=Reset          F6=Command      F7=Edit         F8=Image
F9=Shell          F10=Exit        Enter=Do
```

Once the principal has been created, an associated DCE account must be created. This can be accomplished by following the SMIT path shown on page 85.

<**UserId**>   This key field specifies a one- to eight-character name for the CICS user being defined.

Principal   This attribute specifies the DCE principal name to be associated with the CICS user. The principal must be specified as either a DCE cell local or cell global name. If no principal name is supplied, the principal used will be / . : /<UserId>.

Priority   This attribute specifies the priority to be defined for the user. The higher the priority, the better is the probability that a request to start a transaction will be processed before others if there is contention. The priority of a user, the terminal it is started from, and the priority of the transaction are combined to calculate an overall transaction start priority.

RSLKeyList   This attribute defines a set of Resource Level Security keys that allow or disallow the user to execute programs which have resource security associated with them. Keys defined by this attribute are separated by the I character and may range from **1** to **24.** The special keyword **none** specifies that no keys are to be associated with the user.

TSLKeyList   This attribute defines a set of Transaction Level Security keys that allow or disallow the user to start transactions. Keys defined by this attribute are separated by the I character and may range from **1** to **64.**

```
smitty dce
    DCE Security & Users Administration
        Accounts
            Add an Account
        [1 user]
```

```
┌──────────────────────────────────────────────────────────────────────────┐
│                          Add an Account                                    │
│                                                                            │
│ Type or select values in entry fields.                                     │
│ Press Enter AFTER making all desired changes.                              │
│                                                                            │
│                                                       [Entry Fields]       │
│ * PRINCIPAL to create account for                     []                +  │
│ * LOGIN user?                                         no                +  │
│ * GROUP to associate with this account               [cics_user]       +  │
│ * ORGANIZATION to associate with this account        []                +  │
│   HOME directory                                      [/]                  │
│   Initial PROGRAM                                     []                   │
│   ACCOUNT information                                 []                   │
│ * Require user to CHANGE PASSWORD on first login?     yes               +  │
│   Allow account to be a SERVER principal?             yes               +  │
│   Allow account to be a CLIENT principal?             yes               +  │
│   Maximum ticket LIFETIME                             [1d]                 │
│   Maximum ticket RENEWABLE lifetime                   [4w]                 │
│   EXPIRATION date ([YY]YY/MM/DD.hh:mm)                [none]               │
│   GOOD SINCE date ([YY]YY/MM/DD.hh:mm)                []                   │
│                                                                            │
│                                                                            │
│ F1=Help          F2=Refresh       F3=Cancel        F4=List                 │
│ F5=Reset         F6=Command       F7=Edit          F8=Image                │
│ F9=Shell         F10=Exit         Enter=Do                                 │
└──────────────────────────────────────────────────────────────────────────┘
```

Name	Default	Summary
OpID	**AIX**	Operator identifier
Principal	**""**	DCE principal name associated with the user
Priority	**0**	Priority associated with user
RSLKeyList	**none**	Resource access keys
TSLKeyList	**1**	Transaction access keys
TraceFile	**""**	AIX file for user trace

Monitoring Definitions (MD)

This resource group contains a single entry that defines if, when, and what data should be written in a CICS monitoring record. The monitoring data output is described in —Heading 'HDMON1' unknown"—. Monitoring data may be written at the completion of every CICS task and contain detailed information on how that task executed. The following attributes are available in a monitoring definition:

TDQ   Name of a CICS locally defined extrapartition transient data queue into which the CICS region will write the monitoring data records.

MonitorStatus   A yes/no attribute that specifies whether monitoring should be started when the region starts. This attribute may be changed dynamically in a running CICS region using the CEMT-supplied transaction with the CEMT SET MONITOR { ON | OFF } command. If this attribute is set to **no,** monitoring will only be started when the CEMT command is executed.

Conversational   This yes/no attribute specifies whether conversational CICS programs (those which prompt the user and then wait for response) should cause separate monitoring records to be written for each pair of send and receive requests.

Exclude   The names of fields or groups of fields to be excluded from the monitoring data output.

Include   The names of fields or groups of fields to be explicitly included in the monitoring data output. The **Exclude** attribute is processed by CICS before the **Include** attribute, allowing large groups of monitoring fields to be excluded and then allowing single fields to be included.

UserMonitorModule   The name of a user written or vendor-supplied program for handling monitoring data collection and disposition.

Name	Default	Summary
Conversational	**no**	Separate records for conversational tasks
Exclude	""	Exclude monitoring field output
Include	""	Explicit inclusion of monitoring fields
MonitorStatus	**no**	Monitoring enabled (**yes**) or disabled (**no**)
UserMonitorModule	""	External monitoring program

CICS Resource Manipulation Command

CICS/6000 supplies a set of commands for adding, deleting, and changing resource definitions within a region. These commands are listed below:

`cicsadd`   This command adds resources to a given resource class in the permanent database and optionally into the runtime database within a running CICS region.

`cicsdelete`   This command deletes resources from the permanent database, the runtime database, or both. Once a resource has been deleted from the permanent database, it is gone until explicitly readded.

`cicsupdate` This command modifies resources in the permanent database, adds them to the runtime database, or both. It is not possible to modify a running resource. To modify the definitions within a running CICS region, the resource must first be deleted and then readded. This command allows it to be readded without changing the permanent database entry.

`cicsget` This command allows an entry in a permanent resource database to be retrieved and displayed. Additionally, a list of resources of a class may be returned.

All the commands listed require two mandatory parameters, the first parameter is the name of the resource class in which the resource being manipulated belongs. The class type is specified by the parameter `-c class`, where *class* is the two- or three-character abbreviation of the class name. The following list defines the allowable class abbreviations:

cd	Communication Definitions, i.e., CICS SysIds
fd	File Definitions, i.e., CICS files
gd	Gateway Definitions, i.e., Encina PPC Gateways
gsd	Gateway Server Definitions, i.e., Encina PPC Gateway Servers
jd	Journal Definitions, i.e., CICS user journals
ld	Listener Definitions, i.e., CICS SNA and TCP/IP listeners
md	Monitoring Definition, i.e., the single CICS monitoring control
pd	Program Definitions, i.e., CICS programs, maps, and tables
rd	Region Definition, i.e., the single CICS region control
scd	Schema File Definitions, i.e., Encina SFS file descriptions
ssd	SFS Server Definitions, i.e., Encina SFSs
td	Transaction Definitions, i.e., CICS transactions
tdd	Transient Data Definitions, i.e., CICS transient data queues
tsd	Temporary Storage Definitions, i.e., CICS temporary storage queues
ud	User Definitions, i.e., CICS userids
wd	Workstation Definitions, i.e., CICS terminals and models
xad	XA Definitions, i.e., CICS database product XA interface definitions

The other mandatory parameter on each resource command names the CICS region being manipulated. This parameter is specified as `-r <region>`, where *<region>* is the name of the CICS region whose resources are being changed. The exception to this are the **ssd, scd,** and **gsd** resource classes, which do not require a region name.

The cicsadd command

The **cicsadd** command adds resource definitions into the permanent database and optionally into the runtime database. An entry cannot be added into the runtime database without first being added to the permanent database. An abbreviated command syntax for the **cicsadd** command is shown below:

```
cicsadd -c class -r region [-P | -B] resource [[name = value] …]
```

The -P flag is the default and instructs the command to add the entry into the permanent database only. The -B flag specifies that both the permanent and runtime databases are to be updated with the new resource. This command is invalid with the Monitoring Definitions and Region Definitions, which only have one entry. To update a runtime database, the executor of the command must be DCE authenticated.

The cicsdelete command

The **cicsdelete** command deletes a resource entry from the permanent database, the runtime database, or both. The command has the following abbreviated syntax:

```
cicsdelete -c class -r region [-P | -R | -B] resource [resource …]
```

The -P flag instructs the command to delete the named resources from the permanent database, the -R flag from the runtime database, and the -B flag from both. Resources may only be deleted from the runtime database at certain points, specifically when doing so would not compromise the integrity or operation of the CICS region. The following resource classes illustrate occurrences of such resources:

Communication Definitions (CD)   Active connections used for ISC such as function shipping, transaction routing, or DTP. The resource may be removed when all conversations using the connection have ended.

File Definitions (FD)   A file may only be removed when it is closed and disabled.

Journal Definitions (JD)   A journal may be removed only when it is closed.

Program Definitions (PD)   A program, mapset, or table may be removed only when it is not currently in use. A program may not be deleted if it is referenced as an abend handler.

Transaction Definition (TD)   A transaction may only be removed when it is not currently in use.

Transient Data Queue (TDD)   A transient data queue may only be removed when it is not being used. A queue may only be deleted when the CICS image of the queue has been deleted with an EXEC CICS DELETEQ TD.

Resource types of Region Definition (RD) or Monitoring Definition (MD) may never be removed. The deletion of a runtime resource is required to update its runtime value. It is first removed and later readded with the **cicsupdate** command.

The cicsupdate command

The **cicsupdate** command can be used to update a permanent definition, a runtime definition, or both. A change to a permanent definition results in a change to the permanent database stanza file. A runtime update is really a dynamic add of the resource into the running region. This requires that the resource in the region be deleted by a **cicsdelete** command if it was installed previously. An abbreviated syntax for the command is shown below:

```
cicsupdate -c class -r region [-P | -R | -B] resource [name = value] …
```

The -P flag modifies the permanent database, the -R flag modifies the runtime database, while the -B flag modifies both.

6

The CICS/6000
Programming Commands

The richness of the CICS programming environment can be seen readily in the CICS Application Programming Interface (API) commands available to a CICS programmer. These commands are the CICS programming statements that may be included in a C or COBOL source program to take advantage of the functions and transactional nature of CICS. The commands are coded in a high-level format known as the *CICS API*. Each command starts with the construct **EXEC CICS** followed by the command name with required and optional parameters. The CICS API is common among all the different implementations of CICS with only slight variations. The compatibility between the API on the different environments allows an application originally written for one environment to be readily ported or migrated to another.

The CICS API Command Summary

The richness of the API prevents the full details and semantics of each command from being discussed completely in this book. Since CICS API is portable and common between all CICS platforms, only the list of specific commands and how they differ or are interesting in CICS/6000 are given in the following sections. These sections may be used as a reference to ensure that a command and its options that are used in a CICS application not already tested on CICS/6000 are available when the program is ported to CICS/6000. Many excellent texts on the CICS API are already available.

Handling Command Errors

Each CICS command is capable of generating an error when executed. An attempt to access a file that is not present, start a transaction without sufficient security access, or communicate with a remote CICS region that is not running are all examples of such errors. The term given to errors such as these is an *exceptional condition* or simply *condition*. Conditions are handled differently in COBOL programs than in C programs. In COBOL, the default action is to terminate the CICS task with a code that indicates the nature of the condition. This code is referred to as an *abnormal end code* or an *ABEND code*. For COBOL programs, a program label can be associated with a specific condition such that if a CICS command generates the condition, control is immediately passed to the label associated with the condition. This is known as *handling* the condition and is described in the EXEC CICS HANDLE CONDITION command. Alternatively, conditions simply may be ignored by issuing the EXEC CICS IGNORE CONDITION command.

The EXEC CICS HANDLE CONDITION and EXEC CICS IGNORE CONDITION commands affect all subsequent CICS commands executed. If a single command is to be handled specially, the NOHANDLE option may be coded on that command. This option disables any special handling of conditions and ABENDs for the duration of that command.

The use of program labels within the C language, although present, is strongly discouraged because it is widely believed that the use of GOTOs promotes poor programming practices and unstructured code. As such, each CICS command executed by a C language program has an implicit NOHANDLE associated with it. To allow a program to determine the outcome of a CICS command, each CICS command executed will return a response code by updating a field in the EXEC Interface Block (EIB) and optionally in the variables specified in the RESP option available on all CICS commands. The RESP option allows any condition raised by a CICS command to be returned to the program for subsequent logic processing. The RESP command is also available to COBOL CICS commands and implies the NOHANDLE option.

The values returned by the RESP option or in the EIB are 32-bit integer values. Coding comparisons against numeric values on return from CICS commands would result in very unreadable code. CICS/6000 provides a macro that may be coded within an application to convert a symbolic representation of a condition to its numeric value. The macro DFHRESP() takes a condition name as a parameter and is expanded by the CICS translator to the numeric value prior to final compilation. If no condition is raised by a CICS command, the condition value will be set to NORMAL.

The following code fragments illustrate the use of the RESP option and the DFHRESP macro:

```
COBOL:
01 resp-code PIC S9(8) COMP-5.

EXEC CICS LINK PROGRAM(program) RESP(resp-code) END-EXEC.
IF resp-code = = DFHRESP(NOTAUTH) THEN ...

C:
int resp_code;
EXEC CICS LINK PROGRAM(program) RESP(resp_code);
if (resp_code = = DFHRESP(NORMAL)
{
....
}
```

Like condition handling, ABEND handling can be used to handle ABENDs caused by unhandled conditions or other reasons that may cause a transaction to fail. The EXEC CICS HANDLE ABEND command may be used to specify a CICS program to be executed when an ABEND occurs or, in the case of COBOL, a program label to which control is to be given.

CICS Constants and Value Data Areas

Many of the CICS command allow a program to inquire or change parameters associated with a CICS resource, CICS task, or the CICS region itself. The majority of these commands expect the values of parameters to be predefined constants. Examples of such values include the language of a CICS program (either C or COBOL), the state of a file (OPEN or CLOSED), and whether a transient data queue is INPUT or OUTPUT. Coding values as numeric constants would make programs unreadable similarly to coding numeric values for possible condition values.

CICS provides a macro called DFHVALUE() that takes a symbolic description of the value of an attribute which is converted into its numeric equivalent by the translator. The following is an example of this macro's use:

```
int status;
EXEC CICS INQUIRE PROGRAM(program) STATUS(status);
if (status = = DFHVALUE(DISABLED))
{
...
}
```

CICS/6000 Commands

The remainder of this chapter details the available CICS commands for CICS/6000.

EXEC CICS ABEND

Cause a CICS transaction to terminate abnormally.

Syntax

```
EXEC CICS ABEND
[ABCODE(name)]
[CANCEL]
```

This command cause the CICS program in which it is executed to ABEND. The ABCODE parameter specifies the four-character ABEND code associated with the end of the program. The CANCEL option causes any handles set up by the EXEC CICS HANDLE ABEND command to be ignored. A transaction that has been started at a CICS terminal will receive the ABEND code. The ABEND also will be logged in the CSMT.out file. The following messages are written to CSMT when a program performs an ABEND:

```
ERZ014016E Transaction 'TEST', Abend 'ABCD', at 'CA00'.
ERZ016050W Logical unit of work for transaction 'TEST' has been backed out;
Distributed Transaction Service (TRAN) reason 'ENC-tra-1025: A client
(not the transaction service) aborted'
```

Any recoverable work performed by the program or transaction is rolled back. Both the ECI and EPI client programming interfaces can receive the ABEND code of the ABEND for front-end processing.

EXEC CICS ADDRESS

Allow access to CICS data structures from an application.

Syntax

```
EXEC CICS ADDRESS
[COMMAREA(ptr-ref)]
[CWA(ptr-ref)]
[EIB(ptr-ref)]
[TCTUA(ptr-ref)]
[TWA(ptr-ref)]
```

Using this command allows a CICS program to access data structures managed by CICS. These include

- *COMMAREA: Communication Area* This is an area of storage used to pass information from one CICS program to another. This could be as part of an EXEC CICS LINK or EXEC CICS XCTL command or as data passed from one of the CICS user exit programs. Data modified in the COMMAREA will be passed back to the caller.

- *CWA: Common Work Area* This is an area of storage that is available to all the CICS programs executing in a single region. The size of the CWA area is specified in the Region Definition (RD) attribute **CWASize.** Applications executing in a CICS region must cooperate to maintain storage in this area.

- *EIB: Execution Interface Block* The EIB contains information on a per-CICS task basis relating to the state and attributes of the task. Error codes from CICS commands, current terminal name, and many other task specific attributes are kept here and are accessible to the program. Access to this structure varies by language. This structure is similar in concept to the "sqlca" structure in most SQL database languages.

- *TCTUA: Terminal Control Table User Area* This is an area of storage that is available to all CICS tasks that execute against the same CICS terminal. It may be used to save information from one task to another. Its size is specified in the model definition in the Workstation Definition (WD) for the terminal being used.

- *TWA: Transaction Work Area* This area of storage is available to a program within the same task. It is similar to the COMMAREA except that the EXEC CICS XCTL or EXEC CICS LINK must execute a program within the same region as the caller.

On return from the EXEC CICS ADDRESS command, the pointer to the storage returned should be tested to determine if there actually was a storage area of this type. The pointer value `0xFF000000` is used to denote that no storage of this type was available. As an example, the following C source shows a CICS C language program testing for the existence of a COMMAREA:

```
main()
{
   void *commarea;
   EXEC CICS ADDRESS COMMAREA(commarea);
   if (commarea = = (void *)0xFF000000)
   {
   .... No commarea
   }
   ....
}
```

EXEC CICS ALLOCATE

Allocate a conversation between the CICS program and a DTP back-end program.

Syntax

```
EXEC CICS ALLOCATE
SYSID(name)
[PROFILE(name)]
[NOQUEUE | NOSUSPEND]
[STATE(cvda)]
```

When communicating with a back-end DTP application, this command allocates the conversation.

EXEC CICS ASKTIME

Obtain the current date and time.

Syntax

```
EXEC CICS ASKTIME
[ABSTIME(data-area)]
```

This command modifies the EIBDATE and EIBTIME fields within the EIB. Optionally, the ABSTIME parameter may be used to specify an 8-byte data area in which to store a date/time coding. The time stored is the number of milliseconds since January 1, 1900 and is represented in packed decimal format. On other CICS platforms, operating system functions such as obtain the system date/time would cause adverse interaction with CICS. On CICS/6000, AIX native functions may be used to obtain the time but must be known to be AIX thread safe.

EXEC CICS ASSIGN

Obtain attributes of the current CICS environment.

Syntax

```
EXEC CICS ASSIGN
[ABCODE(data-area)]            [APPLID(data-area)]            [BTRANS(data-area)]
[COLOR(data-area)]             [CWALENG(data-area)]           [EXTDS(data-area)]
[FACILITY(data-area)]          [FCI(data-area)]               [GCHARS(data-area)]
[GCODES(data-area)]            [HILIGHT(data-area)]           [KATAKANA(data-area)]
[MAPCOLUMN(data-area)]         [MAPHEIGHT(data-area)]         [MAPLINE(data-area)]
[MAPWIDTH(data-area)]          [MSRCONTROL(data-area)]        [NETNAME(data-area)]
[OPCLASS(data-area)]           [OPERKEYS(data-area)]          [OPID(data-area)]
[OPSECURITY(data-area)]        [OUTLINE(data-area)]           [PRINSYSID(data-area)]
[PS(data-area)]                [QNAME(data-area)]             [RESTART(data-area)]
[RESTART(data-area)]           [SCRNHT(data-area)]            [SCRNWD(data-area)]
[SIGDATA(data-area)]           [SOSI(data-area)]              [STARTCODE(data-area)]
[SYSID(data-area)]             [TCTUALENG(data-area)]         [TERMCODE(data-area)]
[TWALENG(data-area)]           [UNATTEND(data-area)]          [VALIDATION(data-area)]
```

The EXEC CICS ASSIGN command allows a CICS program to interrogate its own operating environment. The following list highlights values that are possibly different in a CICS/6000 environment from some other CICS environments:

- APPLID   The name of the CICS/6000 region. This is not necessarily the same as the SNA LU name of the region.
- CWALENG   The size of the Common Work Area is specified in the CICS/6000 Region Definition (RD) attribute **CWASize.**
- SYSID   Local region's own SYSID as specified in the Region Definition (RD) attribute **LocalSysId.**
- TCTUALENG   The size of the current Terminal Control Table User Area is specified in the Terminal Definition (WD) for the current terminal in the **TCTUALeng** attribute.
- USERID   The user name of the currently signed on user. This is the CICS user name and not the underlying DCE user identity. It is not possible from a CICS/6000 application to determine the DCE principal name of the underlying DCE user.

EXEC CICS CANCEL

Stop a previously requested START or DELAY command.

Syntax

```
EXEC CICS CANCEL
REQID(name)
[TRANSID(name)]
[SYSID(name)]
```

This command can be used to interrupt or stop the execution of another CICS task. For an asynchronously started task, if the time at which it is to start has not yet passed, the task can be removed from the queue of tasks waiting to start. This command also can be used to wake another task that has paused itself with an EXEC CICS DELAY command. The program shown below suspends itself for 5 minutes using a REQID value derived from the TERMID of the terminal on which the transaction was executed. If another transaction issues an EXEC CICS CANCEL with this REQID, the transaction will unblock early.

```
#include <stdio.h>

main()
{
   char reqid[9];

   EXEC CICS ADDRESS EIB(dfheiptr);
   sprintf(reqid, "DLAY%4.4s", dfheiptr->eibtrmid);
   fprintf(stderr, "About to DELAY, REQID = %s ...\n", reqid);
   EXEC CICS DELAY FOR MINUTES(5) REQID(reqid);
   fprintf(stderr, "... returned from DELAY [resp = %d]\n", dfheiptr->eibresp);
   EXEC CICS RETURN;
}
```

EXEC CICS COLLECT STATISTICS

Return current CICS operational statistics to the calling program.

Syntax

```
EXEC CICS COLLECT STATISTICS
SET(ptr-ref)
[LASTRESET(hhmmss) |
LASTRESETHRS(data-area)
LASTRESETMINS(data-area)
LASTRESETSEC(data-area)]
{ DUMP | FILE(data-value) | INTERSYSTEM(data-value) |
JOURNAL | PROGRAM[(data-value)] | RUNTIMEDB | STORAGE | TASK |
TDQUEUE[(data-value) | TERMINAL(data-value) | TRANSACTION(data-value) |
TSQUEUE | UNITOFWORK] }
```

This command returns statistics on the resource type specified in the command pointer. In addition to the statistics data, the time that the statistics were last reset can also be returned.

This command is highly nonportable to other CICS family products. The types and content of statistics are not architected for all CICS products, and each separate CICS implementation will return its own data and types. Programs ported from other CICS environments that include statistics queries should be examined carefully and modified.

EXEC CICS CONNECT PROCESS

Specify the connection attributes on a DTP conversation.

Syntax

```
EXEC CICS CONNECT PROCESS
CONVID(name)
PROCNAME(data-area)
PROCLENGTH(data-value)
SYNCLEVEL(data-value)
[PIPLIST(data-area) PIPLENGTH(data-value)]
[STATE(cvda)]
```

When initiating a back-end DTP conversation, this command will be used to specify some of the major attributes of the connection, including the name of the back-end transaction program to invoke and the SyncLevel of the conversation.

EXEC CICS CONVERSE (with an APPC partner)

Send and then receive data from a partner DTP program.

Syntax

```
EXEC CICS CONVERSE
[CONVID(name)]
FROM(data-area)
{ FROMLENGTH(data-value) | FROMFLENGTH(data-value) }
[INTO(data-area) | SET(ptr-ref)]
[TOLENGTH(data-area) | TOFLENGTH(data-area)]
[MAXLENGTH(data-value) | MAXFLENGTH(data-value)]
[NOTRUNCATE]
[STATE(cvda)]
```

Use this command to send and then receive data from a partner DTP application.

EXEC CICS CONVERSE (with a terminal)

Send and receive information from a CICS-attached terminal.

Syntax

```
EXEC CICS CONVERSE
FROM(data-area)
{ FROMLENGTH(data-value) | FROMFLENGTH(data-value) }
[{ INTO(data-area) | SET(ptr-ref) }
 { TOLENGTH(data-area) | TOFLENGTH(data-area) }]
[{ MAXLENGTH[(data-value)] | MAXFLENGTH[(data-value)] }]
[NOTRUNCATE]
[ERASE]
[CTLCHAR(data-value)]
```

This command communicates with a CICS-attached terminal. The command optionally sends data to the terminal and then awaits a user response. This command would be used with low-level CICS terminal control operations.

EXEC CICS DELAY

Suspend a CICS program from executing for a period of time.

Syntax

```
EXEC CICS DELAY
[INTERVAL(hhmmss) | TIME(hhmmss) |
FOR  [HOURS(data-value)]
     [MINUTES(data-value)]
     [SECONDS(data-value)] |
UNTIL [HOURS(data-value)]
      [MINUTES(data-value)]
      [SECONDS(data-value)]]
[REQID(name)]
```

This command stops the execution of the calling program until

- An absolute wall-clock time has passed.
- A relative time interval has passed.
- Another CICS application has issued an EXEC CICS CANCEL command against this EXEC CICS DELAY command.

Although AIX provides other delay primitives such as sleep() these should not be used unless they can be guaranteed to be thread safe. Using CICS statements allows portability, functional correctness, and increased CICS control for the executing applications.

EXEC CICS DELETE

Delete a record from a CICS file.

Syntax

```
EXEC CICS DELETE
FILE(name)
[SYSID(name)]
[RIDFLD(data-area)
[KEYLENGTH(data-value)
[GENERIC [NUMREC(data-area)]]]]
[RRN]
```

This command deletes one or more records from a CICS KSDS or RRDS type file. The actual records will be removed from the underlying SFS file. The records to be deleted are specified with the RIDFLD option.

EXEC CICS DELETEQ TD

Delete the contents of a CICS intrapartition transient data queue.

Syntax

```
EXEC CICS DELETEQ TD
QUEUE(name)
[SYSID(name)]
```

This command deletes the contents of a CICS intrapartition transient data queue. If the queue is defined locally on the CICS/6000 region, the records for this queue will be removed from the underlying SFS file.

EXEC CICS DELETEQ TS

Delete a temporary storage queue.

Syntax

```
EXEC CICS DELETEQ TS
QUEUE(name)
[SYSID(name)]
```

Deletes either a main or auxiliary temporary storage queue. Temporary storage queues can be created dynamically by a CICS application. These queues consume CICS resources. Main storage queues are maintained in CICS memory, whereas auxiliary queues are stored within SFS files. In both cases, poor programming or transaction failure may result in queues being created but not destroyed correctly.

CICS/6000 will automatically delete TS queues that have not been accessed in a period of days. The number of days till queue deletion is specified in the Region Definition (RD) by the **TSQAgeLimit** attribute. Specifying a value of **0** disables CICS from automatically deleting queues.

EXEC CICS DEQ

Release a CICS transaction lock.

Syntax

```
EXEC CICS DEQ
RESOURCE(data-area)
[LENGTH(data-value)]
```

This command unlocks a previous transaction lock taken by this program with an EXEC CICS ENQ command. For those familiar with multithreaded programming, this command is similar to the mutex() locking commands. If a CICS program needs to access a resource such as shared storage with integrity, a lock should be taken on the storage before its use and released with this command when the storage updates have completed. Another program that also may update the storage also should attempt to take the same lock. The program that executes the command first will obtain the lock, while the other program will block until the original program has released the lock with this command. Only the program that has issued the original EXEC CICS ENQ command should attempt to release the lock with an EXEC CICS DEQ command. All locks taken by a transaction are released automatically when the transaction ends.

EXEC CICS DUMP

Obtain a CICS internal storage dump.

Syntax

```
EXEC CICS DUMP
DUMPCODE(name)
FROM(data-area) { LENGTH(data-value) | FLENGTH(data-value)]
[COMPLETE]
[TASK]
[STORAGE]
[PROGRAM]
[TERMINAL]
[TABLES]
[DCT]
[FCT]
[PCT]
[PPT]
[SIT]
[TCT]
```

This command requests that CICS internal and user-specified storage be dumped to disk. The data are written as AIX files that may be formatted using the CICS-supplied dump formatting program. The data and contents written in a CICS/6000 dump are very different from dump data written by other CICS systems.

EXEC CICS ENDBR

End a browse operation on a CICS file.

Syntax

```
EXEC CICS ENDBR
FILE(name)
[REQID(data-value)]
[SYSID(name)]
```

This command ends a browse operation previously started by an EXEC CICS STARTBR command. Using this command allows CICS to free internal resources used to track the current record pointer when the file is browsed. Multiple browses can be in process for the same file if the REQID option is specified on the STARTBR.

EXEC CICS ENQ

Attempt to take a transaction lock.

Syntax

```
EXEC CICS ENQ
RESOURCE(data-area)
[LENGTH(data-value)]
[NOSUSPEND]
```

Executing this command results in the transaction attempting to take an exclusive lock named by the RESOURCE option. If another CICS transaction has already taken the lock on the same named resource, the EXEC CICS ENQ command will block until the lock is released. A lock may be released with the EXEC CICS DEQ command or the transaction that took the lock terminating or syncpointing. The NOSUSPEND option may be used to cause the command to return immediately; even if the lock is held by another transaction, the ENQBUSY condition will be raised.

EXEC CICS ENTER

Write a trace entry from within a CICS program.

Syntax

```
EXEC CICS ENTER
TRACEID(data-value)
[FROM(data-area)]
[RESOURCE(name)]
[ENTRYNAME(name)]
[ACCOUNT]
[MONITOR]
[PERFORM]
```

This command allows a CICS program to write a trace record to the trace and monitoring output containing application-specific data. The trace is directed to the USER trace output and is only written if both the MASTER and USER trace flags are ON and the program containing the EXEC CICS ENTER command has issued an EXEC CICS TRACE SINGLE ON command. The FROM and RESOURCE options may be used to log up to 8 bytes each of additional data to the trace output. The TRACEID additionally may be used to specify an additional byte of trace information. User trace may only be sent to AIX files and cannot be used with the AIX trace facility.

EXEC CICS EXTRACT ATTRIBUTES

Extract the state of a DTP connected conversation.

Syntax

```
EXEC CICS EXTRACT ATTRIBUTES
[CONVID(name)]
STATE(cvda)
```

This command returns the state of a DTP-connected conversation with its partner.

EXEC CICS EXTRACT PROCESS

Extracts information about the invoker of a DTP-initiated back-end.

Syntax

```
EXEC CICS EXTRACT PROCESS
[PROCNAME(data-area) PROCLENGTH(data-area)]
[CONVID(name)]
[SYNCLEVEL(data-area)]
[PIPLIST(ptr-ref) PIPLENGTH(data-area)]
```

This command may be executed by a program that has been invoked as a back-end partner in a DTP conversation. The values returned may be used by the application to control its operation, such as syncpoint processing for a SyncLevel 2 back-end.

EXEC CICS FORMATTIME

Format a date/time value into a human-readable form.

Syntax

```
EXEC CICS FORMATTIME
ABSTIME(data-area)
[YYDDD(data-area)]
[YYMMDD(data-area)]
[DDMMYY(data-area)]
[MMDDYY(data-area)]
```

```
[DATE(data-area)]
[DATEFORM(data-area)]
[DATESEP(data-value)]
[DAYCOUNT(data-area)]
[DAYOFWEEK(data-area)]
[DAYOFMONTH(data-area)]
[MONTHOFYEAR(data-area)]
[YEAR(data-area)]
[TIME(data-area) [TIMESEP [(data-value)]]]
```

This command formats an 8-byte packed decimal date/time encoding as
returned by the EXEC CICS ASKTIME command into one of a number of different formats. Although AIX provides a number of similar date/time formatting functions, this command should be used for CICS portability and to prevent problems due to thread safety of the AIX-supplied functions.

EXEC CICS FREE

Terminate a DTP conversation.

Syntax

```
EXEC CICS FREE
[CONVID(name)]
[STATE(cvda)]
```

This command terminates the specified DTP conversation and releases the
resources associated with it.

EXEC CICS FREEMAIN

Return application-allocated storage to CICS.

Syntax

```
EXEC CICS FREEMAIN
DATA(data-area)
```

Storage may be allocated to a CICS program by executing the EXEC CICS
GETMAIN command. This command returns the storage back to CICS for
possible subsequent reallocation to another task. For storage allocated without the SHARED option by the EXEC CICS GETMAIN command, storage is
released automatically at the end of a task. It is good programming practice
to issue explicit FREEMAIN commands when storage is no longer required.
This storage is owned and managed by CICS. It is not storage allocated by
the CICS malloc() system call. The AIX free() system call should never
be used to attempt to release CICS-allocated storage.

EXEC CICS GETMAIN

Allocate application storage to a program.

Syntax

```
EXEC CICS GETMAIN
SET (ptr-ref)
{ LENGTH(data-value) | FLENGTH(data-value) }
[INITMSG(data-value)]
[NOSUSPEND]
[SHARED]
```

This command allocates storage to the application that issues the command. The storage may be used for any purpose within the application. This command is the CICS equivalent of the AIX `malloc()` system call, which should never be used within a CICS environment. The storage allocated by the application is available until either the application issues an EXEC CICS FREEMAIN command or the task ends. If the SHARED option is specified, the storage is not released at task termination but is available until some other application issues an EXEC CICS FREEMAIN command. Care should be taken to ensure that storage allocated by EXEC CICS GETMAIN with the SHARED option is executed but is never released. Shared GETMAIN storage is a finite resource.

EXEC CICS HANDLE ABEND

Handle an abnormal CICS program termination.

Syntax

```
EXEC CICS HANDLE ABEND
[PROGRAM(name) | LABEL(label) | CANCEL | RESET]
```

This command specifies the actions to be taken when a CICS program detects an error condition and would normally ABEND. This command allows only some of the options in the C language.

EXEC CICS HANDLE AID

Pass control to a code segment when an AID key is pressed.

Syntax

```
EXEC CICS HANDLE AID
[ANYKEY [(label)]]
[CLEAR [(label)]]
[CLRPARTN [(label)]]
[ENTER [(label)]]
[LIGHTPEN [(label)]]
[OPERID [(label)]]
[PAn [(label)]]
[PFn [(label)]]
[TRIGGER [(label)]]
```

This command allows program control to be transferred to a specified label within a COBOL program (this function is not supported for C language programs). When an EXEC CICS RECEIVE is issued and the AID is handled, control is passed to the specified label. Such explicit GOTOs promote poor programming in the C environment and are excluded. Good programming promotes modular and structured programs.

EXEC CICS HANDLE CONDITION

Pass program control when a CICS error condition is raised.

Syntax

```
EXEC CICS HANDLE CONDITION
condition [(label)]
```

This command allows control to be passed to the specified label when the specified error occurs during execution of a CICS command. All CICS commands may return errors, which are known as *conditions*. This command is not available to C programs because GOTOs do not promote structured programming.

EXEC CICS IGNORE CONDITION

Ignore the default action when a CICS error condition is raised.

Syntax

```
EXEC CICS IGNORE CONDITION
condition
```

For some CICS error conditions, the default action on a CICS command is to ABEND the program. This command allows the specified error conditions to be ignored and no ABEND to occur. The condition may still be tested in code following a CICS command by examining the RESP field in the EIB.

EXEC CICS INQUIRE CONNECTION

Examine the status or obtain a list of connections.

Syntax

```
EXEC CICS INQUIRE CONNECTION(name)
[NETNAME(data-area)]
[SERVSTATUS (cvda)]
```

```
EXEC CICS INQUIRE CONNECTION [START | NEXT | END]
[NETNAME(data-area)]
[SERVSTATUS (cvda)]
```

This command allows the status and netname of a CICS-to-CICS connection to be queried. Unlike other implementations of the CEMT transaction, this command is not provided via CEMT. The connections returned are those which are defined in the Communication Definitions (CD) and those dynamically installed by the CCIN transaction as part of CICS client installation.

EXEC CICS INQUIRE FILE

Examine the status of a CICS file.

Syntax

```
EXEC CICS INQUIRE FILE(name)
[ACCESSMETHOD(cvda)]
[ADD(cvda)]
[BASENAME(data-area)]
[BROWSE(cvda)]
[DELETE (cvda)]
[EMPTYSTATUS(cvda)]
[ENABLESTATUS(cvda)]
[FILESERVER(cvda)]
[INDEXNAME(cvda)]
[KEYLENGTH(data-area)]
[KEYPOSITION(data-area)]
[OPENSTATUS(cvda)]
[READ(cvda]
[RECORDFORMAT(cvda)]
[RECORDSIZE(data-area)]
[RECOVSTATUS(cvda)]
[REMOTENAME(data-area)]
[TYPE(cvda)]
[UPDATE(cvda)]
```

This command returns various attributes of a CICS-defined file. Among those specific to CICS/6000 are

FileServer   The Encina SFS name specified as a DCE CDS location string.

BaseName   The name of the Encina file corresponding to the CICS file. This file is located on the SFS returned in the **FileServer** attribute.

IndexName   The name of the Encina SFS file index used to index data within the file.

EXEC CICS INQUIRE JOURNALNUM

Examine the attributes of a CICS journal definition.

Syntax

```
EXEC CICS INQUIRE JOURNALNUM(data-value)
[OPENSTATUS(cvda)]
[DISKASTATUS(cvda)]
[DISKBSTATUS(cvda)]
```

This command returns the attributes for a CICS-defined journal.

EXEC CICS INQUIRE PROGRAM

Examine the attributes of a CICS-defined program.

Syntax

```
EXEC CICS INQUIRE PROGRAM(name)
[LANGUAGE(cvda)]
[PROGTYPE(cvda)]
[STATUS(cvda)]
```

This command returns attribute information on a CICS-defined program, mapset, or table. The languages supported by CICS are C and COBOL.

EXEC CICS INQUIRE STATISTICS

Return the times and status of CICS statistics generation.

Syntax

```
EXEC CICS INQUIRE STATISTICS
[ENDOFDAY(hhmmss) |
 ENDOFDAYHRS(value)
 ENDOFDAYMINS(value)
 ENDOFDAYSECS(value)]
[INTERVAL(hhmmss) |
 INTERVALHRS(value)
 INTERVALMINS(value)
 INTERVALSECS(value)]
[NEXTTIME(hhmmss) |
 NEXTTIMEHRS(value)
 NEXTTIMEMINS(value)
 NEXTTIMESECS(value)]
[RECORDING(cvda)]
```

This command returns the end of day time, interval time, and next time at which statistics are to be collected. The status of interval and unsolicited recording is also returned.

EXEC CICS INQUIRE SYSTEM

Examine CICS systemwide attributes.

Syntax

```
EXEC CICS INQUIRE SYSTEM
[AKP(data-area)]
[APPLID(data-area)]
[DATEFORM(data-area)]
[INTROINTVL(data-area)]
[LOCALE(data-area)]
[MAXREGIONPOOL(data-area)]
[MAXTASKSHPOOL(data-area)]
[OPREL(data-area)]
[OPSYS(data-area)]
[REGIONTHRESH(data-area)]
[RELEASE(data-area)]
[SYSID(data-area)]
[TASKSHTHRESH(data-area)]
```

The information returned by this command is highly CICS/6000 specific. Included in the retrieved data is the operating system type and release level and various memory thresholds.

EXEC CICS INQUIRE TASK

Examine information about a specific CICS task.

Syntax

```
EXEC CICS INQUIRE TASK(data-value)
[FACILITY(data-area)]
[FACILITYTYPE(data-area)]
[RUNSTATUS(cvda)]
[UOWSTATE(cvda)]
[STARTCODE(data-area)]
[TCLASS(data-area)]
[TRANSACTION(data-area)]
[PROCID(data-area)]
[USERID(data-area)]
```

This command returns information about a specific CICS task. The **PROCID** attribute returns the AIX processid of the CICS application server executing the task. The STARTCODE option returns an indication of how and why the task was started. Possible reasons include a DPL request, a transid entered at the terminal, a pseudoconversational return, or a transient data queue–triggered transaction.

The task number of the current task can be obtained from the EXEC INTERFACE BLOCK (EIB) in the EIBTASKN field.

EXEC CICS INQUIRE TASK LIST

Return a list of CICS tasks.

Syntax

```
EXEC CICS INQUIRE TASK LIST
LISTSIZE(data-area)
[DISPATCHABLE]
[RUNNING]
[SUSPENDED]
[SET(ptr-ref)]
[SETTRANSID(ptr-ref)]
```

This command returns a list of current CICS tasks selectable by various attributes. The list returned is an array of 32-bit integers with the number of tasks returned in the **ListSize** parameter.

EXEC CICS INQUIRE TDQUEUE

Return information about a transient data queue.

Syntax

```
EXEC CICS INQUIRE TDQUEUE(name)
[ATIFACILITY(cvda)]
[ATITERMID(data-area)]
[ATITRANSID(data-area)]
[EMPTYSTATUS(cvda)]
[ENABLESTATUS(cvda)]
[INDIRECTNAME(data-area)]
[IOTYPE(cvda)]
[NUMITEMS(data-area)]
[OPENSTATUS(cvda)]
[RECORDFORMAT(cvda)]
[RECORDLENGTH(data-area)]
[RECOVSTATUS(cvda)]
[REMOTENAME(data-area)]
[REMOTESYSTEM(data-area)]
[TRIGGERLEVEL(data-area)]
[TYPE(cvda)]
```

This command returns data about a specific transient data queue. Some of the options apply to intrapartition queues only, extrapartition queues only, or indirect queues only.

Option	Type of queue	Description
ATIFACILITY	Intrapartition	Value of TERMINAL or NOTERMINAL. If TERMINAL, a triggered transaction will execute against a terminal
ATITERMID	Intrapartition	The name of the terminal (or session) against which a triggered transaction will be started
ATITRANID	Intrapartition	The name of the transaction to be started for a trigger associated with the queue.
EMPTYSTATUS	Extrapartition	Status of the queue
ENABLESTATUS	Not indirect	Enabled status of the queue
INDIRECTNAME	Indirect	Name of the indirect queue
IOTYPE	Extrapartition	Is the queue defined for input or output?

Option	Type of queue	Description
NUMITEMS	Intrapartition	Number of items in the queue
OPENSTATUS	Extrapartition	Is the queue open or closed?
RECORDFORMAT	Extrapartition	Does the queue have fixed- or variable-length records?
RECORDLENGTH	Extrapartition	Size of a record within the queue
RECOVSTATUS	Intrapartition	Recovery status of the queue
TRIGGERLEVEL	Intrapartition	Trigger status of the queue
TYPE	All	Type of the queue, such as intrapartition, extrapartition, or indirect

EXEC CICS INQUIRE TERMINAL

Return information about a specific CICS-defined terminal.

Syntax

```
EXEC CICS INQUIRE TERMINAL(name)
[NETNAME(data-area)]
[ATISTATUS(cvda)]
[DEVICE(cvda)]
[GCHARS(data-area)]
[GCODES(data-area)]
[OPERID(data-area)]
[REMOTESYSTEM(data-area)]
[SCREENHEIGHT(data-area)]
[SCREENWIDTH(data-area)]
[SERVSTATUS(cvda)]
[TERMMODEL(data-area)]
[TERMPRIORITY(data-area)]
[TRANSACTION(data-area)]
[TTISTATUS(cvda)]
[USERAREA(ptr-ref)]
[USERAREALEN(data-area)]
[USERID(data-area)]
```

This command returns details of the specified CICS installed terminal.

Option	Description
NETNAME	The netname associated with the terminal.
ATISTATUS	An indication of whether or not asynchronous transactions may be started against the terminal as a result of an EXEC CICS START or transient data queue trigger.
DEVICE	The terminal or session type.
GCHARS	The Graphic Character Set Global Identifier for the terminal.
GCODES	The Code Page Global Identifier for the terminal.
OPERID	The 3-byte OPERID associated with the user that owns the terminal. The OPERID value is specified in the User Definitions (UD).
REMOTESYSTEM	The SYSID of the remote system if this terminal is actually an APPC connection.
SCREENHEIGHT	The height in characters of the terminal.
SCREENWIDTH	The width in characters of the terminal.
SERVSTATUS	The inservice or outservice status of the terminal.
TERMMODEL	The 3270 terminal model number.
TERMPRIORITY	The priority of transaction starts associated with the terminal.
TRANSACTION	The name of the currently executing transaction for the terminal.

Option	Description
TTISTATUS	Whether or not transactions can be started by a user entering a transaction code at the terminal.
USERAREA	A pointer to the TCTUA (Terminal Control Table User Area) associated with the terminal.
USERAREALEN	The 2-byte length of the TCTUA storage. The size of the TCTUA is controlled in the Terminal Definitions (WD).
USERID	The CICS userid associated with the terminal. This is the user that was either used for signon or changed with the CESN transaction.

EXEC CICS INQUIRE TRANSACTION

Return information about a CICS transaction.

Syntax

```
EXEC CICS INQUIRE TRANSACTION(name)
[REMOTESYSTEM(data-area)]
[PROGRAM(data-area)]
[STATUS(cvda)]
[PRIORITY(data-area)]
```

This command returns information about a CICS transaction. Any transaction defined in the CICS/6000 Transaction Definitions (TD) may be queried by this command.

Option	Description
REMOTESYSTEM	The SYSID of the remote system if the transaction is defined as being remote.
PROGRAM	The name of the CICS program associated with the transaction.
STATUS	The enabled or disabled status of the transaction.
PRIORITY	The priority of the transaction.

EXEC CICS ISSUE ABEND

ABEND a DTP transaction pairing.

Syntax

```
EXEC CICS ISSUE ABEND
[CONVID(name)]
[STATE(cvda)]
```

This command causes a DTP-based CICS application to ABEND and ABEND its APPC-connected partner.

EXEC CICS ISSUE CONFIRMATION

Send a positive response in a DTP-based application.

Syntax

```
EXEC CICS ISSUE CONFIRMATION
[CONVID(name)]
[STATE(cvda)]
```

This command is used to send a positive response to a DTP partner application when the partner issues an EXEC CICS SEND CONFIRM command.

EXEC CICS ISSUE ERROR

Send an error indication to a back-end DTP partner.

Syntax

```
EXEC CICS ISSUE ERROR
[CONVID(name)]
[STATE(cvda)]
```

This command is used to send an error indication to a partner DTP application.

EXEC CICS ISSUE PREPARE

Syncpoint prepare for a DTP-based application.

Syntax

```
EXEC CICS ISSUE PREPARE
[CONVID(name)]
[STATE(cvda)]
```

This command is used to issue the first part of a syncpoint request to a partner DTP application.

EXEC CICS ISSUE SIGNAL

Send a change of flow direction request.

Syntax

```
EXEC CICS ISSUE SIGNAL
[CONVID(name)]
[STATE(cvda)]
```

This command requests a change of direction from a DTP transaction that is in SEND state to a partner.

EXEC CICS JOURNAL

Write a journal record to a CICS journal file.

Syntax

```
EXEC CICS JOURNAL
JFILEID(data-value)
JTYPEID(data-value)
FROM(data-area)
[LENGTH(data-value)]
[REQID(data-area)]
[PREFIX(data-value) [PREFIXLENG(data-value)]]
[STARTIO]
[WAIT]
[NOSUSPEND]
```

This command writes a journal record to the CICS journal facility.

EXEC CICS LINK

Call another CICS program.

Syntax

```
EXEC CICS LINK
PROGRAM(name)
[COMMAREA(data-area) [LENGTH(data-value)]]
[SYSID(name)]
[SYNCONRETURN]
[TRANSID(data-value)]
[DATALENGTH(data-value)]]
```

This command transfers control within a CICS program to another CICS program. When the called CICS program issues an EXEC CICS RETURN command, control is transferred back to the original caller. If the program is defined as remote or the SYSID option is used, the program called will execute on the remote CICS region.

If the SYNCONRETURN option is specified, on return from the linked-to program, the transaction issuing the LINK command will perform a CICS SYNCPOINT. If this option is not specified, **SyncPoint** will occur later in the transaction. The TRANSID option may be specified to name the mirror transaction from which the called program will be executed. The transaction name specified here must be a valid mirror transaction.

EXEC CICS LOAD

Load a table or map into memory.

Syntax

```
EXEC CICS LOAD
PROGRAM(name)
[SET(ptr-ref)]
[LENGTH(data-area) | FLENGTH(data-area)]
[ENTRY(ptr-ref)]
[HOLD]
```

This command loads an AIX file into CICS storage or loads a BMS map into storage. The ENTRY field is provided for CICS compatibility but is redundant in CICS/6000 because programs may not be loaded using this command. If the program being loaded is defined in the Program Definitions (PD) with the **ProgType** = **table** attribute, the file specified by the **PathName** attribute is pulled into CICS memory and its address is returned by the SET pointer. If the HOLD option is set, the data loaded will be held in memory until explicitly released by the EXEC CICS RELEASE command. If the HOLD option is not set, the data are only guaranteed to be held in memory until the end of the task that issued the LOAD.

EXEC CICS PERFORM STATISTICS RECORD

Record named statistics types.

Syntax

```
EXEC CICS PERFORM STATISTICS RECORD ALL [RESETNOW]
EXEC CICS PERFORM STATISTICS RECORD
[DUMP]
[FILE]
[INTERSYSTEM]
[JOURNAL]
[PROGRAM]
[RUNTIMEDB]
[STORAGE]
[TASK]
[TDQUEUE]
[TERMINAL]
[TRANSACTION]
[TSQUEUE]
[UNITOFWORK]
```

This command allows some or all of the CICS-maintained statistics to be written immediately to the statistics output file. If the RESETNOW option is specified, the statistics will be reset. This command may be executed before and after some complex CICS task to determine the resource utilization imposed by that task.

EXEC CICS POP HANDLE

Restore the previous EXEC CICS HANDLE command settings.

Syntax

```
EXEC CICS POP HANDLE
```

This command restores the states of all the CICS condition handling functions to the values last saved with an EXEC CICS PUSH HANDLE command. This command is only valid for COBOL programs and may not be used within a C language program.

EXEC CICS PUSH HANDLE

Save current EXEC CICS HANDLE command settings.

Syntax

```
EXEC CICS PUSH HANDLE
```

This command saves the states of all active condition handles that may be restored by an EXEC CICS POP HANDLE command.

EXEC CICS READ

Read a record from a CICS file.

Syntax

```
EXEC CICS READ
FILE(name)
{ INTO(data-area) | SET(ptr-ref) }
[LENGTH(data-area)]
RIDFLD(data-area)
[KEYLENGTH(data-value) [GENERIC]]
[SYSID(name)]
[RBA | RRN]
[GTEQ | EQUAL]
[UPDATE]
```

This command reads a record from a CICS file. The record read is either stored in a data area specified by the INTO option or in CICS storage with a pointer to that storage returned if the SET option is used. The record retrieved is specified by the RIDFLD attributed. The RIDFLD may be used to find exact matches to a record or records that have partial or greater matches to the key supplied. The UPDATE option reads the record and flags it for possible update using the CICS REWRITE command or for deletion using the CICS DELETE command. A lock is taken on the record and held until either the record is explicitly unlocked with the CICS UNLOCK command or the record is updated or deleted.

EXEC CICS READNEXT

Read the next record from a CICS file.

Syntax

```
EXEC CICS READNEXT FILE(name)
[INTO(data-area) | SET(ptr-ref)]
[LENGTH(data-area)]
RIDFLD(data-area)
[KEYLENGTH(data-value) | RSA | RRN]
[REQID(data-value)]
[SYSID(name) KEYLENGTH(data-value)]
```

This command reads the next record from a CICS file. The CICS command EXEC CICS STARTBR should be issued prior to this command to position the logical file pointer for subsequent reads. Following this command, the file pointer is incremented to point to the next record to be read. The EXEC CICS ENDBR command should be issued when browsing of the file is complete.

EXEC CICS READPREV

Read the previous record from a CICS file.

Syntax

```
EXEC CICS READPREV FILE(name)
{ INTO(data-area) | SET(ptr-ref) }
[LENGTH(data-area)]
RIDFLD(data-area)
[KEYLENGTH(data-value) | RBA | RRN]
[REQID(data-value)]
[SYSID(name) KEYLENGTH(data-value)]
```

This command reads the previous record from a CICS file. The CICS command EXEC CICS STARTBR should be issued prior to this command to position the logical file pointer for subsequent reads. Following this command, the file pointer is decremented to point to the next record to be read. The EXEC CICS ENDBR command should be issued when browsing of the file is complete.

EXEC CICS READQ TD

Read a record from a transient data queue.

Syntax

```
EXEC CICS READQ TD QUEUE(name)
{ INTO(data-area) | SET(ptr-ref) }
[LENGTH(data-area)]
[SYSID(name)]
[NOSUSPEND]
```

This command reads the next record from the specified transient data queue. If the queue is intrapartition and recoverable, any records read will be returned to the queue if the transaction ABENDs or is otherwise rolled back. If there are no records left to be read from the queue, the QZERO condition will be raised.

EXEC CICS READQ TS

Read a record from a temporary storage queue.

Syntax

```
EXEC CICS READQ TS QUEUE(name)
{ INTO(data-area) | SET(ptr-ref) }
[LENGTH(data-area)]
[NUMITEMS(data-value)]
[ITEM(data-value) | NEXT]
[SYSID(name)]
```

This command reads the next record from a temporary storage queue. Each queue maintains a pointer to the next record to be read from the queue. After reading the next record, the queue pointer is advanced. The NUMITEMS option specifies the number of items contained in the whole queue. If the ITEM option is specified, that item will be returned from the queue and the queue pointer positioned to the record following that item. Since there is only a single queue pointer associated with the queue, any transaction reading a record will modify the queue pointer and hence the next record returned across the whole region.

EXEC CICS RECEIVE (from APPC partner)

Receive data from a DTP application partner.

Syntax

```
EXEC CICS RECEIVE
[CONVID(name)]
[INTO(data-area) | SET(ptr-ref)]
[LENGTH(data-area) | FLENGTH(data-area)]
[MAXLENGTH(data-value) | MAXFLENGTH(data-value)]
[NOTRUNCATE]
[STATE]
```

This command is used to receive data from a DTP-connected CICS application that is in RECEIVE state. The data received will have been sent from the partner application using an EXEC CICS SEND command.

EXEC CICS RECEIVE (from terminal)

Receive data directly from a CICS terminal.

Syntax

```
EXEC CICS RECEIVE
[{ INTO(data-area) | SET(ptr-ref) }
 { LENGTH(data-area) | FLENGTH(data-area) }]
[MAXLENGTH(data-value) | MAXFLENGTH(data-value)]
[NOTRUNCATE]
[ASIS]
[BUFFER]
```

This command receives raw 3270 data from the terminal. If no data are currently available, the command blocks awaiting response back from the terminal when an AID key is next pressed. The BUFFER option allows the whole terminal buffer to be returned immediately to the caller.

EXEC CICS RECEIVE MAP

Receive a formatted 3270 screen into a BMS map.

Syntax

```
EXEC CICS RECEIVE MAP(name)
[MAPSET(name)]
[INTO(data-area) | SET(ptr-ref)]
[FROM(data-area) LENGTH(data-value) | TERMINAL [ASIS]]
```

This command requests that data be returned from the terminal and stored in a CICS BMS map structure. The data returned from the terminal is 3270 format, and CICS will map the response into the C or COBOL language structures corresponding to the symbolic map.

EXEC CICS RELEASE

Release a table or mapset from CICS storage.

Syntax

```
EXEC CICS RELEASE PROGRAM(name)
```

This command releases storage allocated to a table or mapset that had been loaded previously into memory using the EXEC CICS LOAD command with the HOLD option. Once this command has been issued, storage pointed to by a previous EXEC CICS LOAD should not be referenced because CICS may release the storage immediately.

EXEC CICS RESETBR

Reset the start of a browse operation.

Syntax

```
EXEC CICS RESETBR FILE(name)
RIDFLD(data-area)
[KEYLENGTH(data-value) [GENERIC] | RBA | RRN]
[REQID(data-value)]
[SYSID(name)]
[GTEQ | EQUAL]
```

This command resets the file pointer associated with a CICS file browse previously initiated by an EXEC CICS STARTBR command. The file pointer can be moved forward or backward in the file.

EXEC CICS RETRIEVE

Return information stored for a CICS task.

Syntax

```
EXEC CICS RETRIEVE
[INTO(data-area) | SET(ptr-ref)]
[LENGTH(data-area)]
[RTRANSID(data-area)]
[RTERMID(data-area)]
[QUEUE(data-area)]
```

This command retrieves data associated with an asynchronously started transaction requested by the EXEC CICS START command.

EXEC CICS RETURN

End a CICS program or return control to a previous LINK.

Syntax

```
EXEC CICS RETURN
[TRANSID(name) [COMMAREA(data-area) [LENGTH(data-value)]]]
```

This command terminates a CICS program. If the program was called from an EXEC CICS LINK command, control is returned to the calling program. If the return is executed at the top level of a program, the command terminates the transaction as a whole. If the TRANSID option is specified at the top-level return, the transaction specified will be the next transaction started at the terminal following the user pressing an AID key. This functionality allows pseudoconversational applications to be written. If data are to be passed to the next transaction or back to the calling program of an EXEC CICS LINK, the COMMAREA option may be used. Data supplied to the COMMAREA is passed back to the previous level.

A transaction scheduled to execute psuedoconversationally by this command may not be the next transaction actually executed if an intervening EXEC CICS START command is issued against the terminal.

EXEC CICS REWRITE

Modify the contents of a CICS file record.

Syntax

```
EXEC CICS REWRITE FILE(name)
FROM(data-area)
[LENGTH(data-value)]
[SYSID(name)]
```

This command updates or rewrites a previously read record from a CICS file. The record that is updated must have been accessed previously by an EXEC CICS READ with UPDATE option.

EXEC CICS SEND (to APPC partner)

Send data to a partner DTP application.

Syntax

```
EXEC CICS SEND
[CONVID(name)]
[FROM(data-area) { LENGTH(data-value) | FLENGTH(data-value) }]
[INVITE | LAST]
[CONFIRM | WAIT]
[STATE(cvda)]
```

This command is used to send data to a DTP application that has issued an EXEC CICS RECEIVE command.

EXEC CICS SEND (to terminal)

Send data directly to a CICS-attached terminal.

Syntax

```
EXEC CICS SEND
FROM(data-area) { LENGTH(data-value) | FLENGTH(data-value) }
[WAIT]
[ERASE]
[CTLCHAR(data-value)]
```

This command sends data directly to the terminal. The data sent will be interpreted by the terminal as 3270 data stream. Valid 3270 commands and orders may be included in the data sent to format or otherwise control the display. The CTLCHAR command allows the 3270 Write Control Character to be set. The ERASE option specifies that the 3270 data stream command sent is ERASE WRITE as opposed to the WRITE command. The data sent must be ASCII format 3270 data.

EXEC CICS SEND CONTROL

Send control information to a CICS-attached terminal.

Syntax

```
EXEC CICS SEND CONTROL
[CURSOR [(data-value)]]
[FORMFEED]
[ERASE | ERASEUP]
[PRINT]
[FREEKB]
[ALARM]
[FRSET]
```

This command allows a transaction to send control information to the display against which it is being executed. The following options may be specified:

CURSOR   This option allows the input cursor to be positioned at a specified location on the display. The cursor is specified as an offset into the display.

FORMFEED   Specifies a new page.

ERASE   Erases the screen. The 3270 command sent is set to ERASE WRITE as opposed to a simple WRITE.

ERASEUP   This option erases all the unprotected fields on the display.

PRINT   Specifies the start of a print operation.

FREEKB   Unlocks the keyboard.

ALARM   Sounds the terminal audible alarm.

FRSET   This command resets the modified data tags of any unprotected fields on the display.

EXEC CICS SEND MAP

Send a BMS map to a CICS terminal.

Syntax

```
EXEC CICS SEND MAP(name)
[MAPSET(name)]
[FROM(data-area) [LENGTH(data-value)] [DATAONLY] | MAPONLY]
[CURSOR [(data-value)]]
[FORMFEED]
```

```
[ERASE | ERASEAUP]
[PRINT]
[FREEKB]
[ALARM]
[FRSET]
```

This command sends 3270 data stream to the display. The data stream is obtained from either the physical map, logical map, or both. Various 3270 control orders also may be specified.

EXEC CICS SEND TEXT

Send formatted data to a CICS terminal.

Syntax

```
EXEC CICS SEND TEXT
FROM(data-area)
[LENGTH(data-value)]
[CURSOR(data-value)]
[FORMFEED]
[ERASE]
[PRINT]
[FREEKB]
[ALARM]
[NLEOM]
```

This command sends 3270 data stream to the terminal. The data sent are pre-formatted such that words are not split across lines.

EXEC CICS SET CONNECTION

Change attributes of a CICS connection.

Syntax

```
EXEC CICS SET CONNECTION(name)
[SERVSTATUS(cvda)]
```

This command allows a CICS connection to a remote CICS region to be inservice (enabled) or outservice (disabled).

EXEC CICS SET FILE

Change attributes of a CICS file.

Syntax

```
EXEC CICS SET FILE(name)
[BASENAME(data-value)]
[FILESERVER(data-value)]
[INDEXNAME(data-value)]
[EMPTYSTATUS(cvda)]
```

```
[READ(cvda)]
[UPDATE(cvda)]
[BROWSE(cvda)]
[ADD(cvda)]
[DELETE(cvda)]
```

This command allows the attributes of a CICS file to be modified or changed. The following attributes may be modified:

Option	Description
BASENAME	The name of the file as held by the SFS. The name of the SFS file may be different from that of the CICS file itself.
FILESERVER	This attribute defines the server name of the SFS on which the file is held.
INDEXNAME	The name of the primary index to be used with the file.
EMPTYSTATUS	This attribute specifies whether the file should be emptied next time it is opened.
READ	This attribute controls whether the file may be read or is to prevent reading.
UPDATE	This attribute controls whether the file may be updated or is to prevent updating.
BROWSE	This attribute controls whether the file may be browsed or is to prevent browsing.
ADD	This attribute controls whether the file may have records added to it or is to prevent new records from being added.
DELETE	This attribute controls whether the file may have records deleted from it or is to prevent records from being removed.

EXEC CICS SET JOURNALNUM

Change the open status of a CICS journal.

Syntax

```
EXEC CICS SET JOURNALNUM(data-value)
[OPENSTATUS(cvda)]
```

This command may be used to open or close a CICS journal. If the journal file is already open, this command also may be used to switch the AIX operating system journal files.

EXEC CICS SET PROGRAM

Change attributes of a CICS program, mapset, or table.

Syntax

```
EXEC CICS SET PROGRAM(name)
[STATUS(cvda)]
[NEWCOPY]
```

This command allows a CICS program or mapset to be flagged for reloading at next execution or reference by specifying the NEWCOPY command. Additionally, the status of the program may be changed with the STATUS option. Possible values for the status of the program are

ENABLED   The program or mapset may be used.

DISABLED   The program or mapset is disabled.

EXEC CICS SET STATISTICS

Change attributes of CICS statistics collection.

Syntax

```
EXEC CICS SET STATISTICS
[ENDOFDAY(hhmmss) |
 [ENDOFDAYHRS(value)]
 [ENDOFDAYMINS(value)]
 [ENDOFDAYSECS(value)]]
[INTERVAL(hhmmss) |
 [INTERVALHRS(value)]
 [INTERVALMINS(value)]
 [INTERVALSECS(value)]]
[RECORDING(cvda)]
```

This command may be used to change the CICS statistics characteristics. The time used for end-of-day statistics and the period for interval statistics may be modified. The automatic recording of interval and unsolicited statistics also may be enabled and disabled by this command.

EXEC CICS SET TASK

Purge a CICS task.

Syntax

```
EXEC CICS SET TASK(data-value)
PURGETYPE(cvda)
```

This command can be used to purge a CICS task. The purge type may be either PURGE or FORCEPURGE. The PURGE option causes the task to ABEND when data integrity can be maintained. The FORCEPURGE option may result in data inconsistency and usually should be avoided.

EXEC CICS SET TDQUEUE

Change the attributes of a CICS transient data queue.

Syntax

```
EXEC CICS SET TDQUEUE
[ATIFACILITY(cvda)]
[ATITERMID(data-value)]
[ATITRANID(data-value)]
[ENABLESTATUS(cvda)]
```

```
[OPENSTATUS(cvda)]
[TRIGGERLEVEL(data-value)]
```

Option	Description
ATIFACILITY	This attribute specifies whether a triggered transaction from this queue should be associated with a terminal or an APPC conversation.
ATITERMID	This attribute specifies the terminal or conversation identifier that is to be associated with a triggered transaction.
ATITRANID	This attribute defines the transaction name that is to be started when the trigger level for an intrapartition queue has been reached.
ENABLESTATUS	This attribute specifies whether the queue is disabled or enabled.
OPENSTATUS	For extrapartition queues only, this attribute specifies whether the queue should be opened or closed.
TRIGGERLEVEL	For intrapartition queues only, this attribute specifies the trigger level after which a transaction will be started.

EXEC CICS SET TERMINAL

Change the attributes of a CICS terminal.

Syntax

```
EXEC CICS SET TERMINAL
[TERMPRIORITY(data-value)]
[SERVSTATUS(cvda)]
[ATISTATUS(cvda)]
[TTISTATUS(cvda)]
[PURGE]
```

Option	Description
TERMPRIORITY	The priority associated with the terminal.
SERVSTATUS	Whether the terminal should be inservice or outservice.
ATISTATUS	Should asynchronous transactions be allowed to start against this terminal?
TTISTATUS	Should user transactions be allowed to be submitted directly from the terminal?
PURGE	Any transaction associated with the terminal is to be purged.

EXEC CICS SET TRANSACTION

Change the attributes of a CICS transaction.

Syntax

```
EXEC CICS SET TRANSACTION(name)
[STATUS(cvda)]
[PRIORITY(data-value)]
[PURGEABILITY(cvda)]
```

Option	Description
STATUS	Should the transaction be enabled or disabled?
PRIORITY	The priority of the transaction.
PURGEABILITY	Can the transaction be purged by request?

EXEC CICS START

Request that a CICS transaction be asynchronously started.

Syntax

```
EXEC CICS START
[INTERVAL (hhmmss) |
 AFTER [HOURS(data-value)]
       [MINUTES(data-value)]
       [SECONDS(data-value)] |
 AT [HOURS(data-value)]
    [MINUTES(data-value)]
    [SECONDS(data-value)]]
TRANSID(name)
[REQID(name)]
[FROM(data-area) LENGTH(data-value)]
[TERMID(name)]
[SYSID(name)]
[RTRANSID(name)]
[RTREMID(name)]
[QUEUE(name)]
[NOCHECK]
[PROTECT]
```

This command allows a new transaction to be started by the currently executing program. The transaction to be started is supplied by the TRANSID option. The transaction is started asynchronously, and its final outcome is not known by the starting program unless some explicit intertransaction synchronization is employed. Optionally, a time specified as either an interval or an absolute time may be supplied. The transaction is not actually started until either the interval has passed or the absolute time is reached. The transaction may be started on a remote CICS system by specifying a SYSID.

Data may be passed from the current transaction to the newly started transaction by using the FROM and LENGTH options.

EXEC CICS STARTBR

Begin a browse operation on a CICS file.

Syntax

```
EXEC CICS STARTBR FILE(name)
RIDFLD(data-area)
[KEYLENGTH(data-value) [GENERIC] | RBA | RRN]
[REQID(data-value)]
```

```
[SYSID(name) [KEYLENGTH(data-value)]]
[GTEQ | EQUAL]
```

This command specifies that a browse operation is to begin on a CICS file. Following this command, EXEC CICS READNEXT and EXEC CICS READPREV commands are valid. Following a browse, the EXEC CICS ENDBR command should be used to terminate the browse operation.

EXEC CICS SUSPEND

Suspend the execution of a CICS task.

Syntax

```
EXEC CICS SUSPEND
```

On CICS/MVS, all CICS tasks execute under one MVS address space. Context switching from one CICS task to another is handled by CICS itself as opposed to MVS. This command allowed a CICS task to voluntarily relinquish its use of CICS in favor of another CICS task. On CICS/6000, execution of CICS transactions is managed by the AIX operating system. This command is available within CICS/6000 for compatibility but is effectively a no operation.

EXEC CICS SYNCPOINT

Commit or roll back the work of a CICS transaction.

Syntax

```
EXEC CICS SYNCPOINT
[ROLLBACK]
```

This command instructs CICS to commit or roll back the changes made by the current transaction. Once committed or rolled back, the transaction continues and may make additional transactional changes that will be committed or rolled back at the next EXEC CICS SYNCPOINT or task exit commands.

EXEC CICS TRACE

Control CICS trace output.

Syntax

```
EXEC CICS TRACE
[ON | OFF]
[SYSTEM]
[EI]
[USER]
[SINGLE]
```

This command controls CICS/6000 trace output and its content. Internally, CICS maintains a set of boolean flags that may be on or off. These flags control the content of CICS trace output. The flags may be switched on or off with this command. CICS maintains the following flags:

MASTER   Master trace output flag. When this flag is off, all the other CICS trace flags are ignored, and no trace output is generated. Trace will only be written when the master trace flag and one or more of the other trace flags are turned on. To turn on the master trace flag, no other options should be specified on the command. EXEC CICS TRACE ON will turn on the master trace flag, and EXEC CICS TRACE OFF will turn it off.

SYSTEM   CICS System trace flag. This flag specifies that internal CICS trace is to be generated. When this flag is on and the EI flag is off, CICS/6000 will generate internal CICS trace showing the internal operation of CICS. The primary purpose of this trace output is for IBM to perform diagnosis of CICS internal problems.

EI   EXEC Interface trace flag. When this flag is turned on in conjunction with the SYSTEM flag, trace output will contain entry and exit records from every EXEC CICS command executed. This trace may be particularly useful in obtaining performance numbers and for user-based diagnostics.

USER   Control USER trace flag. When this flag is on in conjunction with the MASTER trace flag, user-based trace through the EXEC CICS ENTRY command is written. When the flag is off, no user-based trace is collected.

SINGLE   Controls output of the EXEC CICS ENTER trace command.

EXEC CICS UNLOCK

Unlock a previously locked CICS file record.

Syntax

```
EXEC CICS UNLOCK
FILE(name)
[SYSID(name)]
```

This command unlocks a CICS file record that may have been locked previously with an EXEC CICS READ UPDATE command.

EXEC CICS WAIT CONVID

Wait for data to be sent to a DTP partner.

Syntax

```
EXEC CICS WAIT CONVID(name)
[STATE(cvda)]
```

In CICS DTP operation, data being sent may be buffered. This command flushes the data to the partner immediately.

EXEC CICS WAIT JOURNAL

Force Journal output to disk.

Syntax

```
EXEC CICS WAIT JOURNAL
JFILEID(data-value)
[REQID(data-value)]
[STARTIO]
```

This command forces journal data to be written to disk before returning.

EXEC CICS WAIT TERMINAL

Force terminal data to the terminal.

Syntax

```
EXEC CICS WAIT TERMINAL
```

This command causes buffered terminal data to be sent to the terminal immediately and waits for the data to be sent before completing.

EXEC CICS WRITE

Write a record to a CICS file.

Syntax

```
EXEC CICS WRITE FILE(name)
FROM(data-area)
[LENGTH(data-value)]
RIDFLD(data-area)
[KEYLENGTH(data-value) | RBA | RRN]
[SYSID(name)]
[MASSINSERT]
```

This command writes a record into a CICS file. The MASSINSERT option is ignored by CICS/6000 and causes a warning message to be generated by the CICS translator. It is provided for CICS language compatibility and is a no operation.

EXEC CICS WRITEQ TD

Write a record into a CICS transient data queue.

Syntax

```
EXEC CICS WRITEQ TD QUEUE(name)
FROM(data-area)
[LENGTH(data-value)]
[SYSID(name)]
```

This command writes a record into a CICS transient data queue defined as either intrapartition or extrapartition. Extrapartition queues on CICS/6000 are defined as AIX files. This command allows CICS to write data in various formats to AIX files.

EXEC CICS WRITEQ TS

Write a record into a CICS temporary storage queue.

Syntax

```
EXEC CICS WRITEQ TS QUEUE(name)
FROM(data-area)
[LENGTH(data-value)]
[ITEM(data-area) [REWRITE]]
[SYSID(name)]
[MAIN | AUXILIARY]
[SUSPEND]
```

This command writes a record into a CICS-defined temporary storage queue. If the queue has not been written previously, this command will create the queue. If the MAIN operand is specified, the queue will be created in CICS memory, whereas if the AUXILIARY operand is specified, the queue will be mapped onto an SFS file.

Records within the queue will be appended at the end of the queue for a simple write, and the item or index number of the newly added record will be returned in the ITEM operand. A record written previously may be updated by specifying the REWRITE option along with the ITEM option.

EXEC CICS XCTL

Transfer control to another CICS program.

Syntax

```
EXEC CICS XCTL
PROGRAM(name)
[COMMAREA(data-area) [LENGTH(data-value)]]
```

This command transfers control from the current CICS program to another. In other environments such a transfer may be considered a GOTO. Any recoverable changes made by the first program are still outstanding in the second.

Developing CICS Applications

The task of developing a CICS/6000 application may be divided, like any software development activity, into planning, design, implementation, and testing phases. In order to plan and design a CICS/6000 application, the functions and characteristics of CICS should be understood. With a grasp of the functions that CICS provides, the design of an application can be modeled on characteristics such as user presentation, business rules, and data manipulation. The presentation of information can be handled by CICS through terminal control and Basic Mapping Support, the business rules through the program algorithms, and the data manipulation through CICS data types such as queues and files. If data are maintained by a database, CICS also will assist by ensuring that data modified within the database are kept consistent with data updated in CICS data constructs

Numerous texts have been written on CICS application programming. The following chapters summarize some of the key constructs of CICS applications including presentation, data constructs of CICS, and some specifics of CICS/6000. The IBM-supplied manuals should be consulted for more detailed information on specific commands and data types.

Translating and Compiling

A CICS/6000 application can be written in either the C or the COBOL programming languages. No support is currently provided for other languages, such as 370 assembler, PL/I, C++, or RPG. The source code of a CICS program may be entered into an AIX file using an editor such as vi supplied with the operating system. Source code may be written on a separate machine such as a PC workstation or even under a mainframe environment but must be copied to AIX before it can be used with CICS/6000. Source programs containing CICS statements have CICS-defined file suffixes. There is one suffix for COBOL language programs and a separate suffix for C language programs. For COBOL, the suffix is .ccp, and for C language programs the suffix is `.ccs`. These suffixes allow pretranslated and posttranslated programs to be differentiated.

A CICS source program contains a mixture of native language calls and CICS command level statements. Native language calls are programming constructs such as "if" statements, "move" statements, and other C or COBOL constructs. The CICS commands are specified as

```
EXEC CICS <command> <options ...>
```

In the C language, each EXEC CICS command is terminated with a semicolon (;), while in COBOL, each command is terminated with an "END-EXEC." parameter.

Once a CICS source program has been written and entered as an AIX file, it must be processed by a CICS-supplied translator and finally compiled by a compiler. These tasks are further described in the following sections and are illustrated in Fig. 7.1.

The EXEC CICS commands are not understood by the C or COBOL compilers. As such, the program source files are required to be translated before compilation. The translation step removes each occurrence of an EXEC CICS command and replaces it with either C or COBOL code that performs the same function as the original EXEC CICS statements. The newly inserted code is usually a function or procedure call to a "stub" function that is linked into the final program which gives control to CICS/6000 code to handle the CICS command.

The translation step for CICS/6000 programs is achieved by the CICS/6000-supplied command **cicstran.** Cicstran takes as input a source program that may contain EXEC CICS calls and writes as output an equiva-

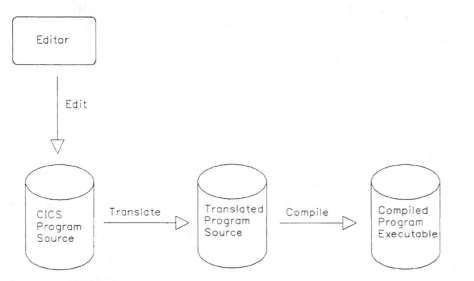

Figure 7.1 CICS source.

lent source program with the EXEC CICS calls replaced with native code. The basic syntax of the **cicstran** command is

```
For COBOL source programs:
cicstran -lCOBOL program

For C source programs:
cicstran -lC program
```

The translation produces either a pure COBOL source program ending with a `.cbl` suffix or a pure C source program ending with a `.c` suffix depending on the original source language. If the translation completes without error, the following message will be produced:

```
ERZ004060I/5015: cicstran translation ended: 0 error(s), 0 warning(s).
```

Any errors detected during translation will still result in the target source file being produced, but this source file should not be compiled. The source file will contain the error messages detected by the translator.

On a successful translation, the **cicstran** command will return an AIX return code of 0 and a nonzero return code for a translation error. This can be used by an AIX shell script or Makefile to direct processing.

Error, warning, and information messages produced by cicstran are directed to the AIX error file stream `stderr`. These messages can be captured in a file by redirecting `stderr` through normal shell redirection facilities.

The format of an error message produced by the translator is as follows:

```
ERZ004xxxxx/xxxx: NNNNN: MMMMMMMMMMMMMMMM
```

where

    xxxxx   Message number from CICS. The message number may be looked up in the messages and codes manual for additional explanation of the error and how to correct it.

    NNNNN   Line number in original source at which error was detected.

    MMMMMM   Message text describing the error.

It is important to make any code changes required to fix translation errors in the original source (the files ending in `.ccs` or `.ccp`) rather than in the translated source output (the files ending in `.c` or `.cbl`). Changes made in these files will be meaningless, because the next translation of the original source will cause the translated output to be overwritten.

Once the source programs containing the EXEC CICS statements have been translated, they must be compiled to executable code. The steps required for compilation vary depending on the language type being compiled.

To compile a C language program, the AIX C compiler must be used. This compiler is supplied with the AIX base operating system. Since CICS/6000 applications execute in a multithreaded environment, the code generated by the compiler must be thread-safe. To achieve this, special versions of the compiler are supplied to generate thread-safe code. The compilers are named cc_r and xlc_r. The _r suffix stands for *reentrant*. The difference between the cc and xlc compilers relates to the level of C language supported. The cc compiler compiles to the original Kernighan and Ritchie level of the language, while the xlc compiles with the newer and stricter ANSI definition level of the language. It is recommended that the xlc_r compiler be used because this performs the strictest correctness checking.

To compile a translated CICS C program, use the following command structure:

```
xlc_r \                                  # Use the xlc_r C compiler
/usr/lpp/cics/lib/libcics_api.a \        # Link with the CICS library
-I/usr/lpp/cics/include \                # Set the search path for CICS include
progname.c \                             # The name of the source program to be
-o progname                              # The name of the target executable
```

COBOL programs may be compiled with the MicroFocus COBOL compiler. This compiler can produce different types of executables for different purposes. For CICS/6000, two types of compiled output are meaningful. These are intermediate code and intermediate code with Animator support. The COBOL intermediate code allows code to be finally executed under a separate COBOL runtime. CICS uses this technique to include CICS logic into a special instance of the COBOL runtime created with the **cicsmkcobol** command discussed later. The intermediate code with Animator support produces additional logic in the resulting executable that allows the program to be debugged in conjunction with the MicroFocus source level debugger.

To compile a translated CICS COBOL program, the following compilation commands must be used:

```
For non-Animator:
COBCPY = /usr/lpp/cics/include; cob -u progname.cbl

For Animator:
COBCPY = /usr/lpp/cics/include; cob -A progname.cbl
```

The default output file name for a C compilation is a.out. The -o filename option should always be used with C compilation to give the program a more meaningful name. It is suggested that the output name be the same as the original but with no suffix.

The output of a COBOL compilation varies depending on whether Animator support is required. If no Animator is required, the output will be a single file ending with the .gnt suffix. The file name will be the same as the original source program. When compiling with Animator, the output will consist of two files ending with the .int and .idy suffixes. Both files should be moved and treated as a single unit.

The CICS/6000 product supplies a utility tool called **cicstcl** to translate and then subsequently compile and link a program in a single step. If an error is encountered during translation, subsequent compilation is not attempted. The **cicstcl** command has the following syntax:

```
For C source programs:
cicstcl -lC program

For COBOL source programs (no Animator):
cicstcl -lCOBOL program

For COBOL source programs (with Animator)
cicstcl -lCOBOL -a program
```

During the execution of cicstcl, the translated program will be generated temporarily on disk. This is removed at the successful generation of the program. If an error occurs during translation, the translated output will be left on disk. When using cicstcl to generate a COBOL program for use with Animator, the translated COBOL program is always left.

If additional compilation flags or libraries are required for compiling and linking, these may be specified by setting the required parameters in AIX environment variables. For C, the environment variable is CCFLAGS. For COBOL, the variable is COBOPTS. These variables may be used to specify additional link libraries such as database-supplied libraries.

If the program being compiled contains any syntax errors or other problems that will cause the compilation to fail, the compiler will generate the error and warning messages. These messages typically have the source file line number at which the error was detected. It is important to note that the line number displayed is the line number in the translated source and not the line number in the original source program containing the EXEC CICS statements. The translated source may be viewed to find the source of the error, but once discovered, the original, pretranslated source must be modified to correct the problem. Any changes made to the translated source will be undone next time the original program is translated. Translation of a CICS program usually causes the program to expand. This means that an error reported at line 1000 in the translated source may be an error at some other line in the pretranslated source, usually much further back in the original source.

Maintaining Source Programs

The development of an application requires some mechanism for maintaining source programs and executables. AIX provides a number of tools to perform these tasks including **make** and **sccs**.

AIX supplies a productivity tool called **make** for describing rules for building programs and executables from source. The **make** tool is very powerful and can be used with CICS/6000. **Make** is driven from a control file called

`Makefile` that is located in the same directory as the source files. Each entry in the `Makefile` specifies how to build one program from another, e.g., an entry of the following format

```
a: b
    compile b to produce a

b: c
    translate c to produce b
```

states that program "a" depends on program "b." This means that if the file containing "a" is older than the file containing "b," then compile "b" to produce "a." Before performing this rule, the other rules in the `Makefile` are scanned to see if there are additional rules for building program "b." In the example, there is a rule for building "b" that depends on "c." Since there are no "c" rules, the time stamp checking is all that is performed. If the time stamp on "c" is newer than that on "b," the rule is performed, and "c" is translated to produce "b."

This is only an abstracted flavor of the **make** program, but its power becomes quickly apparent. If a CICS application consists of many source files all of which need to be translated and compiled, building a `Makefile` containing rules for these usually will be advantageous, since **make** will then be able to track the dependencies and the commands needed to build.

The following example shows a CICS program that includes a symbolic map (C include file) generated from a CICS BMS source file. If the BMS source has been changed after the CICS program has been compiled, the program will be recompiled.

```
# The executable "program" depends on its source and the BMS
# generated include file.
program: program.ccs maps.h
    cicstcl -lC program.ccs

# The "maps.h" include file depends on the BMS source file.
maps.h: maps.bms
    cicsmap maps.bms
```

Makefiles also can be used to group together a sequence of commands to perform tasks other than building programs; the following illustrates the use of a `Makefile` that contains commands to define resources to a CICS region and another set of commands for installing them into a running region. Other sets of commands could be defined to delete resources from a running region or from the resource database.

```
install:
    cicsadd -c pd -r $(CICSREGION) PROGRAM PathName = $(PWD)/program
    cicsadd -c pd -r $(CICSREGION) TRAN ProgName = PROGRAM
    cicsadd -c pd -r $(CICSREGION) MAPSET \
        PathName = $(PWD)/maps.map \
        ProgType = map
```

```
runtime:
    cicsupdate -c pd -r $(CICSREGION) -R PROGRAM
    cicsupdate -c pd -r $(CICSREGION) -R TRAN
    cicsupdate -c pd -r $(CICSREGION) -R MAPSET
```

By performing the AIX command **make install,** the `Makefile` is searched for rules to "build" install. Since it depends on nothing, the rules will always be executed.

Rules within a `Makefile` must *always* be indented with a tab character. Environment variables are expanded by surrounding them with parenthesis and prefixing with a dollar symbol.

A rule to translate CICS source to its native format is shown in the following:

```
.SUFFIXES: .ccs

.ccs.c:
    cicstran -1C $<
```

A more meaningful but complex example is now described. The example illustrates a `Makefile` to build two CICS executables called **program1** and **program2.** "program1" is built from two C source files called `main.ccs` and `func.ccs`, while "program2" is built from the single source file called `program2.ccs`. These files are shown below:

```
/* main.ccs */
main()
{
    /* Some business logic */
    function2();
    /* Some more business logic */
    EXEC CICS RETURN;
}
/* func2.ccs */
int function2()
{
    /* Some business logic */
    return;
}
/* program2.ccs */
main()
{
    EXEC CICS RETURN;
}
```

The `Makefile` to build the programs and track the dependencies is shown next:

```
.SUFFIXES:
.SUFFIXES: .ccs .o

TRANSLATE_FLAGS = -d -e

SOURCE = main.o func2.o
```

```
all: program program2

program: $(SOURCE)
        xlc_r -o program $(SOURCE) /usr/lpp/cics/lib/libcics_api.a

.ccs:
        cicstcl $(TRANSLATE_FLAGS) -lC $@

.ccs.o:
        cicstran $(TRANSLATE_FLAGS) -lC $<
        xlc_r -c -I/usr/lpp/cics/include $*.c
        rm $*.c
```

This `Makefile` illustrates two generic rules, one to build an AIX object from a CICS source file and one to build an executable from a CICS source file. The `Makefile` rules follow the following logic:

```
program -> main.o func2.o
 /* Is program older than either main.o or func2.o? If yes
 /* or program does not exist, execute the rule to build
 /* program from main.o and func2.o
main.o -> main.ccs
 /* Is main.o older than main.ccs? If yes or main.o does not
 /* exist, execute the rule to build main.o from main.ccs
func2.o -> func2.ccs
 /* Is func2.o older than func2.ccs? If yes of func2.o does not
 /* exist, execute the rule to build func2.o from func2.ccs

program2 -> program2.ccs
 /* Is program2 older than program2.ccs? If yes, or program2
 /* does not exist, execute the suffix rule to create program2
 /* from program2.ccs
```

C Language Considerations

When writing a C language CICS application, the following must be considered.

CICS API data type mappings

The CICS API defines its arguments in terms of 16-bit data values, 32-bit data values, data areas, CVDAs, and other CICS data types. These map to C language data types as follows:

CICS parameter type	C language data type
16-bit data value	Short
32-bit data value	Long
16-bit data area	Short
32-bit data area	Long
CVDA	Long
pointer-ref	Any C language pointer type
name	A C language character array; this may be specified as a constant string (text surrounded by double quotes).
label	Not supported for C language programs
hhmmss	Not supported for C language programs

Using EIB and RESP commands

The Exec Interface Block (EIB) is not automatically addressable by CICS C language programs. To obtain addressability to the EIB, the CICS/C program must execute an EXEC CICS ADDRESS EIB command. This command expects a pointer to an EIB data structure as a parameter. The CICS-supplied typedefed structure called DFHEIBLK may be used. During translation, CICS declares a variable called dfheiptr of this type that may be used. The following code fragment illustrates the use of this command:

```
EXEC CICS ADDRESS EIB(dfheiptr);
```

Prior to issuing this command, the RESP values returned from CICS commands must be ignored because execution of the command causes the EIB to be updated, which if not mapped into the program results in undefined values on RESP value testing.

Structure packing

The C programming language provides a data type known as *struct* or *structure*. This data type allows multiple data elements called *fields* to be grouped together. The combined fields constitute a structure that may be manipulated as a single entity. The fields within a structure are themselves data typed and may be of any valid C language type including structures themselves. As an example, consider a file record containing a name, an address, and an account balance. This may be described as a C language struct as follows:

```
struct record
{
    char    name[30];      /* 30 byte name field    */
    char    address[90];   /* 90 byte address field */
    char    credit;        /* 1 byte credit rating  */
    int     balance;       /* 4 byte balance        */
};
```

From the contents of the record, the total size of the data type can be seen as 125 bytes (30 + 90 + 1 + 4). Unfortunately, the C compiler attempts to locate fields in structures on even or full-word boundaries and instead of generating

```
      30          90        1        4
+ ------- + ------- + ------ + ------ +
|  name   | address | credit | balance |
+ ------- + ------- + ------ + ------ +
```

may generate:

```
      30          90        1          1          4
+ ----- + -------- + ---------- + -------- + ----- +
| name  | address  |  credit    |  filler  | balance |
+ ----- + -------- + ---------- + -------- + ----- +
```

This results in an unexpected 126-byte structure. The impact of this is most apparent if a CICS file is defined that has records of only 125 bytes in size and an attempt to write an instance of this C language structure is made. Fortunately, the C compiler provides a compilation control command to force the compiler to not inject filler information to align on even or full-word boundaries.

The following statement may be included in C language programs to specify that all structures are compiled for single-byte alignment.

```
#pragma options align = packed
```

To reset the packing to its previous value, the following command may be used:

```
#pragma options align = reset
```

COBOL Language Considerations

When writing a COBOL language CICS application, the following must be considered.

CICS API data type mappings

CICS parameter value	COBOL language data type
16-bit data value	PIC S9(4) COMP
32-bit data value	PIC S9(8) COMP
16-bit data area	PIC S9(4) COMP
32-bit data area	PIC S9(8) COMP
CVDA	PIC S9(8) COMP
pointer-ref	A COBOL pointer variable or variable preceded by the COBOL "ADDRESS OF" qualifier
label	A COBOL paragraph or section name
hhmmss	PIC S9(7) COMP-3

CICS program path names

When defining a program to CICS/6000 and the program source language is COBOL, care should be taken not to include the compiled program suffix, which is either .gnt or .int. Specify only the path name of the file without the suffix. The program location is specified in the **PathName** attribute of the program definition.

Language restrictions

Certain COBOL commands are invalid within a CICS/6000 environment. Some of these statements are listed below:

- **STOP RUN** Use EXEC CICS RETURN or EXEC CICS ABEND instead.
- **DISPLAY** Do not attempt to use screen output commands from within a COBOL application.

Calling other COBOL programs

A COBOL program can invoke either another C or COBOL program as a sub-program by using the EXEC CICS LINK command. Alternatively, a COBOL program can invoke another COBOL program using the COBOL language CALL facility. Using the CALL command allows additional parameters to be passed to the program other than just the Exec Interface Block and a COMMAREA. When calling another COBOL program, the program must be called using the following format:

```
CALL 'PROGRAM' USING DFHEIBLK DFHCOMMAREA
```

The called program must have its procedure division coded as follows:

```
PROCEDURE DIVISION USING DFHEIBLK DFHCOMMAREA
```

If the called program contains CICS statements or has been translated by the CICS command translator, the two parameters previously mentioned need not be explicitly coded; they will be inserted into the program by the translator.

When calling a program using CALL from a non-CICS program, the search directories for the called program are specified by the COBPATH environment variable. This mechanism may not be used with CICS/6000. The called program must be located either in the `/usr/lpp/cics/bin` directory or the `/var/cics_regions/<region>/bin` directory. If the called program is specified as a full path name, the program may be located in any AIX directory accessible by the AIX CICS userid.

Calling C functions from COBOL

The MicroFocus COBOL compiler and runtime requires that any C functions that are to be called from a COBOL application must be linked into the COBOL runtime support module. This is the module generated as part of the **cicsmkcobol** command used to generate a COBOL runtime that includes the calls to the CICS/6000 runtime.

To add a C function into the COBOL runtime, the source containing the C code must be compiled to an AIX object file. Once the object file has been created, it must to be linked into the COBOL runtime.

To compile a C source file to an AIX object file, issue the command:

```
$ xlc_r -c <C-Source file>.c
```

This will create a new AIX object file with the same name as the C language source file. The fill suffix will be `.o`.

The new COBOL run-time can now be created by executing the **cicsmk-cobol** command as follows:

```
# cicsmkcobol <AIX Object file>.o
```

A new COBOL runtime called `cicsprCOBOL` will be created in the current directory. This should be moved to the `/usr/lpp/cics/bin` directory and the CICS region restarted for the new runtime to take effect.

The following illustrates this process with a simple example of adding a function called *cfunc* into the COBOL runtime used by CICS. A sample COBOL program and procedure show a call to this function.

A sample AIX shell script to build and install the sample is given below. The sample should be compiled and installed as the root user.

```
#!/bin/ksh
# Script to:
#
# o Compile a C source file
# o Add the C function to the COBOL runtime
# o Copy the new run-time to the CICS expected location
# o Compiled the COBOL program
# o Define the COBOL program to CICS by resource definitions
#
xlc_r -c cfunc.c
cicsmkcobol cfunc.o
cp cicsprCOBOL /usr/lpp/cics/bin

cicstcl -d -e cobc.ccp

cicsadd -c td -r ${CICSREGION} COBC ProgName = COBCPROG
cicsadd -c pd -r ${CICSREGION} COBCPROG PathName = ${PWD}/cobc
```

Next, the C language function to be added into the COBOL runtime:

```
/*
 * C Language function to be called from a CICS COBOL application
 */

#include <stdio.h>

int cfunc(char *string, int *intPointer, int localInt)
{
    fprintf(stderr, "C function called: %s, %d, %d\n",
        string, *intPointer, localInt);
    return(99);
}
```

Finally, a COBOL program that calls the C language function:

```
000010 IDENTIFICATION DIVISION.
000020 PROGRAM-ID. COBC.
000030 ENVIRONMENT DIVISION.
000040 DATA DIVISION.
```

```
000050 WORKING-STORAGE SECTION.
000060 01 STR.
000070    03 STR-TEXT PIC X(12) VALUE "COBOL String".
000080    03 FILLER   PIC X     VALUE X"00".
000090 01 NUMBER-1    PIC S9(8) COMP-5 VALUE 34.
000100 01 NUMBER-2    PIC S9(8) COMP-5 VALUE 56.
000110
000120 PROCEDURE DIVISION.
000130    CALL "cfunc" USING STR, NUMBER-1 BY VALUE NUMBER-2.
000140    DISPLAY "Return code from C: " RETURN-CODE UPON SYSERR.
000150    EXEC CICS RETURN END-EXEC.
```

8

CICS/6000 Display Programming

This section discusses the principles of interacting with a user through a CICS/6000 application. A description of 3270 terminals is given, including the data stream expected by such a terminal. Programming directly with a 3270 data stream is then discussed, and finally, use of CICS Basic Mapping Support (BMS) is addressed.

The 3270 Terminal Model

As described previously, CICS/6000, like the other members of the CICS family of products, uses the 3270 terminal model to interact with a user. The layout of a 3270 display as seen by a user is that of a series of fields of data on the display. A field can be flagged as either allowing input (unprotected) or not allowing input (protected). A field on the display is created by the CICS/6000 application sending control information to the display in a language known as *3270 data stream*. The 3270 data stream language consists of an initial command such as **write** or **erase/write** followed by a set of control orders that create or change the layout of the display.

A 3270 display can be pictured as a rectangular array of characters or cells on the screen (usually 80 columns by 24 rows). Each cell may contain either a printable character or a field control character. The control characters determine the attributes of the following characters until the next control character is found.

The following control characters may be imbedded into 3270 data stream:

Value	Description
0x1D	Start Field
0x10	Start Field Extended
0x11	Set Buffer Address
0x1F	Set Attribute
0x13	Insert Cursor

A 3270 terminal handles all keystroke processing until one of a set of keys, called an *Action IDentifier* or *AID* key, is pressed. The AID keys consist of the enter key, the F1 to F24 keys, the clear key, and some other 3270 keyboard-specific keys. Until the AID key is pressed, no key strokes flow between the terminal and the CICS/6000 transaction.

When an AID key is pressed on a 3270 terminal, any characters in the unprotected fields that have been modified by the user are returned to the CICS/6000 application. The format of the inbound 3270 data stream is a series of cell addresses followed by the data returned.

Programming with 3270 Data Stream

Programming with 3270 data stream directly is a relatively low-level interface between CICS and the terminal but may be used to produce more powerful effects than can be achieved otherwise.

The following CICS commands may be used directly within a CICS/6000 application that has a 3270 terminal attached to send or receive 3270 data stream directly with the terminal:

EXEC CICS SEND   Send 3270 data from a CICS application to the 3270 terminal. The data can include any of the valid 3270 orders to format the display.

EXEC CICS SEND CONTROL   This command sends control information to the 3270 terminal such as commands to erase the screen or position the cursor.

EXEC CICS RECEIVE   Receive data from the terminal when an AID key is pressed. This command causes the CICS/6000 application to block until data are available from the terminal.

EXEC CICS SEND TEXT   Sends 3270 data from a specified area to the 3270 terminal but formats the data before transmission.

EXEC CICS CONVERSE   Sends 3270 data to the terminal and then performs a wait until data are available to be returned. This command is equivalent to performing an EXEC CICS SEND followed by an EXEC CICS RECEIVE.

EXEC CICS WAIT TERMINAL   Suspends the CICS/6000 application until the data sent to the terminal have been processed by the terminal. This option also can be specified as part of the EXEC CICS SEND command.

The 3270 terminal buffer

The 3270 terminal maintains a logical view of what the screen looks like. This is maintained as an array of character cells, one cell for each position on the screen. This screen representation is called the *screen buffer*. Changing the value of an element in the screen buffer causes a corresponding change on the value of the screen. The size of the buffer is the number of columns times the number of rows (e.g., an 80 × 24 screen has a size of 1920).

The position of an arbitrary cell is given by the row value multiplied by the number of cells in a row plus the column value. In most CICS/6000 instances, the number of cells in a row will be the constant 80. For example, the buffer position corresponding to row 6, column 25 will be 6*80 + 25, which equals 505. Modifying buffer cell 505 will modify the character at row 6, column 25. Figure 8.1 illustrates the 3270 terminal buffer. 3270 control orders take effect from the point at which the current logical buffer pointer is set. The buffer pointer may be positioned by specifying the SBA order discussed in the next subsection.

Setting the buffer address in 3270 programming

When 3270 data stream is sent to the terminal, the data stream causes changes to occur from the position specified by the current buffer address (initially 0). To position the 3270 buffer address at a different location, the 3270 order called *Set Buffer Address* or *SBA* must be sent. The SBA order code has a value of **0x11** and is followed by the 2-byte value of the position in the buffer where the following data stream is to take effect. Unfortunately, the buffer address is not as simple as its raw buffer index value. An algorithm must be followed to convert a buffer address into the 3270 data stream

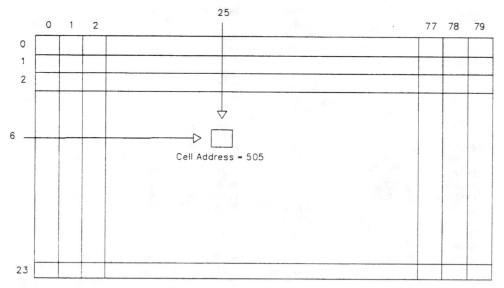

Figure 8.1   3270 buffer address.

coding. To calculate the 3270 data stream buffer address of a row, column value:

1. Calculate the buffer index position by multiplying the row number by the number of cells in a column (80) and adding the column value.
2. Calculate the two 6-bit values that correspond to the least significant 6 bits and the next 6 bits. Call these values *low* and *high*.
3. Look up the corresponding values indexed by each of these two 6-bit values in the SBA lookup table (Fig. 8.2).
4. Return these values as the 2-byte pair high-low.

The diagram in Fig. 8.3 illustrates the process of determining the 3270 SBA codes for a position on the screen.

Bit value	ASCII byte value	ASCII character value	Bit value	ASCII byte value	ASCII character value
00 0000	0x20	space	10 0000	0x2D	'-'
00 0001	0x41	'A'	10 0001	0x2F	'/'
00 0010	0x42	'B'	10 0010	0x53	'S'
00 0011	0x43	'C'	10 0011	0x54	'T'
00 0100	0x44	'D'	10 0100	0x55	'U'
00 0101	0x45	'E'	10 0101	0x56	'V'
00 0110	0x46	'F'	10 0110	0x57	'W'
00 0111	0x47	'G'	10 0111	0x58	'X'
00 1000	0x48	'H'	10 1000	0x59	'Y'
00 1001	0x49	'I'	10 1001	0x5A	'Z'
00 1010	0x5B	'['	10 1010	0x7C	'|'
00 1011	0x2E	'.'	10 1011	0x2C	','
00 1100	0x3C	'<'	10 1100	0x25	'%'
00 1101	0x28	'('	10 1101	0x5F	'_'
00 1110	0x2B	'+'	10 1110	0x3E	'>'
00 1111	0x21	'!'	10 1111	0x3F	'?'
01 0000	0x26	'&'	11 0000	0x30	'0'
01 0001	0x4A	'J'	11 0001	0x31	'1'
01 0010	0x4B	'K'	11 0010	0x32	'2'
01 0011	0x4C	'L'	11 0011	0x33	'3'
01 0100	0x4D	'M'	11 0100	0x34	'4'
01 0101	0x4E	'N'	11 0101	0x35	'5'
01 0110	0x4F	'O'	11 0110	0x36	'6'
01 0111	0x50	'P'	11 0111	0x37	'7'
01 1000	0x51	'Q'	11 1000	0x38	'8'
01 1001	0x52	'R'	11 1001	0x39	'9'
01 1010	0x5D	']'	11 1010	0x3A	':'
01 1011	0x24	'$'	11 1011	0x23	'#'
01 1100	0x2A	'*'	11 1100	0x40	'@'
01 1101	0x29	')'	11 1101	0x27	'''
01 1110	0x3B	';'	11 1110	0x3D	'='
01 1111	0x5E	'^'	11 1111	0x22	'"'

Figure 8.2   SBA lookup table.

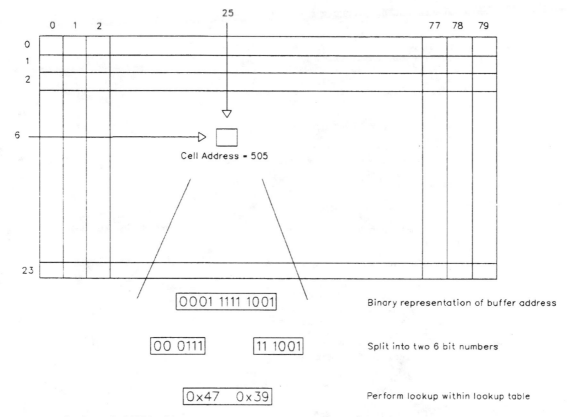

Figure 8.3   Lookup of an SBA address.

Sample use of the SBA addressing

The sample program shown below is an example of a CICS terminal control program that uses the 3270 SBA order to display a character at a random position on the screen. The program draws random bar charts.

Note: The program is illustrative only. Sending 3270 data a few bytes at a time is *very* inefficient. The program also contains an algorithm implementation for the SBA address calculation. The function containing this is called **CalculateSBA().**

```
#include <stdio.h>
#define CICS_3270_SBA 0x11

/*
 * Function: CalculateSBA
 * Given the row and column information, calculate the ASCII 3270 buffer
 * address used to reference the screen position. Row ranges from 0-24 and
 * column ranges from 0-79 are valid.
 */
void CalculateSBA(int row, int column, unsigned short *sba)
{
```

```
            static int sbaLookup[64] = {
            0x20, 0x41, 0x42, 0x43, 0x44, 0x45, 0x46, 0x47,
            0x48, 0x49, 0x5b, 0x2e, 0x3c, 0x28, 0x2b, 0x21,
            0x26, 0x4a, 0x4b, 0x4c, 0x4d, 0x4e, 0x4f, 0x50,
            0x51, 0x52, 0x5d, 0x24, 0x2a, 0x29, 0x3b, 0x5e,
            0x2d, 0x2f, 0x53, 0x54, 0x55, 0x56, 0x57, 0x58,
            0x59, 0x5a, 0x7c, 0x2c, 0x25, 0x5f, 0x3e, 0x3f,
            0x30, 0x31, 0x32, 0x33, 0x34, 0x35, 0x36, 0x37,
            0x38, 0x39, 0x3a, 0x23, 0x40, 0x27, 0x3d, 0x22 };

            unsigned int bufferAddress;

            bufferAddress = row * 80 + column;
            *sba = sbaLookup[(0x3f & (bufferAddress>>6))]<<8 |
                   sbaLookup[(0x3f & bufferAddress)];
            return;
}
/*
 * Function: PlotPoint
 * This function places a '*' character at the specified row and column
 * position.
 *
 *
 * The 3270 data stream sent consists of the following:
 *
 *
 *        1 byte            2 bytes        1 byte
 * +--------------+-------------+-----+
 * | 3270 SBA (0x11) |  SBA address  |  '*'  |
 * +--------------+-------------+-----+
 */
void PlotPoint(int Row, int Column)
{
    unsigned short sba;
    char data[4];

    data[0] = CICS_3270_SBA;
    CalculateSBA(Row, Column, &sba);
    *(unsigned short *)(&data[1]) = sba;
    data[3] = '*';
    EXEC CICS SEND FROM(data) LENGTH(4);
    return;
}
/*
 * Function: DrawBar
 * Draws a bar starting at column x with height specified.
 */
void DrawBar(int x, int height)
{
    int Row,Column,i;

    Row = 22;
    Column = 5 + x * 2;

    for (i = 0; i<height; i++)
    {
        PlotPoint(Row, Column);
        Row-;
    }
    return;
}
/*
 * Function: main
 * Draws random bar charts on the display
 */
```

```
main()
{
    int x,height;
    for (x = 0; x<10; x++)
    {
        height = rand()%20;
        DrawBar(x,height);

    }
    EXEC CICS RETURN;
}
```

Creating 3270 fields

A field may be created on a 3270 display. A *field* is an area of the display that has specific attributes. The 3270 data stream order code for a Start Field (SF) is 0x1D followed by the field attribute byte. A field attribute specifies the attributes of the field, including

- Is input allowed in the field (protected versus unprotected)?
- Is the field numeric only (alphanumeric versus numeric)?
- Is the field defined as autoskip (protected and numeric)?
- Is the field intensified or nondisplay?
- Is the modified data tag set on or off?

The field attribute is a single-byte value with bit fields with the following meanings:

Bits 0-1	2	3	4, 5	6	7
Graphic Convertor	U/P	A/N	D/SPD	unused (0)	MDT

Bits	Meaning
0,1	Ignored bits but used to make character in the printable range
2	0 Field is unprotected and allows user input
	1 Field is protected and prevents user input
3	0 Field allows alphanumeric input
	1 Field allows numeric input only
4,5	00 Light pen (not used with CICS/6000)
	01 Light pen (not used with CICS/6000)
	10 Intensified field
	11 Nondisplay, field is dark
6	Not used, must be set to 0
7	Modified data tag bit
	0 Field has not been modified
	1 Field has been modified by user or by program

When the appropriate bit mask for the attribute field has been determined, it should be converted to the code shown in Fig. 8.2 by taking the lowest 6 bits and performing a lookup in the table.

Once converted, if the Start Field (SF) order byte followed by the field attribute is sent to the 3270 terminal, a new field will be created at the current buffer location. The SBA order may be used prior to sending the SF order to position the buffer location pointer to a new position on the screen.

When a field is created on the terminal, the attributes of the field will remain in effect until another field is created. When a field is created, the position that starts the field is displayed as a blank character. For example, to create a field that is a protected label, followed by an input area of 10 bytes, the 3270 data sent may be as

```
0x11 0x3C 0x2D 0x1D 0x2D "Enter data" 0x1D 0x20 0x11 0x3C 0x36 0x1D 0x2D
```

This 3270 data stream consists of an SBA order to position the next buffer location, an SF order to create a protected field, some text that is displayed, a second SF order to create an unprotected field, a second SBA order to position the buffer location, and a last SF order to create a protected field to bracket the input field.

CICS Basic Mapping Support

The preceding subsection described the principles behind 3270 data stream programming. 3270 programming can be complex and requires a tight correlation between the application and the way the end user perceives the application. Modification and readability of 3270 data stream are difficult. The next section describes the principals of Basic Mapping Support (BMS) and how it may be used to provide a much higher level interface onto 3270 data stream programming, effectively hiding most of the details of the output control data and allowing the application programmer to concentrate on the presentation interface as opposed to the details of how it will be achieved.

Basic Mapping Support (BMS)

Basic Mapping Support (BMS) is the name given to the functionality of CICS to display information to the user and obtain a response. Historically, CICS has employed 3270 data stream terminals for interacting with the user. These terminals understand 3270 data stream and interpret the contents for display. The CICS/6000-supplied cicsterm and cicsteld client programs provide 3270 emulation capabilities.

The BMS screens are called *panels* or *maps* and may be displayed on the CICS/6000 clients. The definitions of these maps are specified in a language called *BMS macro*. These statements look like mainframe macro language and are portable across the CICS family of products. A single BMS source file contains three types of entries:

1. Mapset definition
2. Map definitions

3. Field definitions

Each BMS source file contains one or more maps, each map usually corresponding to a complete screen destined for the end user. The collection of maps in a source file is called a *mapset*. When displaying a map to the user, both the map and the mapset containing the map must be specified. Each BMS map consists of field definitions specifying the layout of a particular field in the map. Mapsets, maps, and fields are all named items. A map may be presented to the user by instructing CICS to display the map by name. Within the map, individual fields may have their contents changed or read from by specifying their symbolic names. The actual location of the field on the screen need not be known to the program.

Translating BMS source maps

The source of a BMS mapset must be translated for use with CICS/6000. The translation takes as input the source file containing the BMS macro definitions and produces as output two new files known as the *symbolic* and *physical map files*.

The physical map contains the 3270 data for each of the maps in the mapset. Its internal format is hidden from the programmer. The physical mapset is defined to the CICS/6000 region in the program definitions with a **ProgType** attribute of **map.** When a CICS application issues an EXEC CICS SEND MAP command, the contents of the physical map is used to build the 3270 data stream to be sent to the display.

The symbolic map is a C or COBOL data structure definition used to allow the program to modify or retrieve data either sent or received from the terminal. For output, any changes to the data structure within the program are combined with the 3270 data in the physical map and the combined output displayed on the terminal. If an application modified any of the fields in the data structure, these changes are reflected in the final output. If the EXEC CICS RECEIVE MAP command is issued, the 3270 data stream received from the terminal results in the data structures being modified to reflect changes from the display.

CICS/6000 supplies a utility called **cicsmap** that takes as input a BMS source file and produces the symbolic and physical mapset files. The symbolic mapset produced will either be a C include file or a COBOL language copybook depending on the setting of the **LANG** attribute in the BMS macro definitions.

The BMS Macro Language

Originally developed for assembly by a mainframe assembler, the BMS macro language is a relatively low-level interface for describing the layout of information on a display. With the availability of high-level interfaces such as the cicssda described in "CICS Screen Design Aid" on page 160, little coding of direct BMS macro language is required. An appreciation of the format of the language and its capabilities can still be highly useful to CICS programmers. An understanding of the types of BMS macro commands available also assists in determining the degree of difficulty in porting or migrating a CICS application from another CICS environment to CICS/6000.

Overview of BMS macro language

The BMS macro language consists of three basic "commands":

DFHMSD   Define a BMS mapset. This command appears at the beginning and end BMS macro source. At the beginning, it names the mapset being defined. At the end, it marks the end of mapset definition.

DFHMDI   Define a BMS map. This command starts a BMS map definition. It follows a DFHMSD statement and describes the nature of the map. Following statements describe the details of the map until a subsequent DFHMDI statement, which terminates the previous map and begins a new map.

DFHMDF   Define a map field. This command describes a specific field within a map. The field applies to the map specified in the previous DFHM-DI statement in the macro source.

The format of a BMS macro source program is very important. The DFHMSD, DFHMDI, and DFHMDF commands are expected to start in specific columns of the file, as are the other constructs. There are three defined column positions.

- *Label column*   Labels or names of specific mapsets, maps, or fields must start in column 1. The length of a label may be 1 to 7 characters for mapsets and maps and 1 to 31 characters for fields. For portability, labels should be entered as uppercase names only.

```
MAPSET DFHMSD
MAP1   DFHMDI ....
       DFHMDF ....
LABEL1 DFHMDF ....
       DFHMDF
LABEL2 DFHMDF ....
              ....
MAP2   DFHMDI ....
LABEL3 DFHMDF ....
              ....
MAP3   DFHMDI ....
       DFHMDF ....
MAPSET DFHMSD TYPE=FINAL
```

Figure 8.4 BMS macro layout.

- *Command column* The command column starts after the label (if one is present).

- *The continuation column.* If a macro line is longer than 70 characters, a continuation character must be added at column 71, and the line must be continued in column 16 of the following line.

An example of a BMS macro layout is illustrated in Fig. 8.4.

BMS macro statement syntax

The BMS macro syntax for each of the BMS commands is described below.

DFHMSD

```
mapset DFHMSD
TYPE = {DSECT|MAP},
TIOAPFX = YES,
[MODE = {IN  |  OUT  |  INOUT},]
[LANG = {C  |  COBOL },]
[FOLD = {LOWER  |  UPPER},]
[STORAGE = AUTO  |  BASE = NAME],
[CTRL = ([PRINT],  [length],  [FREEKB],  [ALARM],  [FRSET])]
[EXTATT = {NO  |  MAPONLY  |  YES},]
[COLOR = {DEFAULT  |  color},]
[HILIGHT = {OFF  |  BLINK  |  REVERSE  |  UNDERLINE},]
[PS = {BASE  |  psid},]
[VALIDN = ( [MUSTFILL], [MUSTENTER], [TRIGGER] )]
[TERM = type,  |  SUFFIX = n,]
[MAPATTS = (attr1, attr2, ...),]
[DSATTS = (attr1, attr2, ...),]
[OUTLINE = {BOX  |  ( [LEFT], [RIGHT], [OVER], [UNDER] ) }]
[SOSI = {NO  |  YES},]
[TRANSP = {YES  |  NO },]
[DATA = {FIELD  |  BLOCK}]
```

TIOAPFX Specifies fillers be used in symbolic maps. This is required for CICS/6000 but should cause no portability problems. If omitted, a warning is produced and the map processed as if this attribute were present.

MODE Specifies whether the mapset should is to be used for input, output, or both input and output. If not specified, the default is output only. When using cicssda to create BMS maps, this is also the default.

LANG Specifies whether the symbolic mapset generated should be either a COBOL copybook or a C include file.

FOLD For **LANG** = **C** mapsets only, specifies whether labels are to be translated into lowercase or uppercase. Lowercase conversion is the default.

STORAGE Controls how the storage for the maps are allocated. If **STORAGE** = **AUTO,** storage is allocated for the maps. If **STORAGE** = **BASE,** the memory for the maps must be allocated elsewhere.

CTRL Specifies control options (see EXEC CICS SEND CONTROL) that are sent whenever a map in the mapset is displayed. If an individual map in the mapset has its own **CTRL** = ... options, these are processed in place of the options specified here.

EXTATT Supported for compatibility only. This option is now replaced with the MAPATTS and DSATTS options.

COLOR Specifies the default color for the mapset. This option will not be used if either a map or field in a map also has a COLOR option.

HILIGHT Specifies the default highlighting of the maps and fields unless the maps or fields have their own HILIGHT option.

PS Specifies a programmable symbol set to use. This option is ignored in CICS/6000.

VALIDN Specifies the type of validation of a map or field. This option is ignored in CICS/6000.

TERM Specifies the type of terminal for which the mapset has been written. This option is intended primarily for use with mapset suffixing.

MAPATTS The types of 3270 data stream attributes supported for the physical map.

DSATTS The types of 3270 data stream attributes supported for the logical map.

OUTLINE This attribute allows fields to have outlined characteristics. This is currently not supported on CICS/6000.

SOSI Specifies whether multibyte character data may be entered in the map.

TRANSP Ignored for CICS/6000.

DATA Specifies that the data is to be either block or field utilized.

DFHMDI

```
map DFHMDI
[,SIZE = (line,column)]
[,CTRL = ([PRINT][,length][,FREEKB][,ALARM][,FRSET])]
[,EXTATT = {NO | MAPONLY | YES}]
[,COLOR = {DEFAULT | color}]
[,HILIGHT = {OFF | BLINK | REVERSE | UNDERLINE)]
[,PS = {BASE | psid}] [,VALIDN = ([MUSTFILL][,MUSTENTER][,TRIGGER])]
[,COLUMN = number]
[,LINE = number]
[,FIELD = NO]
[,MAPATTS = (attr1, attr2, ...)]
[,DSATTS = (attr1, attr2, ...)]
[,OUTLINE = {BOX | ([LEFT][,RIGHT][,OVER][,UNDER])}]
[,SOSI = {NO | YES}]
[,TRANSP = {YES | NO}]
[,JUSTIFY = BOTTOM]
[,DATA = {FIELD | BLOCK}]
```

SIZE   Specifies the size of the map.

CTRL   Specifies control options (see EXEC CICS SEND CONTROL) that are sent whenever a map in the mapset is displayed. This attribute overrides attributes specified in a CTRL option in a DFHMSD definition statement.

EXTATT   Supported for compatibility only. This option is now replaced with the MAPATTS and DSATTS options.

COLOR   Specifies the default color for the map. This option will not be used if a field in a map also has a COLOR option.

HILIGHT   Specifies the default highlighting fields unless the fields have their own HILIGHT option.

PS   Specifies a programmable symbol set to use. This option is ignored in CICS/6000.

VALIDN   Specifies the type of validation of a map or field. This option is ignored in CICS/6000.

COLUMN   Specifies the column on the display at which the map is to start.

LINE   Specifies the line on the display at which the map is to start.

FIELD   This option is ignored on CICS/6000.

MAPATTS   The types of 3270 data stream attributes supported for the physical map.

DSATTS   The types of 3270 data stream attributes supported for the logical map.

OUTLINE   This attribute allows fields to have outlined characteristics. This is currently not supported on CICS/6000.

SOSI   Specifies whether multibyte character data may be entered.

TRANSP   Ignored for CICS/6000.

JUSTIFY   Specifies that the map is to be located at the bottom of the screen.

DATA   Specifies that the data are to be either block or field utilized.

DFHMDF

```
[field] DFHMDF
[,POS = {number | (line,column)}]
[,ATTRB = ([[{ASKIP | PROT | UNPROT,[NUM]}]
[,(BRT | NORM | DRK)]
[,DET][,IC],[,FSET])]
[,COLOR = {DEFAULT | color}]
[,JUSTIFY = ([[{LEFT | RIGHT}][,{BLANK | ZERO}]])]
[{,INITIAL = `data' | XINIT = hex data | GINIT = `graphic'}]
[,HILIGHT = {OFF | BLINK | REVERSE | UNDERLINE}]
```

```
[,PS = {BASE | psid}]  [,VALIDN = ([MUSTFILL][,MUSTENTER][,TRIGGER])]
[,LENGTH = number]
[,GRPNAME = group-name  |  ,OCCURS = number]
[,PICIN = `value']
[,PICOUT = `value']
[,OUTLINE = {BOX  |  ([LEFT][,RIGHT][,OVER][,UNDER])}]
[,SOSI = {NO | YES}]
[,TRANSP = {YES | NO}]
[,CASE = MIXED]
```

POS   Specifies the location of the field within the map. This may be coded as the number of characters relative to 0 from the start of the map or a row and column position relative to 1.

ATTRB   Specifies field characteristics and attributes.

COLOR   Specifies the color for the field.

JUSTIFY   Specifies whether the field is to be left or right justified when data are entered and whether any remaining space is to be blank filled or zero character filled.

INITIAL   Specifies initial data for the field.

LENGTH   Specifies the length of the field.

HILIGHT   Specifies the highlighting to be used for the field.

PS   Specifies a programmable symbol set to use. This option is ignored in CICS/6000.

VALIDN   Specifies the type of validation of a map or field. This option is ignored in CICS/6000.

GRPNAME   Group name of related BMS fields.

PICIN   Specifies a COBOL language picture for formatting data received as input in the symbolic map.

PICOUT   Specifies a COBOL language picture for formatting data sent as output in the symbolic map.

OUTLINE   This attribute allows fields to have outlined characteristics. This is currently not supported on CICS/6000.

SOSI   Specifies whether multibyte character data may be entered in the field.

TRANSP   Ignored for CICS/6000.

CASE   Used for multibyte character set transformation.

CICS/6000 screen design aid

A powerful utility called **cicssda** is supplied with CICS/6000. This utility allows programmers to create and modify BMS maps for use with CICS using a graphic interface. Through cicssda, a programmer or an end user can design and develop BMS maps without having to know the BMS macro language. The inputs and outputs from the cicssda are regular BMS macro source files. This allows BMS maps that had been developed previously on other CICS family members to be modified using cicssda. Conversely, maps created with CICS/6000 can be used on other CICS platforms.

Through cicssda, all the attributes and parameters that are available through hand-coded BMS macro programs are also available. Cicssda must be invoked within an X-Windows environment. When started, the window shown in Fig. 8.5 will be displayed.

New fields may be entered into the maps by positioning the cursor with the mouse and entering the text or size of the field. The attributes of the fields may be changed. Such attributes include naming, color, unprotected, and others. The field dialog window is illustrated in Fig. 8.6 (see page 162).

The BMS mapset source generated from the panels shown is included below:

```
**********************************************************************
*  cicssda  MAP1  -- Fri Jun 23 16:06:17 CDT 1996
**********************************************************************
MAP1     DFHMSD TYPE=&SYSPARM,MODE=OUT,LANG=COBOL,STORAGE=AUTO,          X
                TIOAPFX=YES
MAP1     DFHMDI SIZE=(24,80),LINE=1,COLUMN=1
         DFHMDF POS=(3,3),LENGTH=20,ATTRB=(PROT,NORM),CASE=MIXED,INITIALX
                ='Enter Customer Name:'
NAME     DFHMDF POS=(3,25),LENGTH=20,ATTRB=(UNPROT,NORM,IC),CASE=MIXED
         DFHMDF POS=(22,2),LENGTH=8,ATTRB=(PROT,NORM),CASE=MIXED,INITIALX
                ='PF3=Exit'
MAP1     DFHMSD TYPE=FINAL
```

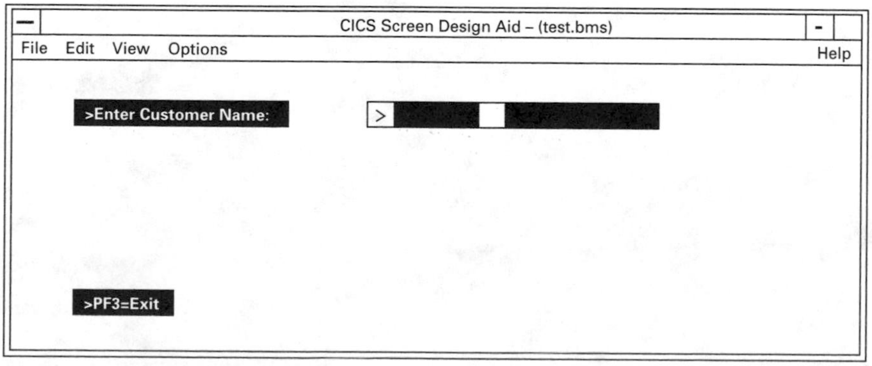

Figure 8.5 Cicssda main panel.

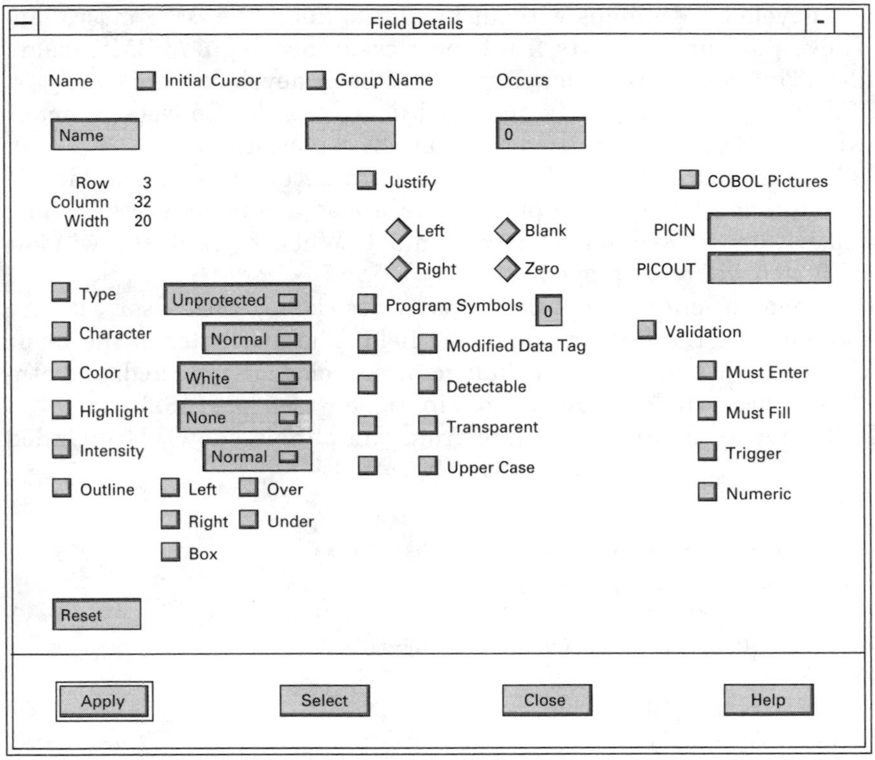

Figure 8.6 Cicssda field definitions.

Passing Options
to CICS Transactions

When a CICS/6000 transaction is started from a blank terminal, any parameters passed to the newly started transaction may be retrieved by using the EXEC CICS RECEIVE command. The data returned contain the initial transaction name followed by the parameters. These parameters may be parsed by the application to obtain initial start-up options or other application specific options. The parsing of these data may be performed by application-specific code or assisted by AIX-supplied parsing functions and tools. For C language programs executed under native AIX, parameters are supplied to the main() function of the program in the first two parameters normally known as argc and argv. In CICS, argc is set to the value 1, meaning one parameter has been supplied. The argv array has only one parameter, the name of the transaction that caused the program to start.

For advanced AIX and C programmers, AIX supplies a tool called *lex* that allows data to be parsed into tokens for easier interpretation. For example, if a transaction is defined that expects to receive parameters of the form

```
NAME = "VALUE"  NAME = "VALUE"  NAME = "VALUE"  ...
```

where NAME may be "STREET" or "SURNAME," lex will be able to determine that the character string "STREET" matches a keyword and that the next VALUE passed should be associated with streets. Lex is a complex tool but very powerful when used by itself or with a companion program called yacc which parses complete structures.

The following illustrates a sample parsing program utilizing lex. The transaction, called *LEXT,* expects parameters such as STREET and SURNAME with supplied values. The program parses these data and prints what it has found.

```
%{

/* Source file cicslex.l */

#undef input
#undef unput

char *data;

enum {none, street, surname} state = none;

char streetValue[50];
char surnameValue[50];
char *errorValue;
%}
%%

SURNAME {
    if (state ! = none)
    {
        errorValue = yytext;
        return(1);
    }
    state = surname;
}
STREET {
    if (state ! = none)
    {
        errorValue = yytext;
        return(1);
    }
    state = street;
}
"\""[A-Za-z0-9]+"\"" {
    switch(state)
    {
        case street:
            strcpy(streetValue, yytext);
            break;
        case surname:
            strcpy(surnameValue, yytext);
            break;
        default:
            printf("Error\n");
            errorValue = yytext;
            return(1);
    }
    state = none;
}

" = " ;

[A-Za-z0-9]* {
    errorValue = yytext;
    return(1);
}
[ \t\n] ;
%%
int yywrap()
{
    return(1);
}
```

```
char input()
{
    char character;

    character = *data;
    data++;
    return(character);
}
void unput(char character)
{
    data-;
    *data = character;
    return;
}

main()
{
    int    rc;
    short  length;
    char   response[100];
    char   inputData[200];
    /*
    * Get data from the terminal
    */
    length = sizeof(inputData);
    EXEC CICS RECEIVE INTO(inputData) LENGTH(&length);
    inputData[length] = '\0';
    data = inputData;

    /*
    * Skip the transaction name
    */
    data+ = 4;
    rc = yylex();
    if (rc != 0)
    {
        sprintf(response, "Error found at: %s", errorValue);
    }
    else
    {
        sprintf(response, "Street found is: %s, Surname found is: %s",
            streetValue, surnameValue);
    }
    EXEC CICS SEND FROM(response) LENGTH(strlen(response)) ERASE;
    EXEC CICS RETURN;
}
```

A suitable AIX `Makefile` for building this program is shown below:

```
CC = cc_r

cicslex: lexyy.ccs
    cicstran -lC -d -e lexyy
    $(CC) -o cicslex lexyy.c \
        -I/usr/lpp/cics/include \
        -L/usr/lpp/cics/lib \
        -lcics_api

lexyy.ccs: cicslex.l
    lex cicslex.l
    mv lex.yy.c lexyy.ccs
```

```
install:
    -cicsadd -c td -r $(CICSREGION) LEXT ProgName = "CICSLEX"
    -cicsadd -c pd -r $(CICSREGION) CICSLEX PathName = $(PWD)/cicslex

runtime:
    cicsupdate -c td -r $(CICSREGION) -R LEXT
    cicsupdate -c pd -r $(CICSREGION) -R CICSLEX
```

Debugging Applications

If an application fails to execute, CICS/6000 provides a number of mechanisms to enable problem determination. Each of these will be covered in turn and the merits of each described. The following list shows some of the available diagnostic tools:

- CEDF: Execution Diagnostic Facility
- COBOL Animator
- CICS/6000 Trace
  - User Trace Points
  - EXEC Interface Trace
  - System Trace
  - Inserting diagnostic information

CEDF: Execution Diagnostic Facility

CICS/6000 provides the CEDF transaction found on other CICS platforms. CEDF allows transaction programs to be stepped through and stopped before and after each CICS command is executed. Using CEDF, the logic flow through an application may be examined and the parameters and response codes from each CICS command modified. CEDF does not show the native C or COBOL code between each CICS command; only the CICS commands themselves may be viewed. To use CEDF, the programs that are to be examined must be translated with the -e option and optionally the -d option of the CICS translator cicstran. These options enable CEDF debugging and source line number inclusion in CEDF output. During application development, it is good practice to compile with these flags enabled. There is virtually no performance degradation when executing programs translated using these flags.

To use CEDF, the user must have access to two CICS terminals; either cicsterm or cicsteld sessions will do. Once these sessions have started, the terminal on which the user wishes to execute the transaction to be diagnosed should be chosen. On the other terminal, CEDF should be invoked, passing the TERMID name of the terminal on which the transaction will execute. When a transaction is next executed on that terminal that has been compiled for CEDF debugging, CEDF output will be presented on the terminal at which CEDF was started. CEDF on CICS/6000 does not support a single-screen session; two terminals are required to use CEDF. On a system that supports X-Windows, this can be achieved by starting two instances of an aix-term terminal window and attaching to CICS/6000 using cicsterm from both.

The CEDF transaction requires security access to all the CICS resources that the transaction under examination may access. If CEDF is not given access, it may fail with a security check. For a development environment, it is good practice to disable security checking of CICS resources by changing the CEDF transaction attribute governing RSL checking. Changing the Transaction Definition (TD) resource attribute to **RSLCheck = none** for CEDF will accomplish this.

COBOL Animator

The Micro Focus COBOL product provides a powerful menu-driven debugging tool called the *Animator*. With the Animator, COBOL programs can be viewed as COBOL source as the program executes. Variables may be viewed as they change, break points inserted, and many other control functions executed. CICS/6000 provides a mechanism to invoke the Animator for COBOL programs.

When a COBOL program is to be animated by CICS/6000, a terminal or AIX window must be available for the Animator output to be displayed. The diagram in Fig. 10.1 illustrates the relationship between CICS/6000, the Animator, and the COBOL runtime.

It is not necessary to have two physical terminals to utilize the Animator. If X-Windows is available, two windows may be opened, one for interacting with CICS through 3270 terminal emulation and the other for interacting with Animator control. If X-Windows is not available, a PC with Windows or OS/2 and TCP/IP connectivity to a machine with CICS/6000 client services will suffice. In this case, two telnet sessions must be started with the AIX operating system.

The terminal (window or telnet session) must be prepared for Animator output before use. The Animator expects complete control of the terminal, which includes both input from the keyboard and output to the display. Normally, an unused terminal leaves the user with an AIX shell prompt and awaits input. This must be prevented to allow the Animator to receive all the keystrokes from the keyboard. If this is not achieved, both the shell and the Animator will receive keystrokes in an unspecified manner.

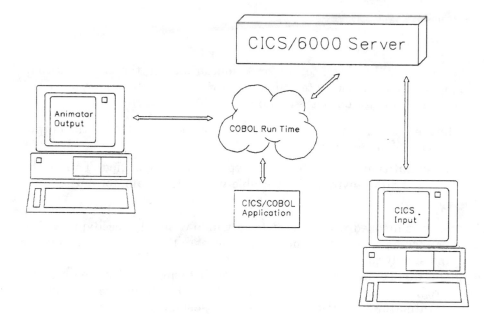

cicsterm −A < terminal name >

Figure 10.1   CICS/6000 and the Animator.

The AIX command **sleep** suspends a process for a specified number of seconds. This is ideal for suspending input to the AIX shell. The **sleep** command may be interrupted at any time with an AIX interrupt signal (normally CTRL + C).

To allow the Animator access to the terminal, it usually will be required to change the access permissions for the terminal. To do this, the name of the terminal must be determined. This name also must be specified to CICS so that the Animator output may be sent to the correct terminal. To determine the name of a particular terminal, execute the AIX command **tty** on that terminal. The name returned will be an AIX file name corresponding to the terminal. The name may be of the form /dev/ttyXX for ASCII attached terminals or /dev/pts/XX for X-Windows and telnet sessions.

To change the permissions on the terminal, execute the following command:

```
chmod 777 <terminal name>
```

The shell script shown in below should be used to set the terminal permissions, display the terminal name, and suspend input from the terminal. This script should be executed on the terminal where Animator output is desired.

```
#!/bin/ksh
chmod 777 $(tty)
tput clear
```

```
echo "Terminal type is: $TERM"
echo "About to suspend terminal: $(tty)"
sleep 999999
```

When a terminal has been set up for Animator output, the **cicsterm** command may be used to attach a terminal to CICS. Two additional options must be specified if Animator output is required:

-A <terminal>   The terminal name must be specified. This is the output from the **tty** command.

-T <terminal type>   The terminal type must be specified. This is the value of the TERM environment variable within the animator output window.

If cicsterm is invoked within an aixterm window, simply specifying -A- to cicsterm will create a new aixterm window, prepare the window for Animator output, and supply the necessary information.

Once the **cicsterm** command has caused a terminal attachment, any COBOL program started at the 3270 terminal that has been compiled for use with the Animator will cause an Animator session to be started at the Animator terminal.

Preparing a program for animation

Before a program can be executed under the Animator, it must be compiled specially for the Animator. This may be achieved by specifying the -a flag to the **cob** compiler command or more simply by specifying the -a flag at the **cicstcl** command. This process is illustrated in Fig. 10.2.

The three output files from the compilation process must be located in the directory referenced by the **PathName** attribute in the Program Definition for the program in CICS. If the COBOL program included copybooks, these copybooks also must reside in the same directory.

COBOL Animator restrictions

- The terminal on which Animator output is to be displayed must be local to the CICS/6000 server. Remote terminals are only available through telnet and rlogin.

- The telnet tn3270 interface to CICS/6000 does not support the Animator; cicsterm must be used instead.

CICS/6000 trace

CICS/6000 provides a powerful trace capability to allow various internal trace-related items to be produced. CICS/6000 trace captures information that shows the flow of control, data values, and user-specifiable information. Trace can be used to perform both CICS system and user application problem

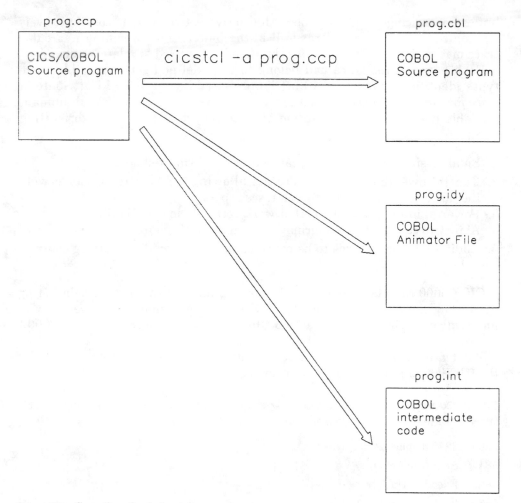

Figure 10.2 Compiling for Animator.

determination. The trace entries also have time stamps and can be used to identify bottlenecks or other performance-related timing items.

CICS/6000 trace utilizes the services provided by the AIX operating system's trace capabilities. To understand CICS/6000 trace, it is helpful to understand AIX trace.

AIX trace. AIX trace executes by collecting trace information in a memory buffer of trace entries. Each trace entry consists of an identifier called a **hookid,** a time stamp, and some additional information. These trace entries are a small number of bytes in length. One of the primary objectives of trace is that it should have as low an overhead as possible. As trace entries accumulate in the trace buffer, they may be written to disk or left in the buffer. Depending on how the AIX trace buffer was configured, the trace may fill the buffer and tracing then be stopped. Alternatively, tracing may continue, over-writing the oldest trace records still in the buffer, thus providing a circular trace mechanism. The trace buffer can then be captured at a later time.

Each entry in the trace will belong to a predefined set of possible trace types identified by the **hookid** attribute. Based on the **hookid** attribute, a *trace formatter* tool may be used to format the trace into meaningful, human-readable messages. The separation of trace collection from trace formatting allows

1. Smaller-sized trace entries because they are formatted off-line.
2. Control over the output generated, allowing a formatter to selectively include or exclude entries from a trace report.
3. Powerful interrogation tools that work better on low-level data.
4. Ability to capture trace information from multiple sources.
5. Additional trace entries to be collected and additional formatting controls to be defined.

CICS/6000 collects trace entries by writing them to the AIX trace buffer or by writing the entries directly into AIX files. The format of a trace entry is identical in each case. Figure 10.3 illustrates the collection of CICS/6000 trace and other trace entries.

The trace entries written may be formatted by the AIX **trcrpt** utility or by the CICS/6000-provided **cicstfmt** command.

CICS/6000 trace hookids.   CICS/6000 generates trace entries with specific AIX trace hookids. The hookids and their explanations are as follows:

580   3270 display device driver
581   Significant events
582   Exec Interface trace entry
583   Exec Interface trace exit
584   Application trace entries
585   CICS internal function entry
586   CICS internal function exit
587   Trace of CICS messages
588   CICS Internal trace errors

CICS/6000 trace control.   The collection of trace information is an overhead on CICS transaction execution time and resources. It is unlikely that trace will be collected continuously. Trace should only be collected when a problem has been encountered or when performance information or bottleneck detection is required.

CICS/6000 provides control over the collection of traces by a series of switches or flags known as *trace control*. The trace control flags determine

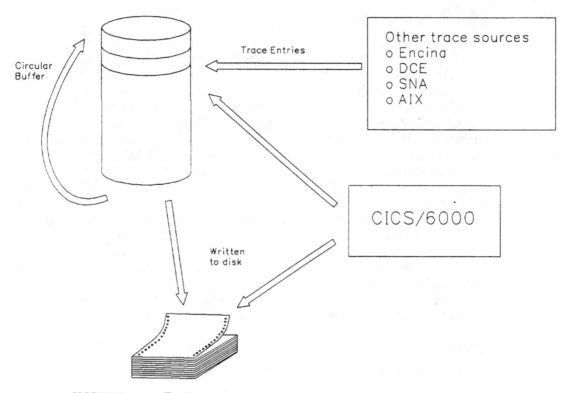

Figure 10.3   CICS/6000 trace collection.

whether trace will be produced and what kind of trace types will be accumulated. Other CICS resource definitions control the amount and destination of CICS trace.

The CICS/6000 trace flags are controlled by the EXEC CICS TRACE command. This command allows the different trace flags to be turned on or off independently. Whenever one of the CICS trace flags is turned ON or OFF, its new state is written into the CICS console log file.

MASTER trace flag.   Since the collection of CICS traces is somewhat of an overhead, this flag controls whether CICS will collect any trace information. If this flag is OFF, no trace data will be collected at all. If the trace flag is ON, the trace written will be based on the settings of the other trace flags. To set this flag ON, the following command should be issued:

```
EXEC CICS TRACE ON
```

To disable all trace collection, issue the command:

```
EXEC CICS TRACE OFF
```

SYSTEM trace flag. The SYSTEM trace flag controls CICS internal trace output. If this flag is OFF, no CICS internal trace is produced. If the flag is ON, trace of CICS's internal operation is produced. It is unlikely that this trace is meaningful to anyone but CICS developers and product service personnel. This flag also must be ON if EXEC interface trace is to be produced.

EXEC INTERFACE trace flag. The EXEC INTERFACE trace flag specifies whether CICS statement trace is to be produced. If this flag is ON, entry and exit trace from each CICS command is written. For EXEC Interface trace to be produced, the SYSTEM trace flag also must be ON.

USER trace flag. The USER trace flag controls the output of user-based trace. This is trace that is written by a single application into a specific trace output file for the execution of that application. User trace is used in conjunction with the SINGLE trace flag and the EXEC CICS ENTER command.

SINGLE trace flag. The SINGLE trace flag controls the output of the EXEC CICS ENTER command. If this flag is OFF for an application, any EXEC CICS ENTER commands within that program will cause no trace output to be produced. If the flag is ON and the USER and MASTER trace flags are ON, both EXEC Interface and EXEC CICS ENTER trace will be logged to the trace file. The trace files are user-configurable.

Trace flag tables

Master trace	System trace	EXEC Interface trace	Description
OFF	X	X	No trace of any type is produced.
ON	ON	OFF	CICS internal system trace is produced.
ON	ON	ON	CICS EXEC Interface trace is produced.

Any other combination of the preceding trace flags results in no system or EXEC INTERFACE trace being produced.

Master trace	User trace	Single trace	Description
OFF	X	X	No trace of any type is produced.
ON	ON	ON	A new trace file is created and written to by the application containing both EXEC INTERFACE trace and the output of EXEC CICS ENTER commands.

Any other combination of the preceding trace flags results in no user or EXEC Interface trace being produced.

User trace points. User trace is designed to allow collection of trace either inserted into an application by a programmer or to collect EXEC Interface trace for one application without necessarily collecting EXEC Interface trace for a whole CICS region. CICS/6000 provides user trace through the use of the USER and SINGLE trace flags and through the EXEC CICS ENTER command. When user trace is to be produced, the application that wishes to have the trace written must execute an explicit EXEC CICS TRACE SINGLE ON command. If both the MASTER and USER trace flags are ON, trace will be produced. The location of the trace output is controlled by a number of resource definitions.

The AIX directory into which the user trace is to be written is specified by the **UserTraceDirectory** attribute in the Region Definition (RD). By default, this directory is the publicly writable /tmp directory. The directory used must have write permission for either the AIX "cics" userid or the AIX "cics" groupid. The name of the AIX file used to hold the trace is specified in the User Definition (UD) of the CICS user that is executing the program. The **TraceFile** attribute specifies the file name. By default, the name used is blank, in which case the file name used is the one specified in the Region Definition (RD) by the **PublicUserTraceFile** attribute. This defaults to the file cicspubl.

Each trace file written is suffixed with a sequence number to allow separate trace files to be maintained. The first trace file written will have a suffix of 001, followed by 002, and so on. User trace cannot be written to the AIX trace facility; it will always be written directly to AIX files.

To include a user trace entry, the EXEC CICS ENTER command may be used. The program in Fig. 10.4 illustrates the use of user trace. The output of the user trace is shown in the following sample:

```
main()
{
char     fromData[8] = "FFFFFFFF";
char     resourceData[8] = "RRRRRRRR";
char     message[] = "User trace test";

EXEC CICS TRACE ON SINGLE;

EXEC CICS ENTER TRACEID(45) FROM(fromData) RESOURCE(resourceData);
EXEC CICS SEND TEXT FROM(message) LENGTH(strlen(message));
EXEC CICS ENTER TRACEID(45) FROM(fromData) RESOURCE(resourceData);

EXEC CICS RETURN;
}
```

System trace. The CICS system trace writes the internal operation of CICS. This trace was written for IBM personnel to diagnose problems with CICS operation. If a problem occurs within CICS that is felt to be a defect in CICS and cannot be attributed to programming use, system trace may be obtained and examined by someone knowledgeable in CICS internals. Submitting this trace to IBM may significantly aid in the diagnosis and resolution of a system problem. To obtain CICS system trace, the MASTER trace flag must be ON, the SYSTEM trace flag must be ON, and the EXEC INTERFACE trace flag

```
583  CICS Fri Mar 31 11:59:46 1995 GMT 636248576   22217/1                UTRC(55 54 52 43) nkolban  cicsas  EI< Returning from EXEC CICS TRACE
582  CICS Fri Mar 31 11:59:46 1995 GMT 639490816   22217/1                UTRC(55 54 52 43) nkolban  cicsas  EI> Entering EXEC CICS ENTER
                                       Function        = 19
                                       Option Mask     = 20000013
                                       Aggregate Count = 0

584  CICS Fri Mar 31 11:59:46 1995 GMT 642329344   22217/1                UTRC(55 54 52 43 46 46 46 46) nkolban  cicsas  ++ User Trace Id(45)
                                       From          = FFFFFFFF  (46 46 52 52 52 52 52 52)
                                       Resource      = RRRRRRRR  (52 52 52 52)

583  CICS Fri Mar 31 11:59:46 1995 GMT 644933120   22217/1                UTRC(55 54 52 43) nkolban  cicsas  EI< Returning from EXEC CICS ENTER
582  CICS Fri Mar 31 11:59:46 1995 GMT 647756288   22217/1                UTRC(55 54 52 43) nkolban  cicsas  EI> Entering EXEC CICS SEND TEXT
                                       Function        = 109
                                       Option Mask     = 21000014
                                       Aggregate Count = 0

583  CICS Fri Mar 31 11:59:46 1995 GMT 709121536   22217/1                UTRC(55 54 52 43) nkolban  cicsas  EI< Returning from EXEC CICS SEND TEXT
582  CICS Fri Mar 31 11:59:46 1995 GMT 712669696   22217/1                UTRC(55 54 52 43) nkolban  cicsas  EI> Entering EXEC CICS ENTER
                                       Function        = 19
                                       Option Mask     = 20000013
                                       Aggregate Count = 0

584  CICS Fri Mar 31 11:59:46 1995 GMT 715312128   22217/1                UTRC(55 54 52 43 46 46 46 46) nkolban  cicsas  ++ User Trace Id(45)
                                       From          = FFFFFFFF  (46 46 52 52 52 52 52 52)
                                       Resource      = RRRRRRRR  (52 52 52 52)

583  CICS Fri Mar 31 11:59:46 1995 GMT 717921024   22217/1                UTRC(55 54 52 43) nkolban  cicsas  EI< Returning from EXEC CICS ENTER
582  CICS Fri Mar 31 11:59:46 1995 GMT 720966144   22217/1                UTRC(55 54 52 43) nkolban  cicsas  EI> Entering EXEC CICS RETURN
                                       Function        = 72
                                       Option Mask     = 20000000
                                       Aggregate Count = 0

583  CICS Fri Mar 31 11:59:46 1995 GMT 724270848   22217/1                UTRC(55 54 52 43) nkolban  cicsas  EI< Returning from EXEC CICS RETURN
```

Figure 10.4 User trace.

must be OFF. The settings of the other flags are unimportant. System trace may be obtained by the execution of the following commands:

```
EXEC CICS TRACE SYSTEM ON
EXEC CICS TRACE EI OFF
EXEC CICS TRACE ON
```

A sample of CICS system trace is illustrated in Fig. 10.5.

CICS/6000 EXEC Interface trace.   CICS/6000 EXEC Interface trace provides the collection of the trace entries relating to entry and exit from CICS commands. An example of such a trace is shown in Fig. 10.6.

CICS EXEC Interface trace provides an excellent device for the collection of both diagnostics and performance information. The entries show both entry and exit from commands. In the event of a CICS application ABEND or loop, the trace may be examined to determine the previous CICS commands executed. EXEC Interface trace also may be directed to the AIX trace buffer for continuous collection. This provides the ability to continuously capture trace in an effort to resolve problems that may be caused by adverse interaction or timing problems between multiple programs. For example, if one program writes a record into a transient data queue while another attempts to read the queue, it is possible for the two programs to execute for quite some time before the reading program reads from the queue and before the writing program has written the record. Poor programming or design in the reading program may not account for this possibility, and a CICS program failure may result. Such a failure, by its nature, may not occur on every execution. A CICS EXEC Interface trace will aid in the determination of this problem.

Using the AIX trace facility for CICS trace

This subsection describes the process to capture and format CICS/6000 trace using the AIX trace facility. By using the AIX operating system–supplied trace collection mechanism, CICS can have its trace data collected by the AIX trace program. This trace program is highly optimal in terms of resource consumption, and little degradation of CICS should be noticed. The AIX trace program also allows a circular in-memory buffer to be maintained of the last trace collected. Using this facility, trace may be collected from CICS/6000 in memory without it being written into a file. When a significant event (such as an error) occurs, the trace may be stopped and the buffer then written to a file.

The output from the AIX trace program is highly compressed and must be formatted before being viewed by an end user. AIX supplies a trace formatting program called **trcrpt** that takes the raw AIX-written trace as input and formats it into human-readable output.

```
585  3.379297024  0.210176  CICS  29715/1  UTRC(55 54 52 43) nkolban cicsas  E>  StoRE_RegionAllocate (40,0,16,2FF7BBD8)
585  3.379479808  0.182784  CICS  29715/1  UTRC(55 54 52 43) nkolban cicsas  E>  StoMA_Alloc (a00012e8 68)
581  3.379586816  0.187008  CICS  29715/1  UTRC(55 54 52 43) nkolban cicsas      Common Storage Control Module (StoMA)
     Memory Allocation Request
       Size     = 68
       Handle   = 0xA00012E8
       Result   = SUCCESSFUL
     Memory Allocated = 0xA006BC80
586  3.379668480  0.081664  CICS  29715/1  UTRC(55 54 52 43) nkolban cicsas  E<  StoMA_Alloc return(0xA006BC80)
581  3.379768576  0.100096  CICS  29715/1  UTRC(55 54 52 43) nkolban cicsas      Region Related Storage Control Module (StoRE)
     Region Related Storage Control Request
       Result   = Allocated
       Pool     = Region
       Size     = 68
       Address  = 0xA006BC98
       Pool State = OK
586  3.379846400  0.077824  CICS  29715/1  UTRC(55 54 52 43) nkolban cicsas  I<  StoRE_RegionAllocate return(1, RSN_3)
586  3.379927296  0.080896  CICS  29715/1  UTRC(55 54 52 43) nkolban cicsas  I<  TasLU_Register return(1, RSN_3)
586  3.380005376  0.078080  CICS  29715/1  UTRC(55 54 52 43) nkolban cicsas  I<  TerBM_FlushTIOA return(0, RSN_28)
585  3.380409856  0.404480  CICS  29715/1  UTRC(55 54 52 43) nkolban cicsas  I>  TerBM_OptionsToControl (...)
586  3.380507648  0.097792  CICS  29715/1  UTRC(55 54 52 43) nkolban cicsas  I<  TerBM_OptionsToControl return(void)
585  3.380753664  0.246016  CICS  29715/1  UTRC(55 54 52 43) nkolban cicsas  I>  TerBM_SendText (....)
585  3.380945408  0.191744  CICS  29715/1  UTRC(55 54 52 43) nkolban cicsas  I>  TerBM_InsertCursor (0xa006b398)
586  3.381041152  0.095744  CICS  29715/1  UTRC(55 54 52 43) nkolban cicsas  I<  TerBM_InsertCursor return(0, RSN_1)
586  3.381263616  0.222464  CICS  29715/1  UTRC(55 54 52 43) nkolban cicsas  I<  TerBM_SendText return(0, RSN_12)
586  3.381357568  0.093952  CICS  29715/1  UTRC(55 54 52 43) nkolban cicsas  I<  TerBM_ECSend return(1, RSN_24)
585  3.381535232  0.177664  CICS  29715/1  UTRC(55 54 52 43) nkolban cicsas  E>  PinCA_EIBfnToStr (0x20351223)
586  3.381689856  0.154624  CICS  29715/1  UTRC(55 54 52 43) nkolban cicsas  E<  PinCA_EIBfnToStr return(0xD129B9D0)
581  3.381783296  0.093440  CICS  29715/1  UTRC(55 54 52 43) nkolban cicsas      API Module (PinCA)

EIBRESP(0) returned by EXEC CICS SEND TEXT : EIBFN(0x1806)
```

Figure 10.5 CICS system trace.

ID	ELAPSED_SEC	DELTA_MSEC	APPL	SYSCALL	KERNEL	INTERRUPT			
582	2.175853056	2175.853056	CICS	29715/1		UTRC(55 54 52 43)	nkolban	cicsas	EI> Entering EXEC CICS TRACE
		Function = 100							
		Option Mask = 20000021							
		Aggregate Count = 0							
583	2.281689856	105.836800	CICS	29715/1		UTRC(55 54 52 43)	nkolban	cicsas	EI< Returning from EXEC CICS TRACE
582	2.300106752	18.416896	CICS	29715/1		UTRC(55 54 52 43)	nkolban	cicsas	EI> Entering EXEC CICS ENTER
		Function = 19							
		Option Mask = 20000013							
		Aggregate Count = 0							
583	2.334688768	34.582016	CICS	29715/1		UTRC(55 54 52 43)	nkolban	cicsas	EI< Returning from EXEC CICS ENTER
582	2.349701120	15.012352	CICS	29715/1		UTRC(55 54 52 43)	nkolban	cicsas	EI> Entering EXEC CICS SEND TEXT
		Function = 109							
		Option Mask = 21000014							
		Aggregate Count = 0							
583	2.366515328	18.814208	CICS	29715/1		UTRC(55 54 52 43)	nkolban	cicsas	EI< Returning from EXEC CICS SEND TEXT
582	2.383386624	14.871296	CICS	29715/1		UTRC(55 54 52 43)	nkolban	cicsas	EI> Entering EXEC CICS ENTER
		Function = 19							
		Option Mask = 20000013							
		Aggregate Count = 0							
583	2.412257536	28.870912	CICS	29715/1		UTRC(55 54 52 43)	nkolban	cicsas	EI< Returning from EXEC CICS ENTER
582	2.426329344	14.071808	CICS	29715/1		UTRC(55 54 52 43)	nkolban	cicsas	EI> Entering EXEC CICS RETURN
		Function = 72							
		Option Mask = 20000000							
		Aggregate Count = 0							
583	2.441249536	14.920192	CICS	29715/1		UTRC(55 54 52 43)	nkolban	cicsas	EI< Returning from EXEC CICS RETURN

Figure 10.6 EXEC Interface trace.

Configuring CICS/6000 for trace collection

By default, CICS/6000 will log trace directly to an AIX file. To have the trace directed to the AIX trace program, a CICS resource in the CICS Region Definition (RD) table must be modified to enable external trace. To accomplish this, the following command may be issued to change the **ExternalTrace** attribute:

```
cicsupdate -c rd -r <region> ExternalTrace = yes
```

The next time the CICS region is cold started, any trace generated will be directed to the AIX trace program.

CICS/6000 trace collection

Although CICS may be writing trace, if the AIX trace program is not running, the trace information will not be collected. To start the AIX trace command, the invoker must be logged into AIX as the root user. By default, the **trace** command collects trace from all possible sources; this includes the AIX operating system. This quickly becomes unmanageable, and for CICS usage, trace collection should be restricted to just the CICS trace information. Trace information is written in tagged categories. Each category is known as a *hook identifier* or *hookid*. The AIX trace program allows the specification of the hookids on which it will collect trace.

The following example illustrates use of the **trace** command to start the AIX trace demon for CICS trace collection for just the CICS components:

```
trace -a -l -j "581,582,583,584,585,586,587,588" \
-o cicstrace.raw
```

This command may be saved in an AIX shell script for multiple executions. The flags illustrated tell the AIX trace program to

- Execute in the background.
- Log trace to the in-memory buffer.
- Collect trace only for CICS/6000.
- Write the final trace output to a file called `cicstrace.raw` in the current directory.

Once started, the AIX trace will immediately collect CICS-generated trace in its own memory buffer. The trace is not written to the output file until the trace program is stopped by issuing the **trcstop** command. Once issued, the output file will contain the trace most recently captured by the trace program, and the trace program will have stopped. Restarting the trace program will immediately start collecting more data and overwrite the last trace file written.

Formatting CICS/6000 trace

Once the raw trace output had been generated, it must be formatted into a human-readable form before it can be used. AIX provides the AIX trcrpt program for formatting trace output. This program takes a raw trace file name as input and writes the formatted output to the screen. This output should be redirected into a file and then viewed with an editor because trace output may be quite large. The following command illustrates formatting trace output:

```
trcrpt cicstrace.raw > cicstrace.fmt
```

Advanced tracing

Through the use of the AIX trace demon and other techniques, additional trace items may be collected that will be of use in developing and debugging CICS/6000 applications. From both the C and the COBOL programming languages, it is possible to include additional trace entries that will be sent to the AIX trace facility for collection. The overhead of collecting these entries is relatively small.

To include new trace entries in a CICS application, the AIX hookids that will be associated with the new entries must be chosen. AIX provides a set of hookids for user applications; these range from hex 0x010 through to 0x0FF, a total of 240 different trace types. Once the hookid corresponding to the new trace entry is chosen, it may be used as a parameter to the AIX macro TRCGENT to cause data to be written and associated with the hookid. The TRCGENT macro may be found in the AIX include file <sys/trchkid.h>. The parameters to TRCGENT are as follows:

Channel   The AIX trace channel on which the trace is to appear; this should always be coded as **0.**

Hookid   The hookid corresponding to the trace data to be written. The hookid is the most significant 12 bits of a 32-bit word. To convert the hookid in the range 0x010 to 0x0FF into the required format type, it must first be moved 20 bits to the left.

Data word   A mandatory 32-bit value that is stored in the trace entry.

Length   The length of the following data to be stored in the trace entry. The data pointed to by the following parameter must be at least this length.

Data pointer   Additional data to be stored in the trace entry. The length of the trace data is specified by the previous **Length** parameter.

AIX trace example.   If a trace record is to be written that includes the AIX process ID of the process writing the entry plus a fixed length character string:

```
/*
 * Sample AIX program to generate a trace entry.
 *
 * Format of output data is:
 *
 *        4 Bytes              8 Bytes
 *    + ---------- + ----------------- +
 *    | Process Id | 8 character string |
 *    + ---------- + ----------------- +
 */

#include <sys/trchkid.h>

main(int argc, char *argv)
{
TRCGENT(0, 0x099 << 20, getpid(), 8, "ABCDEFGH");
}
```

When compiled and executed, the program will generate a trace entry. For
the trace entry to be collected, the AIX trace collection demon must be executing. The trace demon can be started to collect this trace using the following
command:

```
trace -a -j 099 -o trace.out
```

This command causes the trace demon to be started in the background, to collect trace for hookid 099 only and to place the trace output in the file called
`trace.out` in the current directory.

   If the program is executed, its trace entries will then be logged to the output file. The trace demon uses an internal memory buffer to hold the trace
data temporarily. The trace data are only written when the trace demon is
stopped. The trace demon may be stopped by the command **trcstop.**

   Once stopped, the trace file will contain the raw trace entries. The contents
of this file are not readable and must be formatted with the **trcrpt** command.
Since the trace contains hookids that are not known to AIX, a new trace template entry must be created to explain how the data should be formatted. The
discussion of writing AIX trace templates is beyond the scope of this book but
may be found in the AIX documentation and in the commentary in the
`/etc/trcfmt` file. An example trace format template is shown below:

```
#
# Sample format template for hookid 099 used as an example in the book
#
099 1.1 L = APPL "@Test Trace Entry" \
   D4 A8
```

The trace template should be entered into a file that is referenced by the -t
parameter on trcfmt. If the program is executed a number of times and formatted using the preceding template, the following output may be obtained:

```
099    1.569996800    0.000000    18786 ABCDEFGH
099    3.304898816    1734.902016    18787 ABCDEFGH
```

```
099    6.987762944    3682.864128    18789 ABCDEFGH
099   10.813143296    3825.380352    18791 ABCDEFGH
```

The first column shows the hookid responsible for the trace entry. This will always be 099 for the current example. The second parameter shows the elapsed seconds at which the trace entry was written from the start of the trace collection. The third column shows the number of milliseconds from the previous trace entry. This is particularly useful for gathering performance information. Bracketing a command or function call with two AIX trace statements allows the exact elapsed time in between to be gathered. The rest of the line shows any additional data gathered with the trace that has been formatted according to the format template for that hookid.

In the preceding output, the program was executed four times in the space of just over 10 seconds. The four different process IDs for the different program runs also can be seen.

Inserting diagnostic information

A CICS/6000 application interacts with the display using BMS or direct terminal control facilities. It is thus difficult to display diagnostic information from a program directly to the display. One way that may be used to determine the state of variables or location of execution of the program is to insert diagnostic points in the code. These points will write some information when they are encountered. The information may contain variable contents, counters, or simply just the fact that the diagnostic point has been reached. This is similar to the user trace mechanism.

To write information to the user, data may be written to the CICS-defined extrapartition transient data queue called *CSMT*. CSMT is defined as being an external AIX file called CSMT.out located in the /var/cics_regions/ <region>/data directory. Information written to this queue will be written immediately to the AIX file. The AIX file can be examined or be followed using the AIX **tail -f** command. To write information to the queue, issue the following command from within a CICS application:

```
EXEC CICS WRITEQ TD QUEUE("CSMT") FROM("message to be written")
```

When developing C programs, the following function may be useful:

```
void CICS_WriteQ(char *message)
{
    EXEC CICS WRITEQ TD QUEUE("CSMT") FROM(message) LENGTH(strlen(message));
    return;
}
```

This function takes a NULL terminated string as a parameter and writes its contents to the CSMT queue. The function may be called from different points in the C program. An example of its use is shown below:

```
char message[200];
...
EXEC CICS READ FILE("myfile") INTO(mydata) RESP(resp);
sprintf(message, "Response code from READ: %d", resp);
CICS_WriteQ(message);
```

Debug points in a program can be removed once the problem has been determined. Another alternative to removing the debug points is to have them conditionally activated by the presence of some external condition such as an environment variable.

It is also possible to write diagnostic information to the output streams of the applications. AIX defines two output streams called *stdout* (standard output) and *stderr* (standard error). When a CICS program is started, it is executed in a CICS application server process. The standard output and standard error streams for this process are inherited from the main cics process that was started initially by the AIX SRC demon. This in turn has had its stdout and stderr directed to AIX files. By default, the AIX SRC subsystem entries for a CICS/6000 region are directed to the AIX file called /var/ cics_regions/<region>/console.msg. This file contains all the stdout and stderr from CICS and its applications. It is common for this file to be followed with the **tail** command to check for CICS start-up and other information, warning, or error messages.

When CICS starts, stderr and stdout are opened against this file and have their file pointers positioned at the beginning of the file. As CICS operates, it writes error messages to stderr, thus advancing the stderr file pointer. CICS does not write any data to stdout. If a CICS application attempts to write information to the stdout stream, this will be written to the same file but, unfortunately, not at the end of the file. It will be written at the file pointer for stdout, which will not be the same as stderr. As such, data will either be overwritten or a jumble of data will appear. Figure 10.7 illustrates the relationship with file pointers and SRC.

The CICS/6000 regions defined to AIX SRC can have their attributes within SRC changed; this includes the location of the stderr and stdout output streams. If the AIX stdout stream is directed to a different AIX file from that of stderr, it may be used to collect diagnostic information from a CICS application if that application writes output to the stdout stream.

To redirect the stdout output stream, the user must be logged into AIX as the root user and issue the following AIX command:

```
# chssys -s cics.<region> -o <AIX path name for stdout>
```

It is recommended that the path used for stdout collection should be a file in the CICS region directory, /var/cics_regions/<region>/stdout.out, for example.

When the CICS/6000 region is started, any data written to stdout will result in data being collected in this file. In a C language application, this may be a command such as

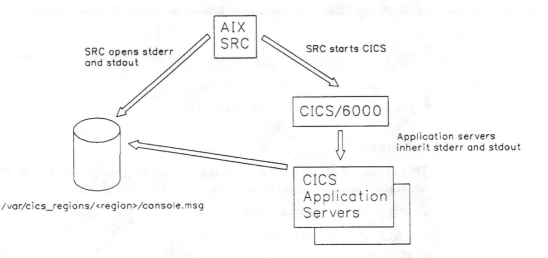

AIX file pointers over time

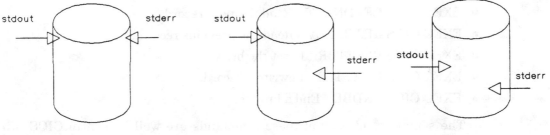

Figure 10.7 AIX SRC, stderr, and stdout.

```
...
printf("Hello world! This is transaction: %4.4s\n", eibptr->eibtrnid);
...
```

In a COBOL language application, the DISPLAY command may be used:

```
...
DISPLAY "Hello world! This is transaction: " EIBTRNID.
...
```

If the stdout stream is not redirected to a separate file, it is still possible to collect information. If data are written to the stderr stream, it will be appended to the contents of the console.msg file in the CICS/6000 region directory. Samples for C and COBOL are shown below:

```
C language

#include <stdio.h>
...
fprintf(stderr, "Hello World!");

COBOL language

DISPLAY "Hello World!" UPON SYSERR.
```

CICS/6000 File Control

This section discusses CICS/6000 file control in greater depth. The CICS API provides a set of commands to manipulate CICS files. These include

- EXEC CICS DELETE   Delete a record.
- EXEC CICS READ   Read a record.
- EXEC CICS WRITE   Write a record.
- EXEC CICS UNLOCK   Unlock a record.
- EXEC CICS STARTBR   Start a browse.
- EXEC CICS READNEXT   Read the next record.
- EXEC CICS READPREV   Read the previous record.
- EXEC CICS RESETBR   Reset the browse.
- EXEC CICS REWRITE   Rewrite a record.
- EXEC CICS ENDBR   End a browse.

The semantics of each of these commands are well known to CICS programmers and are coded in many CICS applications. To be able to provide the same semantics for these commands on CICS/6000 as provided on other CICS platforms, recoverable, record-oriented files are required. The AIX file system does not have the concept of records and does not lend itself to implementing a recoverable interface.

The Encina Structured File Server (SFS) provides a record-oriented, recoverable view of files. The SFS is used as the file manager for CICS files.

CICS versus SFS file types.   CICS provides a model of files where an individual file can belong to one of three different types of file. The file types known to CICS are

- *Key-sequenced data sets* (*KSDS*)   Records contain one or more fields known as the *key* which may be used to retrieve the record. Browsing through the file returns the records in a sorted order based on the key. Records in a KSDS file may be retrieved, updated, or deleted in a random order.
- *Entry-sequenced data sets* (*ESDS*)   Records written to the file are assigned a value know as a *relative bytes address* or *RBA*. This RBA value may be

specified when reading the record back. New records inserted into the file will be added at the end of the file and be assigned an RBA value higher than the last RBA value.

- *Relative record data sets (RRDS)*   Records are inserted into the file in fixed slot locations. These locations are known as *relative record numbers* or *RRNs*. The RRDS file is similar to that of an array data structure. Records written to the file are written in the slot or location specified and are read from the file by those slots.

The SFS provides similar file types for SFS files. CICS/6000 maps the three types of CICS files to the three types of available SFS files. The semantic operations on the three SFS file types are the same as those for the CICS types.

The following table shows the mapping between CICS file types and the corresponding SFS file types:

CICS file type	SFS file type
Key-sequenced data sets (KSDS)	Clustered files
Entry-sequenced data sets (ESDS)	Entry-sequenced files
Relative record data sets (RRDS)	Relative files

Concepts of KSDS files.   Key-sequenced data set (KSDS) files allow records to be inserted into the file at random positions. One or more fields within the records known as *key fields* specify the relative order of the records within the file. KSDS files may have records added, deleted, or updated by specifying the key field in the CICS RIDFLD option on CICS file commands.

Multiple CICS files may be defined against a single underlying KSDS file but with alternate indices specified. The alternate indices allow different orderings to be associated with the file.

The record length of KSDS files may be defined as variable, allowing more efficient use of file storage than only allowing records to be of a fixed, maximum size.

Concepts of ESDS files.   Entry-sequenced data set (ESDS) files allow records to be inserted into the file without a key field being specified. Records are always added at the end of the file. When a record is added, a 32-bit value known as the *relative byte address* (RBA) is returned. This returned value may be used as the key field when retrieving the record at a later point. The numerical value of the RBA will always increase for new records being added. Other than as a key to retrieve or update a previously added record, no other meaning should be used with an RBA value.

Records added to an ESDS file may not be deleted, but the read, browse, and update commands may still be used.

Concepts of RRDS files. Relative record data set (RRDS) files can be thought of as files containing arrays of fixed-size records. Each record is inserted into the file at a position specified by an index value known as the *relative record number* or *RRN*. These RRN values are 32-bit integers ranging from 1 upward. The index is not part of the data record but is supplied separately in the RIDFLD with the RRN option being specified on the CICS command.

Operation of the SFS

The SFS operates as a server process as part of the Encina product. It uses the services of the DCE RPC and DCE Security Services components and is a server for client requests to access files maintained by it. CICS/6000 becomes a client of the services it provides.

The SFS maintains an area of physical storage on AIX known as a *logical volume.* The logical volume must be created by an AIX administrator before starting the SFS. The SFS uses this physical storage to store SFS files and other SFS housekeeping information. The use of raw physical storage allows the SFS to access the data without the overhead of having to go through the AIX file system drivers. Unfortunately, this means that few AIX commands may be used with the actual underlying data of the SFS. AIX commands such as **ls, chmod,** and other file-related commands may not be used with SFS files.

SFS files have one or more indices associated with them. These indices are named entities and are used to impose an ordering on the records within the file. An SFS file may be thought of logically as a random collection of records where the organization of the records is specified by the indices. Indices use one or more fields within the record to form the key field on which the records are ordered. The diagram shown in Fig. 10.8 illustrates an SFS file with two indices. Each index imposes a different ordering on the file.

When first started, the SFS has no files to manage. The files managed by the SFS must be defined to it. When a new CICS/6000 region is created, one of the tasks of creating that new region is to create new files on the SFS. These files are used by the CICS/6000 region to maintain CICS-recoverable resources such as queues, interval control starts, and installed terminals. When querying the files being maintained by the SFS after configuring for a CICS region, the following files may be found:

<region>cicsnlqfile   This file contains locally queued requests to asynchronously start CICS transactions that are unprotected.

<region>cicsplqfile   This file contains locally queued requests to asynchronously start CICS transactions that are protected.

<region>cicsnrectsqfil   This file holds all the queues and records for nonrecoverable auxiliary temporary storage queues.

<region>cicsrectsqfile   This file holds all the queues and records for recoverable auxiliary temporary storage queues.

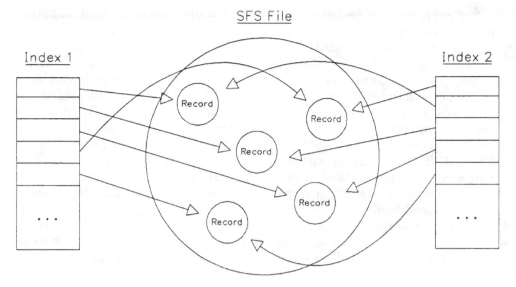

Figure 10.8   Logical SFS files and indices.

<region>cicstdqlgfile   This file holds all the queues and records for logically recoverable intrapartition transient data queues.

<region>cicstdqnofile   This file holds all the queues and records for non-recoverable intrapartition transient data queues.

<region>cicstdqphfile   This file holds all the queues and records for physically recoverable intrapartition transient data queues.

When a client wishes to access a file within the SFS, it must first issue an SFS call to create a handle to that file that it may use in subsequent calls to refer to that file. These file handles are known as *open file descriptors* (OFDs) and may be seen when querying an SFS. An OFD has many attributes associated with it when it is created; these include whether the file should be accessed in a recoverable mode, what kind of record locking should be used, and what access requests are allowed. CICS/6000 creates OFDs when it wishes to access the SFS files. The act of writing new records or reading old records causes OFDs to be created by CICS/6000 against the SFS.

Defining new files for CICS/6000

To create a new file for use with CICS/6000, the SFS file must be created on the SFS and a File Definition (FD) must be made within CICS/6000 to associate the CICS file with the SFS file. The file may be created on the SFS by using either the Encina-supplied administration commands or the CICS/6000 higher-level utilities. In both cases, it is essential to understand the structure and use of the new file.

Before creating an SFS file, attributes of the file must be decided on so that it can be defined. These attributes and their types will vary depending on the type of SFS file being created.

Before any new file can be created of any CICS file type, its record structure should be decided on. CICS views file records as fixed- or variable-length records of unformatted, contiguous byte data. No knowledge of fields within a record is available to CICS. Any data structure may be imposed on the sequence of bytes, although there are requirements made by different file types. If porting an application from another CICS environment such as CICS/MVS, record layout within files may be preknown. Alternatively, for new and ported applications, if the data content of a record is known in terms of its constituent application record fields, the record format for the file may be determined easily.

For example, if a file is to contain customer information including Social Security Numbers, names, addresses, and account balances, it may be decided that the fields within the file will be composed of the following:

Field Type	Data Type	Length in bytes
Social Security Number	Character	11
Surname	Character	30
Address	Character	90
Account balance	Integer	4

In a C language program, this may be mapped with a structure such as

```
struct fileRecord {
    char ss_number[11];
    char surname[30];
    char address[90];
    int balance;
};
```

In a COBOL program, it may be defined as

```
01 file-record.
   02  ss-number pic x(11).
   02  surname   pic x(30).
   02  address   pic x(90).
   02  balance   pic s9(8) comp-5.
```

In both cases, the size of an individual file record is 139 bytes in length.

When a file is defined to SFS, an index is also associated with the file to impose a record ordering and lookup mechanism. To achieve this, one or more fields within an SFS record are identified as key fields to compose the index. When deciding on the record layout within the SFS, the location of indices associated with the file also must be considered.

In the example, if the Social Security Number were to be the only component of the index, it must be defined as a separate SFS file field, whereas the other logical fields could be stored on the SFS as a single field. The SFS record layout would then be composed of two fields, the first field being 11 bytes in length and associated with the file index and the second field being 128 bytes in length to hold all the other logical fields.

The SFS allows many varied data types to be associated with SFS file fields. For CICS/6000 usage, it is strongly recommended that the only data types used be those for the fixed- and variable-length unformatted sequences of bytes. SFS names these data types sfs_byteArray and sfs_varLenByteArray. For the example, the SFS record structure used when creating the SFS file for CICS usage would be

```
+ -------------------- + ----------------------- +
|   sfs_byteArray[11]   |    sys_byteArray[128]    |
+ -------------------- + ----------------------- +
```

When creating an SFS file, each field within a file's record must be named. The names given to the fields are unused by CICS, which only utilizes the record's structure. Arbitrary names may be given to the record's fields. The name or names given to the fields that constitute the index associated with the file must be specified when the file and index are created.

Creating new files for CICS/6000.   To create a new file on an SFS, a number of different commands and techniques exist. Before the file can be created, a series of questions must be answered relating to its type, structure, and access. Some of these areas were discussed in the preceding section. What follows is a checklist of facts that must be gathered before a file can be created:

SFS name   To create a file on an SFS, the actual server on which the file is to be created must be known. The commands that will be executed later to create the file require the name of the SFS upon which to act. An SFS is specified by the DCE Cell Directory Service name. For CICS/6000, this is usually /.:/cics/sfs/<name>. When the connection between the SFS file and the CICS/6000 file is made within the CICS File Definitions (FD), the SFS name is specified, allowing each CICS file to be located on arbitrary SFS.

SFS file name   All files managed by an SFS have unique names within the server. To create a file on the server, the name of the file must be chosen. File names may be up to 254 character in length. When the connection between the SFS file and the CICS/6000 file is made in the CICS File Definitions (FD), the SFS file name will be specified to CICS.

Field names, types, and sizes   For fixed- and variable-length file record layouts, the field names, types, and sizes must be specified. These attributes allow the SFS to manage organization of the files through indices based on one or more fields. Since CICS does not distinguish between field types within a record but simply returns and takes untyped data for the record, fields need not be defined within a record if they are not to be used for indexing. The length of a record must match the expected size of a record as used by CICS. Field names are used when defining any indices for the file but are transparent to CICS. The names of the fields are local to the file, and field names need not be unique among files but must be unique within a single file.

Index name   For all SFS file types, a named index is created and associated with the file. The purpose of the index is to organize and access the file's records in a predefined order. The index has a name associated with it to allow additional, differently named indices to be created associated with different fields within the record. Accessing a particular file through one index would return records in one order, while accessing the same file through an alternate index allows the records to be accessed in a different order. From the example discussed previously, one index may be associated with a Social Security Number, while another index may be associated with a surname. Such indices allows records to be retrieved directly by either Social Security Number or surname. Adding or modifying records in an SFS file either through CICS or by Encina SFS commands results in changes to the index that are performed automatically by the SFS itself. When the mapping from CICS files to SFS files is specified in the CICS File Definitions (FD), the index name used to access the file for the CICS file also must be specified.

Volume name   The data for the SFS file must reside on physical disk storage. The storage used to hold SFS file data is known as a *logical volume.* Logical volumes are defined to an SFS at initialization of the server and may be added or expanded after start-up. When a file is created on an SFS, the logical volume on which the file's data are to be stored is specified. An SFS file may not span logical volumes and must be contained within a single volume.

Additional options also may be specified when creating SFS files, including maximum records within a file, amount of logical volume storage to be allocated initially to the file, and whether records within a file should be unique or allow duplicates based on key values of an index.

To create an SFS file, CICS SMIT panels and commands may be used. The SMIT panels allow all the previous definitions of an SFS file to be saved in an AIX file. Once the file has been created, the definitions within the file can be applied to an actual SFS to create the file. The files that hold the definitions for an SFS file are known as *schema files.* To utilize the SMIT panels for creating such a file, the following tasks must be done:

1. Create a blank schema file.
2. Select the schema file for use.
3. Define the SFS file structure within the AIX schema file.
4. Apply the SFS file descriptions contained within the schema file to the SFS.

A schema file can be used to hold multiple SFS file descriptions, and each file description may be applied to the SFS separately. The benefit of using a schema file to contain the descriptions of the file is that in the event of a catastrophic failure, the SFS files can be recreated quickly by reapplying the file descriptions against a new SFS.

To navigate to the SFS schema files panels in SMIT, follow the path

```
smit cics
    Manage Encina SFS Servers
        Manage Schemas for Encina SFS Servers
```

The resulting panel is shown below. From this panel, all SFS schema commands may be executed.

```
                    Manage Schemas for Encina SFS Servers

Move cursor to desired item and press Enter.

   Change Working Schema File
   Create empty Schema File
   Destroy a Schema File
   Add a new Schema
   Delete Schemas
   Show/Change a Schema
   Apply Schemas to an Encina SFS Server (with all Indexes)
   Apply a Schema to an Encina SFS Server (with selected Indexes)


F1=Help            F2=Refresh         F3=Cancel          F8=Image
F9=Shell           F10=Exit           Enter=Do
```

The first task when working with schema files is to create a new blank schema file that initially contains no actual file definitions. This file contains the template used for creating subsequent file definitions. The "Create Empty Schema File" menu option should be chosen, which will display the following panel. The name of the AIX schema file to be created can be entered and the file then created.

```
                       Create empty Schema File

Type or select values in entry fields.
Press Enter AFTER making all desired changes.

                                              [Entry Fields]
* Schema File                                 [/u/user/test.sc]


F1=Help            F2=Refresh         F3=Cancel          F4=List
F5=Reset           F6=Command         F7=Edit            F8=Image
F9=Shell           F10=Exit           Enter=Do
```

Once an empty schema file has been created, file definitions for the files to be created in the SFS may be added. Before adding entries, the actual AIX schema file to be used must be specified either through the "Change Working Schema File" panel entry or by setting the CICS_SCHEMA environment variable to the name of the schema file. The panel to create a new schema entry contains the following fields:

```
                         Add a Schema Entry

Type or select values in entry fields.
Press Enter AFTER making all desired changes.

[TOP]                                        [Entry Fields]
* SFS File Name                            [ 1 ]
* Model SFS File Name                       ""
* Schema File to use                       [ 2 ]
  Resource description                     [SFS Schema File]
* Number of updates                         0
  Protect resource from modification?       no                    +
  Type of SFS File                          clustered
  Volume Name                              [sfs_%S]
  Number of Pages to Preallocate           [100]                  #
  Maximum Number of Records                [10000]
  Primary Index Name                       [ 3 ]
  Is Primary Index Unique?                  yes                   +
  Field Names for Primary Index            [ 4 ]
  Descending Field Names for Primary Index []
  Field 1 - Name                           [ 5 ]
  Field 1 - Type                            none  6        +
  Field 1 - Length                         [0]  7         #
  Field 2 - Name                           []
  Field 2 - Type                            none                  +
  Field 2 - Length                         [0]
  ...
  Variable Field - Name                    []
  Variable Field - Type                     none                  +
  Variable Field - Length                  [0]                    #
  Secondary Index 1 - Name                 []
  Secondary Index 1 - Volume Name          []
  Secondary Index 1 - Preallocated Pages   [20]                   #
  Secondary Index 1 - Is it Unique?         yes                   +
  Secondary Index 1 - Field Names          []
  Secondary Index 1 - Descending Fields    []
  ...

F1=Help          F2=Refresh        F3=Cancel        F4=List
F5=Reset         F6=Command        F7=Edit          F8=Image
F9=Shell         F10=Exit          Enter=Do
```

The fields in the schema file define the characteristics of the file created on SFS.

1 The name of the SFS file to be created on the SFS. This does not include the SFS name itself.

2 The name of the schema file being used to hold the definition. This field cannot be changed and will be what was set by the previous panel or environment variable.

3 The name of the primary index associated with the file.

4 The names of the fields within the file that will constitute the key value for the index. Each field name should be later defined within the record.

5 The name of the first field within the record.

6 The SFS field type of the field being defined. A suitable value is `sfs_byteArray`.

7 The length of the field in bytes being defined.

Once one or more file definitions are described in the schema files, the definitions may be applied to the SFS. This may be achieved by executing the "Apply Schemas to an Encina SFS Server" panel. The files described in the schema file may then be selected individually for creation on the SFS. Before performing this step, the user must be DCE authenticated with sufficient permissions to create a file on the server.

The diagram show in Fig. 10.9 illustrates the process of defining a file on the SFS using schema files.

Creating a clustered file: KSDS. A clustered file will correspond to the CICS file type of KSDS and will be used to access the file in a random fashion. When creating an SFS clustered file, the format of the record structure of the file must be predefined. The record structure is composed of named fields within the record. An index also must be associated with the file that defines the ordering and access methods for the file.

Creating an entry-sequenced file: ESDS. When creating an ESDS file for CICS/6000 on an SFS, the corresponding SFS file type should be **sequential.** To create an SFS sequential file, the following attributes of the file must be specified:

- File name
- Field names
- Field types
- Field sizes
- Primary index name
- Logical volume for data

The field types used when defining the file should be `sfs_byteArray`, with the last field in the record optionally being `sfs_varLenByteArray` if

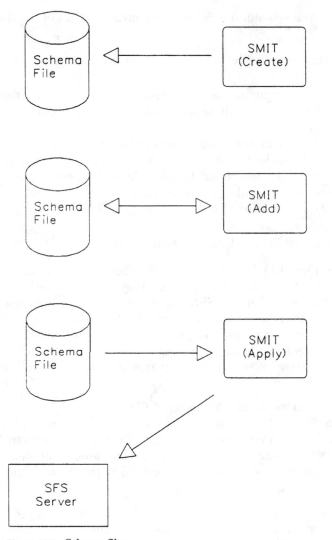

Figure 10.9 Schema files.

variable-length records are desired. Note that unlike the other SFS file types, the index need not be associated with a key field in the record; the index of sequential files is implied by the order of insertion of records into the file.

Creating a relative file: RRDS. An RRDS file is created on an SFS by creating an SFS file of file type **relative.** When creating such a file, a field with the record format of SFS field type `unsignedInt32` must be created and used as the primary key field. Although the records contained within the SFS file contain the RRN key, when written or read from within CICS, this field is not visible in CICS file records.

Alternate indices. Certain types of CICS files may have alternate indices associated with them. The alternate index specifies a different set of fields within the record that are to be used as the key fields. When accessing a CICS file by an alternate index, the ordering of the records inserted and returned will be different.

An example of the use of alternate indices would be a file that contains fields of customer names and customer account numbers. If a query is desired against a specific customer, the customer name or the customer number is known. The CICS file could be defined as having two indices, one that relates to the customer name and another relating to the customer number. A CICS application could then read the file through the most appropriate index to optimize the search.

An alternate index is created by defining the name of the new index to be created and the fields that are to comprise the key for the new index. These are defined to the SFS, which manages both the original file, its contents, the original index, and the newly created index.

Alternate indices may be created through the CICS schema files when creating the original file. This is accomplished by defining the index name, fields, whether the index should contain only unique keys, and the SFS logical volume used for holding the index data. The Encina-supplied **sfsadmin** command also may be used to add a secondary index to a preexisting file. The command **sfsadmin add index** allows an additional index to be created for an SFS file. The command expects the same types of information as the schema definitions.

Once the SFS file has an additional index associated with it, a new CICS file definition must be defined that specifies the name of the CICS file that is to be associated with the alternate index access to the original file. The new file definition will specify the same details as the original file definition, except that the index name used will be that of the new index.

Variable-length records. CICS KSDS files may be defined as having variable-length records. The length of the record is specified when it is written initially. Using variable-length records can significantly reduce the amount of disk space used to hold file data, since the alternative to variable-length records would be defining fixed-size records large enough to hold the largest record.

Variable-length record files are created by defining a field in an SFS file as being of SFS data type `sfs_varLenByteArray`. The value of this field should be defined as the maximum length that the varying record can be.

CICS requires that there be only one instance of a variable-length field within a record and that it be the last field in the record.

CICS/6000 File API

The API available for accessing files allows record to be written, read, updated, and deleted.

Writing CICS files.   The EXEC CICS WRITE command may be used to insert a new record into a file. For KSDS files, the record is inserted into the file at the position specified by the index such that the ordering of the file is maintained. If the file is defined to the SFS as having unique keys in the index, the write of the record will fail, and the DUPREC condition be raised. The contents of the record are taken from the data pointed to by the FROM option. The key field for the record should be specified in the RIDFLD option.

If the file is defined to CICS as recoverable, the record will be written but not committed until the end of the transaction. If any other transaction attempts to read for update or browse through the position of the newly inserted record, the other transaction will block until the write is committed or rolled back.

Reading CICS files.   The EXEC CICS READ command may be used to directly read an arbitrary record by key. For KSDS files, the key of the record to be obtained is specified in the RIDFLD option. If a record with the specified key is not found, the NOTFND condition will be raised. The GTEQ option may be specified to read the next higher record in the file if a direct match with the key is not found. The key specified in the RIDFLD may be specified shorter than actual keys by using the KEYLENGTH and GENERIC options. The first record that includes the specified key as a prefixed string will be returned if one exists. The RIDFLD will be updated with the complete key of the returned record.

If the UPDATE option is specified, the record will be read and a lock placed on the record to prevent other reads also with the update option. A read with update is a requirement for a subsequent EXEC CICS REWRITE command used to update the record. Locks are held on a record with the read for update command until

- An EXEC CICS UNLOCK command is executed by the locking transaction.
- The transaction is committed or rolled back.
- The transaction issues a subsequent read for update without first having rewritten the previously locked record.

Browsing CICS files.   CICS files may be browsed sequentially starting at a specified point. The browsing of files is initiated by an EXEC CICS STARTBR command and a record key specified in a similar manner to that for reading files. The execution of this command does not read a record but simply positions a file pointer at the next record to be returned. Records may be read sequentially in either a forward (EXEC CICS READNEXT) or a backward (EXEC CICS READPREV) direction. The EXEC CICS ENDBR command ends a browse operation and frees internal CICS resources related to tracking the current file browse. No browse should be in effect while a modification of the file is being undertaken. Specifically, a transaction should not attempt a read with update, delete, or write after a **start browse** command but before an **end browse** command.

The **start browse** command can be used to position the file pointer at the beginning or end of the file by specifying all binary zeros (0x00) or all binary ones (0xff) as the RIDFLD values. If the file pointer is positioned at the beginning of the file, the **read next** command may be used to traverse the file. If the file pointer is positioned at the end of the file, the file may be scanned backwards with the **read previous** command.

Using sfsadmin to administer the SFS. Encina supplies a utility called **sfsadmin** to perform administrative tasks against an Encina SFS. The **sfsadmin** command allows files to be created and queried, disk space examined, and many other SFS administrative operations to be initiated.

To utilize the **sfsadmin** command, the user must be sufficiently authenticated with DCE to perform the requested tasks. This will usually require authenticating as the DCE principal cell_admin. The SFS name may be specified on the **sfsadmin** command with the -s server_name option or by specifying the name of the SFS in the ENCINA_SFS_SERVER environment variable.

The options of the **sfsadmin** command include

Option	Description
add index	Create a secondary index for an SFS file.
add lvol	Define a new logical volume for an SFS.
copy file	Copy an SFS file to another file on the same server.
create clusteredfile	Create an SFS clustered-ordered file (KSDS).
create relativefile	Create an SFS relative-ordered file (RRDS).
create sequentialfile	Create an SFS sequential file (ESDS).
deactivate index	Deactivate a secondary index associated with an SFS file. Deactivating an index causes the SFS not to update the index when changes are made to the file. This can improve file performance.
delete index	Delete a secondary index associated with an SFS file.
destroy file	Destroy an SFS file. All storage associated with the file is released.
empty file	The contents of the SFS file are emptied. Following this command, no records are left in the file.
enable server	Enable an SFS for full operation.
expand file	The disk space associated with the SFS file is increased. Disk space is automatically increased as records are added to a file and the disk space allocated to the file is insufficient. This command allows space to be preallocated to a file and can prevent errors if insufficient space for the file as a whole does not exist.
expand index	The disk space associated with a secondary index for an SFS file is increased.
export file	The contents of an SFS file are exported to an AIX file.
import file	A previously exported Encina SFS file is repopulated.
list files	The names of the SFS files held on the SFS are returned.
list ofds	The currently open file descriptors to SFS files are listed.
query export	The status of an SFS file export is displayed.
query file	The status of an SFS file is displayed. This includes the file name and type, the record format, number of records, and last access times.
query filelock	Display information about locks currently held on the SFS file.

Option	Description
query index	Information about the secondary index of an SFS file is displayed.
query lvol	Information about an SFS logical volume is returned.
query server	Information about the SFS is returned.
query tranlock	The status of locks held by a specified transaction is returned.
rebuild index	The SFS secondary index is rebuilt from the data in the file. This command may be used following a previous **deactivate index** command to reset the index contents and make the index available for use.
rename file	The name of the SFS file is changed to a new value.
rename index	The name of an SFS file index is changed to a new value.
reorganize file	The contents of a sequential SFS file are reordered to reclaim unused space on the logical volume holding the file.
set recordlimit	The maximum number of records for the SFS file is set.
terminate ofd	The specified open file descriptor is closed. Any work previously performed on the file through the OFD will be backed out.

A complete list and description of all **sfsadmin** commands may be found in the CICS/6000 manual *Encina for CICS,* available from IBM.

Using cicssdt to administer the SFS.   CICS/6000 supplies a command similar in function to that of the Encina **sfsadmin** command. The **cicssdt** command may be used to work directly with an SFS. Unlike sfsadmin, cicssdt provides enhanced user interaction and a set of SFS access functions related to CICS's use of the SFS. To utilize cicssdt, the user must have sufficient DCE authority to access the SFS. The name of the SFS against which cicssdt operates may be specified by the environment variables CICS_XDT_SERVER and CICS_SFS_SERVER or by specifying the server name explicitly on the **cicssdt** command.

The **cicssdt** utility provides the following subcommands for performing work against an SFS:

Option	Description
setopen	This command specifies how **cicssdt** should open files against the SFS. Options include exclusive/shared, timeout for operations, transactional/nontransactional, and lock modes.
list	This command lists SFS files maintained by the SFS. Files may be listed by name or include additional information such as the index name and number of records contained within the file.
create	This command allows a new SFS file to be created. The field and index names as well as all the other file attributes may be specified.
read	This command allows all or some of the records within an SFS file to be read, displayed, and altered.
write	This command allows records to be inserted into an SFS file.
empty	This command allows an SFS file to have its contents emptied.
delete	This command deletes an SFS file from the SFS.
free	This command terminates open file descriptors (OFDs) currently open on an SFS file. This may be used to release and terminate locks on an SFS file in the event that the CICS region terminates unexpectedly.
addindex	This command allows an additional secondary index to be created against an associated SFS file.
delindex	This command allows a secondary index to be deleted from an SFS file.

Option	Description
info	This command displays detailed information about an SFS file being maintained by an SFS. The output includes the file fields and organization, number of records, and currently open file descriptors.
server	This command allows the name of the SFS currently the target of SFS commands to be changed.
qtos	This command loads an AIX file in QSAM format into the SFS as an SFS file.
stof	This command writes the contents of an SFS file into an AIX file either as straight data or in a format suitable for reloading by the **ftos** subcommand.
ftos	This command loads data into an SFS file from an AIX file in a suitable format.
quit	This command ends the **cicssdt** utility.

Full information on the options of the **cicssdt** command may be found in the CICS/6000 *Administration Reference Manual*.

Backing up an SFS file. The individual files being managed by the SFS contain data used by the CICS applications executing on the system. In case of a system failure or other catastrophe, it is advisable to take frequent backups of the SFS files for subsequent restoration. The following illustrates some techniques to enable SFS files to be backed up.

Backing up files with cicssdt

The **cicssdt** command provides a mechanism to write the contents of an SFS file to an AIX file. The format of the AIX data in the file may be either cicssdt format or raw data format. The cicssdt format includes the description of the original file structure as well as the file record contents. This format also allows variable-length records to be written and later reloaded. The raw format is a byte stream of data taken record by record from the SFS file. This format does not allow reloading if the file structure contains variable-length records because there are no record terminators in the data.

To create an AIX file from an SFS file, the cicssdt subcommand **stof** (SFS to Flat) may be used. This command prompts for the name of the SFS file to be dumped, the name of the AIX file to contain the dumped contents, and whether the data should be written in cicssdt format or raw format.

Once the AIX file has been created, it may be reloaded subsequently using the cicssdt command **ftos** (Flat to SFS). If the AIX flat file format is cicssdt format, the file being reloaded need not be previously defined. If raw format, the SFS file must be initially created.

Using the sfsadmin export capability

The **sfsadmin export** command allows the contents of an SFS file to be written to an AIX file, tape, raw disk, or stdout. The data written can be reread subsequently with the **sfsadmin import** command. The **sfsadmin export** command has a number of parameters, some of which are described below:

devicetype   This parameter specifies the type of output generated by the **sfsadmin export** command. Allowable values include **disk** for raw disk output, **file** for AIX file output, and **tape** for spooling to tape.

target   The target parameter specifies the name of the output destination. The type of target output should correspond to the **devicetype** parameter. The special value **stdout** specifies that the data will be sent to the sfsadmin stdout stream.

checkpointsize   The number of bytes written during the export before a checkpoint is taken. Checkpoints are taken to allow the export to be restarted at points during the output in case the export is interrupted.

locktype   This parameter specifies the locking to be used on the file during a file export. Possible values include **filelock,** which specifies that the whole file should be locked preventing access by other applications; **recordlock,** which specifies that the record should be locked during output; and **nolock,** which specifies that the no locks should be taken on the file or records. Uncommitted (dirty) records may be exported.

CICS/6000 Queues

CICS/6000 provides both the temporary storage and transient data types of CICS queues. The differences between the two types and how they exist on an AIX CICS system are discussed.

Temporary storage queues

The logical model of a temporary storage queue is that of an array of variable-length records into which the queue items are placed sequentially. Subsequent queue reads can retrieve the records written by either the current task or from some other task. CICS defines two types of temporary storage queues, *main storage queues* and *auxiliary storage queues*. The main storage queues are, as their name implies, held in the memory of the CICS system. As new records are added to the queue, the queue grows in CICS memory. Main storage temporary storage queue data are always lost when a CICS region is restarted.

Auxiliary storage temporary storage queues behave as their main storage equivalents except that the record data are held on an external, nonmemory storage destination. CICS/6000 utilizes the Encina SFS to hold auxiliary temporary storage queues. With auxiliary temporary storage, the queues may be present after a CICS restart if the region is autostarted. Both types of temporary storage queues will be lost if the region is cold started. The diagram in Fig. 10.10 shows the logical format for temporary storage queues.

The queues will retain the records until either

- The queue is explicitly deleted with the EXEC CICS DELETEQ TS command.

Temporary Storage Queue

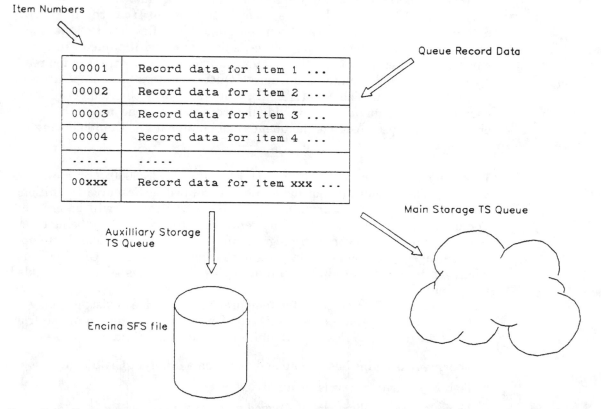

Figure 10.10 Temporary storage.

- The CICS system is restarted (main storage temporary storage queues).
- The CICS system is cold started (both types of temporary storage queues).
- The queue has been inactive for the queue age limit time period.

Temporary storage queue API. The API for temporary storage consists of the following commands:

- EXEC CICS WRITEQ TS
- EXEC CICS READQ TS
- EXEC CICS DELETEQ TS

The WRITEQ command allows the specification of either main storage or auxiliary storage queues. The first write to the specified queue creates the queue and attributes it with either main or auxiliary storage. When the record is written, the index into the queue is returned in the ITEM operand. The first record written into the queue is item 1. If a record already in the queue is to be updated, the ITEM operand can be combined with the REWRITE operand to replace the record within the queue.

The READQ command allows records to be read from the queue. By default, the next item is read from the queue. The first read of the queue returns item 1. A single queue pointer is associated with a queue such that when a queue record is read, the pointer is advanced. If any transaction reads a record, the queue pointer is advanced. Queue pointers have scope across a whole CICS region. The NUMITEMS attribute returns the number of items currently in the queue. An individual record can be read using the ITEM operand. This also positions the queue read pointer to the item following the item just read.

Temporary storage queue definitions.   Unlike other CICS/6000 resources, temporary storage queues do not have to be predefined in Resource Definitions. The first time a temporary storage queue is written, it will be created. Temporary storage queues are named entities, with their names being exactly eight characters. A common programming error is to not make the temporary storage queue name exactly eight characters, and thus CICS will use whatever characters are in the trailing bytes. The names should be padded with blanks.

A Resource Definition class for temporary storage does exist and may be used to specify alternate characteristics of a temporary storage queue from those of the default. A Resource Definition would be required if

- The queue is defined as remote and exists on a different CICS region.
- Tighter security access is required.
- The queue is auxiliary and is flagged as recoverable.

CICS/6000 supplies a transaction called *CEBR* to allow on-line browsing of temporary storage queues. CEBR also can be used to destroy a queue.

Transient data queues

CICS provides a data queueing mechanism known as *transient data queues*. These queues allow data to be written into them and subsequently processed off-line or by another CICS transaction. Two types of transient data queue are defined, namely, intrapartition queues and extrapartition queues.

Intrapartition transient data queues.   Intrapartition queues are queues managed internally by CICS. They are not visible externally to CICS by AIX applications. An intrapartition queue can be written by one transaction and read by another. This type of queue is rich in functionality and has many uses.

Intrapartition queue recovery. Intrapartition queues may be defined as recoverable using the **RecoveryType** attribute in the Transient Data Queue Resource Definitions (TDD). This attribute can have various values that are described below:

none No queue recovery is required. A record that is written into the queue is immediately inserted into the queue. If the transaction that writes the record abends, the queue still contains the record. Two transactions writing into the queue simultaneously will have their records written in the order that the commands were received. Any transaction that reads the queue immediately obtains the next record. If the reading transaction abends, the records read are not returned to the queue. The actual queues and records in the queues are stored in an SFS file called <region>cicstdqnofile.

physical Same as **none,** but in the event that the region as a whole abnormally terminates, the queue is returned to the state that it was in immediately preceding the region failure. Additionally, the last record read from the queue is returned to the queue, assuming that the transaction that last read it has not completed its processing. The actual queues and records in the queues are stored in an SFS file called <region>cicstdqphfile.

logical Full recovery is performed on the queue. For records to be finally added to the queue, the transaction that writes the records must complete or sync point. If the transaction abends, any records written to the queue will be removed. If a transaction reads from the queue and subsequently abends, the records are returned to the queue for later processing. A lock is held on the queue by any transaction that successfully reads or writes a record. This lock is required to prevent out-of-order records from being processed. The actual queues and records in the queues are stored in an SFS file called <region>cicstdqlgfile.

Intrapartition triggered transactions. An intrapartition queue can have a trigger level associated with it. This is an action to be performed when the trigger level number of committed records has been added to the queue. The trigger level is specified in the **TriggerLevel** attributed in the Transient Data Queue Resource Definitions (TDD). A value of **0** disables the queue triggering. If a trigger is defined, when the trigger level is reached, a transaction is automatically started. This transaction is specified in the **TriggeredTransId** attribute. The transaction executes in one of three modes depending on the setting of the **FacilityType** attribute. The values of this attribute are

file The triggered transaction executes in the background with no terminal or other facility associated with it. It may not perform any terminal IO.

terminal The triggered transaction is scheduled to execute against the terminal specified by the **FacilityId** attribute. This transaction may use terminal IO.

system   A distributed transaction processing link is formed between this transaction and a remote CICS system specified by the **FacilityId** attribute.

The trigger-started transaction is expected to empty the queue by performing EXEC CICS READQ commands until the QZERO condition is raised. Only when the queue is emptied and once again reaches the threshold is a new triggered transaction started.

Extrapartition transient data queues.   The other type of transient data queue is the extrapartition queue. This is accessed by the same API as intrapartition queues. Extrapartition queues are either read only or write only in nature depending on the setting of the **IOMode** attribute, which can have a value of either **input** for read only or **output** for write only. These queues manifest themselves as AIX files that may be processed outside the CICS environment. The **ExtrapartitionFile** attribute specifies the name of an AIX file to be mapped against the queue. Reading from the queue causes the next record to be read from the file. Writing to the queue causes a new record to be added to the file. Unlike intrapartition queues, the records are not deleted once read. If the queue is closed and later reopened, the records can be reread starting from the very beginning. Since a particular queue can be either input or output only, it is not possible to both read and write from the same queue. It is allowed to define the same underlying AIX file associated with two separate queues, one for input and one for output.

AIX files in an AIX file system are not naturally record format files but are simply byte streams or arrays of contiguous bytes. Since the semantics of writing a record to an extrapartition transient data queue are that a record will be written externally to CICS, a method of writing records into AIX files is required. CICS/6000 allows configuration of the record format on a per-queue basis when writing a record. The type of record format is defined by the **RecordType** attribute in the Transient Data (TDD) Resource Definition for the queue. This attribute may be assigned one of the following types:

fixed_length   Fixed-length records are written into the AIX file. The length of each record is specified by the **RecordLen** attribute in the Resource Definition. Records written by a CICS application should be of exactly the record length size.

variable_length   Variable-length records are written with the length of the record preceding the actual record data. The length is specified by a 2-byte binary integer value with the most significant byte first.

byte_terminated   Byte-terminated records are written to the file with a terminator byte appended at the end. The terminator byte is specified by the **RecordTerminator** attribute of the Resource Definition. The record data should not contain an instance of the record terminator byte itself or else confusion will occur on rereading.

line_oriented Line-oriented records are a specific case of byte-oriented records where the terminator byte is the AIX end of line character or \n. This type of record allows the output to be processed by other AIX commands that expect end of lines such as editors.

null_terminated Null-terminated records are again a specific case of byte-oriented records where the terminator byte is the binary 0 byte. This is the C language end of string character allowing the resulting file to be processed by AIX programs that are looking for arrays of strings.

The diagram shown in Fig. 10.11 illustrates the different types of extrapartition queue formats available.

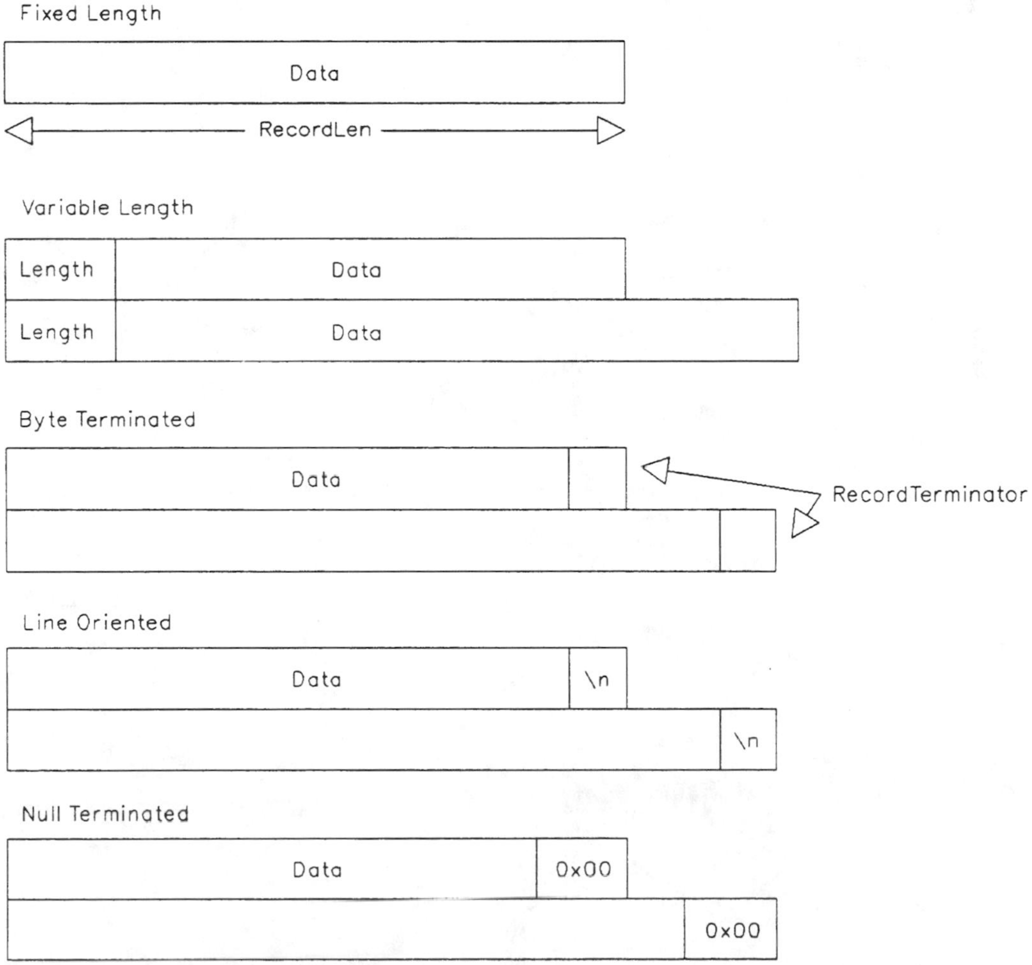

Figure 10.11 Format of extrapartition records.

No matter which record type is used for queues, the data read back from such a queue through CICS do not include any record control information such as the length or terminator byte. The data read from the queue are exactly the data that were written to the queue.

CICS/6000 Journaling

This chapter describes the facility of CICS/6000 known as *journaling*. In CICS, journaling was introduced to allow an application to log information outside the CICS environment that could be used to record changes to recoverable resources such as files. Journaling also could be used as a mechanism to act as an audit trail for the activity of applications. For example, an application could record the Social Security Number or bank account number of any updates it had processed against a customer's address or bank account balance.

In CICS environments other than CICS/6000, the journal numbered '1' is used internally for the operation of CICS itself. It is allowable to use journal '1' within a CICS/6000 application, but this could cause serious problems if the application were ported or migrated to another CICS platform. For this reason, journal '1' should not be used within a CICS/6000 application.

The following table describes the format of an individual journal record:

Offset	Length	Description
0	2	Length of the following record fields
2	2	Journal ID
4	2	The year that the record was written (e.g., 1995)
6	2	The month that the record was written (e.g., 02 = February)
8	2	The day that the record was written (e.g., 14 = 14th day of month)
10	2	The hour that the record was created (e.g., 15 = 3 P.M.)
12	2	The minute that the record was written (e.g., 47 = 47 minutes past the hour)
14	2	The second that the record was written (e.g., 13 = 13 seconds into the minute)
16	2	The specified journal type as specified by the JTYPEID on the EXEC CICS JOURNAL COMMAND
18	2	The specified user prefix length as specified by the PFXLENG option on the EXEC CICS JOURNAL COMMAND
20	2	The user data length
22	p	Prefix data as specified by the PREFIX option on the EXEC CICS JOURNAL COMMAND
22+p	u	User data

Note: In the preceding table, the date is recorded in Unix UTC, which is GMT time and not necessarily local time.

The CICS command to write a journal record is as follows:

```
EXEC CICS JOURNAL
JFILEID(data value)
JTYPEID(data value)
FROM(data areas)
[LENGTH(data value)]
[REQID(data area)]
[PREFIX(data value)
[PFXLENG(data value)]]
[STARTIO]
[WAIT]
[NOSUSPEND]
```

On other CICS systems, I/O is under the direct control of CICS, and thus the output of the journal records could be controlled and buffered by the application. The options REQID, STARTIO, WAIT, and NOSUSPEND are primarily present for compatability.

Example journal browser. The following program is an example journal file browser. When compiled, it may be used to browse the journal file specified by the file name given as the first parameter.

```c
#include <stdio.h>
struct journalRecord
{
    unsigned short journalID;
    unsigned short year;
    unsigned short month;
    unsigned short day;
    unsigned short hour;
    unsigned short minute;
    unsigned short second;
    unsigned char journalType[2];
    unsigned short prefixLength;
    unsigned short dataLength;
    unsigned char prefixData[1];
};
int main(int argc, char *argv[])

{
    FILE                *file;
    unsigned short      length;
    struct journalRecord    *record;

    /*
     * Check that a journal file was specified; print an error and exit
     * otherwise.
     */
    if (argc < 2)
    {
        fprintf(stderr, "Usage: %s fileName\n", argv[0]);
        exit(1);
    }
```

```
    /*
     * Open the journal file for reading.
     */
    file = fopen(argv[1], "rb");
    if (file = = NULL)
    {
        perror("Error opening file");
        exit(1);
    }

    /*
     * While there are more records to process ....
     */ while( fread(&length, 2, 1, file) > 0)
    {
    /*
     * Allocate enough storage for the record
    */ record = (struct journalRecord *)malloc(length);

    /*
     * Read the record into memory
     */
        fread(record, length, 1, file);

    /*
     * Display the contents of the record
     */

        printf("- Start of journal record -\n");
        printf("Journal ID: %d\n", record->journalID);
        printf("Year/Month/Day: %d/%d/%d\n",
            record->year,
            record->month,
            record->day);
        printf("Hour/Minute/Second: %d/%d/%d\n",
            record->hour,
            record->minute,
            record->second);
        printf("Journal Type: '%c%c'\n",
            record->journalType[0],
            record->journalType[1]);
        printf("User prefix length: %d\n", record->prefixLength);
        printf("User data length: %d\n", record->dataLength);
        printf("- End of journal record -\n");

        free(record);
        }
    fclose(file);
    return(0);
}
```

Application Access
to CICS/6000 Information

From within a CICS/6000 application, it is often useful to determine information about the application and about the surrounding CICS and AIX environment. CICS provides a series of commands to return information. Additionally, a data structure know as the Execution Interface Block is available to a program to determine additional information.

Using EXEC CICS ASSIGN

The CICS command EXEC CICS ASSIGN is available to be called and return many useful pieces of information about the CICS system as a whole but specifically about the program's own operating environment. The following list illustrates some of the attributes returned by this command and how they may be utilized by an application:

ABCODE   This operation returns the last ABEND code generated in the program. This may be utilized in a HANDLE ABEND command to produce additional information as to why the abend handler was called. If the abend handler is utilized to handle multiple types of abends, this value can be used to direct program logic based on the specific type of abend raised.

APPLID   This attribute returns the APPLID of the CICS/6000 region in which the program is executing. The APPLID of a CICS/6000 region is the name of the region itself. This operand may be used by an application to determine the region it is actually executing in and change logic flow. A program or transaction may execute in multiple regions based on a definition of remote in a Resource Definition, an explicit route in the program, or by being routed by one of the routing user exits.

CWALENG   This attribute returns the length of the common work area, an area of storage shared between all CICS applications within the same

CICS region. This attribute may be queried by an application to determine the size or existence of the CWA, which may not be large enough for a program's needs.

FACILITY This attribute returns the name of the CICS terminal or the conversation identifier of the terminal or communication channel against which the program is executing. If a transaction needs to know the name of its own terminal, it can execute this command to determine the value. The terminal against which a program is executing is used by programs for such purposes as creating unique, referencable temporary storage queues.

NETNAME This attribute returns the NETNAME of the terminal against which the transaction is executing. The netname may be used by the program for logging or enhanced security. The internal logic of the program may allow or disallow execution based on the netname.

OPERKEYS This attribute returns a 64-bit integer value representing the set of TSL security keys associated with the current user. This attribute may be used by a program to query the current state of keys, perhaps across a communications link.

QNAME This attribute returns the transient data queue name that caused the transaction to be started if the transaction is started by the triggering of a queue.

STARTCODE This attribute returns the reason why a transaction was started. Possible reasons include terminal entry, asynchronous start, transient data trigger, and a distribute program link. A program may use this value to handle starts from various sources.

SYSID This attribute returns the SYSID of the region in which the program is executing. This may be used by an application to explicitly route a request to the local region if a remote sysid must be supplied.

TCTUALENG This attribute returns the length of the terminal control table user area used to hold data specific to the terminal. This attribute may be used by an application to determine if a terminal user area is even defined.

TWALENG This attribute returns the length of the transaction work area.

USERID This attribute returns the name of the CICS user under which the program is actually executing.

Other options exist for this command and should be examined.

The Execution Interface Block

When a CICS program starts, a data structure known as the *Execution Interface Block* (EIB) is created. The EIB stores information about the CICS region and the transaction. The EIB may be accessed from an application to determine current values for various important attributes. The following list illustrates some of the more important fields within the EIB data structure:

EIBAID   This field contains the Attention IDentifier value of the last AID received from the terminal. The values of this field are defined as symbolic constants in the dfhaid.h file. An application can use this field to take different actions on a receive of data from the terminal based on which key was pressed to return the data. For example, an enter key may be defined to return data normally, a PF3 key to quit the program, and the clear key to request to redraw the display.

EIBCALEN   This field contains the length of the COMMAREA used to pass data from one program to another. If this field is zero, no COMMAREA is defined. Applications typically may use this field to determine if this is the first or subsequent time the program has been invoked in a pseudoconversational environment.

EIBCPOSN   This field contains the cursor position in effect the last time data were received from the terminal. Applications may use this field to perform various logic tasks based on cursor location. Usually such applications would have a model of what the screen looked like.

EIBDATE   This field contains the date a task was started or the last time an application issued a CICS ASKTIME command.

EIBFN   This field contains an encoding of the last CICS command issued by the program. Each time the program issues a new CICS command, this field is updated. This field may be used for advanced debugging.

EIBRESP   This field contains the error code returned from the last CICS command invoked. On a normal command return, the value stored here will be **0x00** or the NORMAL value. Each new command updates this field. Applications may use this field following a CICS command to test for an error condition. A set of symbolic constants is defined for all possible errors and may be specified with the **DFHRESP(value)** macro. This macro is expanded at CICS source translate time into an integer.

EIBTASKN   This field contains the CICS task number for the CICS task currently executing the program. Each new CICS task is assigned a unique task number in this field.

EIBTIME   This field contains the time at which the task was first started or the time at which the last EXEC CICS ASKTIME command was issued.

EIBTRMID   This field contains the terminal name of the currently executing program's terminal or communication ID.

EIBTRNID   This field contains the transaction name associated with the currently executing program.

Not all the fields in the EIB were discussed; the *Application Programmer's Reference Manual* should be consulted for all possible fields. Wherever possible, an equivalent EXEC CICS ASSIGN command should be utilized as opposed to direct access to the EIB. Using ASSIGN promotes higher level language programming that is more structured and readable.

For C language applications, the EIB is not immediately addressable, and a pointer to the EIB must be created. The CICS command EXEC CICS ADDRESS EIB(pointer) should be used to obtain addressability. The C language data type DFHEIBLK describes the layout of the EIB. A pointer variable called **dfheiptr** is included in translation and may be used in the ADDRESS command, e.g.,

```
EXEC CICS ADDRESS EIB(dfheiptr)
```

Failure to gain addressability to the EIB in a C language application may cause unexpected failures when examining RESP codes from CICS commands as the RESP code returned from a command is stored in the EIB.

Determining AIX Information

Execution of a CICS/6000 program occurs within an AIX process environment. Such programs can make use of AIX-supplied function calls and facilities to obtain status of the operating system or other non-CICS applications. If such calls are to be used, thought must be given to the portability of the application. Inclusion of AIX- or UNIX-specific calls may make the application nonportable to other CICS environments. Calls made to AIX functions also must be thread safe or else they may interfere with the operation of CICS itself.

A CICS application can call AIX functions such as getrusage() to obtain the CPU and other AIX process utilization for performance tuning. The application may call file access functions such as stat() and access() to determine information about AIX-defined files in the AIX file system.

An application also may interrogate the settings of AIX environment variables using the AIX-supplied getenv() function. Applications can access the values of variables and change their business logic based on these values.

AIX environment variables accessible to a CICS region must either be set within the AIX standard environment file /etc/environment or in the region specific environment file /var/cics_regions/<region>/environment.

13

CICS/6000 User Exits

CICS/6000 provides a mechanism by which programs may be written that are given control by the system before, during, or after some CICS operation. These programs are called *user exits*. A user exit may exist already and is called for some CICS function; these exits may be replaced by programs written to perform some more specific tasks. These exists are called *replaceable exits*. The other type of exit programs are those which are not necessarily present but may be added to perform additional tasks.

This chapter describes the user exits available within CICS/6000 and provides guidance on how to write new ones.

Terminal Installation

CICS/6000 terminals are the primary devices for submitting transaction start requests and for interacting with the user. When a terminal is connected to CICS/6000, it is entered into the running CICS/6000 region in an internal table. On host CICS systems, this table is known as the *terminal control table* (TCT). The equivalent table in a CICS/6000 system is known as the *Workstation Definitions* (WD). This internal table holds the characteristics and definitions for all currently connected terminals. In addition to terminals that have been installed while the system is running, predefined terminals known as *hard-defined terminals* are also held in the table. Terminals that have been connected during the running of the system are known as *autoinstalled terminals*.

When a terminal is connected, it is assigned a four-character terminal name by CICS. These terminal names are known as the *terminal identifiers* or *TERMIDs*. Hard-installed terminals are allocated constant TERMIDs, while autoinstalled terminals are assigned TERMIDs dynamically. The selection of the TERMID is governed by the network name of the terminal being installed. On an SNA network associated with CICS on the host, the network names of terminals are always unique. For CICS/6000, network names must be specified by the terminals themselves (cicsterm and cicsteld). If they are not specified, the network names are dynamically generated and guaranteed to be unique.

The algorithm used to generate the TERMID for an autoinstalled terminal is governed by a replaceable program called the *autoinstall user exit*. This program is called during the dynamic installation of a terminal when connected and again when the terminal is disconnected. Parameters specifying the netname and models are passed in a COMMAREA to the program that will execute as a CICS task.

When a terminal is autoinstalled, a list of one or more model definitions characterizing the attributes of the terminal to be installed is included in the COMMAREA. One of these models must be returned by the autoinstall exit along with the TERMID. The attributes of a terminal model include

- The color of error messages
- Transaction and resource security keys for the terminal
- Number of lines and columns
- Uppercase translation required
- Netname for hard-installed terminals
- Model entry (**DevType**)

The CICS/6000-supplied autoinstall exit

The purpose of the autoinstall program is to select the TERMID and the model to be used to select attributes of the autoinstalled terminal. The CICS/6000-supplied exit uses the first two and last two characters of the netname passed from the clients or generated as unqiue with CICS/6000 as the four-character TERMID. The model chosen is the first model in the list of models contained in the COMMAREA.

Replacing the autoinstall-supplied exit

The autoinstall exit program may be replaced with an alternate program. This program must select a model and generate a TERMID just like the CICS/6000-supplied program. In addition, it may perform any user-driven logic. This logic could include

- Additional logging information including the CICS user name that is associated with the terminal, the date and time, and the duration for which the terminal is installed.
- Setting the TERMID to known values. The TERMID could be obtained through algorithms or by making calls via TCP/IP sockets or DCE RPC calls to other applications.
- Restricting the number of concurrently installed terminals. The autoinstall exit allows terminals to be rejected during the install. A count of currently

installed terminals could be incremented when a terminal is installed and decremented when the terminals are deinstalled.

The autoinstall exit program supplied with CICS/6000 is called *DFHCHATX*. Autoinstall exit programs are defined in the CICS/6000 Program Definitions (PD). If DFHCHATX is replaced with a new program, this new program will be called during the autoinstall processing. If multiple autoinstall exits are required, the name of the program to be called during autoinstall processing may be specified with the CEMT-supplied transaction.

```
SET AUTOINSTALL
STATUS:  RESULTS - OVERTYPE TO MODIFY

 Aut  Pro( DFHCHATX )                                   NORMAL




                                              APPLID=<region>
 RESPONSE:  NORMAL
 PF 1 HELP      3 END                    9 MSG
```

A new version of the autoinstall program should accept the same format COMMAREA as expected by the supplied exit. The new program also should return the data expected by the running CICS system.

CICS/6000 supplies a C language header file called `cics_aut.h` in the CICS include directory. This file contains definitions for the layout of the COMMAREA passed in a terminal install and uninstall. Figure 13.1 illustrates the autoinstall format.

The fields contained in these definitions are as follows:

Operation   This is a byte value describing the operation to be performed. The ASCII character **0** defines an install operation, while the character **1** defines an uninstall operation. Note that these are character codes and not byte values.

FullWord2   This is a pointer to the netname passed.

FullWord3   This is a pointer to the list of install model names passed.

FullWord4   This is a pointer to the data to be returned by the autoinstall exit.

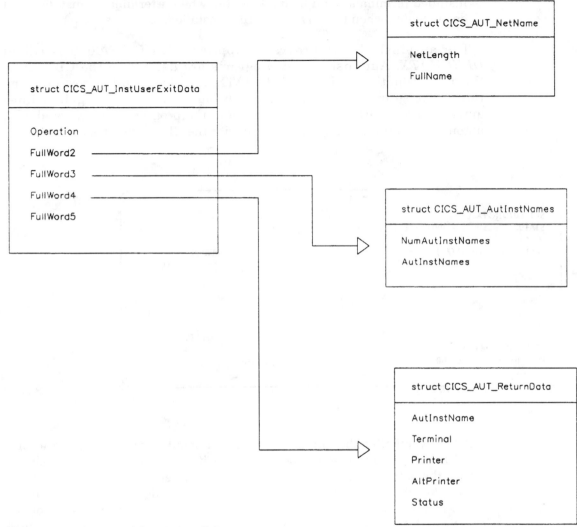

Figure 13.1 Description of the autoinstall format.

FullWord5   This is for compatibility with the CICS host autoinstall exit and may be ignored.

NetLength   This is the length in bytes of the netname contained in the **FullName** parameter.

FullName   This is the netname passed to the autoinstall exit. It may be a maximum of 8 bytes long.

NumAutInstNames   This is the number of install models in the **AutInstNames** list.

AutInstNames   This is an array of 8-byte install model names.

AutInstName   This is the 8-byte name of the install model selected for this install.

Terminal   Not used.

Printer   Not used.

AltPrinter   Not used.

Status   This is a status byte indicating success or failure. The byte value **0** indicates success. The value **1** indicates failure. If the value **1** is returned, the terminal requesting the install will be rejected.

If a terminal name (TERMID) is returned that has the same name as a current terminal in the WD table, the terminal being installed will be failed. Only one terminal at a time with a particular TERMID may be installed.

During a terminal deinstall, the autoinstall exit program is called again; the format of the COMMAREA passed to the program is illustrated in Fig. 13.2.

Generating known TERMIDs

Many CICS applications require that TERMIDs be assigned to particular terminals. This may be used to restrict certain CICS programs to only execute on well-known terminals. The CICS application could determine its own TERMID from the EIB or from an EXEC CICS ASSIGN command. This TERMID could be compared within a program's logic for correctness.

To be guaranteed a known TERMID, a netname may be specified with either **cicsterm** or **cicsteld.** This netname must correspond to a hard-installed terminal definition made in the region Workstation Definitions (WD) with the same netname specified. The TERMID included in the WD table will be used when an install takes place for a terminal with the given netname.

Using cicsterm.   When cicsterm is invoked without a netname (the -n parameter), a netname is generated by cicsterm and passed to the CICS/6000 region for use in the autoinstall process. The netname is composed of the first four characters of the AIX hostname on which cicsterm is executed and the last four characters of the AIX tty name of the terminal in which it will perform.

```
struct CICS_AUT_UnInstUserExitData

Operation

Terminal
```

Figure 13.2   Format of deinstall COMMAREA.

If the `-n netname` is included in the invocation of cicsterm, the netname supplied will be used instead of the generated version. This netname must have been defined to CICS/6000 previously in a WD.

Using cicsteld.   Unlike cicsterm, cicsteld allows the CICS/6000 region to generate a random, unique netname to be passed to the autoinstall process unless it is invoked with the `-n netname` parameter. This is of limited value to cicsteld because it is usually configured to AIX inetd and hence will be invoked multiple times with the same parameters. An attempt to install multiple terminals with the same netname is invalid and will cause the second terminal to fail its installation.

To use cicsteld to specify known netnames and hence known TERMIDs, it is necessary to wrap the invocation of cicsteld into an AIX shell script that causes the actual execution of cicsteld to have different netnames supplied.

An example of how this may be used would be to assign a known TERMID to a CICS/6000 terminal installed through cicsteld from specific personal computers or workstations. When the telnet client connects to cicsteld over TCP/IP, it is possible for the application receiving the initial connect request to determine the TCP/IP address of the TCP/IP host executing the telnet client. The TCP/IP address could be used as the netname during the cicsteld terminal autoinstall. The result of this mechanism would be to prevent multiple terminals from being installed from the same personal computer simultaneously as well as to provide a constant TERMID for each of those terminals.

Client Autoinstall User Exit

When a non-AIX CICS client such as a PC CICS client makes a request to a CICS/6000 system, an entry is added dynamically to the Communication Definitions table stored in memory for runtime usage. This is the internal representation of the Communication Definitions (CD) database. The client passes a netname or APPLID parameter to the CICS/6000 region to identify the client. A CICS Client Autoinstall exit is provided to allow the client to be installed or rejected. The exit also allows specification of the four-character SYSID parameter used by CICS and to modify the APPLID. Knowing the SYSID allows incoming transactions to be debugged using the CICS-supplied diagnostic transaction CEDF, the exit is the program to be executed by the CICS-defined DFHCCINX program. The default program allows CICS to specify the SYSID based on the APPLID passed. The default algorithm uses the first two and last two characters of the APPLID as the SYSID. A user-replaceable program may be written to change the default logic. A sample CICS Client Autoinstall program is found in the `/usr/lpp/cics/src/samples/client` directory.

The exit passes a COMMAREA storage structure that contains the following fields:

Name	Offset	Length	Description
Length	0	2	Length of the COMMAREA data used for the autoinstall
Type	2	1	INSTALL (**0**) or UNINSTALL (**1**) request
ApplidLen	3	2	Length of the APPLID passed from the client
Applid	5	8	APPLID the client passed. The exit may modify this value.
SysidLen	13	2	Length of the SYSID returned
Sysid	15	4	SYSID to be used for this client
ReturnCode	19	1	OK (**0**) or REJECT (**1**)

The layout of the COMMAREA is further illustrated in Fig. 13.3.

```
struct CICS_CLIENT_InstUserExitData
{
    unsigned short    Length;
    unsigned char     Type;
    unsigned short    ApplidLen;
    char              Applid[8];
    unsigned short    SysidLen;
    char              Sysid[4];
    unsigned char     ReturnCode;
};
```

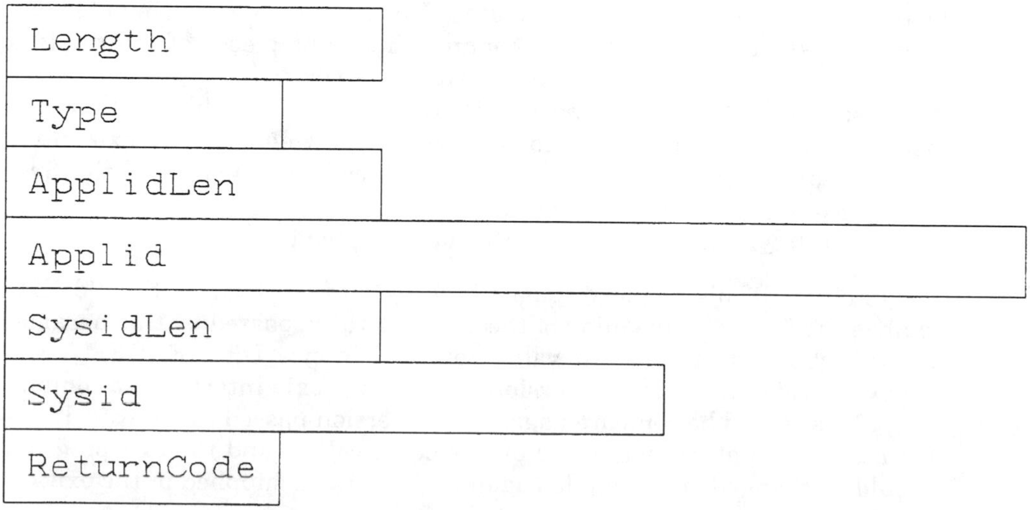

Figure 13.3 COMMAREA layout for DFHCCINX exit.

The exit may be used to allow or deny installation of the client or modify the SYSID value or APPLID value. If the exit modifies the APPLID or SYSID to a value already contained within the communication database, the client connection will fail.

The exit is also invoked when a client terminates the connection.

The Generic User Exit

CICS/6000 provides an architected user exit interface. This interface provides a consistent and extensible way for IBM to provide additional exits and allows multiple exits to refer to the same programs.

A number of user exits are already supplied in CICS/6000, and these include

- UE014015   Task end user exit
- UE052017   Dump control user exit
- UE014025   Dynamic transaction routing user exit
- UE015050   Dynamic DPL user exit

Each of these user exits is designed to integrate with the Generic User exit interface.

A Generic User exit is implemented in the C programming language. A C source file containing the logic and function interface must be compiled and defined as a user exit program. This program will then be called whenever the user exit function is invoked.

The Generic User exit header control block

The first parameter passed to the Generic User exit interface is a pointer to a C language structure that contains many important pieces of information relating to the task or program that is invoking the exit.

CICS supplies a C language header file called `cicsue.h` that contains the constant and type definitions used throughout the Generic User exit interface. The data type `cics_UE_header_t` defines the structure of the first parameter passed to each exit program.

The `cics_UE_header_t` contains the following fields:

`UE_Version`   This is the version of the user exit interface. Should IBM change the format or meaning of the exit, the value passed by this parameter will changed. A constant value specified in cics_UE_HEADER_VERSION provides the current version of the user exit interface at compile time. This should be compared against the version passed in the exit. If different, a different version of the exit is being called, and the exit program should be changed or recompiled against the version supplied in the exit.

`UE_ProcessId`   This is the AIX process number for the CICS application server (cicsas) that is executing the task.

`UE_Thread`   This is the DCE thread identifier for the thread that is running the user exit program.

`UE_Number`   This is the number of the user exit. This will be the value defined in the Program Definition (PD) resource for the exit.

`UE_Name`   This is the NULL terminated string name for the user exit being called.

`UE_TransId`   This is the NULL terminated string name for the transaction that is invoking the user exit.

`UE_TaskNo`   This is the CICS task identifier for the task running the user exit.

`UE_Workarea`   This is an area of storage shared by all user exits called by the same CICS task. It may be used to pass data from one exit program to another for the same task.

`UE_Workarea_Size_t`   This is the length in bytes of the UE_Workarea storage provided by the user exit interface.

`UE_TraceOn`   This parameter allows the call to the exit plus its parameters to be traced by the CICS trace facilities if they are enabled. When called, this parameter has the value `UE_No` but may be set to `UE_Yes` before return from the user exit program.

The second parameter passed to the user exit function by CICS is a pointer to exit specific data. The format and meaning of the data will vary by the user exit being invoked.

Building a User Exit Program

A user exit program must be written in the C programming language and has a number of restrictions placed on it. Like all CICS programs, it must be *thread safe*. Specifically, it must not block the AIX process, cause the process to exit, or change the state of its process-wide environment. Additionally, the program must not

- Make any EXEC CICS calls.
- Change the state of the AIX process.

The program should be compiled with the xlc_r version of the C compiler to ensure that the thread-safe properties are adhered to.

Defining the exit to CICS

Each architected exit program has a name and an exit identifier code. The exit name is of the form UEmmmmNN, where mmmm refers to the class of exit and NN is the exit identifier code.

Each exit program is defined to CICS as a separate CICS program definition. If the **UserExit** value is not **0,** the exit will be installed and will be called corresponding to the two-digit exit identifier code. For example, when defining the Transaction Routing exit, its name is UE014025 and its identifier code is 25. When a CICS program definition with **UserExit** = **25** is specified, any transaction that has the **Dynamic** = **yes** attribute set in the Transaction Definitions will cause the exit program to be called.

A single exit program may be defined multiple times, each with a different **UserExit** value. For each different exit value, the exit program will be called. In this case, it is the responsibility of the exit program logic to determine how the specific exit code should be processed. When compiling an exit program, the program usually does not have a C language main() function. The entry point into the program should be defined as the user exit function to be called when the exit is invoked. The entry point into a program may be specified at compile time by specifying the C compiler flag -e function_name.

An example AIX Makefile is shown in Fig. 13.4.

Task End User Exit: UE014015

This user exit program is called at the end of a CICS task. If the task ends normally or ends abnormally with an ABEND, the task is still called. The exit-specific data are defined in the cics_UE014015_t, which is a C language structure defined in the cics_ue.h include file. This structure contains the following fields:

UE_Version   Version number of the exit program interface. Initially **1**.

UE_Terminationtype   The type of task termination. This will either be **0** to indicate a normal task termination or **1** to indicate an abend occured.

This exit may be used to perform an additional action in the event of an abnormal task termination. The action could be to signal an administrator by AIX mail or log additional information to a message log.

```
# Build the user exit executable called ueprogram from the C
# source file called ueprogram.c which has the function "ueentry"
# defined within.
build: ueprogram

ueprogram: ueprogram.c
    xlc_r -o ueprogram -I /usr/lpp/cics/include ueprogram.c -e ueentry

# Install the program into the region specified by the CICSREGION
# environment variable.  The <exitno> parameter to UserExit should be
# changed to the specific exit number for the exit defined.
install:
    cicsadd -c pd -r $(CICSREGION)
        UserExit=<exitno> \
        PathName=$(PWD)/ueprogram
```

Figure 13.4 Compiling a user exit.

Dump Control User Exit: UE052017

This user exit is called whenever a request to dump a portion of CICS is made. The exit-specific data are defined in the `cics_UE052017_t`, which is a C language structure defined in the `cics_ue.h` include file. This structure contains the following fields:

`UE_Version`   Version number of the exit program interface. Initially **1.**

`UE_User`   This is the CICS userid that requested the dump.

`UE_Term`   The is is the four-character terminal identifier for the task that invoked the dump request. If the dump was not requested by a terminal task, this value is "".

`UE_Prog`   This is the name of the CICS program that requested the dump.

`UE_Dumpcode`   This is the dump code associated with the dump.

`UE_DumpReason`   This is the reason that the dump occurred.

`UE_CWA`   Pointer to CWA.

`UE_CWALEN`   Length of CWA.

`UE_TCATWA`   Pointer to TWA.

`UE_TCATWA_LEN`   Length of TWA.

`UE_TransDump`   For transaction dumps, specifies the **TransDump** field in the Transaction Definitions.

There are two possible return codes from this exit that effect the outcome of the dump request:

`UE_normal`   Continue processing the dump request.

`UE_bypass`   Suppress the creation of the dump.

Dynamic Transaction Routing User Exit: UE014025

This exit is called whenever a transaction is invoked which has the **Dynamic = yes** attribute defined in the Transaction Definitions (TD) table. The exit allows the dynamic selection of the CICS region, program name, and transaction name. When the exit is called, the values contained in the local transaction definition are supplied. These values may be changed within the exit and are acted on when the exit returns. The exit may be called again optionally for the same transaction routing request when the transaction ends normally or abnormally and in the event that the routing of the transaction failed because of a connection failure to the remote CICS system.

The exit may be used to provide a workload-balancing mechanism. The selection of the remote CICS system on which to execute the transaction may be based on the load on various candidate CICS systems, the one chosen being the least utilized.

The exit specific data are defined in the `cics_UE014025_t`, which is a C language structure defined in the `cics_ue.h` include file. This structure contains the following fields:

`UE_Version`   Version number of the exit program interface. Initially **1.**

`UE_Dyrfunc`   The reason for the invocation of this user exit; possible values include

- UE_ROUTESEL (0)   Transaction routing.
- UE_RTESELERR (1)   Error in route selection; see the `UE_Dyrerror` field for more information.
- UE_ROUTETERM (2)   Previously routed transaction ended normally.
- UE_RTEABEND (4)   Previously routed transaction ended abnormally.

`UE_Dyropter`   Should the user exit be reinvoked when the task terminates? Possible values are `UE_No` and `UE_Yes`. The default value is `UE_No`. This field may be modified before the exit ends.

`UE_Dyrretry`   Should the user exit be reinvoked when a routing error occurs? Possible values are `UE_No` and `UE_Yes`. The default value is `UE_No`. This field may be modified before the exit ends.

`UE_Dyrlclsys`   Local SYSID value.

`UE_Dyrlclapl`   Local APPLID name.

`UE_Dyrprog`   The initial program name for the transaction taken from the **ProgName** attribute of the Transaction Definition. This parameter may be changed to execute a different program before the exit terminates.

`UE_Dyrsysid`   This field contains the name of the CICS system (SYSID) on which the transaction is to execute. This may be changed before the exit terminates to select an alternate SYSID.

`UE_Dyrcount`   Count of the number of times the user exit has been called to route this transaction.

`UE_Dyrerror`   Error code if the `UE_Dyrfunc` value is UE_RTESELERR. Possible values for this field are

- UE_SYSID_UNKNOWN (0)   The SYSID returned in a previous call to the exit is not defined on the CICS region. The SYSID returned is supplied in the `UE_Dyrsysid` field and may be changed to a new value.
- UE_SYSID_OUT_SRV (1)   The SYSID returned in a previous call to the exit is not currently in service. The SYSID returned is supplied in the `UE_Dyrsysid` field and may be changed to a new value.
- UE_CON_FAILURE (2)   The SYSID used produced a connection failure and may be retried.

- UE_NO_ERROR (3)   There is no error.

UE_Dyrabcde   ABEND code if the transaction abends.

The possible return codes from the dynamic routing exit are as follows:

UE_Normal   Continue processing the routing request.

UE_Terminate   Terminate the routing request without a transaction ABEND being raised.

UE_Term_Abend   Terminate the routing request with an ABEND.

When invoked, the exit can be used to change the program name, transaction name, or remote CICS system on which it should execute. When first invoked for the starting of a new transaction, the UE_Dyrfunc field will be set to UE_ROUTESEL and will modify the CICS system (UE_Dyrsysid), program (UE_Dyrprog), and transaction name (UE_Dyrtran). The exit also may set the UE_Dyropter field to indicate whether or not the transaction should be reinvoked on normal or abnormal termination of the transaction. The UE_Dyrretry field also may be set to indicate whether or not the exit should be reinvoked if an error occurs with routing.

An area of CICS-maintained storage is supplied and pointed to by the UE_Dyruser field of a length contained in the UE_Dyrusersize field that is

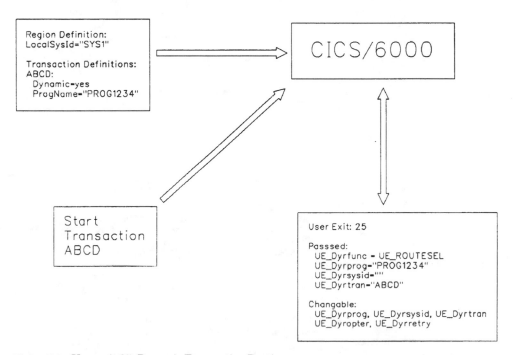

Figure 13.5 User exit 25: Dynamic Transaction Routing.

available to store transaction instance–specific data used between the start and end of a transaction. Figure 13.5 illustrates an invocation of the user exit.

The following program shows a sample user exit that displays all the parameters passed to the exit.

```c
#include <stdio.h>
#include <cicstype.h>
#include <cicsue.h>

cics_UE_Return_t   UE014025(  cics_UE_Header_t   *UE_header,
                              cics_UE014025_t    *UE_specific)
{
    FILE *file;

    file = stderr;

    fprintf(file, "+------------------------------+\n");
    fprintf(file, "| UE014025: Dynamic Transaction Routing |\n");
    fprintf(file, "+------------------------------+\n");
    fprintf(file, "Version:            %d\n", UE_header->UE_Version);
    fprintf(file, "ProcessID:          %d\n", UE_header->UE_ProcessId);
    fprintf(file, "Thread:             %d\n", UE_header->UE_Thread);
    fprintf(file, "Number:             %d\n", UE_header->UE_Number);
    fprintf(file, "Name:               %s\n", UE_header->UE_Name);
    fprintf(file, "TransId:            %s\n", UE_header->UE_TransId);
    fprintf(file, "Task No:            %d\n", UE_header->UE_TaskNo);
    fprintf(file, "Work Area:          %p\n", UE_header->UE_Workarea);
    fprintf(file, "Work Area Size:     %d\n", UE_header->UE_WorkareaSize);
    fprintf(file, "UE Version:         %d\n", UE_specific->UE_Version);
    fprintf(file, "Abend Code:         %s\n", UE_specific->UE_Dyrabcde);
    fprintf(file, "Count:              %d\n", UE_specific->UE_Dyrcount);
    fprintf(file, "User area length:   %d\n", UE_specific->UE_Dyrusersize);
    switch(UE_specific->UE_Dyrfunc)
    {
        case UE_ROUTESEL:
            fprintf(file, "Function: UE_ROUTESEL\n");
            break;
        case UE_RTESELERR:
            fprintf(file, "Function: UE_RTESELERR\n");
            fprintf(file, ">Error: ");
            switch(UE_specific->UE_Dyrerror)
            {
                case UE_SYSID_UNKNOWN:
                    fprintf(stderr, "Unknown sysid\n");
                break;
                case UE_SYSID_OUT_SRV:
                    fprintf(stderr, "Sysid outservice\n");
                    break;
                case UE_CON_FAILURE:
                    fprintf(stderr, "Connection failure\n");
                    break;
                case UE_NO_ERROR:
                    fprintf(stderr, "No error\n");
                    break;
                default:
                    fprintf(stderr, "Unknown error code: %d\n",
                        UE_specific->UE_Dyrerror);
                break;
            }
            break;
```

```
        case UE_ROUTETERM:
            fprintf(file, "Function: UE_ROUTETERM\n");
        break;
        case UE_RTEABEND:
            fprintf(file, "Function: UE_RTEABEND\n");
            break;
    }
    fprintf(file, "Local System:      %s\n", UE_specific->UE_Dyrlclsys);
    fprintf(file, "Local APPLID:      %s\n", UE_specific->UE_Dyrlclapl);
    fprintf(file, "Initial Prog:      %s\n", UE_specific->UE_Dyrprog);
    fprintf(file, "SysId:             %s\n", UE_specific->UE_Dyrsysid);
    fprintf(file, "Remote Tranid:     %s\n", UE_specific->UE_Dyrtran);
    fprintf(file, "Reinvoke at end?  %s\n",
        UE_specific->UE_Dyropter = = UE_No?"No":"Yes");
    fprintf(file, "Reinvoke at route err? %s\n",
        UE_specific->UE_Dyrretry = = UE_No?"No":"Yes");
    if (UE_specific->UE_Dyrcount>4)
    {
        return(UE_Term_Abend);
    }
        return(UE_Normal);
}
```

Dynamic DPL User Exit: UE015050

The Dynamic Distributed Program Link exit is called whenever a link to a CICS program is invoked via an EXEC CICS LINK command. The exit also can be reinvoked to determine the outcome of the link. Other than installing the user exit, no other resource changes are required to take advantage of the exit. Since the exit is called on every LINK command, it should be as efficient as possible.

The exit also may be used to handle an attempted link to a program that is not defined.

The exit may be used to provide a workload-balancing mechanism. The selection of the remote CICS system on which to execute the program may be based on the load on various candidate CICS systems, the one chosen being the least utilized.

The exit-specific data are defined in the `cics_UE015050_t` C language data structure defined in the `cics_ue.h` include file. This structure contains the following fields:

UE_Version   Version number of the exit program interface. Initially **1.**

UE_Dplcomptr   A pointer to the COMMAREA passed on the CICS LINK.

UE_Dplcomlgth   The length of the COMMAREA data passed on the CICS LINK.

UE_Dplcwaptr   A pointer to the CICS Common Work Area (CWA).

UE_Cplcwalgth   The length of the CICS Common Work Area (CWA).

UE_Dplfunc   The reason that the exit was invoked. Possible values include

- UE_LINKSEL (0)   Selection of the destination of the CICS LINK.
- UE_LINKSELUNKNOWN (1)   Selection of the destination of the CICS LINK when the program is not defined in the Program Definitions (PD).
- UE_LINKTERM (2)   Indication of a successful return from a previous LINK command where the DPL exit was requested to be re-invoked on completion by the UE_Dplopter field.
- UE_LINKABEND (3)   Indication of an unsuccessful return from a previous LINK command where the DPL exit was requested to be reinvoked on completion by the UE_Dplopter field.

UE_Dpllclsys   The system identifier of the local CICS system.

USE_Dpllclapl   The APPLID of the local CICS system.

UE_Dplopter   Should this exit be reinvoked when the linked program ends either normally or abnormally? Possible values are UE_No to specify that the exit should not be reinvoked and UE_Yes to specify that the exit should be reinvoked. This value may be changed before returning from the exit. The default value is UE_No.

UE_Dplprog   The name of the CICS program that is being linked. This value may be changed before returning from the exit.

UE_Dplsysid   The SYSID name of the CICS system on which the program should be executed. This value may be changed before returning from the exit.

UE_Dpltptr   A pointer to the Terminal Control Table User Area (TCTUA).

UE_Dpltlgth   The length of the Terminal Control Table User Area (TCTUA).

UE_Dplmirtran   The name of the mirror transaction on the remote system. This value may be changed before returning from the exit.

UE_Dpluser   A pointer to storage that the exit program can use to save state information about this link request. If the UE_Dplopter value is set to UE_Yes, any data saved in this memory area will be passed back to the reinvoked DPL exit when the link request completes.

UE_Dplusersize   The length of the storage area associated with the link.

The possible return codes that may be returned from the exit program are as follows:

UE_Normal   The exit has completed, and the link should continue.

UE_ProgramNotKnown   The program is unknown and has not been handled. Returning this value will result in an APCT ABEND (Program not found).

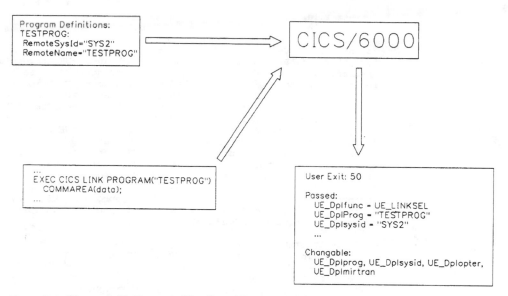

Figure 13.6 User exit 50: Dynamic Distributed Program Link.

When invoked, the exit can be used to change the program name, SYSID of the remote CICS system, and the mirror transaction used to start the program. The mirror transaction passed to the exit in the UE_Dplmirtran field usually will be blank, specifying that the default mirror transaction (CPMI) should be used. If this field is changed, the transaction specified should have the same characteristics as CPMI; specifically, the program invoked by the transaction should be DFHMIRS.

The name of the program that is to be executed also can be changed by modifying the UE_Dplprog field. If the program being linked is not defined in the Program Definition (PD) of the local CICS system and no SYSID(...) option was specified on the EXEC CICS LINK command, the UE_Dplfunc field will be set to UE_LINKUNKNOWN. It is the responsibility of the exit function to either rename the program or select a CICS region on which the program is defined. Figure 13.6 illustrates an invocation of the user exit.

The following program shows a sample user exit that displays all the parameters passed to the exit:

```
#include <stdio.h>
#include <cicstype.h>
#include <cicsue.h>

cics_UE_Return_t  UE014050(  cics_UE_Header_t  *UE_header,
                             cics_UE015050_t   *UE_specific)
{
    FILE *file;

    file = stderr;
```

```
fprintf(file, "+----------------------- +\n");
fprintf(file, "| UE014050: Dynamic Program Link |\n");
fprintf(file, "+----------------------- +\n");
fprintf(file, "Version:          %d\n", UE_header->UE_Version);
fprintf(file, "ProcessID:        %d\n", UE_header->UE_ProcessId);
fprintf(file, "Thread:           %d\n", UE_header->UE_Thread);
fprintf(file, "Number:           %d\n", UE_header->UE_Number);
fprintf(file, "Name:             %s\n", UE_header->UE_Name);
fprintf(file, "TransId:          %s\n", UE_header->UE_TransId);
fprintf(file, "Task No:          %d\n", UE_header->UE_TaskNo);
fprintf(file, "Work Area:        %p\n", UE_header->UE_Workarea);
fprintf(file, "Work Area Size:   %d\n", UE_header->UE_WorkareaSize);
fprintf(file, "UE Version:       %d\n", UE_specific->UE_Version);
fprintf(file, "Commarea         %p\n", UE_specific->UE_Dplcomptr);
fprintf(file, "Commarea length:  %d\n", UE_specific->UE_Dplcomlgth);
fprintf(file, "Program:          %s\n", UE_specific->UE_Dplprog);
fprintf(file, "Sysid:            %s\n", UE_specific->UE_Dplsysid);
fprintf(file, "Mirror Tran:      %s\n", UE_specific->UE_Dplmirtran);
switch(UE_specific->UE_Dplfunc)
{
    case UE_LINKSEL:
        fprintf(file, "Function: UE_LINKSEL\n");
        break;
    case UE_LINKUNKNOWN:
        fprintf(file, "Function: UE_LINKUNKNOWN\n");
        break;
    case UE_LINKTERM:
        fprintf(file, "Function: UE_LINKTERM\n");
        break;
    case UE_LINKABEND:
        fprintf(file, "Function: UE_LINKABEND\n");
        break;
}
fprintf(file, "Local System:    %s\n", UE_specific->UE_Dpllclsys);
fprintf(file, "Local APPLID:    %s\n", UE_specific->UE_Dpllclapl);
fprintf(file, "Reinvoke at end?  %s\n",
    UE_specific->UE_Dplopter = = UE_No?"No":"Yes");
fprintf(file, "Size of user storage: %d\n", UE_specific->UE_Dplusersize);
return(UE_Normal);
}
```

A suitable AIX Makefile for building and installing the user exit is shown below:

```
CC = xlc_r

ue: ue.c
$(CC) -o ue -D_POSIX_SOURCE -e UE014050 -I /usr/lpp/cics/include ue.c

install:
    cicsadd -c pd -r $(CICSREGION) UE014050 \
        UserExitNumber = 50 \
        PathName = $(PWD)/ue

    runtime:
        cicsupdate -c pd -r $(CICSREGION) -R UE014050
```

CICS/6000 Communications

CICS provides functions to allow it to communicate with other CICS family members. This communication may be used to distribute work from a local CICS region to a remote CICS region. There are many circumstances in which this may be very advantageous. Data that are being manipulated by a CICS region may reside in a remote CICS region. Instead of copying the data to the local CICS system, it may be accessed remotely. Alternatively, requests may be sent to a remote CICS region for processing because the data are logically owned and administered by that remote region.

CICS Connectivity Options

Before CICS/6000 can send requests to a remote CICS system or receive requests from a remote CICS system, connectivity must be achieved between the local CICS system and the remote CICS system. This may be over either the TCP/IP protocol or over the SNA communication protocol. Selecting which protocol to use will be based on the type of CICS systems with which connectivity is required. If the remote system is another CICS/6000, TCP/IP will probably be used. CICS/6000 is able to use the Encina Peer-to-Peer Communications functionality to allow SNA-like flows to be transmitted over TCP/IP. Currently, if TCP/IP is used, the partner may only be another CICS/6000 system or an AIX application that is coded to utilize the Encina PPC functionality. This is described in "Using Encina PPC Executive with DTP" later in this chapter.

When using TCP/IP, CICS/6000 regions that wish to communicate with each other must be in the same DCE cell. This is required because the communication between the regions, although carried over TCP/IP, utilizes DCE RPC as the higher-level transport.

For all other CICS systems such as CICS/ESA, CICS/MVS, CICS OS/2, and others, the connectivity protocol must be SNA.

CICS/6000 provides two distinct access methods to the SNA protocol. The first type is termed *local SNA*. With this method of SNA communication, the CICS/6000 product communicates directly with the SNA Server product to achieve communication over SNA. Local SNA supports SyncLevel 1 communication only. The other type of CICS communication over SNA involves the use of the Encina PPC Gateway product. Using the Gateway allows full SyncLevel 2 communication to be achieved. Which one is used will depend on the synchronization level, desired use of PPC Gateway, and availability of the SNA Server product. Figures 14.1 through 14.3 illustrate the different CICS communication types available.

The two methods provide the same access over SNA, but only one method provides SyncLevel 2 capability. "CICS Synchronization Level" (later in this chapter) describes CICS SyncLevel processing.

Defining a TCP/IP Connection

Defining a TCP/IP connection between two CICS/6000 regions is the simplest communications configuration. CICS ISC between two CICS/6000 regions can be used for testing or development of ISC applications that will eventually be distributed between various CICS platforms. CICS/6000 ISC over TCP/IP is also very fast, allowing production CICS ISC to be performed easily. ISC over TCP/IP also provides full SyncLevel 2 connectivity, guaranteeing data consistency between two CICS regions.

For two CICS/6000 regions to perform ISC functions, they must both be able to reach each other by TCP/IP protocol and both be registered as members of the same DCE cell.

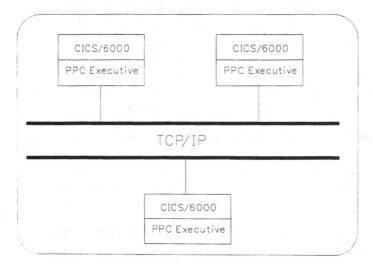

Figure 14.1   TCP/IP ISC.

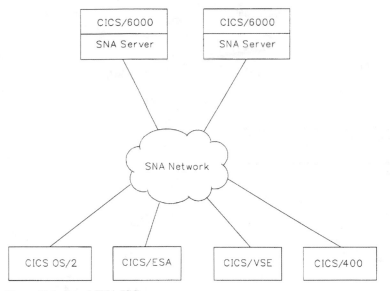

Figure 14.2   Local SNA ISC.

To configure CICS ISC between these regions, each region must have a Communication Definition (CD) entry defining the connection to the other region. The communication attributes that are required for TCP/IP communication are

Communication Definition Key   The name of the communication entry is the one- to four-character SYSID that CICS uses to refer to the remote region. Although not necessary, it is good practice to define the same SYSID value as the remote regions **LocalSysId** attribute in the Region Definition (RD) on the remote region.

RemoteSysType   The type of communication to be used between the two regions. For TCP/IP communication, this value should be **TCP.** For SNA connections, the value **SNA** should be used.

RemoteLUName   The name of the remote CICS/6000 region. This is the name that the remote region will use to advertise itself within DCE CDS. A CICS region allows the specification of an alternate LU name with the **LocalLUName** attribute in the Region Definition (RD). This attribute is only applicable when using SNA connectivity.

RemoteNetworkName   The name of the logical network on which the remote CICS region believes that it is accessible.

Figure 14.4 illustrates resource configuration for two CICS/6000 regions in the same DCE cell that wish to communicate with each other over TCP/IP.

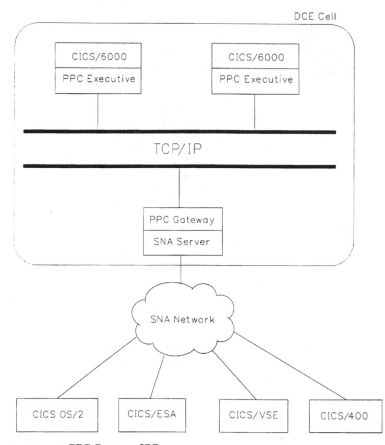

Figure 14.3 PPC Gateway ISC.

Defining an SNA Connection

Access to the SNA network is provided by the IBM AIX SNA Server product. SNA Server provides the services for an application to make SNA requests and for the administrator to define the appropriate SNA definitions.

To communicate over SNA, two possible alternatives exist: CICS/6000 can make SNA calls directly by calling the SNA Server, or it may make requests to the Encina Peer-to-Peer Gateway product (PPC Gateway), which will make the SNA Server calls on behalf of CICS/6000. Using SNA directly is termed *local SNA* by CICS/6000. Local SNA has less overhead and performs better than utilizing the PPC Gateway but only supports SyncLevels 0 and 1. The PPC Gateway access supports SyncLevel 2. The PPC Gateway is a DCE RPC server and receives the requests to make SNA calls by way of DCE RPCs from a CICS/6000 region. The PPC Gateway need not reside on the same AIX machine as the CICS/6000 region. Multiple CICS/6000 regions on separate AIX machines may utilize the services of a single PPC Gateway and need not have SNA locally installed.

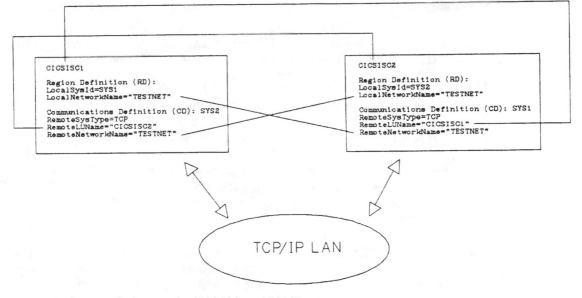

Figure 14.4   Resource Definitions for CICS ISC over TCP/IP.

Configuring the AIX SNA Server

Before utilizing either local SNA or PPC Gateway access to a remote CICS/6000 region, the AIX SNA Server must be configured to allow SNA LU 6.2 sessions to be created between CICS/6000 and the remote region. The configuration of SNA is beyond the scope of this book and is covered in the AIX SNA Server product documentation. Before configuring the AIX SNA Server, a number of parameters must be determined or defined for the network. The following briefly describes these parameters and may be of aid to an SNA network administrator when configuring for CICS/6000.

Network name/netid.   Each SNA network may have its own network name. When configuring SNA, this parameter must be specified. When CICS/6000 advertises itself as an LU partner, it also will specify the network name. The CICS/6000 region must be told the network name in the **LocalNetworkName** attribute in the Region Definition (RD).

Local LU name/region name/applid.   When a partner CICS system attempts to contact the CICS/6000 region, the SNA network will be searched for the LU name of the CICS region. The CICS region has its own LU name specified in a number of ways and can be known by a number of LU names. The order of LU name determination is as follows:

- *Region name*   The name of the CICS region will be used as the LU name if not overridden by one of the following. To be valid, the region name must be uppercase and conform to SNA LU naming standards.

- *Region Definition* (**LocalLUName**)   LU name used for CICS region if not overridden.

- *Gateway Definition* (**GatewayLUName**)   LU name used for access to the CICS region if the PPC Gateway is used for communication.

The LU name of the CICS/6000 region must be specified in the SNA LU 6.2 Local LU Profile and in the LU 6.2 Side Information Profile.

Partner LU name.   To be able to communicate between CICS/6000 and a CICS partner, the CICS/6000 region and SNA definitions must be informed of the full network name and LU name of the partner CICS system. This is specified in the CICS/6000 Communication Definition (CD) for the partner and in the SNA profiles for defining an LU 6.2 Partner Profile and defining an LU 6.2 Partner Location Profile.

Mode name.   The SNA Mode profile defines the characteristics that should be used when communicating from one SNA partner to another. The Mode profile name (**Modename**) must be defined to both the AIX SNA product and the remote SNA service (VTAM). The Mode names must be the same in each case. The Mode name is linked to the CICS/6000 system by a reference to the CICS/6000 LU name in the LU 6.2 Side Information Profile.

Local Transaction Program Name (TPN).   A Transaction Program Name must be defined to accept incoming start requests from remote systems. A TPN is defined to AIX SNA by creating an LU 6.2 TPN Profile. The attributes of this profile should include

- *PIP data:* **no_LU_verification.**
- *Conversation type:* **mapped.**
- *Synchronization level:* **all.**

The profile name defined for this TPN must be associated with all CICS/6000 transactions that may be started from a remote CICS system. This specifically includes those CICS transactions which are started because of inbound function shipping or transaction routing requests. The following transactions must have the TPN Profile defined:

- CRTE
- CPMI
- CVMI
- CSMI
- CSM1
- CSM2

- CSM3
- CSM5
- CRSR

Additionally, any other transactions that may be started through transaction routing and any transaction that is defined as a back-end DTP transaction must have the TPN Profile defined.

The profile is associated with a transaction definition in the **TPNSNAProfile** attribute of the Transaction Definitions (TD).

CICS synchronization level

When making requests to remote CICS systems to perform work on the local region's behalf, a new problem is introduced. If either the local or remote CICS regions ABEND or the program fails, what should happen to resources updated by both the local and the remote CICS regions?

As an example, consider the task of moving funds from one bank account to another. If each bank holds its own data, the transfer of funds requires the debit of one account and the credit of another. If the local bank initiates the request and first debits the local account and makes a request to the remote bank to credit the remote account but the remote bank fails, the account will have lost funds because the local account will have been debited while the remote bank was not credited. If the local bank first requests that the remote bank credit the account and then debits the local account, a failure could occur in the debit of the local account. The account would then have gained funds, since the remote account would have been credited while the local account was not debited.

Neither situation is acceptable. Programming logic could be introduced to send a series of acknowledgments and logging to ensure that either both accounts were updated successfully or neither was. This logic quickly becomes complex.

CICS/6000 provides the ability to extend the transactional "all or nothing" construct out to the communication with other CICS regions. If the local CICS transaction abends, any work requested by the transaction in a remote CICS region also will be backed out. If the remote CICS region abends, the local region that made the request will be informed and also will back out the work for the transaction.

This synchronization of work between multiple CICS regions is available in three levels, each level adding additional consistency but with some additional processing overhead. These levels are termed *synchronization levels* or *synclevels:*

SyncLevel 0   No information about outcome of request

SyncLevel 1   Basic acknowledgment

SyncLevel 2   Full two-phase commit, guaranteed integrity

CICS/6000 provides full SyncLevel 2 over both TCP/IP and SNA protocols. To utilize SyncLevel 2 over SNA, the PPC Gateway must be used. Local SNA connections do not allow SyncLevel 2, only SyncLevels 0 and 1.

The Communications Definition

The Communications Definition (CD) resource class must be configured with details about all the partner CICS regions that may potentially interact with the CICS/6000 region. This is required for TCP/IP connections to other CICS/6000 regions as well as for SNA connections. The Communications Definition must be configured with the following attributes:

<**KEY**>   The four-character key of the communication definition is the SYSID of the remote CICS region. CICS commands and other resource definitions specify a SYSID to refer to a remote CICS region. The SYSID is mapped to the remote region with the details specified in the other resource attributes.

RemoteSysType   This attribute is either **TCP** or **SNA,** specifying whether the connection is to another CICS/6000 region over TCP/IP or to a non-CICS/6000 region over SNA.

RemoteLUName   The LU name of the remote CICS region.

RemoteNetworkName   The network name to which the remote CICS region is attached.

GatewayName   If local SNA is to be used, this attribute should be left blank; otherwise, the name of a PPC Gateway should be specified. The name is not the DCE CDS name of the gateway but rather the key field of a Gateway Definition (GD).

Note: Care should be taken to distinguish a Gateway Definition (GD) from a Gateway Server Definition (GSD). The Gateway Definition defines the CICS/6000 logical characteristics of the PPC Gateway, while the Gateway Server Definition (GSD) specifies the start-up and control attributes of the PPC Gateway itself.

If a PPC Gateway is to be used, the Gateway Definition (GD) must be defined with the following attributes:

<**KEY**>   The name of the Gateway Definition is used as the key in a Communication Definition (CD) **GatewayName** attribute.

GatewayCDSName   This attribute defines the DCE CDS name of a PPC Gateway that is to be the recipient of ISC requests from CICS/6000 out to other CICS regions or from other CICS regions into CICS/6000. The name may be specified as a full DCE CDS name or as just the name of the server that will have /.:/cics/ppc/gateway/ prefixed.

GatewayLUName   This optional attribute defines the LU name that the

PPC Gateway is to know the CICS region as. If not specified, either the CICS region name or the **LocalLUName** attributes will be used.

When CICS/6000 initializes, any PPC Gateways defined in Gateway Definitions are configured with details of the CICS/6000 region, including the LU name of the region and the CICS transactions that may be started on that region for incoming requests. The PPC Gateways defined in the Gateway Definitions should be started prior to starting the CICS/6000 regions.

The PPC Gateway

The Encina PPC Gateway may be used in conjunction with CICS/6000 to provide an alternative path to communicating with a remote CICS system over an SNA network. The PPC Gateway is an executable supplied with the Encina product that provides a gateway for communication with client applications that utilize the Encina PPC Executive calls. When started, the PPC Gateway advertises itself in the DCE Cell Directory Service and allows incoming DCE RPC calls to be accepted. The RPC calls are generated from Encina PPC Executive calls (usually CPIC). On receipt of an RPC call, the PPC Gateway converts the call into a corresponding AIX SNA call to transmit data onto the SNA network. On receipt of a response from the SNA network, the PPC Gateway returns the information on the return of the RPC call. The PPC Gateway can only be used on a machine that also has AIX SNA installed, since it attempts to make direct SNA calls.

If a PPC Gateway is defined to CICS/6000, when the CICS region is started, it informs the PPC Gateway of the region's existence and what it wishes the region's LU name to be. The PPC Gateway then advertises itself on the SNA network as being the endpoint for SNA communications to the LU name defined by CICS. When a remote CICS region wishes to communicate with CICS/6000, it then is able to send an SNA request that is received by the PPC Gateway, which in turn forwards the request to the CICS/6000 region associated with the LU name of the request.

The PPC Gateway provides two advantages over the local SNA–based communications access:

- The PPC Gateway is able to support the SyncLevel 2 protocol required for guaranteed two-phase commit.
- The PPC Gateway need not reside on the same machine as the CICS/6000 regions that are utilizing it. A single PPC Gateway may be used by multiple CICS regions. The machine running the PPC Gateway need be the only machine on which SNA is installed and configured, thus providing a cheaper solution and a single point of administration.

Like the Encina SFS, the PPC Gateway is created and configured through AIX SMIT panels or through the use of the CICS-supplied **cicscp** command.

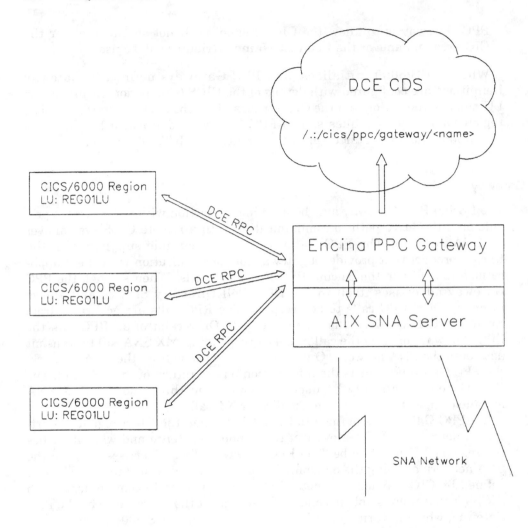

Configuring a PPC Gateway

The Encina PPC Gateway can be configured by using native Encina commands, using CICS-supplied commands, through the AIX SMIT panels, or through the use of the **cicscp** command.

The following commands are provided with CICS/6000 for PPC Gateway administration:

- **cicsppcgwycreate** Create an Encina PPC Gateway definition.
- **cicsppcgwy** Start a previously configured PPC Gateway.
- **cicsppcgwyshut** Stop a running PPC Gateway.
- **cicsppcgwydestory** Unconfigure a PPC Gateway.

The configuration of a PPC Gateway requires that the following be decided on:

DCE CDS name   Name that the PPC Gateway will use to advertise itself within the DCE CDS name space.

Short name   Like the SFS, the PPC Gateway requires a machine-wide "short name" to be associated with it. The short name is used to define the PPC Gateway to the AIX SRC and provide a means of naming other parts of the Gateway's operation. The short name is only used for administration and is transparent to end users or CICS configuration.

Logical volume   The AIX logical volume used to store recovery information needed to restart a Gateway. The default logical volume used is `log_%S`, which is expanded at runtime to include the unique short name.

AIX userid   The PPC Gateway executes under the control of an AIX userid that is specified when the Gateway is configured. The default name is the short name of the Gateway. The AIX logical volume used to manage PPC Gateway–recoverable information needs to be owned by the PPC Gateway AIX userid.

When operating, the PPC Gateway uses an AIX logical volume to store recovery information that it may use to recover from failures such as power losses. This AIX logical volume may be created by an AIX administrator using the following command:

```
mklv -y <volume name> rootvg 1
```

The name of the volume should be `log_<short name>`. The invoker of this command must be **root.** The volume group need not be **rootvg.** The AIX SMIT panels for logical volume creation may be used in place of the AIX command if preferred.

An AIX user with the same name as the short name for the PPC Gateway should be created and be given "cics" as the primary group. Once the AIX userid has been created, the logical volume used by the PPC Gateway should have its ownership given to the new userid. This can be accomplished with the following AIX commands:

```
chown <userid>.cics /dev/log_<short name> /dev/rlog_<short name>
```

Once these prerequisites have been accomplished, the CICS creation and configuration of the PPC Gateway can commence.

The following fastpath will present the AIX SMIT panel for gateway creation:

```
smit cics
    Manage Encina PPC Gateway Servers
        Define Encina PPC Gateway Servers
            Create
```

```
                      Create Encina PPC Gateway Server

Type or select values in entry fields.
Press Enter AFTER making all desired changes.


                                             [Entry Fields]
* PPC Gateway Server Identifier              [/.:/cics/ppc/gateway/GWY1]
* Model PPC Gateway Server Identifier         ""
  Ignore errors on creation?                 no                          +
  Resource description                       [PPC Gateway Server Def>
* Number of updates                          0
  Protect resource from modification?        no                          +
  Protection level                           none                        +
  Number of threads for RPC requests         [10]
  Short name used for SRC                     [shortName]
  AIX user ID for server                     [%S]
  AIX logical volume for logging             [log_%S]




F1=Help            F2=Refresh        F3=Cancel         F4=List
F5=Reset           F6=Command        F7=Edit           F8=Image
F9=Shell           F10=Exit          Enter=Do
```

The name of the Gateway is the name it will use to advertise itself to CICS clients. This name should be /.:/cics/ppc/gateway/<name>. Executing these commands causes the PPC Gateway Definitions to be added to the Gateway Server Definitions (GSD) resource types plus appropriate AIX directories to be created under the /var/cics_servers/GSD directory.

The Gateway is now ready to be started.

Starting a PPC Gateway

The PPC Gateway may be either cold-started or autostarted. The first time the Gateway is started it must be cold-started. Subsequent cold starting will destroy any recoverable information about conversations the Gateway may have been involved in. Normally it will be autostarted subsequently.

When the Gateway is started, it will advertise itself in the DCE CDS name space, allowing CICS to locate and utilize its services. To start the Gateway, the administrator must be a logged in as the AIX root user and be DCE authenticated as cell_admin. The PPC Gateway may be started by following the AIX SMIT panels:

```
smit cics
    Manage Encina PPC Gateway Servers
        Cold start and Encina PPC Gateway Server
```

Administrating a PPC Gateway

The Encina product provides a PPC Gateway administration tool called **ppcadmin.** This command allows various administration and query tasks to be performed against operating PPC Gateway servers. To utilize the command, the administrator must be DCE authenticated as `cell_admin` and have the ENCINA_GWY_SERVER environment variable set to the DCE CDS name of the PPC Gateway server that the administrative commands are to be executed against.

The **ppcadmin** tool provides the following commands:

ppcadmin list luentries   The list of all SNA LUs that the PPC Gateway is listening on behalf of is returned. The LU names and the DCE CDS entry names of the DCE servers for the LUs are returned. For CICS, the DCE CDS names will be `/.:/cics/<region>/ts`, that is the DCE CDS name of the CICS/6000 transaction scheduler.

ppcadmin query luentry   This command allows an individual LU being managed by the PPC Gateway to be queried. The LU name, the DCE CDS name, and the CICS transactions that the Gateway is listening to on behalf of the region are returned.

ppcadmin list convs   This command displays a list of all active conversations at the PPC Gateway.

ppcadmin query conv   This command returns information about a specific SNA conversation at the PPC Gateway.

ppcadmin query stats   This command queries statistics accumulated by the PPC Gateway, including number of conversations, errors, and connections.

The CICS Communication Types

CICS/6000 provides the full set of CICS Intersystem Communications (ISC) functions found on other CICS family members. These functions may be divided into the types of access to the remote systems. CICS provides five different communication types:

- Transaction Routing
- Function Shipping
- Distributed Program Link
- Asynchronous Transaction Start
- Distributed Transaction Processing

Transaction Routing

Transaction Routing allows a CICS transaction to be initiated on a remote CICS region. This can be achieved by defining the transaction as remote in the Transaction Definition (TD) for the transaction. CICS/6000 also provides a transaction called **CRTE** that makes a connection to the remote region from a terminal. Every transaction submitted from the terminal will then be started on the remote CICS region.

Function Shipping

Function Shipping allows access to CICS resources located on a remote CICS region from a local CICS region as through the resources were local. The following CICS resource types may be accessed remotely as though they were local:

- Files
- Temporary storage queues
- Transient data queues

Access to the remote resources may be achieved by defining them as remote in local definitions for the resources. Alternatively, they may be accessed remotely by specifying the remote CICS system identifier within the CICS program statements.

Distributed Program Link

Distributed Program Link allows a CICS EXEC CICS LINK command to execute the program on the remote CICS system. This may be achieved by defining the program as remote in the Program Definitions (PD) for the local definition of the program. Alternatively, the program may be accessed remotely by specifying the remote CICS system identifier within the CICS application program that is making the EXEC CICS LINK call.

Asynchronous Transaction Start

Asynchronous Transaction Start allows a transaction to be started asynchronously with the EXEC CICS START command from within a CICS application. The transaction can start on a remote CICS system. The transaction will start remotely if it is defined as remote in the Transaction Definitions (TD) or a remote system identifier has been specified within the CICS application program.

Distributed Transaction Processing

Distributed Transaction Processing is a CICS API interface to SNA LU 6.2 application programming. Using Distributed Transaction Processing allows a

CICS application to act as a partner application to another LU 6.2 application. This could be a remote CICS transaction or some other SNA application that uses the LU 6.2 protocol for communication.

Distributed Transaction Processing Usage

Distributed Transaction Processing (DTP) is the lowest-level communications API. Use of DTP requires skills in APPC and SNA LU 6.2 programming. CICS/6000 provides the API to allow a CICS application to communicate with another CICS application or a CPI-C application using LU 6.2 communication flows. No data-conversion exits are provided with DTP, as with the other forms of ISC programming. When communicating with a partner application, this requires either an SNA link between the two applications in the case that the partner is not another CICS/6000 system or an Encina PPC application.

Designing DTP applications is very much client/server programming. One side of the pair will be listening for incoming DTP application start requests, while the other will be responsible for issuing the request. The application that initiates the request is termed the *front-end application,* while the application that the front-end application invokes is termed the *back-end.* Once the two applications have started conversing, only one of them may send data while the other receives the data. They may choose to switch this role and let the other send or receive. Information flow between the two applications is strictly one way and then the other. The conversation is unidirectional but has the capability to switch that direction.

Since one end of the conversation has the ability to send while the other only to receive, both sides must be aware of which is which. This is achieved by both sides having *program state* (i.e., being aware of whether they are the sender or the receiver). As well as being able to send or receive, the DTP applications also have additional state characteristics that will be described as they are introduced. A DTP application may query its own state by issuing the EXEC CICS EXTRACT ATTRIBUTE command or by the STATE option on some of the CICS DTP commands.

Programming with DTP may be thought of as talking to someone through an old-fashioned telephone. Before you actually get to talk, the first task is to ask the operator to allocate you a line with the party you wish to speak by means of a switchboard. The switchboard only has room for a certain number of concurrent calls. The first request in a DTP front-end will be to have a line allocated for your conversation. Once the line is allocated, the conversation may begin by asking to be connected to the remote person. The person at the other end hears the telephone ringing and only then answers it. This is analogous to the back-end program initiation. Since the telephone is primitive, only one person can speak at a time, and a strict organization must be imposed to decide who that person will be.

This may appear at first as old-fashioned technology, but it must be remembered that it works and is efficient.

DTP programming

The front-end application must first start by allocating a conversation with the remote back-end. This is achieved with the EXEC CICS ALLOCATE command. On successful completion, a conversation identifier (CONVID) is returned that must be used on all subsequent communications with the back-end. The purpose of this identifier is to distinguish one conversation from another. A front-end application may communicate with multiple back-ends simultaneously. Each conversation will have a separate identifier. Similarly, when the back-end application is started, it too is given a conversation identifier that it will use to communicate with the front-end. Although a back-end application will have only one front-end, it may initiate a conversation with another back-end (and hence be the front-end in that conversation). The different conversation identifiers are used to distinguish the conversations.

The EXEC CICS ALLOCATE command names the remote system with which communication is requested. This is specified as a CICS SYSID value and must have been set up previously in the Communication Definitions (CD). The next task is to actually name the back-end application with which the front-end wishes to converse. This is accomplished with the EXEC CICS CONNECT PROCESS command. This command expects the remote back-end program name to be specified in the PROCNAME option. The communication SyncLevel is also specified on the CONNECT command. Unlike the telephone conversation analogy, the telephone at the other end does not ring until the dialer actually attempts to say something. Realistically, the connect request is not flowed to the back-end system until the first use of the conversation.

When the back-end system receives the CONNECT request, it starts the back-end application. The two applications are now conversing. Initially, the front end is in SEND state, while the back-end is in RECEIVE state.

The back-end transaction may fail to start for a number of different reasons. The front-end application is informed of this via a TERMERR RESP code from the DTP command, and the EIB ERRERRCD is set to a value describing the nature of the error.

Once the front-end and the back-end are in conversation, data may be sent from the sender to the receiver. This is possible using the EXEC CICS SEND command in the sending application and EXEC CICS RECEIVE in the receiver. It is invalid for the EXEC CICS SEND command to be executed when the program is in a state other than the send state. Like the initial CONNECT PROCESS request, the data are not actually transmitted to the receiver until either an explicit EXEC CICS WAIT CONVID command is issued or the WAIT option is included on the SEND command. The receiver must issue the EXEC CICS RECEIVE command to receive the data sent by the sender. The receiver can issue a request to change the direction of a conversation, making the sender the receiver and the original receiver the sender. This may be achieved by the EXEC CICS SEND INVITE command or EXEC CICS ISSUE signal.

The receiver, initially in receive state and executing an EXEC CICS RECEIVE command, will return with the change of state signaled in the EIB. The application will now be in the send state.

The details of the state transitions are discussed in the CICS/6000 communication guide manual. The list of related CICS API commands for DTP programming is

- EXEC CICS ALLOCATE
- EXEC CICS CONNECT PROCESS
- EXEC CICS SEND
- EXEC CICS RECEIVE
- EXEC CICS EXTRACT PROCESS
- EXEC CICS EXTRACT ATTRIBUTES
- EXEC CICS ISSUE ABEND | CONFIRMATION | ERROR | PREPARE | - SIGNAL
- EXEC CICS WAIT CONVID

When sending data from one CICS system to another, it is important to remember that the data are transmitted without modification. If the data are sent or received from an EBCDIC character set environment such as CICS/MVS and received or sent to an ASCII-based system such as CICS/6000, CICS provides no assistance in translating the data. In AIX, a function called `iconv()` is available to convert data from one character set to another. This function can be used to convert ASCII data to and from EBCIDC data. The `iconv()` function is provided as part of the AIX base operating system.

Example DTP applications. The following applications illustrate the use of DTP programming. The applications may execute on separate CICS/6000 regions but could be on the same CICS systems. The example will send a message from one CICS region (SYS1) to the partner CICS region (SYS2). The back-end will receive the message and send a message back to SYS1. This scenario is illustrated in Fig. 14.5. The front-end application is listed in Fig. 14.6. The back-end application is listed in Fig. 14.7. The various Resource Definitions for the programs are illustrated in Fig. 14.8. A DTP application that is to be available as a back-end must be flagged as **BackEnd = yes** in its Transaction Definition (TD) attributes.

Using Encina PPC Executive with DTP

The Encina PPC Executive product provides a mechanism to allow an AIX application to communicate with another AIX application using the CPI-C programming API. The communication between the two applications is carried over a TCP/IP link as opposed to an SNA link, as is more common with

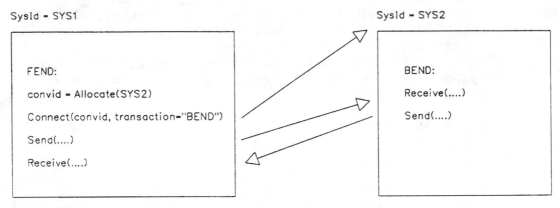

Figure 14.5 DTP sample application.

```c
#include <stdio.h>


main()
{
    char        cnvid[4];
    char        tranId[]="BEND";
    char        message[]="Hello from front-end";
    char        buffer[100];
    short       length;

    EXEC CICS ADDRESS EIB(dfheiptr);

    EXEC CICS ALLOCATE SYSID("SYS2");

    memcpy(cnvid, dfheiptr->eibrsrce, 4);
    EXEC CICS CONNECT PROCESS CONVID(cnvid) PROCNAME(tranId) \
        PROCLENGTH(strlen(tranId)) SYNCLEVEL(0);

    fprintf(stderr, "About to SEND message \"%s\"\n", message);

    EXEC CICS SEND FROM(message) LENGTH(strlen(message)+1)
        CONVID(cnvid) INVITE WAIT;

    fprintf(stderr, "About to RECEIVE\n");

    length = sizeof(buffer);
    EXEC CICS RECEIVE INTO(buffer) LENGTH(length) CONVID(cnvid);

    fprintf(stderr, "RECEIVED: \"%s\"\n", buffer);

    EXEC CICS RETURN;
}
```

Figure 14.6 DTP front-end sample program.

```
#include <stdio.h>

main()
{
    char    buffer[100];
    char    message[]="Hello from backend";
    short   length;

    fprintf(stderr, "BEND Started\n");

    length = sizeof(buffer);
    EXEC CICS RECEIVE INTO(buffer) LENGTH(length);

    fprintf(stderr, "RECEIVED message: \"%s\"\n", buffer);

    EXEC CICS SEND FROM(message) LENGTH(strlen(message)+1) WAIT;

    EXEC CICS RETURN;
}
```

Figure 14.7   DTP back-end sample program.

```
SHELL=/bin/ksh

all: fend bend

fend: fend.ccs
   cicstcl -lC -d -e fend

bend: bend.ccs
   cicstcl -lC -d -e bend

install:
   -cicsadd -c td -r $(CICSREGION1) FEND ProgName="FEND"
   -cicsadd -c td -r $(CICSREGION2) BEND ProgName="BEND" \
       IsBackEndDTP=yes
   -cicsadd -c pd -r $(CICSREGION1) FEND PathName="$(PWD)/fend"
   -cicsadd -c pd -r $(CICSREGION2) BEND PathName="$(PWD)/bend"
   -cicsadd -c cd -r $(CICSREGION1) SYS2 \
       RemoteSysType=TCP \
       RemoteLUName=dtp2 \
       RemoteNetworkName=""
   -cicsadd -c cd -r $(CICSREGION2) SYS1 \
       RemoteSysType=TCP \
       RemoteLUName=dtp1 \
       RemoteNetworkName=""
```

Figure 14.8   Resource Definitions for DTP programs.

```
#include <stdio.h>
#include <utils/trace.h>
#include <ppc/cpic.h>
#include <ppc/ppc.h>
#include <threadTid/threadTid.h>
#include <tran/tran.h>

main()
{
    tran_tid_t  myTid;
    char    conv[8];
    long    rc;
    long    request;
    long    parm;
    long    requested_length;
    long    data_received;
    long    received_length;
    long    status_received;
    long    request_to_send_received;
    char    buffer[100];
    char    message[]="Hello from CPI-C program";

    tran_StandardEnvironment();

    rc = tran_Init(0);

    rc = cpic_Init("TESTNET.CPICTEST");

    rc = tran_Ready();

    rc = tran_Begin(TRAN_TID_NULL, &myTid);

    rc = threadTid_Begin(myTid);

    rc = cpic_ReadConfig("CLIENT_SIDE");

    cminit(conv, "SIDE0001", &rc);

    parm = CM_MAPPED_CONVERSATION;
    cmsct(conv, &parm, &rc);

    slvar = CM_CONFIRM;
    cmssl(conv, &slvar, &rc);

    cmallc(conv, &rc);

    printf ("Sending message: \"%s\"\n", message);
    parm = strlen(message)+1;
    cmsend(conv, message, &parm, &request, &rc);

    requested_length = sizeof(buffer);
    cmrcv(conv,
        buffer,
        &requested_length,
        &data_received,
        &received_length,
        &status_received,
        &request_to_send_received,
        &rc);

    printf("Data received: \"%s\"\n", buffer);

    rc = tran_End(myTid);
}
```

Figure 14.9 CPI-C client program.

```
sideInfo {
     "SIDE0001",
     "",
     "partner",
     "BEND",
     ENCRYPT_NONE,
     SECURITY_NONE,
     "",
     ""
}

partner { "partner",
     CONNECTION_TCP,
     "/.:/cics/dtp2/ts"
}
```

Figure 14.10 Client side profile.

CPI-C conversations. The Encina PPC Gateway allows the Encina CPI-C protocol to be converted from the internal format to the SNA LU 6.2 format and hence to an SNA-connected CPI-C application. CICS/6000 itself can utilize the Encina PPC Executive and its CPI-C API to communicate with other CICS/6000 systems on different systems.

An AIX-based application may be written that utilizes CPI-C calls but is compiled with the Encina PPC Executive. Such an application can converse with a CICS/6000 region if CICS applications are written as DTP back-ends. Figure 14.9 provides an example of such a program, and Fig. 14.10 explains some of the key concepts in writing an Encina PPC Executive CPI-C application.

Edwin N. Strickland

Developing CICS/6000
Client Applications

This chapter describes CICS/6000 client applications. It describes the various models of application design and the different techniques involved in each.

Introduction to Client Applications

Occasionally, a solution to a problem may involve access to CICS/6000 from a non-CICS environment. This may be from a non-AIX machine such as a PC executing OS/2, Windows, or DOS. It may be from a non-AIX Unix machine from a manufacturer such as HP, Digital, or Sun. A graphic interface to a CICS application may be desired or even access to CICS data from a specialized device such as a card swipe or reader.

Each of these cases may require access to CICS functionality from an environment that does not lend itself to the 3270 data stream model of CICS. To facilitate this functionality, a number of "client" interfaces have been developed that allow a non-CICS application to make requests to CICS/6000 to have CICS perform work on behalf of the client application. In this model, CICS/6000 becomes a server of requests originating from a client application.

The client interfaces from CICS/6000 are available on many different platforms. The different types of client interfaces are listed below and will be expanded on in subsequent chapters:

- External Call Interface (ECI)
- External Presentation Interface (EPI)
- TCP/IP sockets
- DCE RPC

CICS/6000 provides all the client interfaces described above. PC-based client interfaces require additional products to facilitate their use. These products provide ECI and EPI interfaces and are known as *CICS clients*.

# Chapter 16

External Call Interface (ECI)

The External Call Interface (ECI) allows a non-CICS application (one that does not include EXEC CICS statements) to make a call to CICS/6000 to have work accomplished. The application can call a CICS program available in a CICS region in a similar way to that of an EXEC CICS LINK call. The calling program is called the *client,* while the region that serves the request is called the *server.* The client program calls the server and passes the name of the program to be executed as well as a set of optional parameters contained in a communication area of storage. This communication area is passed to the server, which may receive the data as a CICS COMMAREA. The server program may modify the area of storage passed, and on return, the client program will be able to receive the modified data.

When a client ECI call is made, parameters such as security, transaction identifier, and other control parameters may be specified optionally.

Logical units of work

When the CICS program executing on the server completes, changes to recoverable resource made by the program may remain uncommitted. The logical unit of work (LUW) of the program is specified by parameters on the call to the CICS server. If the call is made with the **ExtendMode** set **on,** the call will return with the LUW outstanding. Subsequent ECI calls may run additional programs in the LUW, commit the LUW, or cause the LUW to back out. If an LUW is extended, a token or LUW identifier is returned after the first ECI call in the LUW chain. This token is returned in the eci_luw_token parameter. On subsequent calls to the CICS server for the same LUW, the token must be available in the eci_luw_token parameter field. The field must always be zeroed before starting a new LUW.

Alternate transaction names

When a client makes an ECI call to the server, it may specify an optional transaction identifier in the `eci_transid` parameter. This transaction may be returned to the invoked CICS program via a CICS QUERY command. The transaction also may have modified attributes such as security keys or priority. The transaction may be defined in the CICS/6000 region and have the same attributes as the CICS-supplied CPMI transaction, which is invoked if no transaction name is supplied in the ECI call. Specifically, the DFHMIRS program must be defined as the program name for the transaction.

Passing data

Data are passed from the ECI client program to the CICS server by providing a pointer to an area of storage on the client and a length of that storage in the `eci_commarea` and `eci_commarea_length` parameters. The storage is copied to the CICS region and may be modified on return from the CICS program. During transmission of the data from the ECI to CICS and from CICS back to the ECI, the data may be compressed to decrease the amount of network traffic or data flow. The data are compressed by not sending trailing binary zeros in the COMMAREA.

The length of data sent from the ECI client to the CICS program must be sufficient to allow the CICS program to return the maximum amount of data that it wishes to return. The CICS program cannot return more information than was declared initially by the ECI client. The maximum amount of storage that may be sent is 32K.

Synchronous and asynchronous calls

There are two distinct types of ECI calls to invoke a CICS program. These types are the *synchronous* and *asynchronous calls*. The synchronous call waits for the CICS program executing in the CICS region to end before returning control back to the caller of the ECI call in the front-end program. The synchronous call is made by specifying ECI_SYNC as the call type in the `eci_call_type` field in the ECI control structure. Asynchronous calls do not require the front-end program to wait for completion of the CICS program but instead return control back from the ECI call immediately. When the CICS program ends, the outcome of the program must be queried with an ECI REPLY command. Asynchronous calls are made when the call type in the `eci_call_type` field of the ECI control structure is set to ECI_ASYNC. An optional field in the ECI control block called `eci_message_qualifier` may be set to an integer value. This value is returned in the ECI REPLY command and allows an ECI call to be associated with its eventual end. Another optional field used with asynchronous calls is the `eci_callback` field within the ECI control block. This field may be set to a function to be called when the CICS program ends. The function called may examine the passed `eci_message_qualifier` field to determine which asynchronous call has just ended. The set of functions that may be called from within the call-back function is heavily restricted. The intent of this function is to allow it to notify the main execution of the program that an asynchronous call has ended. This may use AIX pipes or DCE synchronization primitives such as mutices or condition variables or simply set a global variable to some value.

Programming with the External Call Interface

ECI programs for AIX must be written in the C programming language. They must be linked with the CICS/6000-supplied library `libcics_eci.a`. A C language header file called `cics_eci.h` is supplied that contains function prototypes, constant definitions, and various type definitions used to make ECI calls.

The following compilation step shows an example of building an ECI application program:

```
xlc_r -o <executable name> \
   <source file>.c \
   -I /usr/lpp/cics/include \
   -L /usr/lpp/cics/lib \
   -lcicseci
```

Before executing an ECI application, the program must either authenticate with DCE security services as an appropriate DCE principal or be executed within a DCE login environment that has sufficient authority.

The ECI call requires that the AIX National Language Support environment be initialized. This environment sets up the collating sequence, message catalogs, and other language-specific requirements before the call to the CICS server is actually made. Failure to set up this environment may result in the CICS region generating messages whose language type is unknown to the ECI client program.

To initialize the National Language Support environment, the following call must be included in the ECI application before making any other ECI calls:

```
#include <locale.h>
...
main(int argc, char *argv[])
{
    ...
    (void) setlocale(LC_ALL, "");
    ...
}
```

Two separate ECI function calls are available from the ECI library:

- `CICS_ExternalCall`
- `CICS_ListSystems`

Each of these calls will be examined in the following sections.

CICS_EciListSystems

The `CICS_EciListSystems()` call provides the application a mechanism to determine the names and descriptions of the available CICS/6000 regions.

The `CICS_EciListSystems()` call has the following call syntax:

```
short_t CICS_EciListSystems(cics_char_t    *NameSpace,
                            cics_ushort_t   *NumSystems,
                            CICS_EciSystems_t *List);
```

Parameters

NameSpace   This parameter specifies the name space in which to search for CICS/6000 regions. Currently, this parameter is unused and should be passed as the NULL pointer (**NULL** or **0**).

NumSystems   On input, this parameter specifies the number of elements that may be returned in the **List.** If more regions are found than space available to be returned, the ECI_ERR_MORE_SYSTEMS return code will be returned from the function call. On return from the call, this parameter is updated with the actual number of CICS regions found and returned.

List   This parameter points to an array of entries that can store the returned names and descriptions of the CICS regions. It is the responsibility of the application to ensure that sufficient storage has been allocated to store at least the number of systems identified by the **NumSystems** parameter.

The `CICS_EciSystems_t` structure contains two fields:

SystemName   A NULL-terminated string containing the name of the CICS/6000 region.

Description   A NULL-terminated string containing the description of the CICS/6000 region defined in the Region Definition (RD).

On return from the call, one of the following codes may be returned; these codes are defined in the ECI header file.

ECI_NO_ERROR   No error was detected and the call returned successfully.

ECI_ERR_MORE_SYSTEMS   More regions were available to be returned than were allowed to be returned by the **NumSystems** parameter.

ECI_ERR_NO_SYSTEMS   No CICS regions were located. The **NumSystems** parameter is set to 0.

ECI_ERR_INVALID_DATA_LENGTH   The **NumSystems** parameter is too large.

ECI_ERR_SYSTEM_ERROR   An internal error occurred. This is usually because the caller has not been authenticated with DCE.

CICS_ExternalCall

The CICS_ExternalCall() makes the call to the CICS server to have the program executed within the server. Additionally, this call allows

- An extend mode LUW to be committed.
- An extend mode LUW to be backed out.
- An extend mode LUW to be extended.
- The status of an asynchronous ECI call to be queried.

The CICS_ExternalCall() has the following call syntax:

```
short CICS_ExternalCall( ECI_PARAMS * )
```

The ECI_PARAMS C language structure controls the execution of the CICS external call and all its associated attributes. If a field in the control block is not set explicitly, its value should be set to binary zeros. This is best achieved by zeroing the whole structure and then filling in the fields that are to be used. The structure may be zeroed with the following C language command:

```
ECI_PARAMS ECI_Control;
memset(&ECI_Control, 0, sizeof(ECI_Control));
```

The following list indicates the fields within the control block:

eci_call_type   The type of ECI call being made. This may be one of the following values:

- ECI_SYNC   This ECI call type make a call to the CICS region in a fully synchronous mode. The ECI client program does not return from the call until the CICS server program has completed.
- ECI_ASYNC   This ECI call type makes an ECI call to the CICS region in an asynchronous mode. The ECI program returns from the call as soon as the CICS region has received the request but usually before the CICS program itself has completed.
- ECI_STATE_SYNC   This ECI call type requests that the status of the ECI interface be returned. The call is synchronous and will not return until the state information is available.
- ECI_STATE_ASYNC   This ECI call type requests that the status of the ECI interface be returned. The call is asynchronous and returns immediately.

- ECI_GET_REPLY   This call returns the response from a previously started ECI request that was asynchronous. If no reply has yet been returned from the CICS region, the ECI_ERR_NO_REPLY code is returned.

- ECI_GET_REPLY_WAIT   This call returns the response from a previously started ECI request that was asynchronous. If the reply has not yet been returned, the call waits for the response to arrive before returning control to the ECI client program.

- ECI_GET_SPECIFIC_REPLY   This call returns the response from a previously started ECI request that was asynchronous. The response returned will match that from a previous start where the `eci_message_qualifier` field matches the value specified in this call. If no reply has yet been returned from the CICS region, the ECI_ERR_NO_REPLY code is returned.

ECI_GET_REPLY_SPECIFIC   This call returns the response from a previously started ECI request that was asynchronous. The response returned will match that from a previous start where the `eci_message_qualifier` field matches the value specified in this call. If no reply has yet been returned from the CICS region, the ECI_ERR_NO_REPLY code is returned.

`eci_program_name`   The name of the CICS/6000 program to be invoked by the ECI call. The program must be defined in the CICS/6000 region but may be defined as remote and exist on another CICS system.

`eci_userid`   The CICS userid that the program is to execute under.

`eci_password`   The password for the CICS user specified in the `eci_password` field. The password is encrypted before transmission over the network.

`eci_transid`   The transaction that the program called is to be executed under. If this parameter is not specified, the transaction used will be the CPMI transaction.

`eci_abend_code`   ABEND code from CICS if the program fails in some manner.

`eci_commarea`   A CICS COMMAREA passed to the program being invoked that may be updated before the program returns. The data will be returned to the ECI caller.

`eci_commarea_length`   The length of the ECI COMMAREA.

`eci_sys_return_code`   Additional information on an ECI system failure return code.

`eci_extend_mode`   This field controls how the logical unit of work should be handled in the CICS region. Options include extending the LUW, committing the LUW, or backing out the LUW.

`eci_message_qualifier`   A 2-byte integer field that may be included in an asynchronous ECI call to allow the response to be paired with the request. The ECI_GET_SPECIFIC ECI call type may be used to wait or obtain a response based on this field.

`eci_luw_token`   This field contains the LUW token used to identify the LUW in progress if the call is being extended. This field should be set to zero before starting a new LUW.

`eci_version`   Version level of the ECI call. This parameter allows the concurrent support of this and possible future versions of the ECI. Future versions would specify a different value for this field, allowing the CICS server to process the parameters correctly while allowing support for back-level versions of the ECI. The current ECI version is ECI_VERSION_1 and must be specified in this field.

`eci_system_name`   The name of the CICS server that is being called. This will be the CICS region name for CICS/6000.

`eci_callback`   This field specifies a callback function that is to be invoked when an asynchronous call returns. The callback function is passed to the `eci_message_qualifier` field from the original ECI request.

`eci_userid2`   Not used.

`eci_password2`   Not used.

The `eci_call_type` field determines the processing nature of each ECI call. For each different call, only some of the parameter fields are valid. Fields that are not valid or are left as default must be set to NULL values before making the ECI call for the specific call type.

The following list illustrates the fields that are valid for each of the different ECI call types:

ECI_SYNC

- `eci_call_type`
- `eci_program_name`
- `eci_userid`
- `eci_password`
- `eci_transid`
- `eci_abend_code`
- `eci_commarea`
- `eci_commarea_length`
- `eci_sys_return_code`
- `eci_extend_mode`

- `eci_luw_token`
- `eci_sysid`
- `eci_version`
- `eci_system_name`

ECI_ASYNC

- `eci_call_type`
- `eci_program_name`
- `eci_userid`
- `eci_password`
- `eci_transid`
- `eci_commarea`
- `eci_commarea_length`
- `eci_sys_return_code`
- `eci_extend_mode`
- `eci_message_qualifier`
- `eci_luw_token`
- `eci_sysid`
- `eci_version`
- `eci_system_name`
- `eci_callback`

ECI_STATE_SYNC

- `eci_call_type`
- `eci_commarea`
- `eci_commarea_length`
- `eci_sys_return_code`
- `eci_extend_mode`
- `eci_luw_token`
- `eci_sysid`
- `eci_version`
- `eci_system_name`

ECI_STATE_ASYNC

- `eci_call_type`
- `eci_commarea`

- `eci_commarea_length`
- `eci_sys_return_code`
- `eci_extend_mode`
- `eci_message_qualifier`
- `eci_luw_token`
- `eci_sysyid`
- `eci_version`
- `eci_system_name`
- `eci_callback`

ECI_GET_REPLY, ECI_GET_REPLY_WAIT

- `eci_call_type`
- `eci_commarea`
- `eci_commarea_length`
- `eci_sysid`
- `eci_version`

ECI_GET_SPECIFIC_REPLY, ECI_GET_SPECIFIC_REPLY_WAIT

- `eci_call_type`
- `eci_commarea`
- `eci_commarea_length`
- `eci_message_qualifier`
- `eci_sysid`
- `eci_version`

17

The CICS/6000 EPI

CICS/6000 first introduced an Application Programming Interface to the CICS product family called the *External Presentation Interface* (EPI). EPI was designed to allow non-CICS applications, those applications which are not designed to run as CICS transactions, to interact with a CICS region to achieve distributed work. The EPI is a set of C language function calls and data types that allows a C language programmer to connect to CICS/6000. Using the EPI requires an understanding of the model of operation of an EPI application and how it interacts with CICS/6000.

From a CICS/6000 perspective, an EPI application looks like an installed CICS terminal. All the attributes of a CICS-attached terminal are associated with an EPI application, including

- A terminal identifier (**TermId**)
- A network name (**NetName**)
- An associated userid
- Security and priority attributes

Any transaction that executes against the EPI-associated CICS terminal that generates output will have that output sent to the EPI application. A request to obtain data from the EPI-associated terminal will result in a request to return data to the CICS region being generated in the EPI application. When a transaction running against the EPI terminal program ends normally or abnormally, the EPI application is informed.

When an EPI application installs itself as a CICS terminal, a handle or index is returned for that installed terminal to the EPI application. Subsequent EPI calls to interact with CICS will require the handle as a parameter to identify the region with which the EPI terminal is communicating. The EPI allows multiple CICS terminal installations to occur, possibly against separate CICS regions. Each installation will return a different handle. This feature allows a single EPI application to install itself as multiple CICS terminals and possibly initiate multiple CICS transactions concurrently against CICS regions from one EPI application.

The EPI executes internally as both a DCE server and a DCE client application. All other application code around the EPI calls must thus conform to the DCE programming requirements. Specifically, only thread-safe programming calls and techniques may be utilized. Since an EPI application is itself a DCE RPC server program, other code in an EPI application cannot attempt to register as a DCE RPC server. This also prevents EPI calls from being executed within a CICS transaction. The EPI can only be used from a native operating system perspective.

Before executing an EPI application, the user must be authenticated as a DCE principal with sufficient authority to connect to the CICS region. Alternatively, DCE security calls may be included to authenticate with the DCE security service by means of a keytab file. An illustration of programmatic DCE authentication is shown on "Programmatic DCE Authentication" later in this chapter.

Uses of the EPI

The EPI allows an application to install and behave as a terminal. This interface opens CICS up to a whole range of new applications.

Since X-Windows and Motif programming are not suited to the short-lived transactional model of CICS programming, providing presentation services in the form of a GUI interface is a primary use of EPI. GUI presentation code can be included in the C language EPI program, which can then make calls to CICS to execute transactions and have the data presented in a GUI format. The data used to present information on the GUI could be derived from 3270 data stream returned from CICS applications executing natively on CICS/6000 or from transactions routed from remote CICS systems. Sample Motif program using EPI later in this chapter describes a use of the EPI for providing graphic interfaces to CICS applications.

Access to nonnative 3270 devices can be achieved through the use of EPI. Some AIX-attached printers allow bar codes to be generated but only if special controls codes are sent to the printer, followed by the bar code data and more control codes. The special codes to control the printer plus the data may not be able to be sent or modeled as 3270 data. CICS applications that would attempt to send data to the printer via an EXEC CICS SEND command would result in sending an invalid 3270 data stream that the cicstermp printer program would not recognize. An EPI application could be developed to accept data sent by a CICS application and feed those data directly to the printer. CICS would not need to be aware that the data were not a valid 3270 data stream.

The EPI Programming Interface

The EPI provides the following API function calls that are available in the C programming language:

CICS_EpiInitialize   Initialize an EPI application.

CICS_EpiTerminate   Terminate an EPI application's usage of EPI resources.

CICS_EpiListSystems   Obtain a list of CICS regions for possible connection.

CICS_EpiAddTerminal   Install the EPI application into a CICS region as a terminal.

CICS_EpiDelTerminal   Delete an EPI application from a CICS region, equivalent to executing the CSSF signoff transaction.

CICS_EpiStartTran   Start a transaction on a CICS region.

CICS_EpiReply   Return data from an EPI application back to a CICS region.

CICS_EpiGetEvent   Get or wait for an event to arrive from the CICS region.

CICS_EpiATIState   Get and set handling of asynchronous transaction starts.

CICS_EpiGetSysError   Obtain underlying operating system reason for a failure from a previous EPI call.

CICS_EPISenseCode   Return an indication of bad data received back to the region.

The standard model of an EPI application is one that initializes the EPI interface with a call to CICS_EpiInitialize(), installs itself as a terminal into CICS/6000 using CICS_EpiAddTerminal(), starts a transaction using CICS_EpiStartTran(), and enters a loop processing events returned from the CICS region using the CICS_EpiGetEvent() call.

The events sent to the EPI application by CICS/6000 inform the application when a change of state has occurred. Additionally, if the CICS application wishes to return data or ask for data from the EPI application, it also will issue an event. The events that may be sent by CICS/6000 include

- The CICS application has sent data.

- The CICS application has requested data.

- The CICS application has ended.

- A new CICS transaction has been started asynchronously against this terminal.

- The terminal is requested to end.
- The CICS application is requesting "help" information.

CICS_EpiInitialize

The `CICS_EpiInitialize()` function initializes the application for subsequent EPI calls. This call must be made before any subsequent EPI calls may be made. The version of the EPI being used is specified as a parameter; the most recent version should be used whenever possible. It is an error to attempt to initialize the EPI more than once within any specific EPI application.

Syntax

```
short CICS_EpiIntialize(/* IN */ cics_ulong_t Version)
```

Parameter

Version   The version of CICS/6000 that the EPI application is coded for and compiled on. There are three current possible values for this:

- CICS_EPI_VERSION_101   This is the version of the EPI API available with CICS/6000 V1.2.
- CICS_EPI_VERSION_100   This is the version of the EPI API available with CICS/6000 V1.1.1.
- CICS_EPI_VERSION_001   This is the version of the EPI API available with CICS/6000 V1.1.0.

Return codes

CICS_EPI_NORMAL   The EPI was initialized successfully.

CICS_EPI_ERR_FAILED   An unspecified error occurred while trying to initialize the EPI interface. The `CICS_EpiGetSysError()` function may be used to determine additional information on the cause.

`CICS_EPI_ERR_IS_INIT`   The EPI is already initialized. It is an error to attempt to initialize the EPI more than once in a single EPI application.

CICS_EPI_ERR_VERSION   The version number specified was invalid or not supported by this instance of the EPI API.

Example

```
#include <cics_epi.h>

main(int argc, char *argv[])
{
    short    returnCode;
```

```
        returnCode = CICS_EpiIntialize(CICS_EPI_VERSION_101);
        if (returnCode != CICS_EPI_NORMAL)
        {
            printf("Unable to initialize EPI: %d\n", returnCode);
            exit(1);
        }
        /* Other processing */
    }
```

CICS_EpiTerminate

This function releases any EPI-related resources acquired as part of a previous `CICS_EpiInitialize()` call. This call should be made when it is absolutely certain that no other EPI calls will be used in subsequent statements in the program. No further EPI calls are permissible other than a call to `CICS_EpiInitialize()` to reinitialize the interface. This call does not release any terminals in the region and should thus only be made once all preceding EPI terminals installed by the EPI program have been deleted with calls to `CICS_EpiDelTerminal()` and the associated `CICS_EPI_EVENT_END_TERM` responses received.

Syntax

```
short CICS_EpiTerminate()
```

Return codes

CICS_EPI_NORMAL Resources associated with EPI have been released successfully.

CICS_EPI_ERR_FAILED An unspecified error occurred while trying to terminate the EPI. The `CICS_EpiGetSysError()` function may be used to determine additional information on the cause.

CICS_EPI_ERR_NOT_INIT The EPI had not been initialized successfully previously with a call to the `CICS_EpiInitialize()` function.

CICS_EPI_ERR_IN_CALLBACK An attempt was made to free the resources consumed by the EPI from within a callback routine associated with EPI.

Example

```
#include <cics_epi.h>

main(int argc, char *argv[])
{
    short returnCode;

    CICS_EpiInitialize(CICS_EPI_VERSION_100);

    /* Some other work */
```

```
returnCode = CICS_EpiTerminate();
if (returnCode ! = CICS_EPI_NORMAL)
{
    printf("Error from CICS_EpiTerminate: %d\n", returnCode);
    exit(1);
}
/* More processing */
}
```

CICS_EpiListSystems

This call searches for suitable CICS/6000 regions in which EPI applications may be installed as terminals. The function works by scanning the DCE CDS name space for CICS regions that are running and have advertised themselves. A list of CICS/6000 regions and their descriptions is returned. The region description is taken from the **ResourceDescription** attribute of the CICS region's Region Definition (RD) resource class. The values returned may be used in a subsequent call to CICS_EpiAddTerminal() to install a terminal into a region.

Syntax

```
short CICS_EpiListSystems
( /* IN     */ cics_char_t *NameSpace,
  /* INOUT */ cics_ushort_t *Systems,
  /* OUT    */ CICS_EpiSystems_t List[])
```

Parameters

NameSpace   This parameter specifies the DCE CDS name space in which to search for CICS regions. If CICS regions are to be located in other DCE cells, the GDS name of the remote cell may be specified. If the local cell is to be searched, the NULL pointer may be used, which is equivalent to specifying / . : / .

Systems   On entry to the call, this parameter specifies the maximum number of entries that may be returned in a single call. This should be equivalent to the number of entries in the **List** parameter array. If too few entries are allocated, the CICS_EPI_ERR_MORE_SYSTEMS return code will be returned, and the parameter will be filled in with actual number of entries found on return. On normal return, the parameter will be filled with the number of valid entries found and returned in the **List** array.

List   An array of CICS_EpiSystem_t structures filled in on return. The number of valid entries in the array are specified by the **Systems** parameter. The storage for the array must be preallocated. The structures contain the name and descriptions for the CICS regions returned.

Data structures

CICS_EpiSystem_t

```
typedef struct
{
   cics_char_t SystemName[CICS_EPI_SYSTEM_MAX+1];
   cics_char_t    Description[CICS_EPI_DESCRIPTION_MAX+1];
} CICS_EpiSystem_t;
```

SystemName   Name of the CICS region. This may be up to eight characters in length and is NULL-terminated. This parameter may be specified as a CICS region name in a call to CICS_EpiAddTerminal().

Description   A NULL-terminated description of the CICS region returned. This is the description string specified in the Region Definition (RD) entry for the CICS region specified by **SystemName.**

Return codes

CICS_EPI_NORMAL   A list of CICS regions was returned successfully.

CICS_EPI_ERR_FAILED   An unspecified error occurred while trying to list the available CICS regions. The CICS_EpiGetSysError() function may be used to determine additional information on the cause.

CICS_EPI_ERR_MORE_SYSTEMS   More region names are available to be returned that were allowed by the **Systems** parameter.

CICS_EPI_ERR_NO_SYSTEMS   No CICS regions were found. The count of returned regions in the **Systems** parameter is set to zero.

CICS_EPI_ERR_NOT_INIT   The EPI interface was not initialized previously by the CICS_EpiInitialize() call

Example

```
#include <cics_epi.h>
#include <stdio.h>
#define MAX_REGIONS 10

main()
{
   CICS_EpiSystems_t  List[MAX_REGIONS];
   cics_ushort_t      count;
   short              returnCode;

   CICS_EpiInitialize(CICS_EPI_VERSION_100);
   count = MAX_REGIONS;
   returnCode = CICS_EpiListSystems(NULL, &count, List);
   if (returnCode != CICS_EPI_NORMAL)
   {
```

```
        printf("Error from CICS_EpiListSystems: %d\n", returnCode);
        exit(1);
    }
    for (index = 0; index<count; index++)
    {
        printf("Region: %s, Description: %s\n", List[index].SystemName,
                                                 List[index].Description);
    }
    /* ... more processing ... */
}
```

CICS_EpiAddTerminal

This function installs the EPI application as a terminal into the specified CICS region. A new handle index is returned that must be used to refer to this specific terminal in future EPI calls. If a callback function is required to handle events for this terminal, it should be specified in the call. The callback function is invoked when the CICS region sends an event to the EPI application. A new thread of control is created to handle the callback function and is terminated at completion of the function. The callback function is not allowed to issue any EPI calls itself; it must indicate back to another, non-EPI-initiated thread that an action is required such as calling CICS_EpiGetEvent() to retrieve the event that caused the callback function to be invoked. The callback function could include either thread signaling calls such as pthread_condsignal() or use AIX methods such as writing into a pipe to indicate to the other threads that the callback has been invoked.

The callback function should return as quickly as possible because the original event may wait on appropriate handling.

Syntax

```
short CICS_EpiAddTerminal
( /* IN */ cics_char_t        *NameSpace,
  /* IN */ cics_char_t        System[CICS_EPI_SYSTEM_MAX+1],
  /* IN */ cics_char_t        NetName[CICS_EPI_NETNAME_MAX+1],
  /* IN */ cics_char_t        DevType[CICS_EPI_DEVTYPE_MAX+1],
  /* IN */ CICS_EpiNotify_t   NotifyFn,
  /* OUT */ CICS_EpiDetails_t *Details,
  /* OUT */ cics_ushort_t     *TermIndex);
```

Parameters

NameSpace   This parameter specifies the DCE CDS name space in which to locate the CICS region. If CICS regions are to be located in other DCE cells, the GDS name of the remote cell may be specified. If the local cell is to be searched, the NULL pointer may be used, which is equivalent to specifying / . : / .

System   The name of the CICS region into which the EPI application is to install itself as a terminal.

NetName   A CICS netname used by the CICS region to select how the terminal shall be installed. This may be up to CICS_EPI_NETNAME_MAX characters in length and be NULL-terminated. If a string is specified, it must match a **NetName** attribute in the terminal definitions (WD). The terminal may be autoinstalled by specifying a NULL pointer in place of a string. The NULL pointer is not the empty string ("").

DevType   This parameter specifies the set of suitable autoinstall models passed to the autoinstall program if no netname is specified in the **NetName** parameter. If this parameter is **NULL,** the default models will be used during autoinstall.

NotifyFn   This parameter specifies a callback function to be invoked when an event arrives from the CICS region for this installed terminal. If the NULL pointer is specified, no callback function is registered, and the event may be detected by a call to CICS_EpiGetEvent(). The callback function is invoked in a thread of control created just for handling the function. No other EPI calls may be made within the callback.

Details   This parameter returns a pointer to a structure holding detailed information about the newly installed terminal.

TermIndex   An index or handle to the newly installed terminal. This parameter should be passed to any other EPI functions that are to correspond directly with this terminal.

Data structures

CICS_EpiNotify_t

```
typedef void (*CICS_EpiNotify_t)(cics_ushort_t TermIndex);
```

TermIndex   The terminal that has had the event posted against it.

CICS_EpiDetails_t

```
typedef struct
{
    cics_char_t    NetName[CICS_EPI_NETNAME_MAX+1];
    short          NumLines;
    short          NumColumns;
    cics_ushort_t  MaxData;
    short          ErrLastLine;
    short          ErrIntensify;
    short          ErrColor;
    short          ErrHilight;
    short          Hilight;
    short          Color;
    short          Printer;
} CICS_EpiDetails_t;
```

NetName   The CICS netname assigned to this terminal. This will be the netname specified by the **NetName** parameter on the

`CICS_EpiAddTerminal` call or the name generated by CICS during an autoinstall.

NumLines   The number of lines known to CICS to be supported by the terminal. Determined by the **NumLines** parameter in the terminal definitions (WD) for the model of terminal chosen for installation.

NumColumns   The number of columns known to CICS to be supported by the terminal. Determined by the **NumColumns** parameter in the terminal definitions (WD) for the model of terminal chosen for installation.

Maxdata   The maximum amount of data that CICS may send to this terminal in one send event.

ErrLastLine   A value of **1** if the terminal should display error messages on the last line, and a value of **0** otherwise.

ErrIntensify   A value of **1** if the terminal should display error messages intensified, and a value of **0** otherwise.

ErrColor   The color in which error messages should be displayed.

ErrHilight   The highlighting attribute for error messages.

Hilight   A value of **1** if the terminal supports extended highlighting, and a value of **0** otherwise.

Color   A value of **1** if the terminal supports color, and a value of **0** otherwise.

Printer   A value of **1** if the terminal is defined to be a printer, and a value of **0** otherwise.

Return codes

CICS_EPI_NORMAL   The terminal has been installed successfully.

CICS_EPI_ERR_FAILED   An unspecified error occurred while trying to initialize the EPI interface. The `CICS_EpiGetSysError()` function may be used to determine additional information on the cause.

CICS_EPI_ERR_MAX_TERMS   The maximum number of installed terminals has already been installed for this EPI application.

CICS_EPI_ERR_NOT_INIT   The `CICS_EpiInitialize()` function has not been called previously, and so the EPI environment is not yet initialized.

CICS_EPI_ERR_SYSTEM   The CICS region specified by the **System** parameter does not exist or cannot be contacted.

Example

```
#include <cics_epi.h>
#include <stdio.h>
```

```
void Notify(cics_ushort_t TermIndex)
{
    printf("An event has arrived from Terminal: %d\n", TermIndex);
    return;
}

main(int argc, char *argv[])
{
    short              returnCode;
    CICS_EpiDetails_t Details;
    cics_ushort_t      TermIndex;

    CICS_EpiInitialize(CICS_EPI_VERSION_100);
    returnCode = CICS_EpiAddTerminal(NULL, argv[1], NULL, NULL, Notify,
                                     &Details, &TermIndex);
    if (returnCode != CICS_EPI_NORMAL)
    {
        printf("Error from CICS_EpiAddTerminal(): %d\n", returnCode);
        exit(1);
    }
    /* ... other processing ... */
}
```

CICS_EpiDelTerminal

This function deletes a previously installed EPI terminal application in the CICS region. The terminal would have been installed by a call to CICS_EpiAddTerminal(), which would have returned a **TermIndex** value. This call is only a request to terminate the terminal. The terminal should not be assumed to have been deleted until an associated CICS_EPI_EVENT_END_TERM has been received. A terminal cannot be deleted until any transactions executing against it have completed.

Syntax

```
short CICS_EpiDelTerminal(/* IN */ cics_ushort_t TermIndex)
```

Parameters

TermIndex   The index or handle value for the terminal to be uninstalled. This value should have been returned previously by a call to CICS_EpiAddTerminal().

Return codes

CICS_EPI_NORMAL   The request to delete the terminal has been delivered successfully.

CICS_EPI_ERR_BAD_INDEX   The **TermIndex** specified does not correspond to a previously installed terminal from this EPI application.

CICS_EPI_ERR_FAILED   An unspecified error occurred while trying to delete the EPI terminal. The CICS_EpiGetSysError() function may be used to determine additional information on the cause.

CICS_EPI_ERR_NOT_INIT   The EPI has not been initialized. A call to `CICS_EpiInitialize()` is required.

CICS_EPI_ERR_TRAN_ACTIVE   A transaction is currently executing against the terminal. A terminal cannot be deleted until it is not associated with a transaction.

Example

```
#include <cics_epi.h>
#include <stdio.h>

main(int argc, char *argv[])
{
   short returnCode;
   CICS_EpiDetails_t Details;
   cics_ushort_t TermIndex;
   CICS_EpiInitialize(CICS_EPI_VERSION_100);
   returnCode = CICS_EpiAddTerminal(NULL, argv[1], NULL, NULL, NULL,
                                    &Details, &TermIndex);
if (returnCode != CICS_EPI_NORMAL)
{
   printf("Error from CICS_EpiAddTerminal(): %d\n", returnCode);
   exit(1);
   }
   /* ... other processing ... */
   returnCode = CICS_EpiDelTerminal(TermIndex);
   if (returnCode != CICS_EPI_NORMAL)
   {
      printf("Error from CICS_EpiDelTerminal(): %d\n", returnCode);
      exit(1);
   }
   /* ... Wait for end of terminal event ... */
   CICS_EpiTerminate();
   exit(0);
}
```

CICS_EpiStartTran

This call causes a CICS transaction to execute in the CICS region. This function may be used to start a transaction only when no transaction is currently executing associated with this terminal. The transaction will be over when a CICS_EVENT_END_TRAN event is returned to the application. Initial data may be supplied to the transaction. This data are expected to contain 3270 data stream as though it had been generated from a 3270 terminal. Specifically, the data stream should contain at least 3 bytes, the first being the AID code for the reason that data are being entered, the next 2 bytes being the SBA address of the cursor location.

Syntax

```
short CICS_EpiStartTran
( /* IN */ cics_ushort_t TermIndex,
  /* IN */ cics_char_t   TransId[CICS_EPI_TRANSID_MAX+1],
  /* IN */ cics_ubyte_t  *Data,
  /* IN */ cics_ushort_t Size);
```

Parameters

TermIndex   The handle or index to the previously installed EPI terminal against which the transaction will execute against in the region.

TransId   A transaction name for the transaction to be started. If this is a NULL parameter, the transaction name will be extracted from the data received by the CICS region in the **Data** parameter.

Data   Initial data to be passed back to the CICS region. These data must contain at least 3 bytes: one byte for the AID key that would have caused the return and 2 bytes for the cursor address.

Size   The size in bytes of the data specified by the **Data** parameter.

Return codes

CICS_EPI_NORMAL   The transaction was submitted to the CICS region correctly.

CICS_EPI_ERR_FAILED   An unspecified error occurred while trying to start a transaction. The `CICS_EpiGetSysError()` function may be used to determine additional information on the cause.

CICS_EPI_ERR_ATI_ACTIVE   An ATI transaction is active for the EPI terminal.

CICS_EPI_ERR_BAD_INDEX   The **TermIndex** specified does not correspond to a previously installed terminal from this EPI application.

CICS_EPI_ERR_NOT_INIT   The EPI has not been initialized. A call to `CICS_EpiInitialize()` is required.

CICS_EPI_ERR_TTI_ACTIVE   A TTI transaction is already active for this terminal.

Example

```
#include <cics_epi.h>
main(int argc, char *argv[])
{
    /* ... EPI and other initialization */
    returnCode = CICS_EpiStartTran(TermIndex, "XYZ", "ABC", 3);
    if (returnCode != CICS_EPI_NORMAL)
    {
        printf("Error from CICS_EpiStartTran(): %d\n", returnCode);
        /* Handle error */
    }
    /* ... More processing ... */
}
```

CICS_EpiReply

This function is used to respond to a CICS transaction that issues an EXEC CICS RECEIVE or EXEC CICS CONVERSE command against an EPI application terminal. The function allows data to be sent back to the CICS/6000 application. The first 3 bytes of data are interpreted by CICS and not returned to the application. The first byte corresponds to the Action Identifier (AID) key pressed that would have caused a real 3270 terminal to return data. The second and third bytes are 3270 buffer coding for the cursor position.

This function should only be called in response to the arrival of a CICS_EPI_EVENT_CONVERSE event.

Syntax

```
short CICS_EpiReply( /* IN */ cics_ushort_t TermIndex,
                     /* IN */ cics_ubyte_t *Data,
                     /* IN */ cics_ushort_t Size);
```

Parameters

TermIndex   The handle or index to the previously installed EPI terminal against which the transaction will execute in the region.

Data   This parameter is a pointer to data to be returned to the CICS/6000 region. It must be at least 3 bytes in length, corresponding to the AID value and the cursor position that would be returned by a real 3270 terminal.

Size   This parameter specifies the length of the data that are to be returned to the CICS application in the **Data** parameter.

Return codes

CICS_EPI_NORMAL   Data were returned to the CICS region successfully.

CICS_EPI_ERR_BAD_INDEX   The **TermIndex** specified does not correspond to a previously installed terminal from this EPI application.

CICS_EPI_ERR_FAILED   An unspecified error occurred while trying to return data. The CICS_EpiGetSysError() function may be used to determine additional information on the cause.

CICS_EPI_ERR_NO_CONVERSE   The CICS region is not currently expecting data to be returned.

CICS_EPI_ERR_NO_DATA   The size of the data returned was zero.

CICS_EPI_ERR_NOT_INIT   The EPI has not been initialized. A call to CICS_EpiInitialize() is required.

CICS_EPI_ERR_IN_CALLBACK   This function was called from within an EPI callback routine; this is invalid.

Example

```
#include <cics_epi.h>
main(int argc, char *argv[])
{
    char data[] = {0x27, 0x20, 0x20}; /*   ENTER key, cursor (0,0) */

    /* ... EPI and other Initialization ... */
    CICS_EpiStartTran(TermIndex, "XYZ", "ABC", 3);
    rc = CICS_EpiGetEvent(TermIndex, CICS_EPI_WAIT, &Event);
    if (Event.Event == CICS_EPI_EVENT_CONVERSE)
    {
        rc = CICS_EpiReply(TermIndex, data, sizeof(data));
    }
    /* .... */
}
```

CICS_EpiATIState

This function allows the handling of Asynchronous Transaction Initiation (ATI) requests to be processed in different ways. ATI requests may originate from a CICS region against a terminal and hence against an EPI application. The EPI has the ability to block the ATI requests such that they are queued against the terminal instead of being executed. Following a CICS_EpiAddTerminal() call, the initial state of ATI handling is that ATI requests will be blocked. They will continue to be blocked until this call is made with the **AtiState** parameter set to CICS_EPI_ATI_ON. Setting the value to CICS_EPI_ATI_HOLD will result in the ATI requests being blocked again. The value CICS_EPI_ATI_QUERY will result in the return of the current state of ATI handling.

Syntax

```
short CICS_EpiATIState
( /* IN */ cics_ushort_t          TermIndex,
  /* INOUT */ CICS_EpiATIState_t *AtiState);
```

Parameters

TermIndex   The handle or index to the previously installed EPI terminal against which the transaction will execute in the region.

AtiState   This parameter specifies the value that ATI handling is to take or a request to query the current value. The values this parameter may take are

- CICS_EPI_ATI_ON   This value specifies that ATI handling is to be enabled for the logical EPI terminal.
- CICS_EPI_ATI_HOLD   This value specifies that ATI handling is to be disabled for the logical EPI terminal.

- CICS_EPI_ATI_QUERY   This value specifies the current state of ATI handling.

Return codes

CICS_EPI_NORMAL   The ATI status was set or queried correctly.

CICS_EPI_ERR_ATI_STATE   The index supplied in the **AtiState** parameter was invalid.

CICS_EPI_BAD_INDEX   The **TermIndex** specified does not correspond to a previously installed terminal from this EPI application.

CICS_EPI_ERR_FAILED   The call failed for an unknown reason.

CICS_EPI_ERR_NOT_INIT   The EPI has not been initialized. A call to CICS_EpiInitialize() is required.

CICS_EPI_ERR_IN_CALLBACK   This function was called from within an EPI callback routine; this is invalid.

Example

```
#include <cics_epi.h>
#include <stdio.h>
main(int argc, char *argv[])
{
   short              returnCode;
   CICS_EpiDetails_t  Details;
   cics_ushort_t      TermIndex;
   CICS_EpiATIState_t ATIState;

   CICS_EpiInitialize(CICS_EPI_VERSION_101);
   returnCode = CICS_EpiAddTerminal(NULL, argv[1], NULL, NULL, NULL,
                                    &Details, &TermIndex);

   ATIState = CICS_EPI_ATI_ON;
   rc = CICS_EpiATIState(TermIndex, &ATIState);
   /* ... other processing ... */
}
```

CICS_EpiSenseCode

This function is used to return an indication to the calling application that the data sent were somehow invalid. This is usually an indication that the 3270 data stream received is not valid.

Syntax

```
short CICS_EpiSenseCode( /* IN */ cics_ushort TermIndex,
                         /* IN */ CICS_EpiSenseCode_t SenseCode);
```

Parameters

TermIndex   The handle or index to the previously installed EPI terminal against which the transaction will execute in the region.

SenseCode   Sense code failure condition; this may be either

- CICS_EPI_SENSE_OPCHECK   Bad 3270 data.
- CICS_EPI_SENSE_REJECT   Bad 3270 command.

Return codes

CICS_EPI_NORMAL   The call informed the CICS region of an error in received data.

CICS_EPI_ERR_BAD_INDEX   The **TermIndex** specified does not correspond to a previously installed terminal from this EPI application.

CICS_EPI_ERR_FAILED   The call failed for an unknown reason.

CICS_EPI_ERR_NOT_INIT   The EPI has not been initialized. A call to CICS_EpiInitialize() is required.

CICS_EPI_ERR_SENSE_CODE   The sense code that the application is attempting to return to the CICS region is invalid.

CICS_EPI_ERR_IN_CALLBACK   This function was called from within an EPI callback routine; this is invalid.

Example

```
#include <cics_epi.h>

main(int argc, char *argv[])
{
    /* ... EPI and other Initialization ... */
    CICS_EpiStartTran(TermIndex, "XYZ", "ABC", 3);

    rc = CICS_EpiGetEvent(TermIndex, CICS_EPI_WAIT, &Event);
    if (Event.Event = = CICS_EPI_EVENT_SEND)
    {
        if ( /* bad data in Event.Data */ )
        {
            rc = CICS_EpiSenseCode(TermIndex, CICS_EPI_SENSE_REJECT);
        }
    }
    /* .... */
}
```

CICS_EpiGetEvent

This function is used to retrieve or wait for an event sent from the CICS region. Events may be generated for a number of reasons.

This is one of the most important of all EPI calls. Understanding this call is essential for successful EPI programming.

The following are some important considerations for using this call:

- The return code CICS_EPI_ERR_MORE_EVENTS indicates that further events are available for retrieval. This return code is not an indication that an error has occurred.

- The **Size** and **Data** parameters of the event data type must be set before calling this function.

Syntax

```
short CICS_EpiGetEvent( /* IN */ cics_ushort_t TermIndex,
                        /* IN */ CICS_EpiWait_t Wait,
                        /* OUT */ CICS_EpiEvent_t *Event);
```

Parameters

TermIndex   The handle or index to the previously installed EPI terminal against which the transaction will execute in the region.

Wait   This parameter specifies whether or not the call is to block waiting for an event to arrive or should return immediately. If no event is available in the nonblocking mode, the CICS_EPI_ERR_NO_EVENT code is returned.

Event   This parameter is a pointer to an event structure that is filled in when an event is available.

Data structures

CICS_EpiEvent_t

```
typedef struct {

    cics_ushort_t    TermIndex;
    CICS_EpiEvent_t  Event;
    CICS_EpiEnd_t    EndReason;
    cics_char_t      TransId[CICS_EPI_TRANSID_MAX+1];
    cics_char_t      AbendCode[CICS_EPI_ABEND_MAX+1];
    cics_ubyte_t     *Data;
    cics_ushort_t    Size; } CICS_EpiEvent_t;
```

TermIndex   The terminal index corresponding to the EPI terminal for which the event arrived.

Event   The reason that the event arrived. This may be one of the following:

- CICS_EPI_EVENT_SEND
- CICS_EPI_EVENT_CONVERSE
- CICS_EPI_EVENT_END_TRAN
- CICS_EPI_EVENT_START_ATI
- CICS_EPI_EVENT_END_TERM
- CICS_EPI_EVENT_HELP

EndReason   Qualifier if the event received was CICS_EPI_EVENT_ END_TERM. The possible reasons that the EPI terminal has been asked to shut down:

- CICS_EPI_END_SIGNOFF
- CICS_EPI_END_SHUTDOWN
- CICS_EPI_END_OUTSERVICE
- CICS_EPI_END_UNKNOWN
- CICS_EPI_END_FAILED

TransId   The name of the next transaction to start if the event was CICS_EPI_EVENT_END_TRAN or the transaction just started if the event was CICS_EPI_EVENT_START_ATI.

AbendCode   The ending ABEND code of the transaction if the event type is CICS_EPI_EVENT_END_TRAN.

Data   3270 data passed to and from CICS.

Size   The length of the 3270 data passed in the **Data** parameter to and from CICS.

Return codes

CICS_EPI_NORMAL   An event was retrieved successfully.

CICS_EPI_ERR_BAD_INDEX   The **TermIndex** specified does not correspond to a previously installed terminal from this EPI application.

CICS_EPI_ERR_MORE_DATA   The data returned in the **Event** structure for an event has been truncated because more data were to be returned than could be stored in the **Event** data type.

CICS_EPI_ERR_MORE_EVENTS   This value is returned if there are additional events ready for return to the EPI application. This return code is *not* an error indication.

CICS_EPI_ERR_NO_EVENT   This value is returned if the nonblocking **Wait** parameter is specified and there are no events available for immediate return.

CICS_EPI_ERR_NOT_INIT   The EPI has not been initialized. A call to CICS_EpiInitialize() is required.

CICS_EPI_ERR_WAIT   The value specified by the **Wait** parameter is neither CICS_EPI_WAIT nor CICS_EPI_NOWAIT.

CICS_EPI_ERR_NULL_PARM   The pointer specified by the **Event** parameter is a NULL pointer.

CICS_EPI_ERR_IN_CALLBACK   This function was called from within an EPI callback routine; this is invalid.

Example

```
#include <cics_epi.h>

main(int argc, char *argv[])
{
    /* ... EPI and other Initialization ... */
    CICS_EpiStartTran(TermIndex, "XYZ", "ABC", 3);

    while(1)
    {
        rc = CICS_EpiGetEvent(TermIndex, CICS_EPI_WAIT, &Event);
        switch (Event.Event)
        {
            case CICS_EPI_EVENT_END_TRAN:
                /* Start a new transaction */

            case CICS_EPI_EVENT_END_TERM:
                /* Exit the program */

            default:
                /* Handle all other events */
        }
        /* .... */
    }
}
```

CICS_EpiGetSysError

This function returns additional information about the nature of a previous CICS_EPI_ERR_FAILED return code from another EPI call.

Syntax

```
short CICS_EpiGetSysError( /* IN */ cics_ushort_t TermIndex,
                           /* OUT */ CICS_EpiSysError_t *SysErr);
```

Parameters

TermIndex   The handle or index to the previously installed EPI terminal against which the transaction will execute in the region.

SysErr   This parameter specifies a pointer to a CICS_EpiSysError_t data structure that is to be filled in with error information about a preceding EPI error.

Return codes

CICS_EPI_NORMAL   The additional error information was returned successfully to the application.

CICS_EPI_ERR_NOT_INIT The EPI has not been initialized. A call to `CICS_EpiInitialize()` is required.

CICS_EPI_ERR_BAD_INDEX The **TermIndex** specified does not correspond to a previously installed terminal from this EPI application.

CICS_EPI_ERR_FAILED The call failed for an unknown reason.

CICS_EPI_ERR_NULL_PARM The pointer specified by the **SysErr** parameter was a NULL pointer.

CICS_EPI_ERR_IN_CALLBACK This function was called from within an EPI callback routine; this is invalid.

Example

```
#include <cics_epi.h>

main(int argc, cahr *argv[])
{
    short              returnCode;
    CICS_EpiSysError_t SysErr;

    returnCode = CICS_EpiInitialize(CICS_EPI_VERSION_100);
    if (returnCode = = CICS_EPI_ERR_FAILED)
    {
        CICS_EpiGetSysError(TermIndex, &SysErr);
        printf("Cause: %d, Value: %d, Msg: %s\n",
            SysErr.Cause, SysErr.Value, SysErr.Msg);
    }
    /* Some other work */
}
```

Compiling and linking an EPI application

The compilation of an EPI application requires the inclusion of a C language header file called `cics_epi.h` and the linking with the CICS-supplied library of EPI routines called `libcicsepi.a`. The following code illustrates the compilation step to build an EPI application:

```
xlc_r -o <executable name> \

   <source file>.c \
   -I /usr/lpp/cics/include \
   -L /usr/lpp/cics/lib \
   -lcicsepi
```

A set of sample EPI applications is supplied with CICS/6000 in the `/usr/lpp/cics/src/samples/epi` directory. These samples illustrate a number of the principles discussed previously.

Other CICS clients

The previous subsections discussed CICS/6000 client access through the EPI and ECI APIs from an AIX environment. The same APIs also may be used to

access CICS/6000 from PC environments executing OS/2, Windows, and DOS, as well as from an Apple MAC. IBM products called *CICS clients* provide access to CICS/6000 through EPI, ECI, and 3270 terminal emulation. The client products also provide access to other CICS servers on other operating environments, including ESA, OS/2, and OS/400.

To connect to CICS/6000, the clients utilize TCP/IP as the transport protocol. The data that flow over TCP/IP are raw TCP/IP datagrams, the content of which is architected into CICS/6000 and the clients. Specifically, unlike EPI and ECI on AIX, these PC- and MAC-based clients do not use or need DCE RPC as the transport.

Application development of ECI or EPI applications on the PC and MAC environments is outside the scope of this book. The APIs are portable, however. An ECI or EPI application developed on AIX should be easily portable to other environments, and vice versa.

Before using CICS/6000 as a server for a PC or MAC client, CICS/6000 needs to be configured to listen for incoming TCP/IP requests to connect a terminal or service an ECI or EPI request. This configuration is achieved by defining a CICS listener using the Listener Definitions (LD) resource class. The Listener Definitions define the TCP/IP ports the incoming clients should use when connecting. A Listener Definition suitable for a PC or MAC client should specify the following:

Protocol   This should be set to **TCP** to indicate that the definition relates to a TCP/IP connection as opposed to an SNA listener used for local SNA ISC communication.

TCPService   This optionally specified parameter defines the TCP/IP port on which CICS/6000 will set up a listener. If this attribute is not specified, the default port of 1435 will be used. If an alternate TCP/IP port is required, a service name as defined in the /etc/services file should be used. The /etc/service file contains a mapping from symbolic names to TCP/IP port numbers that allows applications to determine ports by name. The following example illustrates the definition for a CICS/6000 listener for port 9001:

```
In the /etc/services file:
cicslistener tcp/9001

Define the listener to CICS:
cicsadd -c ld -r $CICSREGION LIS1 \
    Protocol = TCP \
    TCPService = "cicslistener"
```

Programmatic DCE Authentication

As mentioned previously, both an EPI and an ECI application must be executed within a DCE authenticated environment or else authenticate itself through the use of DCE security API.

```
$ rgy_edit
rgy_edit=> ktadd -p <principal> -pw <password> -f <password file>
```

Figure 17.1   Using the **rgy_edit** command to cache passwords.

A DCE context is normally created using the **dce_login** command. This command requires that both a DCE principal name and a password be supplied. DCE security verifies that the password is valid for the principal and creates the security context. For a program to be able to authenticate with DCE, it too must know the principal name and password to be able to supply the information to the DCE security service.

A program could be hard-coded with the password for a principal, but that would defeat the security intent. Storing the password in a file which the program could read would allow the password to be changed but would compromise security if the file were readable by others. DCE itself provides a solution that allows passwords to be stored in files for the retrieval of programs but encrypts the password within the file. Even if someone were to be able to read the password file when he or she should not, the password would still be unknown to him or her because it is encrypted.

The caching of passwords in a file may be accomplished using the DCE **rgy_edit** command. Using this command, the principal name and password can be saved in a file. The **ktadd** (key table add) subcommand takes the principal name, password, and file as parameters and caches the password. If the file did not exist previously, the file is created. A single password file can be used to hold multiple passwords for different principals. The permissions on the file created are set to $-rw ---- $ (read/write for the owner only). If the program that is to read the password file is not going to execute as the AIX user that created the file, permissions or ownership of the file must be changed. The use of **rgy_edit** is illustrated in Fig. 17.1.

The program shown in Fig. 17.2 illustrates how DCE authentication may be performed programmatically. The function DceAuthenticate() is used to authenticate the client program. It takes two parameters, the name of the DCE principal to be authenticated and the name of an AIX keyfile containing the password for the principal.

```
#include <stdio.h>
#include <dce/keymgmt.h>
#include <dce/rpcbase.h>
#include <dce/dce_error.h>
#include <dce/sec_login.h>

/*
 * Utility function to display DCE error messages
 */
void DceError(char *message, unsigned long status)
{
    unsigned char   errorText[dce_c_error_string_len];
    int             status2;

    dce_error_inq_text(status, errorText, &status2);
    fprintf(stderr, "%s: %s\n", message, errorText);
    return;
}


/*
 * DCE Authentication function:
 * Parameters:
 * principal - NULL terminated DCE principal name
 * keyFile   - NULL terminated name of AIX file containing key for principal
 *
 * Return Codes:
 * 0 - succeeded with authentication
 * 1 - failed to authenticate
 *
 */
int DceAuthenticate(unsigned char *principal, unsigned char *keyFile)
{
    sec_login_handle_t      loginContext;
    sec_passwd_rec_t        *passwd;
    sec_login_auth_src_t    authSrc;
    boolean32               resetPasswd;
    error_status_t          status;


    sec_login_setup_identity((unsigned char *)principal,
        sec_login_no_flags,
        &loginContext,
        &status);

    if (status!=0)
    {
        DceError("sec_login_setup_identity", status);
        return(1);
    }

    sec_key_mgmt_get_key(rpc_c_authn_dce_secret,
        keyFile,
        principal,
        0,
        (void **)&passwd,
        &status);

    if (status!=0)
    {
        DceError("sec_key_mgmt_get_key", status);
        return(1);
    }

    sec_login_validate_identity(loginContext,
        passwd,
        &resetPasswd,
        &authSrc,
        &status);

    if (status!=0)
    {
        DceError("sec_login_validate_identity", status);
        return(1);
    }

    sec_key_mgmt_free_key(passwd, &status);

    return(0);
}
```

Figure 17.2 DCE programmatic authentication.

18

CICS/6000 and TCP/IP Sockets

TCP/IP is a communications protocol that allows machines which are LAN-or WAN-attached to communicate with each other. A machine that executes TCP/IP is termed a *host*. TCP/IP applications use an API called *sockets* to communicate with each other. The sockets API is available with all UNIX implementations including AIX.

Sockets is a client/server API. This means that a *server* application listens for incoming requests, and the *client* application originates a request.

There are two flavors of TCP/IP communication, one is connection-oriented and the other is datagram-oriented. The connection-oriented mechanism is known as *TCP,* and the datagram-oriented version is known as *UDP.* The sockets API is almost identical for each type, but some differences exist. The following table outlines the major differences between TCP and UDP:

TCP	UDP
Connection-oriented	Datagram-oriented
Guaranteed delivery	No guaranteed delivery
Byte stream array of data	Discrete packets of data
Indicates loss of server or client	No indication of loss of server or client
Not able to pass connection to other application	Able to pass connection to other application
Not able to broadcast data	Ability to broadcast data

A socket is a notional connection between two TCP/IP applications. These applications may reside on different physical machines (hosts) or be on the same machine. A socket application has two attributes that uniquely specify it. These attributes are its *TCP/IP address* and its *port number* or *port.*

Every host in a TCP/IP network has a 4-byte TCP/IP address. These addresses are usually written as decimal numbers separated by the . (pronounced "dot") character. TCP/IP hosts usually have names (usually called *host names*) that can be used as lookup entries in a database to return the 4-byte TCP/IP address.

A port number is a 2-byte value used to distinguish one application from another on a particular TCP/IP host. The port numbers can be thought off as house numbers on a street, while the TCP/IP address can be thought of as the street name itself. Thus, to send a letter to someone, you would need to know the street name and house number; with TCP/IP, to form a connection with a remote TCP/IP application, you need to know the TCP/IP address and port number.

The sockets API

The sockets API is a set of system calls that can be made from a C language application to form connections between two applications. The following is a list of the sockets calls that are used most commonly:

Call	Description
socket	Create a socket. This call creates a socket descriptor that is used to identify the connection to another application.
bind	Bind the socket to a specified TCP/IP address and port number.
listen	Specify how many connections to accept.
accept	Wait and accept an incoming TCP connection.
sendto	Write data into an unconnected socket.
recvfrom	Receive data from an unconnected socket.
read	Read some data into a socket.
write	Write some data into a socket.
close	Close a socket. This call should be made to close a connection to a socket application. For CICS/6000, this call *must* be made before ending a sockets application.

A sockets application

A sockets server application registers a sockets interface. The interface is specified by the port number and whether it is a TCP or UDP service. Once the server has registered, client applications can make connection requests to the server. The sequence of calls for a TCP server is as follows:

```
main()
{
    s = socket(...)       [1]
    bind(s, ...)          [2]
    listen(...)           [3]
    while (...)
    {
        n = accept(...)   [4]
        Process ...
        close(n)          [5]
    }
}
```

1. Create the TCP/IP socket used by the server to listen for incoming requests. The socket will be specified as being of type SOCK_STREAM, indicating that it is a TCP connection.

2. The previously created socket is associated or bound with the port number on which the application will listen for the incoming requests.

3. The **listen()** call specifies how many connection requests will be handled by the operating system until the **accept()** call is issued to handle the connection directly.

4. Wait for and accept an incoming connection request. This call will block until a client issues a connection request. When the request arrives, a new socket will be returned connected to the client.

5. After processing the client request, the socket allocated for the connection between the server and the client must be released.

The sequence of calls for a UDP server is shown below:

```
main()
{
    s = socket(...)        [1]
    bind(s, ...)           [2]
    while (...)
    {
        recvfrom(s, ...)   [3]
        Process ...
    }
}
```

1. Create the socket for receiving incoming requests from the client. The SOCK_DGRAM attribute will be specified to signify that UDP protocol should be used.

2. The socket is associated or bound with the port number that the client should use to connect to the server.

3. The **recvfrom()** command is issued to block until a message arrives from a client. The message will contain the data and the IP address and port number from the client.

The sequence of calls for a TCP socket client is as follows:

```
main()
{
    s = socket(...)   [1]
    bind(s, ...)      [2]
    connect(s, ...)   [3]
    send(s, ...)      [4]
        Process ...
}
```

1. Create the socket to communicate with the server application. For TCP connections, the SOCK_STREAM attribute must be specified.

2. The socket is associated with the TCP/IP address and port number of the server application.

3. A connection request is made to the server application.

4. Data are sent through the socket from the client to the server.

The sequence of calls for a UDP socket client is as follows:

```
main()
{
    s = socket(...)   [1]
    sendto(s, ...)    [2]
    Process ...
}
```

1. The socket is created for communication from the client to the server. The SOCK_DGRAM attribute is specified for UDP communication.

2. Data are sent from the client to the server. The address and port number of the server are included in the call to send the data.

CICS/6000 and sockets

Within a CICS/6000 application, it is permissible to include sockets calls. A CICS/6000 application may be a socket server or a socket client or both.

There are certain restrictions when using sockets in a CICS/6000 application. The following subsections list some CICS/6000-specific caveats and warnings for CICS/6000 socket programming.

CICS/6000 and socket descriptors

Each CICS/6000 application executes in a CICS application server. These application servers are long-running AIX processes. When a socket is created with the **socket()** call, a socket file descriptor is returned. These socket file descriptors are taken from the pool of AIX file descriptors for a process. A socket descriptor is associated with a process and may be released by a call to the **close()** function or when the process ends. Since a CICS/6000 program runs in a process that normally does not end, it is essential that at the end of a CICS/6000 program all created sockets are explicitly closed. In a socket client application, failure to do this will result in a socket descriptor being used up each application run. Eventually, all available descriptor resources for the CICS process will be used up.

If a socket server application fails to close the socket before the program ends, the operating system will mark the port as in use. An attempt to run the server program again will cause the **bind()** call to fail with an address already in use error.

CICS/6000 and thread-safe socket calls

CICS/6000 applications execute in a DCE multithreaded environment. As a result, the following sockets-related function calls should be replaced by their thread-safe replacements:

Regular function	Thread-safe	Description
gethostbyname	**gethostbyname_r**	Get a TCP/IP address by name
gethostbyaddr	**gethostbyaddr_r**	Get a host name by address
getprotent	**getprotent_r**	Get a TCP/IP protocol entry
getservbyname	**getservbyname_r**	Get a TCP/IP service by name

Note: These calls are *not* parameter equivalents of each other. The parameters for a particular function should be determined from the *DCE Application Programming Reference.*

Compiling CICS/6000 sockets applications

Compiling CICS/6000 sockets applications requires that an additional C language preprocessor definition be made. The _ALL_SOURCE C preprocessor flag must be set. This can be accomplished by setting the CCFLAGS environment variable to -D_ALL_SOURCE before invoking the **cicstcl** CICS translate and compiler command. In an AIX Makefile, this may look as follows:

```
myprog: myprog.ccs
    CCFLAGS = -D_ALL_SOURCE; \
    export CCFLAGS; \
    cicstcl -lC myprog.ccs
```

CICS/6000 socket servers

A socket server is a long-running task. In a CICS/6000 program, a socket server will continue to occupy an application server. This will then consume CICS/6000 resources.

When a client sockets program connects to the CICS/6000 server, the server will usually process the request. While processing the request, no additional connection requests from other clients will be accepted. If the request is potentially long-running or even blocking and many sockets clients are expected to make accepted requests in a short time, the socket server should initiate a new task to handle the request.

If no reply is expected by the client, a new CICS task can be created by simply spawning a new CICS task with the EXEC CICS START command. If a reply is expected, then UDP sockets should be used.

With UDP, the client's return address is returned by the **recvfrom()** call and can be passed to the newly started task. This task can then return the response itself.

Other response mechanisms include

- If the client is a CICS/6000 application, include the SYSID for an ISC response.

- If the client is a UNIX application, it also could be a socket server, in which case the port and host address could be supplied in the initial request.

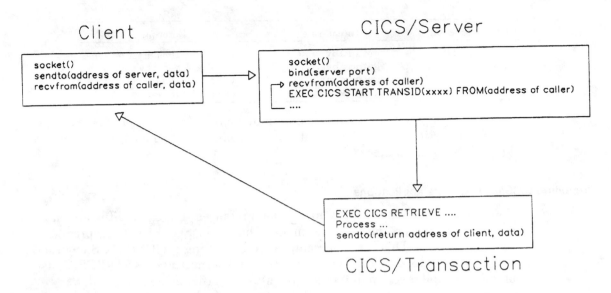

CICS/6000 and socket transactionality

Sockets connections and usage are not transactional. If a sockets call is made and work is done in two separate tasks connected by TCP/IP, an ABEND in one transaction will not cause an ABEND in the other. Great care must be take to ensure that data integrity is maintained when using sockets.

DCE RPC Programming
with CICS/6000

The DCE Remote Procedure Call (RPC) programming interface can be combined with CICS/6000 applications. The basic architecture of a DCE RPC application is that a server application provides a service that a client of that application may make use off. The client RPC application makes what looks like a regular function call within the program but is actually a series of network communications to the server program, which may be located on a separate machine. A DCE RPC server application can advertise its existence in the DCE Cell Directory Service by name. A DCE client application can then query the name space and determine the existence and location of the server. DCE RPC calls also have implied security and data conversion should the machine architecture or character set of the server and client be different from each other. The diagrams shown in Figs. 19.1 and 19.2 illustrate the normal function call paradigm verses DCE RPC.

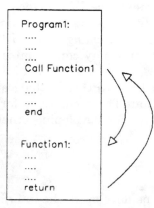

Figure 19.1 Normal function call.

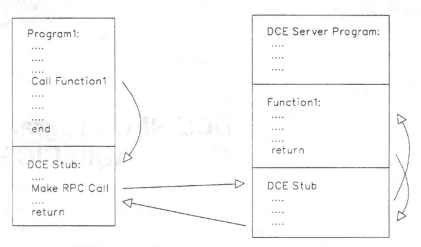

Figure 19.2   RPC function call.

CICS/6000 makes extensive use of DCE RPC technology internally as well as through programming APIs such as EPI and ECI. CICS/6000 sets itself up as a DCE RPC server, allowing client applications such as **cicsterm** and **cicsteld** to make requests to perform work within the CICS region.

The internal design of CICS/6000 requires that it register itself as a DCE RPC server. This currently prevents a CICS application from registering itself as a DCE RPC server because an RPC server may only register once per AIX process, and this privilege has already been made by CICS. For this reason, using CICS/6000 as a DCE RPC server for incoming client requests from DCE RPC clients is not possible.

A CICS/6000 application can utilize the DCE RPC technology to make RPC calls from CICS out to an external RPC server. The outgoing RPC call is not transactional in nature. Any work performed by the remote DCE RPC server would not be backed out if the CICS application were to back out. When an RPC call is made within a CICS environment, the DCE principal associated with the call is the principal of the region that has the name cics/<region>. The principal that CICS executes as must not be changed with DCE API calls or else unpredictable results will occur and may compromise CICS data integrity.

There are few restrictions in the set of DCE RPC calls that can be imbedded within a CICS C language application. The techniques for developing such applications are then similar to those for developing other DCE RPC applications.

Developing a DCE RPC Interface

Before a DCE RPC client and server can be developed, the interface that will be exported by the RPC server and utilized by the RPC client must be decided on. This interface will describe the function names exported by the server and the number and types of parameters expected by these functions. The interface is specified in a DCE RPC description language called the *Interface Definition Language* (IDL). The interface definition is edited into an IDL file and processed by a DCE-supplied utility called the *IDL compiler*. This utility takes the interface definition and produces a C language include file and two compiled object files. The object files contain DCE management code for both the DCE RPC server program and the client program. When these object code modules are linked with the final client and server code, the DCE-compiled objects handle the call and response over the network. The implementation and even operation of these modules are hidden and irrelevant to the development of the client call program and the server handling program.

Figure 19.3 presents an example of an IDL file describing a function called **CallRPC.** This function expects two arguments: The first is a DCE binding handle used by the client to identify the server, and the second parameter is a string that is to be processed. The actual design and implementation of the **CallRPC** function may be performed later. The most important aspect of this phase of DCE RPC programming is that the client and server agree on the names and parameters of functions.

Developing a DCE RPC Server

The development a DCE RPC server consists of three major tasks:

- Development of the service function that is to be actually invoked when a client calls the function to be handled by the server.

- The advertisement of the DCE RPC server service in the DCE CDS name space, allowing the client to locate the server.

- The actual servicing of incoming DCE client requests.

The development of the actual functions to handle the requests sent by the client consists of developing identically named functions to those specified in the IDL file. These functions also must have exactly the same set of parameters. When the server program is finally linked together, these functions will be invoked when the server receives the request from the client.

```
[
uuid(0017471A-A69B-1AC9-ADC9-10005A4F2D61),
version(1.0)
]
interface cicstest
{
    void CallRPC( [in] handle_t binding, [in, string] char *message);
}
```

Figure 19.3   DCE RPC Interface Definition Language sample.

The advertisement of the DCE RPC server consists of choosing a name for it within the DCE name space that should be known by the client. Once the name has been chosen, the server may utilize DCE-supplied CDS registration functions to perform the actual advertisement.

Once the server has advertised its services, it must then wait for incoming requests to actually service. Again, DCE manages this task and provides a function that a server application can call to allow DCE to take control to handle the incoming request.

The server application in Fig. 19.4 illustrates these features.

Developing a DCE RPC Client

A client of a DCE RPC server makes calls to functions defined in the IDL file. These functions will cause the request to be sent to a DCE server for processing and response. It is the responsibility of the client program to select the server to which the request is to be sent. The client will use DCE-supplied calls to interrogate the CDS name space and retrieve a "binding handle." This binding handle is an opaque data type used to direct client requests to specific servers.

Once the binding handle has been determined, the call to the DCE RPC server can actually be performed.

The client application in Fig. 19.5 illustrates these features.

```
#include <stdio.h>
#include <dce/rpc.h>
#include "cicstest.h"

/*
 * The actual function called when an RPC is made to the server.
 */
void CallRPC(rpc_binding_handle_t binding, char *message)
{
    printf("Message: %s\n", message);
    return;
}

main()
{
    unsigned char          *entryName;
    unsigned32              status;
    rpc_binding_vector_t   *bindingVector;

    /*
     * Register the RPC server entry in the DCE CDS name space as /.:/cicstest
     */
    entryName=(unsigned char *)"/.:/cicstest";

    rpc_server_register_auth_info("cell_admin", rpc_c_authn_none,
        NULL, NULL, &status);

    rpc_server_register_if(cicstest_v1_0_s_ifspec,
        NULL,
        NULL,
        &status);

    rpc_server_use_all_protseqs(rpc_c_protseq_max_reqs_default, &status);

    rpc_server_inq_bindings(&bindingVector, &status);

    rpc_ns_binding_export(rpc_c_ns_syntax_default,
        entryName,
        cicstest_v1_0_s_ifspec,
        bindingVector,
        NULL,
        &status);

    rpc_ep_register(cicstest_v1_0_s_ifspec,
        bindingVector,
        NULL,
        NULL,
        &status);

    rpc_binding_vector_free(&bindingVector, &status);

    printf("About to start listening for incoming RPCs ...\n");
    fflush(stdout);

    /*
     * Start listening for incoming server calls ...
     */
    rpc_server_listen(rpc_c_listen_max_calls_default, &status);
}
```

Figure 19.4   DCE RPC server application sample.

```
#include <dce/rpc.h>
#include <stdio.h>
#include "cicstest.h"

main(int argc, char *argv[])
{
    char                    message[100];
    short                   length;
    unsigned32              status;
    rpc_ns_handle_t         importContext;
    rpc_binding_handle_t    binding;

    /*
     * Lookup the binding to the DCE RPC server in DCE CDS name space.  The
     * server should have registered itself at /.:/cicstest.
     */
    rpc_ns_binding_import_begin(
        rpc_c_ns_syntax_default,
        (unsigned char *)"/.:/cicstest",
        cicstest_v1_0_c_ifspec,
        NULL,
        &importContext,
        &status);

    rpc_ns_binding_import_next(
        importContext,
        &binding,
        &status);

    rpc_ns_binding_import_done(&importContext, &status);


    /*
     * Get the parameters passed to the transaction for a message.
     */
    length = sizeof(message)-1;
    EXEC CICS RECEIVE INTO(message) LENGTH(&length);

    message[length] = '\0';
    fprintf(stderr, "About to send message :%s\n", message);

    /*
     * Make the actual RPC call to the server.
     */
    CallRPC(binding, (idl_char *)message);

    strcpy(message, "Message sent via RPC");
    EXEC CICS SEND TEXT FROM(message) LENGTH(strlen(message)) ERASE;
    EXEC CICS RETURN;
}
```

Figure 19.5   DCE RPC client application sample.

20

Graphic User Interface Front Ends

CICS/6000 transactions are usually short-lived applications in terms of their execution duration. Because of this, it is common for front-end applications to provide user interaction. In CICS/6000 and other CICS platforms, user interaction is commonly performed through 3270 terminals or terminal emulators.

In the workstation environment, including AIX, graphic user interfaces for applications are common. The graphic interface provides a high function interface to applications. Such interfaces usually have push buttons, pull downs, menus, and other graphic interface features that are manipulated with a mouse.

In AIX, the graphic user interface (GUI) available is known as *X-Windows*. X-Windows is a client/server-based presentation service. GUI applications, called *clients,* are written that include calls to X-Windows to draw lines or text on the display. The applications send the requests to display output to an X-Window component called the *X-Server*. The X-Server is the software or hardware that the end user directly interacts with. X-Servers are available as dedicated hardware devices or as software that executes within other graphic interface environments such as Windows or OS/2. The client applications communicate with the X-Servers over a TCP/IP network, and hence applications being presented to the user actually may execute on various remote systems.

The actual X-Windows calls are quite primitive and include window creation, line drawing, point plotting, and basic text character output. Using these primitives would be very cumbersome for a programmer to create a complex display. A programming interface called *Motif* was developed to make the creation of complex displays significantly easier than programming to the underlying X-Windows interface directly. Motif provides a rich set of building blocks that can be strung together to create the display. These building blocks include high-level components such as menu bars, pop-ups, push buttons, text entry, scroll bars, and many others. The details of the underlying X-Windows calls are hidden from the Motif programmer.

Within a CICS application, it is possible to use X-Windows and Motif calls with great care. The care is required because of the execution model of Motif. Motif uses a message-driven paradigm of execution. Application calls describe the user interface and the actions taken when a user or some external event causes a change such as a push button press or a mouse click. When the setup is complete, execution control is given to Motif to manage the display. This causes problems for CICS execution because the Motif event controller is not thread-safe and will cause CICS to fail. Additionally, the model of execution does not fit with that of a CICS transaction, which usually only executes for a short period of time. When a transaction completes, the Motif interface would end. A long-running CICS application is possible but would tie up valuable CICS resources and is generally undesirable.

The recognized way of providing a graphic interface to CICS is to develop a non-CICS application that will interact with the user and make requests to CICS to execute transactions on behalf of the user. This may be accomplished using the CICS EPI, ECI, or TCP/IP sockets programming described previously.

Writing a Motif interface to CICS/6000 transactions

As stated in the last section, a Motif interface to CICS/6000 programs should be written outside the CICS/6000 programs themselves. The presentation logic (GUI front-end) will then be separate from the transactional business logic (the CICS/6000 programs). The front-end application will send requests to CICS/6000 when appropriate requests have been entered by the user at the GUI front-end. The requests will use one of the CICS/6000 client interfaces to communicate with CICS. The selection of which interface type to be used will be based on a number of different factors.

Using ECI as the client interface.   The ECI interface provides the call-return paradigm. It is the most natural to program to within a GUI environment. When an event occurs at the GUI interface such as the user selecting a balance enquiry, the request can be sent to CICS/6000, wait for the response, and present the results to the user. The model is in concert with that of current modular programming. An ECI call into CICS/6000 will already assume that presentation logic is being handled by the caller. ECI also has the ability to extend a logical unit of work through many calls that may be required by the GUI front-end. Making ECI calls from CICS/6000 does require that the GUI application be authenticated with DCE. If asynchronous calls are required from the GUI, a special mechanism must be added to the Motif interface to allow notification of the response from the call.

Using EPI as the client interface.   The EPI interface allows the 3270 data stream from the current CICS application to be received by the GUI front-end. The front-end may have imbedded logic to parse this data stream and extract various components or fields from the data. These fields may then be used to build the GUI display presented to the user. Using the EPI in this manner would allow CICS applications to be available for both 3270-style devices and for GUI applications. The parsing of the 3270 data stream is not trivial, and a tight coupling exists between the CICS application that originates the data and the font-end application that presents the data. Changes made to the 3270 output usually will require changes to be made to the GUI front-end application.

Like ECI, EPI front-ends must execute within a DCE authenticated environment and have a special interface set up to handle incoming events with Motif.

Using TCP/IP sockets as the client interface. TCP/IP sockets provides the least overhead and may not require the GUI interface programmer to have to learn new APIs such as ECI or EPI. There is also no requirement to have the GUI interface program authenticated under DCE. Unlike ECI or EPI, a CICS/6000 server application may be required to remain executing to handle incoming sockets requests.

Sample Motif applications using ECI, EPI, and TCP/IP sockets

The following example programs illustrate the use of ECI, EPI, and TCP/IP sockets to present a trivial interface to a CICS/6000 application. The application will simply ask CICS/6000 for the current time and present the time to the user as a GUI front-end. The applications are illustrative only and are unlikely to be end-user applications in their own right. They do serve to describe many of the programming concepts.

The GUI interface presented by the samples is shown in Fig. 20.1.

Each interface method (ECI, EPI, and sockets) will utilize its own version of a CICS program back-end. The ECI CICS program will send responses back to the client through a COMMAREA, the EPI program by sending through the EXEC CICS SEND command, and the sockets application through TCP/IP sockets.

Sample Motif program using ECI. The ECI sample GUI application source code is shown in "CICS/6000 ECI GUI front-end program" later in this chapter. This application sets up the Motif interface with the X-Server using the Motif API and registers a callback function to be called whenever the user presses

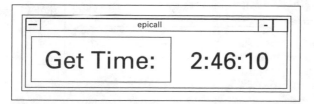

Figure 20.1 Motif front-end.

the "get time" push button. The callback function builds an ECI control block and makes the ECI call to communicate with the CICS/6000 region. When the call is made, the CICS program is invoked to handle the call. The ECI front-end calls a CICS program called *MECIBEND*. The ECI call does not return until the program within the region has completed. On completion, the data returned from the CICS application are used to update the time label field alongside the push button. A diagram showing the relationship is presented in Fig. 20.2.

The application that is invoked within CICS/6000 is called through the ECI interface and thus uses the COMMAREA to receive and pass data. The application called MECIBEND is illustrated in "CICS/6000 ECI back-end program" that follows.

CICS/6000 ECI back-end program

```
/*
 * MECIBEND:
 * CICS/6000 back end program for ECI Motif sample.
 */
DFHEIBLK  *eibptr;

main()
{
    char    timeArea[8];
    char    timeOutput[8]; /* storage to hold "hh:mm:ss"
    char    *commarea;
```

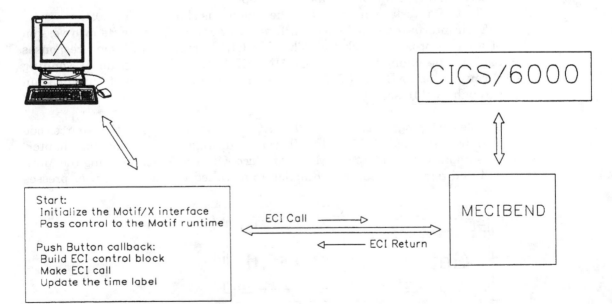

Figure 20.2 Motif and ECI interactions.

```
    /*
     * Get addressability to the COMMAREA and EIB
     */

    EXEC CICS ADDRESS COMMAREA(commarea) EIB(eibptr);
    if (eibptr->eibcalen < 8)
    {
        /*
         * No or insufficient commarea supplied
         */
        EXEC CICS RETURN;
    }

    /*
     * Obtain and format the time. Copy the result into the commarea
     * for return to the GUI front end.
     */
    EXEC CICS ASKTIME ABSTIME(timeArea);
    EXEC CICS FORMATTIME ABSTIME(timeArea) \
        TIME(timeOutput) \
        TIMESEP(`:');

    memcpy(commarea, timeOutput, 8);

    EXEC CICS RETURN;
}
```

CICS/6000 ECI GUI front-end program

```
/*
 * ecicall.c - ECI front end sample program.
 */
#include <Xm/Xm.h>
#include <Xm/Form.h>
#include <Xm/PushB.h>
#include <Xm/Label.h>
#include <locale.h>
#include <cics_eci.h>

/*
 * The following lines define some usefull variables and macros for
 * setting resource attributes of Motif widgets
 */
#define SA(resource,value) {XtSetArg(args[n],(resource),(value));n++;}
static Arg args[20];
static int n;

/*
 * The following variables are global throughout the program
 */
Widget  toplevel;
Widget  labelW;
char    *cicsregion;

/*
 * UpdateTime:
 * This function sets the time display label widget to the new hours,
 * minutes and seconds specified by the paramater. This function is called
 * on successfull return from the ECI call to the CICS/6000 region.
 */
void UpdateTime(char *newTime)
{
```

```
                  XmString  xmstring;

                  xmstring = XmStringCreate(newTime, XmSTRING_DEFAULT_CHARSET);
                  n = 0;
                  SA(XmNlabelString, xmstring);
                  XtSetValues(labelW, args, n);
                  XmStringFree(xmstring);
                  return;
          }
          /*
           * ECICallCB:
           * This function is called as a callback of the get time push button press.
           * When pressed, this function makes an ECI call to CICS/6000 to execute
           * a back-end program called MECIBEND which obtains the time, formats it
           * and returns the result in a commarea. The time is used to update the
           * current time in the motif widget.
           *
           * The CICS region used to service the call is specified by the CICSREGION
           * environment variable.
           */
          void ECICallCB()
          {
                  ECI_PARMS eciParms;
                  short rc;
                  char buffer[9];

                  /*
                   * Build the ECI calling interface
                   */ memset(&eciParms, 0, sizeof(eciParms));
                  eciParms.eci_call_type          = ECI_SYNC;
                  eciParms.eci_version            = ECI_VERSION_1;
                  eciParms.eci_luw_token          = 0;
                  eciParms.eci_extend_mode        = ECI_NO_EXTEND;
                  eciParms.eci_commarea_length    = 8;
                  eciParms.eci_commarea           = buffer;
                  memset(eciParms.eci_system_name, ` `, 8);
                  strcpy(eciParms.eci_system_name, cicsregion);
                  memcpy(eciParms.eci_program_name, "MECIBEND",8);

                  /*
                   * Make the ECI call to the CICS region
                   */
                  rc = CICS_ExternalCall(&eciParms);
                  if (rc == ECI_ERR_SYSTEM_ERROR)
                  {
                      printf("System error: %d\n", eciParms.eci_sys_return_code);
                  }
                  if (rc == ECI_NO_ERROR)
                  {
                      buffer[8] = 0;
                      UpdateTime(buffer);
                  }
                  return;
          }

          /*
           * ecicall:
           * Main entry into the program.
           */
          main(int argc, char *argv[])
          {
              Widget  formW;
              Widget  pushBW;
```

```
        setlocale(LC_ALL,"");

        cicsregion = (char *)getenv("CICSREGION");

        if (cicsregion == NULL)
        {
            printf("The CICSREGION environment variable is not set");
            exit(1);
        }

    /*
     * Create the Motif interface consisting of a container form, a push
     button
     * and a label.
     */
        toplevel = XtInitialize(argv[0], "Xeci", NULL,0,&argc,argv);

        n = 0;
        formW = XmCreateForm(toplevel, "form", args, n);
        XtManageChild(formW);

        n = 0;
        SA(XmNtopAttachment,     XmATTACH_FORM);
        SA(XmNleftAttachment,    XmATTACH_FORM);
        SA(XmNbottomAttachment,  XmATTACH_FORM);
        SA(XmNleftOffset,        5);
        SA(XmNtopOffset,         5);
        SA(XmNbottomOffset,      5);
        pushBW = XmCreatePushButton(formW, "Get Time:", args, n);
         XtAddCallback(pushBW, XmNactivateCallback, ECICallCB, NULL);
        XtManageChild(pushBW);

        n = 0;
        SA(XmNtopAttachment,     XmATTACH_FORM);
        SA(XmNleftAttachment,    XmATTACH_WIDGET);
        SA(XmNleftWidget,        pushBW);
        SA(XmNrightAttachment,   XmATTACH_FORM);
        SA(XmNbottomAttachment,  XmATTACH_FORM);
        SA(XmNrightOffset,       5);
        SA(XmNleftOffset,        5);
        SA(XmNtopOffset,         5);
        SA(XmNbottomOffset,      5);
        labelW = XmCreateLabel(formW, "00:00:00", args, n);
        XtManageChild(labelW);

        XtRealizeWidget(toplevel);
        XtMainLoop();
    }
```

Sample Motif program using EPI. The EPI sample GUI application source code is shown in "CICS/6000 EPI GUI front-end program" later in this chapter. This application, like the ECI front-end, sets up an interface using the Motif API. Additionally, a UNIX pipe is created to allow events originating from CICS/6000 to be received by the Motif interface and have a Motif-registered callback function invoked. When an EPI event arrives from CICS/6000, if an EPI notify function has been registered, the notify function is invoked in a separate thread of the application. It is invalid to either issue the CICS_EpiGetEvent() function to retrieve the event or to make any Motif calls. To circumvent this problem, the UNIX pipe is written to from the EPI notify function, and then the notify function ends. The act of writing into the pipe causes Motif to call a callback function that had been registered previously against the pipe. The callback function should extract the data written into the pipe to prevent the callback from being immediately called again when it returns. After reading from the pipe, the callback function may issue either `CICS_Epi_xxx()` calls or Motif calls since it is executing in the main thread of Motif. The diagram shown in Fig. 20.3 illustrates the interaction between the EPI application and the CICS/6000 region. When the push button is pressed, the callback function associated with the push button makes an EPI call to initiate a transaction in the region. The transaction will send some data back to the application that will be used to update the time label if the event was a send event. Other events such as the end of the transaction are ignored.

CICS/6000 EPI back-end program

```
/*
 * MECIBEND:
 * CICS/6000 back end program for ECI Motif sample.
 */
DFHEIBLK  *eibptr;
```

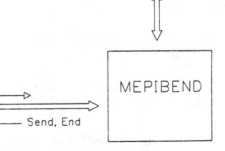

```
Start:
 Initialize the Motif/X interface
 Register pipe as callback source
 Initialize the EPI interface
 Attach to CICS region as terminal
 Pass control to Motif runtime

Push Button callback:
 Make EPI call to start a transaction

EPI Event callback:
 Write a byte into the pipe

Pipe callback:
 Get the EPI event
 If end event, end program
 If send event, update the time label
```

Figure 20.3   Motif and EPI interactions.

```
main()
{
    char   timeArea[8];
    char   timeOutput[8]; /* storage to hold "hh:mm:ss" */
    char   *commarea;

    /*
     * Get addressability to the COMMAREA and EIB
     */

    EXEC CICS ADDRESS COMMAREA(commarea) EIB(eibptr);
    if (eibptr->eibcalen < 8)
    {
        /*
         * No or insufficient commarea supplied
         */
        EXEC CICS RETURN;
    }

/*
 * Obtain and format the time. Copy the result into the commarea
 * for return to the GUI front end.
 */
EXEC CICS ASKTIME ABSTIME(timeArea);
EXEC CICS FORMATTIME ABSTIME(timeArea) \
    TIME(timeOutput) \
    TIMESEP(`:');

    memcpy(commarea, timeOutput, 8);

    EXEC CICS RETURN;
}
```

CICS/6000 EPI GUI front-end program

```
/*
 * epicall.c - EPI front end sample program.
 */
#include <Xm/Xm.h>
#include <Xm/Form.h>
#include <Xm/PushB.h>
#include <Xm/Label.h>
#include <X11/Shell.h>
#include <cics_epi.h>
#include <stdio.h>
#include <locale.h>

/*
 * The following lines define some usefull variables and macros for
 * setting resource attributes of Motif widgets
 */
#define SA(resource,value) {XtSetArg(args[n],(resource),(value));n++;}
static Arg args[20];
static int n;

/*
 * The following variables are global throughout the program
 */
Widget          labelW;
char            *cicsregion;
unsigned short  termIndex;    /* Terminal index for EPI installed pgm   */
int             commsPipe[2]; /* Pipe between the notify func and Mo
```

```
/*
 * UpdateTime:
 * This function sets the time display label widget to the new hours,
 * minutes and seconds specified by the paramater. This function is called
 * when a SEND event has been received from the CICS region.
 */
void UpdateTime(char *newTime)
{
    XmString   xmstring;

    xmstring = XmStringCreate(newTime, XmSTRING_DEFAULT_CHARSET);
    n = 0;
    SA(XmNlabelString, xmstring);
    XtSetValues(labelW, args, n);
    XmStringFree(xmstring);
    return;
}


/*
 * This function is called when an event is passed to the EPI interface by
 * CICS. The function writes a byte into the pipe which causes the Motif
 * main thread run-time to call its registered callback.
 */
void EpiNotifyCallBack(unsigned short termIndex)
{
    char byteValue = 1;
    write(commsPipe[1], &byteValue, 1);
    return;
}


/*
 * This function is called when data is available on the pipe between the
 * notify function and the Motif runt-time. The data is written by the
 * notify function when an event has arrived from the CICS region.
 */
void EpiInputCallBack(XtPointer a, int *fileDescriptor, XtInputId *xtinputid)
{
    char                  byteValue;
    CICS_EpiEventData_t   event;
    unsigned char         buffer[2000];
    short                 rc;

    /*
     * Read the data from the pipe to prevent recursive calls.
     */
    read(commsPipe[0], &byteValue, 1);

    /*
     * Get the EPI event from the CICS region.
     */
    event.Data = buffer;
    event.Size = sizeof(buffer);

    rc = CICS_EpiGetEvent(termIndex, CICS_EPI_WAIT, &event);
    if (rc! = CICS_EPI_NORMAL && rc! = CICS_EPI_ERR_MORE_EVENTS)
    {
        printf("Error with CICS_EpiGetEvent: %d\n", rc);
    }
    switch(event.Event)
    {
    /*
     * 0  1  2  3-10
     * +-----+-----+-----+----------+
     * | AID | SBA | SBA | HH:MM:SS |
     * +-----+-----+-----+----------+
```

```
       *
       */
         case CICS_EPI_EVENT_SEND:
               buffer[10] = `\0';
               UpdateTime((char *)(buffer+3));
               break;

 /*
 * If this is the END TERM event, exit the front-end program. This
 * event may be caused by a region shutdown or an explicit terminal
 * out of service issued for this terminal.
 */
         case CICS_EPI_EVENT_END_TERM:
               CICS_EpiTerminate();
               exit(0);
    }
       return;
    }
 /*
 * This function is called when a push button press has been made.
 * The function starts a transaction in the CICS region called "MEPI".
 */
 void EpiMakeCall()
  {

     unsigned short   rc;
     unsigned char    aid;

     aid = `X';
     rc = CICS_EpiStartTran(termIndex, "MEPI", &aid, 1);
     if (rc != CICS_EPI_NORMAL && rc != CICS_EPI_ERR_TTI_ACTIVE)
     {
          printf("Error with CICS_EpiStartTran: %d\n", rc);
     }
     return;
  }

 main(int argc, char *argv[])
  {
     Widget            toplevel;
     Widget            formW;
     Widget            pushBW;
     unsigned short    rc;
     CICS_EpiDetails_t details;
     unsigned char     aid;

     setlocale(LC_ALL,"");

     cicsregion = (char *)getenv("CICSREGION");

     if (cicsregion == NULL)
  {
          printf("The CICSREGION environment variable is not set");
          exit(1);
  }

 toplevel = XtInitialize(argv[0], "Xeci", NULL,0,&argc,argv);

 n = 0;
 formW = XmCreateForm(toplevel, "form", args, n);
 XtManageChild(formW);

 n = 0;
 SA(XmNtopAttachment,    XmATTACH_FORM);
```

```
          SA(XmNleftAttachment,    XmATTACH_FORM);
          SA(XmNbottomAttachment,  XmATTACH_FORM);
          SA(XmNleftOffset,        5);
          SA(XmNtopOffset,         5);
          SA(XmNbottomOffset,      5);
          pushBW = XmCreatePushButton(formW, "Get Time:", args, n);
          XtAddCallback(pushBW, XmNactivateCallback, EpiMakeCall, NULL);
          XtManageChild(pushBW);

          n = 0;
          SA(XmNtopAttachment,     XmATTACH_FORM);
          SA(XmNleftAttachment,    XmATTACH_WIDGET);
          SA(XmNleftWidget,        pushBW);
          SA(XmNrightAttachment,   XmATTACH_FORM);
          SA(XmNbottomAttachment,  XmATTACH_FORM);
          SA(XmNrightOffset,       5);
          SA(XmNleftOffset,        5);
          SA(XmNtopOffset,         5);
          SA(XmNbottomOffset,      5);
          labelW = XmCreateLabel(formW, "00:00:00", args, n);
          XtManageChild(labelW);

          /*
           * Create the pipe used for communication between the EPI callback
           * and the Motif run-time. Define the pipe to Motif as a source of
           * input.
           */
          pipe(commsPipe);
          XtAppAddInput( XtWidgetToApplicationContext(toplevel),
                         commsPipe[0],
                         (XtPointer)XtInputReadMask,
                         EpiInputCallBack,
                         NULL);
          /*
           * Initialize the EPI interface and define this application as a
           * CICS terminal.
           */
          rc = CICS_EpiInitialize(CICS_EPI_VERSION_101);
          if (rc != 0)
          {
              printf("Error with CICS_EpiInitialize: %d\n", rc);
              exit(1);
          }
          rc = CICS_EpiAddTerminal(NULL, /* Name Space */
              cicsregion,     /* System name */
              NULL,           /* Netname     */
              NULL,           /* DevType     */
              EpiNotifyCallBack,       /* Notify Function */
              &details,       /* Details output */
              &termIndex);    /* Terminal index */
          if (rc != 0)
          {
             printf("Error with CICS_EpiAddTerminal: %d\n", rc);
             exit(1);
          }

          /*
           * Pass application control to the Motif runt-time
           */
          XtRealizeWidget(toplevel);

          XtMainLoop();

      }
```

Sample Motif program using TCP/IP sockets. The sockets sample GUI application source code is shown in "CICS/6000 sockets GUI front-end program" later in this chapter. This application, like the previous ECI and EPI applications, uses Motif to present the user with the GUI interface. It differs from the others in that it uses sockets as the transport communication between the client and the CICS region. The callback function associated with the push button makes a sockets request call to the CICS server and waits for a response. When the response arrives, the data are used to update the time label.

This application does not require that the invoker be DCE authenticated but does expect a parameter. The parameter should be the TCP/IP address in dot-decimal format of the TCP/IP host on which the CICS server is listening. If a request is made when the CICS server is not listening, the application will hang indefinitely waiting for a response. This may be changed in the client logic by introducing a timeout or a retry or using TCP connections as opposed to using UDP.

A functional overview of the components is shown in Fig. 20.4. The CICS back-end program associated with this sample is shown in "CICS/6000 sockets back-end program" that follows. This program should be started before any client requests are submitted. The program listens on a socket for incoming requests and sends back a response when a request arrives.

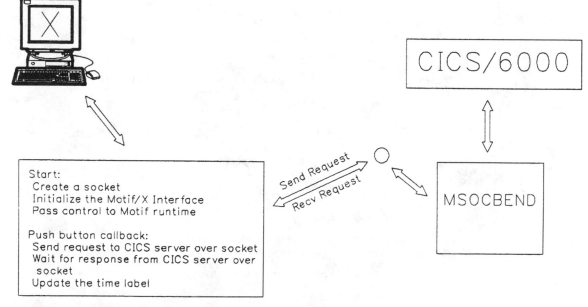

Figure 20.4 Motif and sockets interactions.

CICS/6000 sockets back-end program

```
/*
 * MSOCBEND:
 * CICS/6000 back end program for Sockets Motif sample.
 */
#include <stdio.h>
#include <sys/types.h>
#include <sys/socket.h>
#include <netinet/in.h>
#include <arpa/inet.h>

#define PORT 7777

main()
{
    char    timeArea[8];        /* Storage for CICS returned time/date   */
    char    timeOutput[8];      /* storage to hold "hh:mm:ss"            */
    struct  sockaddr_in address;        /* Address used by the server    */
    struct  sockaddr_in returnAddress;  /* Address of the client         */
    int     returnAddressLength;        /* Length of the client address  */
    char    buffer[10];         /* Storage for received request          */
    int     s;                  /* Socket descriptor                     */
    int     rc;                 /* Function return codes                 */

/*
 * Create a UDP socket to receive the request
 */
s = socket(AF_INET, SOCK_DGRAM, 0);

/*
 * Specify the address on which to receive the request
 */
address.sin_family      = AF_INET;
address.sin_addr.s_addr = htonl(INADDR_ANY);
address.sin_port        = htons(PORT);

/*
 * Bind the socket to the address
 */
rc = bind(s, (struct sockaddr *)&address, sizeof(address));
if (rc < 0)
{
    EXEC CICS RETURN;
}

/*
 * Loop forever ...
 */
while(1)
{
/*
 * Receive data from the client
 */
  returnAddressLength = sizeof(returnAddress);
  rc = recvfrom(s, buffer, sizeof(buffer), 0,

      &returnAddress, &returnAddressLength);
/*
 * Obtain and format the time.
 */
    EXEC CICS ASKTIME ABSTIME(timeArea);
    EXEC CICS FORMATTIME ABSTIME(timeArea) \
        TIME(timeOutput) \
```

```
        TIMESEP(`:');
/*
 * Send the formatted time back to the socket client application.
 */
    sendto(s, timeOutput, 8, 0, &returnAddress, sizeof(returnAddress));
  }
  EXEC CICS RETURN;
}
```

CICS/6000 sockets GUI front-end program

```
/*
 * sockcall.c - Sockets front end sample program.
 */
#include <Xm/Xm.h>
#include <Xm/Form.h>
#include <Xm/PushB.h>
#include <Xm/Label.h>
#include <sys/types.h>
#include <sys/socket.h>
#include <netinet/in.h>
#include <arpa/inet.h>

#define PORT 7777
/*
 * The following lines define some usefull variables and macros for
 * setting resource attributes of Motif widgets
 */
#define SA(resource,value) {XtSetArg(args[n],(resource),(value));n++;}
static Arg args[20];
static int n;

/*
 * The following variables are global throughout the program
 */
Widget          labelW;
char            *cicsregion;
int             s;
struct sockaddr_in serverAddress;

/*
 * UpdateTime:
 * This function sets the time display label widget to the new hours,
 * minutes and seconds specified by the paramater. This function is called
 * on when a response has been received from the CICS region.
 */
void UpdateTime(char *newTime)
{
    XmString  xmstring;

    xmstring = XmStringCreate(newTime, XmSTRING_DEFAULT_CHARSET);
    n = 0;
    SA(XmNlabelString, xmstring);
    XtSetValues(labelW, args, n);
    XmStringFree(xmstring);
    return;
}

/*
 * SockCallCB:
 * Callback function invoked when the push button is prsessed. The callback
 * sends a request to the CICS region over sockets. It is expected that
```

```
* the socket server is running on the CICS region before the request is
* issued. After the request is sent, the program waits for a response
* over the socket. When the response arrives, the label field is updated
* on the display.
*/
void SockCallCB()
{
    char                buffer[9];
    struct sockaddr_in  fromAddress;
    int                 fromAddressLength;
    int                 rc;

    /*
     * Send the request to the CICS server over the socket.
     */
    rc = sendto(s, "X", 1, 0, &serverAddress, sizeof(serverAddress));
    if (rc < 0)
    {
        perror("sendto()");
        exit(1);
    }

    /*
     * Wait for a response from the CICS server.
     */
    fromAddressLength = sizeof(fromAddress);
    recvfrom(s, buffer, 8, 0, &fromAddress, &fromAddressLength);

    /*
     * Update the label with the response.
     */
    buffer[8] = `\0';
    UpdateTime(buffer);

    return;
}
/*
 * sockcall:
 * Main entry into the program. A single parameter is expected which is the
 * IP address of the machine on which the CICS region is listening for
 * incoming requests.
 */
main(int argc, char *argv[])
{
    Widget  toplevel;
    Widget  formW;
    Widget  pushBW;

    if (argc < 2)
    {
        printf("Usage: %s ip_address_of_server\n", argv[0]);
        exit(1);
    }

    /*
     * Create the socket and complete the server address.
     */
    serverAddress.sin_family = AF_INET;
    serverAddress.sin_addr.s_addr = inet_addr(argv[1]);
    serverAddress.sin_port = htons(PORT);

    s = socket(AF_INET, SOCK_DGRAM, 0);
```

```
/*
 * Create the Motif interface consiting off a container form, a push
 * button and a label.
 */
toplevel = XtInitialize(argv[0], "Xeci", NULL,0,&argc,argv);

n = 0;
formW = XmCreateForm(toplevel, "form", args, n);
XtManageChild(formW);

n = 0;
SA(XmNtopAttachment,    XmATTACH_FORM);
SA(XmNleftAttachment,   XmATTACH_FORM);
SA(XmNbottomAttachment, XmATTACH_FORM);
SA(XmNleftOffset,       5);
SA(XmNtopOffset,        5);
SA(XmNbottomOffset,     5);
pushBW = XmCreatePushButton(formW, "Get Time:", args, n);
XtAddCallback(pushBW, XmNactivateCallback, SockCallCB, NULL);
XtManageChild(pushBW);

n = 0;
SA(XmNtopAttachment,    XmATTACH_FORM);
SA(XmNleftAttachment,   XmATTACH_WIDGET);
SA(XmNleftWidget,       pushBW);
SA(XmNrightAttachment,  XmATTACH_FORM);
SA(XmNbottomAttachment, XmATTACH_FORM);
SA(XmNrightOffset,      5);
SA(XmNleftOffset,       5);
SA(XmNtopOffset,        5);
SA(XmNbottomOffset,     5);
labelW = XmCreateLabel(formW, "00:00:00", args, n);
XtManageChild(labelW);

/*
 * Give program control to the Motif runtime.
 */
XtRealizeWidget(toplevel);
XtMainLoop();
}
```

CICS/6000 Performance

Before developing a CICS/6000 application, it is essential to determine if the application will execute within an acceptable time period. CICS/6000 was designed to accommodate multiple users and multiple transactions concurrently. Many attributes affect the responsiveness of a CICS application.

This chapter will identify the factors that affect execution and describe how to measure performance and resolve bottlenecks or other performance hindrances.

CPU Utilization

An AIX application can be in one of many states of execution. Since only one processor is present on each RISC System/6000, only one process may have the CPU's cycles at one time. Other processes may be eligible to run but have to wait until the running process has relinquished its use of the CPU. A process relinquishes the CPU when it either

- Uses its total allowable time with the CPU (preempted)
- Performs some slow I/O operation such as reads or writes from disk
- Performs a network operation such as send a packet
- Voluntarily frees itself

When a CICS region is active and running CICS programs, the CPU will be used to execute those programs. To determine if a CICS region and its applications are CPU-intensive and could benefit from an increased capacity processor, various AIX tools may be used.

Using vmstat to examine the CPU

The **vmstat** command is provided by AIX and reports on both virtual memory utilization and CPU utilization. The output shown in Fig. 21.1 illustrates typical **vmstat** output.

procs		memory		page						faults			cpu			
r	b	avm	fre	re	pi	po	fr	sr	cy	in	sy	cs	us	sy	id	wa
0	0	26752	162	0	0	0	0	0	0	123	19	24	0	1	98	0
0	0	26753	152	0	1	0	0	0	0	134	126	71	13	6	79	1
0	0	26754	135	0	3	0	0	0	0	143	233	88	31	10	56	3
0	0	26754	120	0	3	0	0	0	0	135	185	74	31	7	59	3
0	0	26756	125	0	1	0	3	8	0	138	118	60	16	5	77	2
0	0	26755	120	0	1	0	0	0	0	134	193	73	14	5	80	1
0	0	26755	122	0	1	0	1	6	0	129	176	63	14	4	79	2
0	0	26757	120	0	1	0	1	3	0	131	122	57	14	5	80	1
0	0	26757	124	0	2	0	3	5	0	130	166	69	29	6	63	2
0	0	26758	124	0	3	0	3	8	0	134	172	72	25	7	66	3
0	0	26758	124	0	1	0	1	6	0	133	105	51	14	3	82	2
0	0	26758	120	0	2	0	1	5	0	133	157	68	20	8	70	2
1	0	26760	122	0	4	0	4	17	0	142	398	120	44	13	39	4
0	0	26760	121	0	0	0	0	0	0	127	52	38	2	2	96	0
0	0	26760	123	0	2	0	3	6	0	138	329	101	26	10	61	3

Figure 21.1   vmstat output.

Any user may execute **vmstat.** A parameter can be supplied to control the interval between the **vmstat** output line reports. This interval is specified in seconds. The first output line produced by **vmstat** is a summary showing the average utilizations of the various resources since the machine was last rebooted. Subsequent lines show the resource used over the specified time interval. The last four columns are the most interesting in terms of CPU utilization. The columns are described below:

us   This is the percentage of CPU time utilized over the capture interval used by applications executing user-supplied code.

sy   This is the percentage of CPU time utilized over the capture interval used by applications executing within the kernel on behalf of system calls.

id   This is the percentage of CPU time over the capture interval that was unused. Essentially, the idle time.

wa   This is the percentage of CPU during which the CPU could not execute any application, even though there were applications available to run, because all those applications were awaiting completion of disk I/O.

During the execution of a CICS environment, 0 percent idle time will indicate that the available CPU time has all been utilized. From this, it can be inferred that an increased-capacity CPU would result in an overall increase in the throughput of the environment.

Even if the CPU is 100 percent utilized, the final "wait state" column should be examined to determine what, if any, CPU time was wasted waiting for disk I/O to complete. If this is nonzero, either the applications running on the machine would benefit from improved disks or improved organization of data on the disks or are I/O bound in contention for the data each needs. Additionally, nonzero I/O wait is also symptomatic of AIX operating system paging. This is discussed later.

If zero idle time of the CPU is found, the next step is to determine just what applications are consuming the CPU and in what proportions. If other CPU heavy applications are executing concurrently with CICS, they themselves may be responsible for the majority of CPU utilization. The **netpmon** command may be used to determine what the top CPU utilizing processes actually are.

Using netpmon to determine application CPU usage

AIX provides a command called **netpmon** to determine network usage upon the machine. This command also calculates CPU utilization over the examination period for each process running. **netpmon** utilizes the AIX trace facility for its information capture and hence must execute as the "root" AIX user. Additionally, no other AIX trace program must be running during the **netpmon** data collection period. To execute **netpmon,** the following command may be run:

```
netpmon -o output -O cpu -v
```

This will start **netpmon** collecting CPU information until the AIX **trcstop** command is executed to stop CPU data collection. The statistics are written to the file specified by the -o option. The data in Fig. 21.2 illustrate an output from the **netpmon** command.

Using getrusage() to determine CPU usage within a program

If an approximate CPU utilization, expressed in milliseconds of CPU time used to execute a CICS application, can be determined, the maximum transactions per second throughput rate can be determined. If a single CICS transaction utilizes 50 ms of CPU time, 20 such transactions could be executed in 1 s, resulting in a transaction throughput of 20 transactions per second. It is possible to determine these numbers. Each transaction executes in its own CICS application server process (cicsas). Each AIX process has CPU utilization statistics constantly accumulated for it by the operating system. A system call is available to extract this information from within a process. The **getrusage()** function returns the amount of user space and system space CPU time currently used by the process. *User space CPU time* is the time spent in the application executing user-supplied code and certain operating system–supplied functions. *System space CPU time* is the CPU time spent executing privileged code usually in the kernel of the operating system.

To make use of this information for CICS performance analysis, the **getrusage()** call must be made within the CICS application. Once the call

Fri Aug 25 19:49:10 1995
System: AIX mymachine Node: 3 Machine: 000043971000

22.430 secs in measured interval

==

Process CPU Usage Statistics:

				Network
Process (top 20)	PID	CPU Time	CPU %	CPU %
sfs	18012	3.7823	16.862	0.002
cicsas	22217	0.9388	4.185	0.035
cicsas	14519	0.9259	4.128	0.035
cicsas	21704	0.6118	2.728	0.024
netpmon	15244	0.2363	1.054	0.000
syncd	2605	0.0683	0.304	0.000
netw	771	0.0520	0.232	0.232
rpcd	14817	0.0466	0.208	0.004
trcstop	12173	0.0393	0.175	0.000
cicsic	21189	0.0246	0.110	0.000
rlogind	13156	0.0213	0.095	0.016
swapper	0	0.0208	0.093	0.000
tail	14203	0.0177	0.079	0.000
ksh	10627	0.0171	0.076	0.000
cdsadv	18437	0.0155	0.069	0.002
cdsd	19216	0.0152	0.068	0.002
trace	23942	0.0151	0.067	0.000
aios	16752	0.0129	0.058	0.000
rlogind	4958	0.0119	0.053	0.016
sec_clientd	17400	0.0106	0.047	0.002
Total (all processes)		6.9430	30.953	0.374
Idle time		14.7710	65.852	

Figure 21.2   Output from **netpmon.**

has been executed, the information collected must be externalized for analysis as efficiently as possible. This can be achieved by writing the data collected from **getrusage()** through the AIX trace facility.

The following C language function illustrates use of the **getrusage()** function combined with AIX trace. Associated with the function is an AIX Makefile for building the function code.

```
#include <stdio.h>
#include <sys/types.h>
#include <sys/resource.h>
#include <sys/trchkid.h>
```

```
void PerfTrace(char *data)
{
   struct traceBuffer
   {
       int user; /* Offset 0 CPU used in user space */
       int system; /* Offset 4 CPU used in system space */
       int length; /* Offset 8 Length of following message */
       char text[256]; /* Offset 12 Buffer for message */
   } traceBuffer;

   struct rusage rusage;

   traceBuffer.length = strlen(data);

   getrusage(RUSAGE_SELF, &rusage);
   traceBuffer.system =
       rusage.ru_stime.tv_sec*1000 + rusage.ru_stime.tv_usec/1000;
   traceBuffer.user =
       rusage.ru_utime.tv_sec*1000 + rusage.ru_utime.tv_usec/1000;
   memcpy(traceBuffer.text, data, traceBuffer.length);

   TRCGENT(0, 0x099 << 20, getpid(), 12 + traceBuffer.length, &traceBuffer);
   return;
}
```

The function is passed a single NULL-terminated string of characters that will be included in the output. When called, a trace entry is produced that includes

- The AIX processid of the calling process
- The user space CPU time in milliseconds currently used by the process
- The system space CPU time in milliseconds currently used by the process
- The character string supplied to the function preceded by a length field identifying the size of the string

When trace entries written by this function are collected by the AIX trace facility, they are collected in a raw format that must be processed. A suitable formatting template for producing readable output is illustrated in Fig. 21.3. The actual overhead of executing the function is negligible and may be left safely within production applications without degradation.

Using EXEC Interface Trace to Measure Performance

The CICS EXEC Interface trace, if sent to the AIX trace facility, can be used to gather some excellent performance details of the execution of a CICS program. The EXEC Interface trace includes both absolute time stamps and delta time stamps between the trace entries. With EXEC Interface trace, one

```
099 1.1 L=APPL "@Performance Trace Entry" \
   D4 "["D4","D4"]" S4
```

Figure 21.3 Formatting template.

trace entry is written at the start of a CICS command, while another is written at the end of a CICS command. By subtracting the end of the command time stamp from that of the beginning, the time taken to execute the CICS statement can be calculated. The granularity of the timings is submicrosecond, but because of the time taken to actually collect trace, only microsecond timings are useful.

If the structure of the program being examined with EXEC Interface trace is known, the time between the end of one CICS statement and the start of another also can provide useful information. The time between these trace entries is the time taken to process the intervening logic, which may be complex or involve calls to a database server.

Care should be taken when correlating the pairings between CICS trace entries because multiple executing CICS tasks will have their trace output interleaved. The AIX **grep** command can be used to filter the formatted trace output to include or exclude entries for particular CICS tasks. All output from a particular task will be associated with the same CICS application server and hence the same AIX process indemnifier.

To illustrate CICS EXEC Interface tracing for performance evaluation, the program shown in Fig. 2.1, which was used earlier to show the effect of C program caching, was executed with EXEC Interface tracing turned on. The amount of overhead of such tracing is minimal. The overall times to execute the programs were not found to have changed. The program was executed twice, once with the Program Definition (PD) **Resident** flag set to **yes** and once with the attribute set to **no.** The outputs are illustrated in Fig. 21.4, which shows the EXEC Interface trace with **Resident = no,** and in Fig. 21.5, which shows the EXEC Interface trace with **Resident = yes.**

The trace shows that the elapsed time between the execution of the EXEC CICS LINK command and the first CICS statement executed in the linked program varies from an average of 35 ms for the nonresident program to just

```
001   0.000000000      0.000000                     TRACE ON channel 0
582   4.221609984   4221.609984   CICS   21395/1     CACH(43 41 43 48) cicstest  cicsas   EI> Entering EXEC CICS LINK
582   4.275928832     54.318848   CICS   21395/1     CACH(43 41 43 48) cicstest  cicsas   EI> Entering EXEC CICS RETURN
583   4.276341248      0.412416   CICS   21395/1     CACH(43 41 43 48) cicstest  cicsas   EI< Returning from EXEC CICS RETURN
583   4.279780864      3.439616   CICS   21395/1     CACH(43 41 43 48) cicstest  cicsas   EI< Returning from EXEC CICS LINK
582   4.280425728      0.644864   CICS   21395/1     CACH(43 41 43 48) cicstest  cicsas   EI> Entering EXEC CICS LINK
582   4.314396160     33.970432   CICS   21395/1     CACH(43 41 43 48) cicstest  cicsas   EI> Entering EXEC CICS RETURN
583   4.314809856      0.413696   CICS   21395/1     CACH(43 41 43 48) cicstest  cicsas   EI< Returning from EXEC CICS RETURN
583   4.318724608      3.914752   CICS   21395/1     CACH(43 41 43 48) cicstest  cicsas   EI< Returning from EXEC CICS LINK
582   4.319367168      0.642560   CICS   21395/1     CACH(43 41 43 48) cicstest  cicsas   EI> Entering EXEC CICS LINK
582   4.360807424     41.440256   CICS   21395/1     CACH(43 41 43 48) cicstest  cicsas   EI> Entering EXEC CICS RETURN
583   4.361220864      0.413440   CICS   21395/1     CACH(43 41 43 48) cicstest  cicsas   EI< Returning from EXEC CICS RETURN
583   4.365981440      4.760576   CICS   21395/1     CACH(43 41 43 48) cicstest  cicsas   EI< Returning from EXEC CICS LINK
582   4.366642176      0.660736   CICS   21395/1     CACH(43 41 43 48) cicstest  cicsas   EI> Entering EXEC CICS LINK
582   4.399779840     33.137664   CICS   21395/1     CACH(43 41 43 48) cicstest  cicsas   EI> Entering EXEC CICS RETURN
583   4.400192256      0.412416   CICS   21395/1     CACH(43 41 43 48) cicstest  cicsas   EI< Returning from EXEC CICS RETURN
583   4.403848704      3.656448   CICS   21395/1     CACH(43 41 43 48) cicstest  cicsas   EI< Returning from EXEC CICS LINK
```

Figure 21.4 Nonresident trace.

```
         TRACE ON channel 0
21499/1          CACH(43 41 43 48) cicstest  cicsas   EI> Entering EXEC CICS LINK
21499/1          CACH(43 41 43 48) cicstest  cicsas   EI> Entering EXEC CICS RETURN
21499/1          CACH(43 41 43 48) cicstest  cicsas   EI< Returning from EXEC CICS RETURN
21499/1          CACH(43 41 43 48) cicstest  cicsas   EI< Returning from EXEC CICS LINK
21499/1          CACH(43 41 43 48) cicstest  cicsas   EI> Entering EXEC CICS LINK
21499/1          CACH(43 41 43 48) cicstest  cicsas   EI> Entering EXEC CICS RETURN
21499/1          CACH(43 41 43 48) cicstest  cicsas   EI< Returning from EXEC CICS RETURN
21499/1          CACH(43 41 43 48) cicstest  cicsas   EI< Returning from EXEC CICS LINK
21499/1          CACH(43 41 43 48) cicstest  cicsas   EI> Entering EXEC CICS LINK
21499/1          CACH(43 41 43 48) cicstest  cicsas   EI> Entering EXEC CICS RETURN
21499/1          CACH(43 41 43 48) cicstest  cicsas   EI< Returning from EXEC CICS RETURN
21499/1          CACH(43 41 43 48) cicstest  cicsas   EI< Returning from EXEC CICS LINK
21499/1          CACH(43 41 43 48) cicstest  cicsas   EI> Entering EXEC CICS LINK
21499/1          CACH(43 41 43 48) cicstest  cicsas   EI> Entering EXEC CICS RETURN
21499/1          CACH(43 41 43 48) cicstest  cicsas   EI< Returning from EXEC CICS RETURN
21499/1          CACH(43 41 43 48) cicstest  cicsas   EI< Returning from EXEC CICS LINK
```

Figure 21.5 Resident trace.

a few milliseconds for the resident-defined program. These results are found in the third column of the trace output, which is the milliseconds between the current and the previous trace entries. The second column is the absolute time stamp in seconds that the trace entry was written from the time at which the AIX trace program was started.

Paging Space

Like every other AIX executing process, CICS transactions execute within a virtual memory environment. Each program sees its own address space as independent from that of others. As a program consumes memory for either the code of the application or the memory used for holding the data that the application modifies, the memory used will grow. It is possible for the sum total of memory used by all the programs executing within AIX to exceed the amount of real memory installed on the operating RISC System/6000. When this occurs, memory used by a program is paged out to disk when chunks of real memory are required by other applications. When a memory page is accessed again, it is brought back into memory. The actual algorithms used to decide which pages of memory may be sent to disk and when they are brought back in are under the control of the AIX kernel.

When memory is paged to disk, areas of disk space must be allocated to hold the memory images. These areas are known as *paging spaces* and are defined to AIX by the system administrator. The amount of disk space allocated to paging usually should be twice as much as the real memory installed.

In severe cases, the amount of storage required by all the applications executing in the machine could approach that available from real memory plus the amount of paging space dedicated to holding paged-out memory. In this case, there is little room in which to page out old memory pages. If the situation worsens, a process that requires memory can only obtain that memory at the expense of another process that must release the memory but has nowhere to save its current contents.

In AIX, when the kernel detects low paging space, it signals each of the heaviest users of memory that paging space is low. They then have the choice to release memory or even terminate themselves. If sufficient paging space is still not freed, the kernel may terminate processes to release memory.

In an OLTP environment, it is essential that the transactions should be able to recover themselves gracefully. In CICS/6000, the signal that a process should exit or release memory is trapped by CICS/6000 and handled. Each CICS process that receives the SIGDANGER signal from the kernel handles the signal appropriately. Under no circumstances will the kernel kill a CICS process or application due to low paging space. It must be stressed that in these circumstances, performance of the system will degrade rapidly because almost every operation will require a fetch from disk.

To measure and monitor the amount of paging space available to AIX, the **lsps** command is used:

```
Produce summary: lsps -a
Page Space   Physical Volume   Volume Group   Size    %Used   Active   Auto   Type
hd62         hdisk2            rootvg         104MB   38      yes      yes    lv
hd61         hdisk1            rootvg         64MB    62      yes      yes    lv
hd6          hdisk0            rootvg         24MB    100     yes      yes    lv

Produce detailed: lsps -a
Total Paging Space    Percent Used
      192MB                54%
```

In a system where programs executing use more real memory than is available, performance will be degraded because the operating system will have to continually bring pages of memory into and out of real memory. This situation is known as *thrashing*. Again, the **vmstat** utility may be used to determine the number of pages brought into and sent out of real memory over a given interval. The columns of interest from **vmstat** are

pi   Number of page-ins per second

po   Number of page-outs per second

avm   Number of active virtual memory pages being used on the page space

When a program is newly brought into memory, page-ins will be visible. If significant numbers of page-outs followed by page-ins occurs, the system is thrashing. This usually is also seen in the CPU wait column (**wa**). Since the CPU is available for work, it must await the completion of a program page-in before the CPU can be given to the program to run. Performance degradation due to thrashing may be reduced by increasing the amount of real memory available to the system or by decreasing the amount of memory concurrently required by the running set of applications.

```
Output from: lsps -s
Total Paging Space   Percent Used
        192MB              54%

Output from: vmstat 5 5
procs     memory                    page                  faults         cpu
-----  -----------   -----------------------   ------------   ----------
 r  b    avm    fre  re  pi  po  fr   sr  cy   in    sy   cs  us sy id wa
 0  0  26121   315    0   0   0   0    0   0  123    19   24   0  1 98  0
 0  0  26121   315    0   0   0   0    0   0  123    43   37   1  2 97  0
 0  0  26121   315    0   0   0   0    0   0  121    34   28   0  1 99  0
 0  0  26121   315    0   0   0   0    0   0  120    37   31   1  1 99  0
 0  0  26122   314    0   0   0   0    0   0  128    35   29   0  2 98  0
```

Figure 21.6   Paging space usage.

The output of **vmstat** also shows the count of used paging space pages, where a page is 4 kilobytes. Figure 21.6 illustrates the correlation.

From the figure, the amount of paging space used as shown by the **lsps** command is 54 percent of 192 megabytes, which is 104 megabytes. From the **vmstat** output, 26122 pages of paging space are in use. This equates to 104 megabytes (26122 pages × 4 kilobytes per page). The **vmstat** command may be used to monitor paging space rise and fall. Increased paging space usage over time may be an indication that one or more applications has a memory leak. Knowing the amount of page space allocated to AIX, the total number of 4-kilobyte pages can be calculated. If this number is approached in the **vmstat** output, trouble is close. In the previous example, the total page space available is 192 megabytes, or 50176 pages. The active virtual memory usage of 26122 again shows that approximately 50 percent of paging space is being utilized.

22

Monitoring

CICS/6000 provides a powerful task monitoring capability. As each new CICS transaction executes, various items about that transaction's execution pattern may be collected. These items include its use of system resources, time spent in various CICS functions, time waiting for user input, plus many many more. As each CICS task completes, the data accumulated for that task are then written.

The monitoring data produced by CICS/6000 may be collected in AIX files and analyzed by monitoring data reporting tools. CICS/6000 provides a programmable API to ease the task of writing a monitoring application. A sample monitoring data formatter is supplied and may be used directly or extended for reporting additional monitoring items not reported by default.

Monitoring Data Content

The following table describes the fields in an individual monitoring record written at the end of a CICS task. Individual fields are associated with a field identifier.

Field Id	Description
001	The name of the transaction
002	The terminal name
003	The operator name
004	How the transaction was started; this may be
	■ A Started by an asynchronous start
	■ C Second or subsequent part of a conversational task
	■ D Started by a trigger level being reached on a transient data queue
	■ T Started by a terminal input request
	■ Second or subsequent part of a pseudoconversational task
005	Start time of the transaction
006	End time of the transaction
007	Elapsed time the transaction executed
008	CPU time spent executing the CICS task's user code (This excludes time spent processing CICS statements.)

Field Id	Description
009	Time spent waiting for terminal I/O to complete
010	Time spent waiting for CICS journal I/O to complete
011	Time spent waiting for temporary storage I/O to complete
015	Time spent waiting for terminal I/O to complete
016	Time spent waiting for terminal I/O to complete
024	Time spent in the transaction scheduler
027	Time the task spent voluntarily suspended
029	Number of AIX page faults during the execution of the task that did not require disk I/O
030	Number of AIX page faults during the execution of the task that did require disk I/O
031	The task ID of the CICS task
033	The maximum amount of GETMAIN memory used by the task
034	Number of messages received by the task from the terminal
035	Number of messages sent to the terminal from the task
036	Number of file read requests issued by the task
037	Number of file write requests issued by the task
038	Number of file browses issued by the task
039	Number of file ADDs issued by the task
040	Number of file DELETEs issued by the task
041	Number of transient data GETs issued by the task
042	Number of transient data PUTs issued by the task
043	Number of transient data PURGEs issued by the task
044	Number of temporary storage PUTs issued by the task
046	Number of auxiliary temporary storage PUTs issued by the task
047	Number of main temporary storage PUTs issued by the task
050	The number of BMS map requests issued by the task
051	The number of BMS IN requests issued by the task
052	The number of BMS OUT requests issued by the task
054	The total number of GETMAIN requests issued by the task
055	The number of LINK requests issued by the task (This will always be 1 or greater because the start of the task itself is considered a LINK.)
056	The number of XCTL requests issued by the task
057	The number of LOAD requests issued by the task
058	Number of output journal requests issued by the task
059	The number of START or INITIATE requests issued by the task
060	Number of SYNCPOINT requests issued by the task (This will always be 1 or greater because the end of a task is an implicit syncpoint.)
061	Number of times the task was swapped out of main memory
063	Elapsed time spent waiting for file I/O to complete
064	Signaling conditions
067	Number of messages received from the alternate terminal facility
068	Number of messages sent to the alternate terminal facility
071	Name of the first program invoked at transaction start (This may be blank for some of the internal CICS transactions.)
083	Number of characters received from the primary terminal
084	Number of characters sent to the primary terminal
085	Number of characters received from the alternate terminal
086	Number of characters sent to the alternate terminal
087	Amount of text memory used by the task
088	Amount of memory released by the FREEMAIN command
089	User name
090	Number of BMS requests issued by the task
091	Number of TD requests issued by the task
092	Number of temporary storage requests issued by the task
093	Number of file requests issued by the task

Field Id	Description
094	Time spent in program compression
095	Data segment occupancy of the task
096	Time spent executing CICS statements
097	Terminal name
098	CICS internal task ID used by the Encina transaction manager
101	Elapsed time spent waiting for transient data I/O
103	Elapsed time spent waiting for temporary storage space
108	The text segment occupancy of the task
109	The priority of the transaction
112	Reason the monitoring record was written; this may be one of ■ C Conversational ■ D ULM write request ■ T Task termination
113	First ABEND code for the task
114	Most recent ABEND code for the task
115	Elapsed time spent waiting for the program to load
200	Elapsed time spent in the file manager
202	Total number of FREEMAIN requests issued by the task
203	Total amount of memory obtained from GETMAIN requests
207	Elapsed time spent waiting for an SNA link
208	Elapsed time spent waiting for a TCP/IP link
209	Number of ISC message received by the task
210	Number of ISC message sent by the task
211	CPU time the task was executing within AIX kernel space
212	Numbers of times the task was AIX context switched due to it voluntarily relinquishing control
213	The number of times the task was AIX context switched because it has exceeded its CPU quanta
214	The number of AIX signals received by the task
215	Number of file I/O actions
216	System or user time spent processing CICS statements
217	Elapsed time spent in monitoring ULM

Monitoring data configuration

By default, CICS/6000 does not collect the monitoring data and must be enabled to actually collect such information. The reason for this is that the accumulation and writing of such data consume CPU cycles and will result in a slightly degraded response.

Configuring monitoring data collection requires two modifications to the CICS/6000 resource definitions:

■ A transient data queue needs to be defined that has the following attributes:

  ■ Extrapartition

  ■ Output

  ■ Variable-length records

■ A monitoring definition pointing to the previously defined monitoring definition

```
cicsadd -c tdd -r $CICSREGION MONQ \
    RecordType=variable_length \
    DestType=extrapartition \
    ExtrapartitionFile="mon.out" \
    IOMode=output

cicsupdate -c md -r $CICSREGION \
    TDQ=MONQ
```

Figure 22.1 Monitoring definitions.

The commands illustrated in Fig. 22.1 show the definition of an appropriate extrapartition transient data queue to CICS and its association with the monitoring definition (MD).

The extrapartition transient data queue has the AIX file mon.out associated with it. When CICS monitoring writes a monitoring record, it will be added to this file. Since no absolute path was specified for the file, it will be created in the data subdirectory of the region directory, i.e., /var/cics_regions/<region>/data.

Monitoring Data Formatter

The CICS/6000 sample monitoring formatter is called **cicsmfmt** and is supplied in both source and compiled versions. Unfortunately, it is only capable of formatting a subset of the full monitoring data fields. The following program is a more illustrative and useful sample that takes as input the name of the field to be formatted and the monitoring output file name. Each of the transactions captured in the monitoring output data is listed with a formatted version of the field for each transaction.

The sample program is called **monsamp** and is illustrated below. The program is contained in two C language source files, one called monsamp.c, which is the main driver, and another source file called monutils.c, which contains useful monitoring data formatting fields

```c
/* ------------------------------------------------------ */
/* File: monsamp.c - Monitoring sample program --------- */
/* ------------------------------------------------------ */
#include <sys/types.h>
#include <cics_types.h>
#include <cicsmfmt.h>

main(int argc, char *argv[])
{
    CICS_MFMT_Stream_t              *stream;
    CICS_EMP_TDQ_RecordDetails_t    *ptr;
    char                            buffer[1000];
    enum CICS_MFMT_Status           status;
    /*
     * Check that the required number of parameters have been supplied.
     */
    if (argc < 3)
```

```
    {
        printf("Usage: %s monitor_file field_id\n", argv[0]);
        exit(1);
    }

    /*
     * Open the monitoring file for reading.
     */
    stream = CICS_MFMT_OpenMonitorFile(argv[1], &status);
    if (status ! = CICS_MFMT_STATUS_OK)
    {
        printf("Error: %d opening monitor file\n", status);
        exit(2);
    }

    do
    {
        ptr = CICS_MFMT_FindField(CICS_EMP_FID_TRANS_ ID, stream);
        MonitorExpand(ptr, buffer);
        printf("Transaction: %s", buffer);

        ptr = CICS_MFMT_FindField(atoi(argv[2]), stream);
        MonitorExpand(ptr, buffer);
        printf(" Field: %s: %s", argv[2], buffer);

        printf("\n");

        status = CICS_MFMT_ReadNext(stream);

    } while(status = = CICS_MFMT_STATUS_OK);
    exit(0);
}
/* -------------------------------------------------------- */
/* File: monsamp.c - Monitoring sample program           */
/* -------------------------------------------------------- */
#include <sys/types.h>
#include <cics_types.h>
#include <cicsmfmt.h>

main(int argc, char *argv[])
{
    CICS_MFMT_Stream_t              *stream;
    CICS_EMP_TDQ_RecordDetails_t    *ptr;
    char                            buffer[1000];
    enum CICS_MFMT_Status           status;

    /*
     * Check that the required number of parameters have been supplied.
     */
    if (argc < 3)
    {
        printf("Usage: %s monitor_file field_id\n", argv[0]);
        exit(1);
    }

    /*
     * Open the monitoring file for reading.
     */
    stream = CICS_MFMT_OpenMonitorFile(argv[1], &status);
    if (status ! = CICS_MFMT_STATUS_OK)
    {
        printf("Error: %d opening monitor file\n", status);
        exit(2);
    }
```

```
    do
    {
        ptr = CICS_MFMT_FindField(CICS_EMP_FID_TRANS_ ID, stream);
        MonitorExpand(ptr, buffer);
        printf("Transaction: %s", buffer);

        ptr = CICS_MFMT_FindField(atoi(argv[2]), stream);
        MonitorExpand(ptr, buffer);
        printf(" Field: %s: %s", argv[2], buffer);

        printf("\n");

        status = CICS_MFMT_ReadNext(stream);

    } while(status = = CICS_MFMT_STATUS_OK);
    exit(0);
}
```

The following AIX Makefile is suitable for compiling and linking the mon-samp program.

```
monsamp: monsamp.o monutils.o
    cc -o monsamp monutils.o monsamp.o -L /usr/lpp/cics/lib -lcicsmfmt

.c.o:
    cc -c $< -I /usr/lpp/cics/include

define:
    cicsadd -c tdd -r $(CICSREGION) MONQ \
        RecordType = variable_length \

    DestType = extrapartition \
    ExtrapartitionFile = "mon.out" \
    IOMode = output
cicsupdate -c md -r $(CICSREGION) \
    TDQ = MONQ
```

After compiling the program and having collected some monitor data output, the program may be used to extract individual fields of monitoring data. The following example show the output of the monsamp program after running a set of CICS transactions. The field being extracted is 84, which is the number of characters sent to the users terminal by the transaction:

```
Transaction: CECI Field: 84: 921
Transaction: FILE Field: 84: 589
Transaction: FILE Field: 84: 721
Transaction: CEMT Field: 84: 1324
Transaction: CEMT Field: 84: 256
Transaction: CECI Field: 84: 921
```

23

CICS/6000 Statistics

As CICS/6000 operates, it collects statistics on its own operation. These statistics include the number of transactions executed, amount of memory allocated, and many, many others.

Statistics data from CICS/6000 collect accounting information over periods of time. These data may be used to determine what activity was taking place within a CICS region over that period. These statistics differ from data collected from CICS/6000 monitoring in that statistics are time-oriented, e.g., how many over this time or how much over that time, while monitoring data are specific to particular tasks and not the overall system operation.

CICS collects statistics constantly, and it writes those statistics when various events occur. These events are as follows:

- *Interval* Statistics are written and reset whenever a configurable period of time has passed. The interval between the statistics collection may be set with the SET STATISTICS command.

- *End of day* Statistics are written at the end of each day. The statistics reported are based on the previously written set. End-of-day statistics are also written when the CICS region is stopped.

- *Requested* These statistics are collected when a PERFORM STATISTICS RECORD command is issued.

- *Unsolicited* These statistics are written when a resource for which statistics had been collected is about to be deleted, and the statistics for this resource would otherwise be lost.

CICS/6000 Statistics Commands

CICS/6000 statistics may be controlled from CICS by various CICS commands.

CICS PERFORM STATISTICS RECORD

This command allows some or all of the CICS statistics to be written immediately. This produces the *requested* statistics class of output. If only some of the statistics categories of data are required, they need only be specified. If all categories are written, the statistics values may be reset optionally. By default, the values are not reset. The statistics are written to the file specified in the Region Definition for statistics collection.

EXEC CICS COLLECT STATISTICS

This command allows current statistics to be obtained and returned to the CICS program that executed the command. Some or all of the statistics categories may be obtained. The time at which the statistics values were last reset also may be retrieved.

EXEC CICS SET/INQUIRE STATISTICS

These commands control the operation of statistics recording within CICS. Through the SET command, the interval and end-of-day periods may be changed. Also, interval and unsolicited statistics may be enabled and disabled.

The INQUIRE command allows the interval, end-of-day, recording, and next time at which statistics are to be written information to be retrieved.

Configuring CICS for Statistics

CICS/6000 allows the AIX file that contains the statistics data to be specified. By default, the file is called `statsfile` in the region data directory. If an alternative name or location is required, this may be specified in the Region Definition with the **StatFile** attribute.

Interval and unsolicited statistics can be recorded optionally. If recording of these statistics types is required, then the **StatsRecord** attribute in the Region Definition should be set to **yes.**

Statistics Data Format and Content

The data produced by CICS/6000 statistics consists of two different types of records. One type, the `CICSSTAT_Record`, contains information about the category of statistics data that is to follow. This record type also contains control information as to why the statistics were written.

The other record format is the `CICSSTAT_Detail`, which contains detailed information on the statistic being examined. It also may contain control information if the `CICSSTAT_Record_t` record was itself control information.

The diagram shown in Fig. 23.1 illustrates the structures for data returned from an EXEC CICS COLLECT STATISTICS command. For statistics written to the statistics collection file, the format is the same except that the

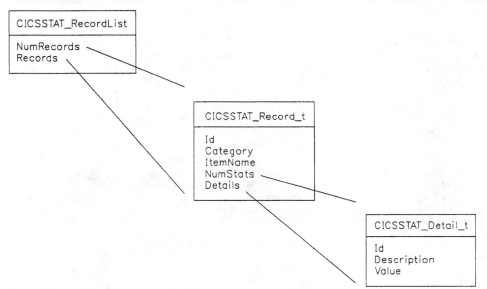

Figure 23.1   Statistics structures layout.

CICSSTAT_RecordList header is omitted because the end of file indicator will show that there are no more records available.

The statistics structures are defined in the C language header file called cics_stat.h in the CICS include directory.

The diagram in Fig. 23.2 shows the memory layout of the data returned by the EXEC CICS COLLECT STATISTICS command.

The **NumRecords** field in the CICSSTAT_RecordList structure holds the number of CICSSTAT_Record_t entries in the data that follow. Immediately after the **NumRecords** field is the first (if any) of the CICSSTAT_Record_t data items. The category of statistics is held in the **Id** field. This field can have a value from the following table:

Id value	Name	Description	Control or Information
010000	DUMP	Dump category	No
020000	FILE	File category	No
030000	ISCM	Intersystem system communication category	No
040000	JOUR	Journal category	No
050000	LUWM	Logical unit of work category	No
060000	PROG	Program category	No
070000	RTDB	Runtime database category	No
080000	STOR	Region storage category	No
090000	STOT	Task private storage category	No
0A0000	TASK	Task category	No
0B0000	TERM	Terminal category	No
0C0000	TDQU	Transient data category	No
0D0000	TRAN	Transaction category	No
0E0000	TSQU	Temporary storage category	No

Id value	Name	Description	Control or Information
0F0000	INTERVAL	Interval statistics collection marker	Yes
100000	ENDOFDAY	End-of-day statistics collection marker	Yes
110000	UNSOLICITED	Unsolicited statistics collection marker	Yes
120000	REQUESTED_RESET	Statistics were reset marker	Yes
130000	REQUESTED	Requested statistics collection marker	Yes
140000	ENDOFREGION	End-of-region statistics collection marker	Yes
150000	END	End-of-statistics collection marker	Yes
160000	TIME_NA	Time unavailable marker	Yes
170000	TIME_START	Time statistics collection started	Yes
180000	TIME_STOP	Time statistics collection stopped	Yes
190000	SUMMARY	Summary statistics collection marker	Yes
1A0000	ALL_DETAILS	All statistics details follow	Yes
1B0000	ONE_DETAIL	One statistics detail follows	Yes

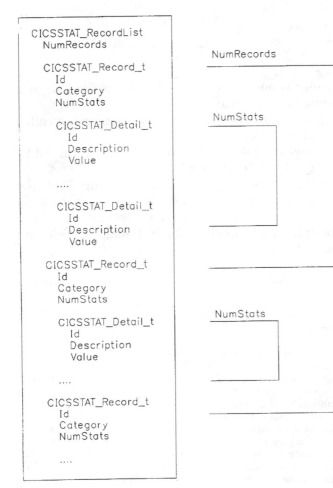

Figure 23.2 Statistics structures layout in memory.

The TIME_START and TIME_STOP category types are not found in the CICSSTAT_Record_t but will be found in the CICSSTAT_Detail_t following REQUESTED, UNSOLICITED, INTERVAL, END, ENDOFDAY, and ENDOFREGION CICSSTAT_Record_t categories.

For CICSSTAT_Record_t categories, which can be records for different items of the same category (e.g., programs, terminals, transactions, etc.), the **ItemName** field contains the NULL-terminated name of the resource or item for which the following CICSSTAT_Detail_t statistics apply.

The structure of the data returned by an EXEC CICS COLLECT STATISTICS call differs from that written in the statistics AIX file. The data returned by the COLLECT call contains only CICSSTART_Record_t category information and details. There are no control or information records included. The number of category records (and hence detail records) can be found in the CICSSTAT_RecordList header.

The data following a CICSSTART_Record_t category record will be a series of CICSSTAT_Field_t records. These records include fields that contain a detail type identifier field (**Id**) and a detail value field (**Value**). The type identifier field contains the type of statistics being returned (e.g., number of file reads), and the value field contains the statistics value for that type.

The following lists show the different detail types split into their distinct categories.

Dump statistics

010000	Number of dumps written
010001	Number of dump write errors

File statistics

020000	Number of file control reads
020001	Number of file control writes
020002	Number of file control browses
020003	Number of file control deletes
020004	Number of file control updates
020005	Number of file control opens
020006	Number of file control closes
020007	Total number of file control reads
020008	Total number of file control writes
020009	Total number of file control browses
02000A	Total number of file control deletes
02000B	Total number of file control updates

02000C	Total number of file control opens
02000D	Total number of file control closes

Intersystem communication statistics

030000	Maximum number of outbound function ship requests
030001	Number of outbound function ship requests
030002	Number of outbound function ship requests transmitted
030003	Number of outbound function ship requests purged
030004	Number of outbound function ship requests
03000B	Number of DTP conversations allocated
03000C	Number of Interval Control Elements on chain
03000D	Total number of resources enqued
03000E	Maximum number of Interval Control Elements on chain
03000F	Number of ENQ requests that waited on a resource
030010	Number of LOCK requests that waited for a resource
030011	Number of inbound function ship requests for file control
030012	Number of outbound function ship requests for file control
030013	Number of forwarded function ship requests for file control
030014	Number of inbound function ship requests for transient data
030015	Number of outbound function ship requests for transient data
030016	Number of forwarded function ship requests for transient data
030017	Number of inbound function ship requests for temporary storage
030018	Number of outbound function ship requests for temporary storage
030019	Number of forwarded function ship requests for temporary storage
03001A	Number of inbound function ship requests for interval control
03001B	Number of outbound function ship requests for interval control
03001C	Number of forwarded function ship requests for interval control
03001D	Number of inbound function ship requests for DPL
03001E	Number of outbound function ship requests for DPL
03001F	Number of forwarded function ship requests for DPL
030020	Number of inbound DL/1 function ship requests
030021	Number of outbound transaction routing requests sent
030022	Number of inbound transaction routing requests received
030023	Number of terminal definitions that were sent
030024	Number of terminal definitions that were received
030025	Number of transaction routing requests that were forwarded
030026	Number of dynamic transaction routing requests

Journal statistics

040000	Number of requests to archive log
040001	Number of journal NOSPACE conditions
040002	Number of journal write retries attempted
040003	Number of CICS checkpoints written
040004	Number of records written to log
040005	Total number of buffered write requests to user journals
040006	Total number of flushed write requests to user journals
040007	Total number of journal IOERR conditions
040008	Total number of unauthorized access attempts on journals
040009	Number of journal write requests to user journal
04000A	Number of flushed write requests to user journal
04000B	Number of journal IOERR conditions
04000C	Number of unauthorized access attempts on journal
04000D	Number of NOSPACE coniditions
04000E	Number of cushion releases
04000F	Number of log forces
040010	Number of log truncates

Logical unit of work statistics

050000	Number of LUWs committed
050001	Number of LUWs aborted
050002	Number of LUWs readonly
050003	Number of hashing algorithm hits
050004	Maximum hash table chain length

Program statistics

060000	Total number of programs run
060001	Number of times program ran

Runtime database statistics

070000	Number of RTDB add requests
070001	Number of RTDB read requests
070002	Number of RTDB pointer get requests
070003	Number of RTDB amend requests

070004	Number of RTDB delete requests
070005	Number of RTDB browse requests
070006	Number of RTDB read next requests
070007	RTDB chain length
070008	Maximum RTDB chain length
070009	Number of RTDB delta requests
07000A	Number of RTDB use requests
07000B	Number of RTDB end use requests
07000C	Number of RTDB exclusive requests
07000D	Number of entries in RTDB
07000E	Number of collisions in RTDB hash chain
07000F	Maximum number of entries in hash chain
070010	Maximum of highest hash chain lengths

Region/Task shared storage statistics

080000	Region pool size
080001	Region pool stress threshold
080002	Number of bytes allocated from Region pool
080003	Number of successful Region pool allocated requests
080004	Number of failed Region pool allocated requests
080005	Number of successful Region pool return requests
080006	Number of failed Region pool return requests
080007	Number of times Region pool was short on storage
080009	Task shared pool size
08000A	Task shared pool stress threshold
08000B	Number of bytes allocated from task shared pool
08000C	Number of successful Task shared pool allocated requests
08000D	Number of failed Task shared pool allocated requests
08000E	Number of successful Task shared pool return requests
08000F	Number of failed Task shared pool return requests
080010	Number of times Task shared pool was short on storage
080011	Longest Task shared pool chain length
080013	Longest Task shared pool hash bucket
080014	Maximum bytes allocated from Region pool
080015	Maximum bytes allocated from Task Shared pool
080016	Total bytes currently allocated from Region pool
080017	Total bytes currently allocated from Task shared pool
080018	Bytes returned to Region pool
080019	Bytes returned to Task shared pool

Task private statistics

090000	Number of successful Task private allocation requests
090001	Number of successful Task private return requests
090002	Number of failed Task private allocation requests
090003	Number of failed Task private return requests
090004	Number of tasks using Task private storage
090005	Number of Task private storage abends
090006	Number of Task private storage abends for transaction

Task statistics

0A0000	Total number of transactions started
0A0001	Total number of transactions which abended
0A0002	Total number of memory violation abends
0A0003	Total number of protection violation abends
0A0004	Total number of operating system error abends
0A0005	Total number of transaction abends due to exceptions
0A0006	Total number of transactions CICS was unable to start
0A0007	Total number of times active transactions reached max application servers
0A0008	Maximum number of tasks
0A0009	Maximum number of running class 1 tasks allowed
0A000A	Current number of class 1 tasks
0A000B	Number of class 1 maximum tasks reached
0A000C	Peak number of class 1 tasks

Transient data statistics

0B0000	Number of EP TDQ reads
0B0001	Number of EP TDQ writes
0B0002	Number of IP TDQ reads
0B0003	Number of IP TDQ writes
0B0004	Number of remote TDQ reads
0B0005	Number of remote TDQ writes
0B0006	Number of times a triggered TDQ was emptied
0B0006	Number of times a triggered TDQ reached trigger level

Terminal statistics

0C0000	Number of input messages received
0C0001	Number of output messages sent

0C0002	Number of terminal transmission errors : . *row
0C0005	Total number of terminal autoinstalls
0C0006	Number of failed terminal autoinstalls
0C0007	Total number of terminal uninstalls

Transaction statistics

0D0000	Number of times transaction started
0D0001	Number of times transaction abended

Temporary storage statistics

0E0000	Number of main TSQ read requests
0E0001	Number of main TSQ write requests
0E0002	Number of main TSQ write requests

Example: Storage statistics

The following program is an example of a CICS transaction that can be used to obtain the statistics for memory utilization. The sizes of the region-wide and task-shared areas of storage are returned. With these data and the statistics illustrating just how much is used, a percentage amount of used storage can be determined. This is the information displayed by the program:

```
#include <cics_stat.h>
main()
{
    long                        tbytesused = 99999;
    long                        rbytesused = 99999;
    long                        rpoolsize = 99999;
    long                        tpoolsize = 99999;
    int                         i,j;
    struct CICSSTAT_RecordList  *ptr;
    CICSSTAT_Record_t           *currentRecord;
    CICSSTAT_Detail_t           *currentDetail;
    char                        message[80];

    EXEC CICS COLLECT STATISTICS SET(ptr)
        STORAGE;
    for (i = 0,currentRecord = ptr->Records; i<ptr->NumRecords; i++)
    {
        currentDetail = currentRecord->Details;
        for (j = 0; j<currentRecord->NumStats; j++)
        {
            switch(currentDetail->Id)
            {
                case CICSSTAT_STOR_RPOOL_SIZE:
                    rpoolsize = currentDetail->Value;
                    break;
                case CICSSTAT_STOR_TPOOL_SIZE:
                    tpoolsize = currentDetail->Value;
                    break;
                case CICSSTAT_STOR_RBYTES_ALLOCSTART:
                    rbytesused = currentDetail->Value;
```

```
                                break;
                        case CICSSTAT_STOR_TBYTES_ALLOCSTART:
                                tbytesused = currentDetail->Value;
                                break;
                    }
                    currentDetail++;
                }
                currentRecord = (CICSSTAT_Record_t *)currentDetail;
        }
        sprintf(message, "Region storage: %d [%d%%], Task shared: %d [%d%%]",
            rbytesused, 100*rbytesused/rpoolsize,
            tbytesused, 100*tbytesused/tpoolsize);
        EXEC CICS SEND TEXT FROM(message) LENGTH(strlen(message)) ERASE;
        EXEC CICS RETURN;
    }
```

# Chapter 24

CICS/6000 Security Considerations

With a transaction processing system such as CICS, security becomes a high consideration. CICS is typically used to manage data critical to an enterprise's operation. The data may include customer orders, payroll, manufacturing information, and many other items of high sensitivity. Security is designed to prevent accidental or malicious access or modification to such data.

CICS/6000 allows restriction of access to CICS-managed resources such as files, queues, transactions, communication links, programs, and mapsets. The restrictions are based on the notion of a CICS user. Different CICS users will be allowed access to different sets of CICS resources. CICS maintains two notions of access, namely, access to CICS transactions and access to CICS-maintained data resources.

CICS Transaction and Resource Security

CICS/6000 has the notion that an individual CICS user should have access to a defined set of CICS resources and transactions. The set of resources may be distinct from that of another user or may overlap in some or all areas. To allow this partitioning, a CICS administrator can define an access key to a CICS resource. This key is an integer value in a predefined range. When a CICS user is defined, the user is given a set of keys in the same range. When the CICS user executes a program that attempts to access the resource, the request will only be allowed if the user has a matching key in the user's key set to that of the resource being accessed. If the user does not have a matching key, the request will be denied. These keys guarding CICS resource access are known as *resource security level (RSL) keys*. A separate set of keys but with the same notion is also defined for transactions. These keys are known as *transaction security level (TSL) keys*. These keys apply to the user's ability to initially execute a given transaction. If the user attempts to execute a transaction for which his or her set of transaction security level keys does not include that for the request transaction, the transaction start request will be denied.

Resource Definitions for security

The set of TSL and RSL keys associated with a user are defined in the user's definition in the CICS User Definition (UD) entry. The **TSLKeys** attribute defines the transaction security level keys, while the **RSLKeys** attribute defines the resource security level keys. TSL keys may be defined in the range 1 to 64, while RSL keys may be defined in the range 1 to 24. Keys are separated by the vertical bar (|) symbol. Only those transactions which have keys that match those in the User Definition may be executed, while only those resources which have matching RSL keys may be accessed.

Each transaction in the Transaction Definitions (TD) has associated with it the type of TSL and RSL checks to be performed by that transaction when it is invoked. For TSL checks, the types may be either **internal** or **external,** signifying whether or not the transaction should use CICS internal security checking or use a possible external security manager program. The TSL checking mechanism is specified by the **TSLCheck** attribute. Additionally, an RSL checking attribute can be set to **internal** or **external** similarly to the TSL checking. A further setting may be specified, which is **none,** to indicate that when the transaction is executed, no RSL checking should be performed. The resource definition attribute for this is RSLCheck.

Individual resources such as queues or programs have an **RSLKey** attribute. This attribute may be set to an individual value defining the RSL key required to access the resource. This attribute may have one of the following values:

1–24   The RSL key that must be held by a user executing a transaction that accesses this resource. The resource also will be accessible from transactions with **RSLCheck** = **none** defined in its Transaction Definition.

public   This resource is accessible by any user from any transaction. Security has been disabled for the resource.

private   This resource may *only* be accessed by transactions that have **RSLCheck** = **none** defined in their Transaction Definitions.

Communications Security

When one CICS region communicates with another, security becomes a high consideration. A remote CICS system may be less securely guarded than a local region. If requests from the remote region arrive and are honored, local CICS security may be compromised. To this extent, CICS provides a set of different security methods to allow implementation of a secure environment for communications requests.

CICS provides three types of security, each providing a different set of secure access. The three types are known as

- *Bind-time security*
- *Link-level security*
- *User-level security*

Bind-time security

Bind-time security is implemented at the SNA level. CICS is unaware of this security method. Bind-time security either allows or disallows an LU 6.2 conversation from being established between two CICS regions. To enable bind-time security, both ends of the SNA conversation must be aware of the passwords defined to their partners at the SNA level. Using this method, CICS regions that are unknown to the target of an ISC request will not be allowed *any* access because they will not know the target's SNA bind password. If this type of security is employed and no other, all requests arriving from the remote system will have the same security access. The other types of communications security operate at a lower level of granularity.

Link-level security

Link-level security specifies the TSL and RSL keys available on the target CICS region from an incoming CICS region request. The TSL and RSL keys in use for an incoming request will be set regardless of the actual user issuing the request. If incoming requests require different levels of TSL and RSL security keys, the link-level security must be set to the most open set of keys that will satisfy the loosest request. Use of this security methodology allows resources and transactions to be restricted but only to a CICS region level. If a lower level of granularity if required, user-level security should be considered.

Link-level security will be used if the CICS/6000 region that receives the request has **RemoteSysSecurity = local** in its Communication Definition for the link to the source CICS region. If this attribute is set, the link-level TSL and RSL keys may be specified by one of two methods.

If the **LinkUserId** attribute is defined with a CICS userid, the TSL and RSL keys in the user's **TSLKeyList** and **RSLKeyList** attributes in the User Definition (UD) for the specified user will be in effect for all incoming requests. The CICS userid that the request will execute as is that user defined in the **LinkUserId** attribute.

If the **LinkUserId** attribute is not defined, the program will execute as the CICS default user, and the keys in effect will be those specified in the **TSLKeyMask** and **RSLKeyMask** attributes in the same Communication Definition (CD).

User-level security

User-level security works by passing the CICS userid of the user issuing the request to the remote CICS region along with the request. On receipt of the request, the RSL and TSL keys defined on the target region are set in effect for the request. This security mechanism allows the tightest level of control. If administered correctly, access to resources and transactions can be governed down to the individual user level. The TSL and RSL keys set for the user on the CICS region that is the target of the request will be used and not necessarily those of the source region. The TSL and RSL keys of the user sending the request are further restricted by a set of link keys. If a key required for access to a resource is not in the set of link keys defined for the communication, the resource will not be accessed.

To implement the flowing of CICS userids from one region to another, the **OutboundUserIds** attribute should be set to **sent.** If no userids should flow, specify **not_sent.** On receipt of a request, if the **RemoteSysSecurity** attribute is set to **trusted,** user security is used. When the request arrives from a remote region, the keys for the passed userid will be used. Any keys belonging to the user not in the same set as those of either the **TSLKeyMask** or **RSLKeyMask** (when **LinkUserid** = **""**) or those of the user specified by the **LinkUserId** will be removed from the effective set.

The following helps to illustrate this idea. A CICS user called *john* is defined that has a TSL key set of 1, 11, and 35 and an RSL key set of 1, 13, and 21. A Communication Definition (CD) has been created between the local region and a remote region. No **LinkUserId** has been defined, and the definition's **TSLKeyMask** is set to **1** and **11,** while the **RSLKeyMask** is set to **1** and **21.** When a request arrives from the remote region from a user on the remote region also called *john,* the effective keys for the request will be 1 and 11 for the TSL key list and 1 and 21 for the RSL key list.

External Security Manager Exit

As an alternative to the CICS/6000 internal security mechanisms of RSL and TSL key checking, an External Security Manager (ESM) may be written to augment the security checking provided by the internal security checks. The purpose of such a program is to allow alternative algorithms or checks to be applied to specify whether a user or program is allowed to access a particular resource.

Examples of the use of such an exit may be

- To allow or disallow access to a CICS transaction or resource based on the time of day or day of week. Some transactions may only be usable during business hours, whereas some others may only be usable outside business hours. These procedures may be set up for business processes or because of the load introduced into the CICS system.

- To allow or disallow access to a CICS transaction or resource based on alternative security parameters. If a more complex mechanism for user access is required other than simple RSL and TSL key checking, the algorithms in the ESM program could be tailored accordingly. Algorithms could involve DCE ACL checking, AIX /etc/passwd checking, or requests to third-party authorization tools such as Kerberos.

- To track or provide other auditing controls to resource and transaction access. Each access to a resource and transaction will cause the ESM to be invoked. The ESM could log or account for this access as well as performing an authorization check.

Writing an ESM program

Some additional points to remember when writing an ESM program include

- Each application server will load its own instance of the ESM program. No assumption about static or shared storage should be made when considering the ESM program as a security program for the whole region.

- Changes to the ESM program take effect only when the application server loads the ESM program, which is when the application server starts. After a change to the ESM program, it is best to shut down the region and restart.

The CICS_ESM_Init() function.   This function should be defined as the main entry point for the executable. It is called by CICS/6000 at ESM initialization and is passed two parameters:

RegionData   This is a pointer to a CICS_ESM_RegionData structure that contains the region name and version of the CICS system.

FnBuf   This is a pointer to a CICS_ESM_FnBuf structure that must be filled in by the ESM with the function entry points for TSL and RSL checking functions.

The function should return CICS_ESM_INIT_OK if the function initialized successfully and return the value !CICS_ESM_INIT_OK if a failure occurs.

The CICS_ESM_TSLCheck function.   This function is called by CICS/6000 whenever a transaction security Level (TSL) check is required before starting a new transaction. The function is passed two parameters:

RegionData   This is a pointer to a CICS_ESM_RegionData structure that contains the region name and version of the CICS system.

ContextData   This is a pointer to a CICS_ESM_ContextData structure that provides additional data relating to the transaction to be authorized for start. The transaction name, userid, terminal, program, and other information can be obtained from this structure and may be used to either grant or deny transaction start authority.

The function may return one of the following values:

CICS_ESM_RETURN_OK   The transaction has passed the TSL check and may be started.

CICS_ESM_RETURN_INVALID   The transaction has failed the TSL check and will not be started.

CICS_ESM_RETURN_FAIL   The function reports an error; the task is abended, and region error messages are issued.

The CICS_ESM_RSLCheck function.   This function is called by CICS/6000 whenever a resource security Level (RSL) check is required before accessing a resource. The function is passed the following parameters:

RegionData   This is a pointer to a CICS_ESM_RegionData structure that contains the region name and version of the CICS system.

ContextData   This is a pointer to a CICS_ESM_ContextData structure that provides additional data relating to the transaction to be authorized for resource access. The transaction name, userid, terminal, program, and other information can be obtained from this structure and may be used to either grant or deny resource access authority.

ResourceData   This is a pointer to a CICS_ESM_ResourceData C language union that contains the details of the resource for which access authority is being requested. The tag for this union structure is supplied in the **ResourceClass** parameter.

ResourceClass   This parameter defines the resource class for the resource being queried. The resource class may take one of the following values:

- CICS_ESM_RESOURCE_CLASS_FD   Files
- CICS_ESM_RESOURCE_CLASS_TSD   Temporary storage
- CICS_ESM_RESOURCE_CLASS_TDD   Transient data
- CICS_ESM_RESOURCE_CLASS_JD   Journals
- CICS_ESM_RESOURCE_CLASS_PD   Program Definitions
- CICS_ESM_RESOURCE_CLASS_TD   Transactions

TaskData   This parameter is a pointer to a CICS_ESM_TaskData structure that contains pointers to the CWA and TCTUA storage areas for CICS.

EIBFn   This pointer points to a 2-byte area that contains the code for the CICS function being requested. Each CICS command has its own code, which is defined in the Exec Interface Block (EIB) documentation in the *Application Programmers Reference.*

The CICS_ESM_FnBuf structure. This structure is passed to the ESM initialization function and should be filled in by that function. The structure contains two fields:

TSLCheckFn   This is a function pointer to a function that will perform the ESM transaction level security checking.

RSLCheckFn   This is a function pointer to a function that will perform the ESM resource level security checking.

The CICS_ESM_RegionData structure. This structure contains information about the CICS region itself. It is primarily used to allow an ESM program to take different logic paths based on the actual region name being used and the version of CICS/6000 itself.

Id   The CICS/6000 region name.

ReleaseNo   The CICS release number. This is a four-character string. For CICS/6000 V1.2, the string returned is "0120." This parameter allows an ESM to be written to handle variations of the ESM in multiple releases should it change.

The CICS_ESM_ContextData structure. This data structure is passed to both the TSL and RSL checking functions to provide a context upon which to base the authorization. The context data include information about the transaction, user, terminal, and program attempting to access the resource or transaction.

TranData   A pointer to a `CICS_ESM_TranData` structure containing transaction information about the transaction requesting authorization for a resource.

UserData   A pointer to a `CICS_ESM_UserData` structure containing user data information about the user requesting authorization.

TermData   A pointer to a `CICS_ESM_TermData` structure containing information about the terminal that is associated with the authorization.

ProgData   A pointer to a `CICS_ESM_ProgramData` structure containing information about the CICS program requesting authorization. For CICS internal transactions, this pointer may be **NULL.**

CommData   A pointer to a `CICS_ESM_CommData` structure containing information about remote communications.

The CICS_ESM_TaskData structure. This data structure is passed to the RSL checking function to allow the ESM program access to the Common Work Area (CWA) and Terminal Control Table User Area (TCTUA) memory areas. The structure contains the following fields:

`CICS_ESM_CWA_Len`   The length of the CWA in bytes.

`CICS_ESM_CWA`   A pointer to the CWA storage.

`CICS_ESM_TCTUA_Len`   The length of the TCTUA in bytes.

`CICS_ESM_TCTUA`   A pointer to the TCTUA storage.

The CICS_ESM_TranData structure.   This data structure contains information about a transaction.

Id   The transaction name making the request.

Type   Either CICS_ESM_TRAN_LOCAL or CICS_ESM_TRAN_REMOTE, which specifies whether the transaction is local or remote.

RemoteName   Name of the remote CICS region if the **Type** is remote.

RemoteSysId   SYSID of the remote CICS region if the **Type** is remote.

The CICS_ESM_UserData structure.   This data structure contains information about the CICS user attempting to access a transaction or be authorized for a resource.

Id   The CICS user name.

Principal   The DCE principal, including the DCE cell name of the underlying DCE user.

The CICS_ESM_TermData structure.   This data type contains information about the terminal associated with the authorization request. Currently only the terminal identifier is supplied.

Id   The terminal name associated with the transaction making the security request.

The CICS_ESM_ProgramData structure.   This data structure contains information about the program requesting authorization or the program that is to be authorized.

Id   The program name associated with the security check.

The CICS_ESM_CommData structure.   This data structure contains information about a remote request.

Id   Communication data.

The CICS_ESM_FileData structure.   This data structure contains information about the file that is to be authorized.

Id   The name of the CICS file being checked.

Type   Either CICS_ESM_FILE_LOCAL if the file is locally defined or CICS_ESM_FILE_REMOTE is the file is defined as being remote.

FileServer   If the file is local, this field contains the name of the SFS containing the underlying SFS file.

FileName   If the file is local, this field contains the name of the SFS file.

FileIndex   If the file is local, this field contains the index name associated with the SFS file.

RemoteName   If the file is remote, this field contains the name of the file on the remote CICS region.

RemoteSysId   If the file is remote, this field contains the name of the CICS region containing the file.

The CICS_ESM_TDQData structure.   This data structure contains information about the transient data queue that is to be authorized.

Id   The name of the transient data queue.

Type   The type of transient data queue; this may be one of

- CICS_ESM_TDQ_INTRAPARTITION
- CICS_ESM_TDQ_EXTRAPARTITION
- CICS_ESM_TDQ_REMOTE
- CICS_ESM_TDQ_INDIRECT

RemoteName   If the queue type is defined as being remote, this field contains the name of the queue on the remote CICS region.

RemoteSysId   If the queue type is defined as being remote, this field contains the SYSID of the remote CICS region containing the queue.

ExtrapartitionFile   If the queue type is extrapartition, this field contains the AIX file name of the queue.

IndirectName   If the queue type is indirect, this field contains the indirect queue name.

The CICS_ESM_TSQData structure.   This data structure contains information about the temporary storage queue that is to be authorized.

Id   The name of the temporary storage queue.

Type   The type of the temporary storage queue; this may be one of

- CICS_ESM_TSQ_MAIN
- CICS_ESM_TSQ_AUXILIARY
- CICS_ESM_TSQ_TEMPLATE
- CICS_ESM_TSQ_REMOTE

RemoteName   If the queue type is defined as being remote, this field contains the name of the queue on the remote CICS region.

RemoteSysId   If the queue type is defined as being remote, this field contains the SYSID of the remote CICS region containing the queue.

The CICS_ESM_JournalData structure.   This data structure contains information about the temporary storage queue that is to be authorized.

Id   The identifier of the CICS journal being checked.

The CICS_ESM_ResourceData union.   A pointer to this C union data type is passed in an RSL check call. The actual field that is to be used from this data type is passed as the **ResourceClass** parameter in the RSL check function. Note that the fields are actual structures and not pointers to structures.

File   An instance of the CICS_ESM_FileData structure for the file being authorized.

TDQ   An instance of the CICS_ESM_TDQData structure for the queue being authorized.

TSQ   An instance of the CICS_ESM_TSQData structure for the queue being authorized.

Jrnl   An instance of the CICS_ESM_JournalData structure for the journal being authorized.

Prog   An instance of the CICS_ESM_ProgramData structure for the program being authorized.

Tran   An instance of the CICS_ESM_TranData structure for the program being authorized.

The data structures and relations just described are shown in the following diagrams. Figure 24.1 illustrates the TSL checking function, while Fig. 24.2 illustrates the RSL checking function.

Resource definition for an ESM

Once an ESM program has been written, the CICS region must be informed of its location. The **ESMModule** attribute of the Region Definition (RD) resource class contains the path name and program name of the ESM program in the AIX file system. Once defined, the **ESMLoad** attribute also must be set to **yes.** This attribute informs the CICS region that it should look for and use the ESM program defined in the **ESMModule** attribute.

The ESM program will be invoked for each transaction and resource access instead of the internal RSL and TSL checking only when the **RSLCheck** and **TSLCheck** attributes of the Transaction Definition (TD) being invoked are set to **external** and the resource checking attributes for the resource class

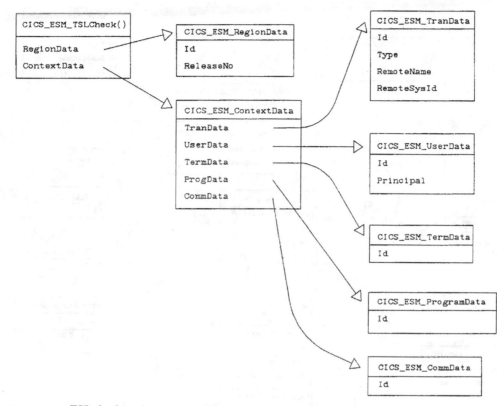

Figure 24.1   TSL checking function and data.

being accessed are set to **external** in the Region Definition. The following list indicates the resource class attributes in the Region Definition (RD).

FileRSLCheck   Type of RSL checking for files, either internal or external.

JournalRSLCheck   Type of RSL checking for journals, either internal or external.

ProgramRSLCheck   Type of RSL checking for programs, either internal or external.

TemporaryStorageRSLCheck   Type of RSL checking for temporary storage queues, either internal or external.

TransactionRSLCheck   Type of RSL checking for transactions, either internal or external.

TransientDataRSLCheck   Type of RSL checking for transient data queues, either internal or external.

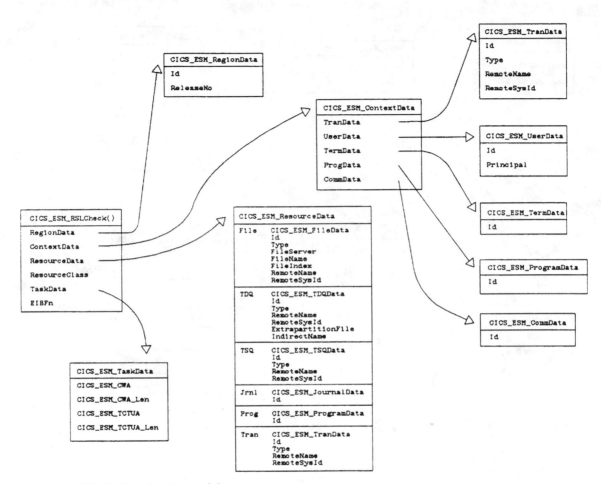

Figure 24.2 RSL checking function and data.

A sample ESM program is supplied with CICS/6000 in the `/usr/lpp/cics/src/samples/esm` directory.

Sample ESM program

The following sample ESM program may be used to display the TSL and RSL checks and data. The program writes the details of all security checks to the `console.msg` file.

```
#include <cics_esm.h>
#include <stdio.h>

void ShowRegionData(struct CICS_ESM_RegionData *RegionData)
{
    fprintf(stderr, "--------------- RegionData ---------------\n");
    fprintf(stderr, "Id: %s\n", RegionData->Id);
    fprintf(stderr, "Id: %s\n", RegionData->ReleaseNo);
```

```
        return;
}
void ShowJournalData(struct CICS_ESM_JournalData *JournalData)
{
    fprintf(stderr, "*** JournalData ***\n");
    fprintf(stderr, "Journal name [Id]: %s\n", JournalData->Id);
    return;
}

void ShowTSQData(struct CICS_ESM_TSQData *TSQData)
{
    fprintf(stderr, "*** TSQData ***\n");
    fprintf(stderr, "Queue name [Id]: %s\n", TSQData->Id);
    switch(TSQData->Type)
    {
        case CICS_ESM_TSQ_MAIN:
            fprintf(stderr, "Type [Type]: Main\n");
            break;

        case CICS_ESM_TSQ_AUXILIARY:
            fprintf(stderr, "Type [Type]: Auxilliary\n");
            break;

        case CICS_ESM_TSQ_TEMPLATE:
            fprintf(stderr, "Type [Type]: Template\n");
            break;

        case CICS_ESM_TSQ_REMOTE:
            fprintf(stderr, "Type [Type]: remote\n");
            fprintf(stderr, "Remote queue name [RemoteName]: %s\n",
                TSQData->RemoteName);
            fprintf(stderr, "Remote SysId [RemoteSysId]: %s\n",
                TSQData->RemoteSysId);
            break;
    }
        return;
}
void ShowTDQData(struct CICS_ESM_TDQData *TDQData)
{
    fprintf(stderr, "*** TDQData ***\n");
    fprintf(stderr, "Queue Name [Id]: %s\n", TDQData->Id);
    switch(TDQData->Type)
    {
            case CICS_ESM_TDQ_INTRAPARTITION:
                fprintf(stderr, "Type [Type]: Intrapartition\n");
                break;

            case CICS_ESM_TDQ_EXTRAPARTITION:
                fprintf(stderr, "Type [Type]: Extrapartition\n");
                fprintf(stderr, "File [ExtrapartitionFile]: %s\n",
                    TDQData->ExtrapartitionFile);
                break;

            case CICS_ESM_TDQ_REMOTE:
                fprintf(stderr, "Type [Type]: Remote\n");
                fprintf(stderr, "Remote queue name [RemoteName]: %s\n",
                    TDQData->RemoteName);
                fprintf(stderr, "Remote SysId [RemoteSysId]: %s\n",
                    TDQData->RemoteSysId);
                break;

            case CICS_ESM_TDQ_INDIRECT:
                fprintf(stderr, "Type [Type]: Indirect\n");
                fprintf(stderr, "Indirect queue name [IndirectName]: %s\n",
```

```
                                TDQData->IndirectName);
                    break;
        }
        return;
}

void ShowFileData(struct CICS_ESM_FileData *FileData)
{
    fprintf(stderr, "*** FileData ***\n");
    fprintf(stderr, "File name [Id]: %s\n", FileData->Id);
    if (FileData->Type = = CICS_ESM_FILE_LOCAL)
    {
        fprintf(stderr, "Type [Type]: Local\n");
        fprintf(stderr, "SFS Server name [FileServer]: %s\n",
            FileData->FileServer);
        fprintf(stderr, "SFS File name [FileName]: %s\n",
            FileData->FileName);
        fprintf(stderr, "SFS Index name [FileIndex]: %s\n",
            FileData->FileIndex);
    }
    else
    {
        fprintf(stderr, "Type [Type]: Remote\n");
        fprintf(stderr, "Remote file name [RemoteName]: %s\n",
            FileData->RemoteName);
        fprintf(stderr, "Remote CICS SYSID [RemoteSysId]: %s\n",
            FileData->RemoteSysId);
    }
    return;
}

void ShowTranData(struct CICS_ESM_TranData *TranData)
{
    fprintf(stderr, "*** TranData ***\n");
    fprintf(stderr, "Transaction name [Id]: %s\n", TranData->Id);
    fprintf(stderr, "Type [Type]: %s\n",
        TranData->Type = = CICS_ESM_TRAN_LOCAL?"LOCAL":"REMOTE");
    if (TranData->Type = = CICS_ESM_TRAN_REMOTE)
    {
        fprintf(stderr, "Remote transaction name [RemoteName]: %s\n",
            TranData->RemoteName);
        fprintf(stderr, "Remote system name [RemoteSysId]: %s\n",
            TranData->RemoteSysId);
    }
    return;
}

void ShowCommData(struct CICS_ESM_CommData *CommData)
{
    fprintf(stderr, "*** CommData ***\n");
    if (CommData = = NULL)
    {
        fprintf(stderr, "No program data available\n");
    }
    else
    {
        fprintf(stderr, "Communication data [Id]: %s\n", CommData->Id);
    }
    return;
}

void ShowProgramData(struct CICS_ESM_ProgramData *ProgData)
{
```

```
        fprintf(stderr, "*** ProgramData ***\n");
        if (ProgData = = NULL)
        {
            fprintf(stderr, "No program data available\n");
        }
        else
        {
            fprintf(stderr, "Program name [Id]: %s\n", ProgData->Id);
        }
        return;
}

void ShowTermData(struct CICS_ESM_TermData *TermData)
{
        fprintf(stderr, "*** TermData ***\n");
        fprintf(stderr, "Terminal Id [Id]: %s\n", TermData->Id);
        return;
}

void ShowUserData(struct CICS_ESM_UserData *UserData)
{
        fprintf(stderr, "*** UserData ***\n");
        fprintf(stderr, "CICS userid [Id]: %s\n", UserData->Id);
        fprintf(stderr, "DCE Principal [Principal]: %s\n", UserData->Principal);
        return;
}

void ShowContextData(struct CICS_ESM_ContextData *ContextData)
{
        fprintf(stderr, "-------------- ContextData --------------\n");
        ShowTranData(ContextData->TranData);
        ShowUserData(ContextData->UserData);
        ShowTermData(ContextData->TermData);
        ShowProgramData(ContextData->ProgData);
        ShowCommData(ContextData->CommData);
        return;
}

CICS_ESM_Return_t CICS_ESM_TSLCheck(
                struct CICS_ESM_RegionData *RegionData,
                struct CICS_ESM_ContextData *ContextData)
{
        fprintf(stderr, "+++++++++++++ TSL Check +++++++++++++++++\n");
        ShowRegionData(RegionData);
        ShowContextData(ContextData);
        return(CICS_ESM_RETURN_OK);
}

void ShowResourceData( union CICS_ESM_ResourceData *ResourceData,
                       enum CICS_ESM_ResourceClass ResourceClass)
{
        fprintf(stderr, "- ResourceData -\n");
        switch(ResourceClass)
        {
          case CICS_ESM_RESOURCE_CLASS_FD:
              ShowFileData(&ResourceData->File);
              break;

          case CICS_ESM_RESOURCE_CLASS_TSD:
              ShowTSQData(&ResourceData->TSQ);
              break;

          case CICS_ESM_RESOURCE_CLASS_TDD:
              ShowTDQData(&ResourceData->TDQ);
```

```
                        break;

            case CICS_ESM_RESOURCE_CLASS_JD:
                ShowJournalData(&ResourceData->Jrnl);
                break;

            case CICS_ESM_RESOURCE_CLASS_PD:
                ShowProgramData(&ResourceData->Prog);
                break;

            case CICS_ESM_RESOURCE_CLASS_TD:
                ShowTranData(&ResourceData->Tran);
                break;
        }
        return;
    }

    CICS_ESM_Return_t CICS_ESM_RSLCheck(
                    struct CICS_ESM_RegionData    *RegionData,
                    struct CICS_ESM_ContextData   *ContextData,
                    union CICS_ESM_ResourceData   *ResourceData,
                    enum CICS_ESM_ResourceClass   ResourceClass,
                    struct CICS_ESM_TaskData      *TaskData,
                    cics_char_t                   *EIBFn)
    {

        fprintf(stderr, "++++++++++++++ RSL Check +++++++++++++++++\n");
        ShowRegionData(RegionData);
        ShowContextData(ContextData);
        ShowResourceData(ResourceData, ResourceClass);
        fprintf(stderr, "CICS Function code: %2.2X%2.2X\n", EIBFn[0], EIBFn[1]);
        return(CICS_ESM_RETURN_OK);
    }

    int CICS_ESM_Init( struct CICS_ESM_RegionData *RegionData,
                    struct CICS_ESM_FnBuf *FnBuf)
    {
        fprintf(stderr, "CICS_ESM_Init called\n");
        ShowRegionData(RegionData);
        FnBuf->TSLCheckFn = CICS_ESM_TSLCheck;
        FnBuf->RSLCheckFn = CICS_ESM_RSLCheck;
        return(0);
}
```

The program may be compiled with the following command:

```
xlc_r -o esm -e CICS_ESM_Init -I/usr/lpp/cics/include ems.c
```

The compilation step compiles the source code contained in the AIX file
`esm.c` and produces an executable called **esm.** The executable cannot be executed directly from AIX because it contains unresolved variables and data. It
should be defined as the ESM program to be used by a CICS region. The following CICS administration command may be used to define the ESM program to CICS:

```
cicsupdate -c rd -r $CICSREGION \
ESMModule = $PWD/esm \
ESMLoad = yes
```

The CICS region must be restarted to take effect. All transaction starts and resource checks for transactions that are defined as having their **RSLCheck = external** and **TSLCheck = external** will be passed through the ESM program. A useful way to test this is to define a new transaction based on the CECI transaction but with **TSLCheck** and **RSLCheck** set to **external.** This may be accomplished by the following command, which creates a new transaction called *MECI* with all the attributes but security the same as the CECI transaction:

```
cicsadd -c td -r $CICSREGION -m CECI MECI \
RSLCheck = external TSLCheck = external
```

25

Batch Programming

CICS/6000 is known as an on-line transaction processing monitor. Programs that are executed outside the context of CICS are often referred to as *batch programs* as opposed to on-line programs. This terminology is somewhat of a legacy in the AIX and CICS/6000 world. CICS on the MVS and ESA operating systems provides the illusion of multiuser access and concurrent task execution. User interaction is also governed by CICS control. In AIX, the shells provide immediate responses to user interactions. When a user enters a command at the shell prompt, the command will appear to execute immediately. Most programs produce some results that are displayed back to the user, again almost immediately.

The following two chapters describe the class of AIX applications that interact with CICS and the underlying Encina and DCE products without being CICS applications themselves.

# Chapter 26

Accessing Encina SFS
through COBOL: EXTFH

Although access to files through the CICS file API is sufficient for the majority of application access, there are many instances when the file data must be accessed through non-CICS or batch applications. These applications can be written in either the C or COBOL programming languages.

This chapter describes developing COBOL applications under AIX that will access Encina SFS files.

COBOL EXTFH

MicroFocus COBOL provides COBOL language file control commands such as

- OPEN   Open a file.
- CLOSE   Close a file.
- READ   Read a record from a file.
- WRITE   Write a record to a file.
- REWRITE   Update a record in a file.
- START   Position the read cursor for reading a record.

In addition to these, MicroFocus COBOL also provides language extensions that specify record locking for concurrent access to a file by multiple applications.

The MicroFocus COBOL product also provides a programmable interface that allows replacement of the underlying file management system. By default, COBOL file operations manipulate files maintained by AIX as AIX file system files. The interface provided by the MicroFocus COBOL product is called the *External File Handler* (EXTFH).

The EXTFH interface works by building a new COBOL language runtime with the native file-handling routines replaced with file-handling routines suitable for other products. The Encina product provides a library of functions that allow access to the Encina SFS through the native COBOL file commands. This is illustrated in Fig. 26.1.

Building an EXTFH COBOL runtime

To use a COBOL application with the Encina EXTFH, a new version of the COBOL runtime must be created for use with compiled COBOL applications. This may be accomplished with the following command:

```
cob -xo newrts $COBDIR/src/rts/ufhtab.o \
   -L /usr/lpp/encina/lib
   -lEncSfsExtfh -lEncSfs -lEncina -ldce -lc_r -lpthreads \
   -m usqfile = cobol_Extfh -m usqfilev = cobol_Extfh \
   -m urlfile = cobol_Extfh -m urlfilev = cobol_Extfh \
   -m uixfile = cobol_Extfh -m uixfilev = cobol_Extfh \
   -e ""
```

The output of this command is a new COBOL runtime called **newrts.** This runtime may be used to execute COBOL programs and, if they contain COBOL I/O calls, will make requests against an SFS.

Since an SFS file must be referenced not only by name but also by the Encina SFS on which the file is located, a mechanism is required to inform the COBOL program on which SFS the files may be found. A COBOL runtime with an Encina EXTFH interface will utilize the ENCINA_EXTFH_SFS environment variable. This variable is expected to contain the DCE CDS name of the SFS. If the COBOL program is to create an SFS file such as with the OPEN OUTPUT command, the name of the SFS logical volume on which to store the SFS file data also must be specified. This is accomplished with the ENCINA_EXTFH_VOL variable, which should be set to the volume name on the SFS.

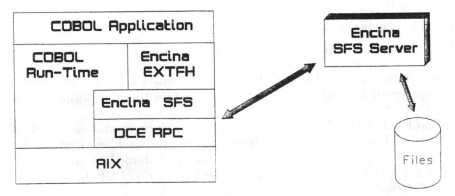

Figure 26.1 Encina EXTFH interface.

Assigning Names to Files

In the COBOL SELECT statement, the ASSIGN TO operands are used to associate a COBOL program file name with a real external file name. When using EXTFH, this may be coded either as an SFS file name, an SFS file name qualified by the file server, or an environment variable that contains the SFS file name or fully qualified file name.

When using environment variables, the SELECT statement should be coded in the application as

```
FILE CONTROL.
   SELECT MY-FILE
      ASSIGN TO EXTERNAL VARIABLE-NAME
      ....
```

The VARIABLE-NAME must exist as an AIX exported environment variable in the environment of the program being executed. The name also must be prefixed by the string dd_. For example, if the environment variable MYFILE is to be used to hold the name that an EXTFH COBOL batch application is to access, the following should be set before executing the program:

```
export dd_MYFILE = "<SFS file name>"
```

Details of COBOL Interfacing to Encina SFS Files

The COBOL language supports four different file types. Only three of these map to Encina SFS file types, and the fourth continues to refer to AIX-based files.

COBOL file type	SFS file type
Line-sequential	No equivalent in SFS
Record-sequential	Entry-sequenced (ESDS)
Indexed	Clustered (KSDS)
Relative	Relative (RRDS)

Sample EXTFH program

The sample described in this section reads all the records from an SFS file and displays them to the user. The records for the sample are assumed to be 10 bytes in length, with the first 5 bytes providing the key field. The SFS file could be mapped to a CICS file in the CICS File Definitions (FD) and may be written to by CICS EXEC CICS WRITE commands. A program such as that described in Fig. 26.2 could easily be used to interrogate or process records written to the file by a CICS application.

```
IDENTIFICATION DIVISION.
    PROGRAM-ID. fileread.
ENVIRONMENT DIVISION.
INPUT-OUTPUT SECTION.
FILE-CONTROL.
    SELECT DATA-FILE
        ASSIGN 'datafile'                          1
        ORGANIZATION IS INDEXED
        ACCESS MODE IS SEQUENTIAL
        RECORD KEY IS USER-KEY
        FILE STATUS IS RECORD-STATUS.
DATA DIVISION.
FILE SECTION.
FD DATA-FILE
    DATA RECORD IS USER-REC.
01 USER-REC.                                       2
    05 USER-KEY   PIC X(05).
    05 USER-DATA  PIC X(05).


WORKING-STORAGE SECTION.
01 RECORD-STATUS PIC XX VALUE IS '00'.


PROCEDURE DIVISION.
0000-MAIN.
    OPEN INPUT DATA-FILE.
    MOVE ZEROS TO USER-KEY.
    START DATA-FILE KEY IS GREATER THAN USER-KEY.
    IF RECORD-STATUS NOT EQUAL '00'
       DISPLAY 'Error positioning, file status =' RECORD-STATUS
       GOBACK.
    PERFORM PROCESS-RECORD
       UNTIL RECORD-STATUS NOT EQUAL '00'.
    IF RECORD-STATUS NOT EQUAL '10'                3
       DISPLAY 'Unexpected error:' RECORD-STATUS.
    DISPLAY 'All Done'.
    GOBACK.


PROCESS-RECORD.
    READ DATA-FILE NEXT RECORD.
    IF RECORD-STATUS EQUALS '00'
       DISPLAY 'Record value:' USER-REC.
```

Figure 26.2 EXTFH sample.

The following key points in the program in Fig. 26.2 help to clarify some of the parts of accessing SFS files through EXTFH.

1. The name of the Encina SFS file.

2. The layout of records in the SFS file.

3. Error code **10** is defined to be no more records.

The program may be executed by performing the following tasks:

```
$ dce_login <principal> <password>
$ export ENCINA_EXTFH_VOL = <volume name>
$ export ENCINA_EXTFH_SERVER = <server name>
$ cob -u readfile.cbl
$ newrts readfile
$ ...
```

Starting AIX Commands from CICS

On occasion, it serves a purpose to initiate a non-CICS application from within the CICS environment. Normally, such programs would be started by the user entering a command at the shell prompt or from a series of commands with an AIX file known as a *shell script*. From within CICS/6000, it is not that simple. CICS/6000 utilizes 3270-style terminals to initiate CICS programs. These 3270 terminals do not lend themselves to the input and output mechanisms expected by most AIX applications.

CICS/6000 also executes its own programs from within the application server processes. These processes allow CICS programs to execute but restrict the set of function and systems calls made by CICS programs to those which are thread-safe. Specifically, the two fundamental AIX system calls used to start new programs, namely, **fork()** and **exec(),** are disallowed. Without the ability to call **fork()** and **exec()** plus the restriction that blocking calls such as **system()** are disallowed, an alternative mechanism must be designed to allow AIX applications to be started.

Using AIX inetd and sockets to start AIX applications

In the cicsteld section (see Chap. 4), the AIX *inetd* demon was introduced. This section will describe more of the capabilities of AIX inetd and how it may be used to start AIX applications at the request of CICS/6000.

The AIX inetd server listens on multiple TCP/IP sockets simultaneously. When a client sockets application makes a TCP/IP sockets call to connect to a TCP/IP socket being listened to by the AIX inetd server, the server starts a new instance of an AIX program corresponding to the socket on which it was listening. The newly started program receives the connection to the client program as its standard input, output, and error streams (stdin, stdout, and stderr). Once the program is started, AIX inetd will then go back to listening for other requests on the socket on which it just received the request as well as all the other sockets with which it has been configured.

Inetd is fully configurable. It can listen on any socket specified by port number, start any command, and execute that command as any defined AIX user. A client application that invokes a program through inetd can pass that newly started program data and receive data back from that program.

Inetd can be thought of as a broker for starting new programs through TCP/IP. Instead of having many server programs all executing and consuming CPU and other resources, the server programs are started only when requested to by the clients and usually terminate when their task has completed. Figure 27.1 illustrates the operation of the inetd demon.

Since inetd has the capability of starting any AIX program including AIX shell scripts, inetd may be configured to start an AIX application on behalf of CICS/6000.

Listening Sockets

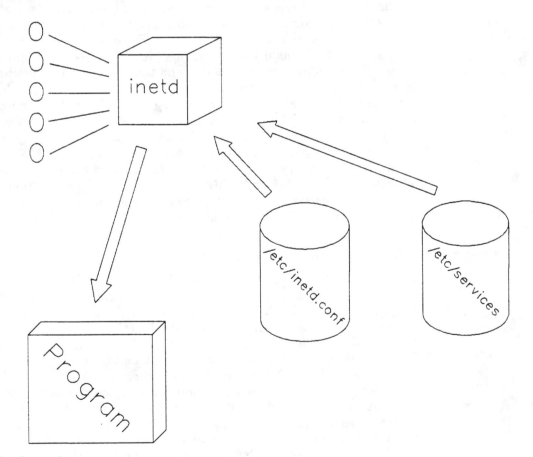

Figure 27.1 Inetd operation.

To allow CICS/6000 to start a program through inetd, three tasks must be accomplished:

1. Develop the program, shell script, or command to be executed by inetd.
2. Configure inetd to start listening on a socket on behalf of the program.
3. Develop a CICS/6000 sockets application to make the request start the program.

Developing inetd programs.   When developing a program that is to be started by AIX inetd, it is important to understand that when the program executes, it has no terminal for output nor a keyboard for input. The program must execute without presenting the user with more data or expecting requestable input. When the program starts, its standard output is directed back to the client application that made the socket request. Programs or commands that would normally send output to the user at the terminal will have their output directed back to the client application. This may be used in many circumstances to good effect. A client program that causes a regular AIX program to be started through inetd can receive the regular output from that program through the socket. The standard error output stream is also directed back to the client application.

The inetd-started application has its standard input source set to the socket connected to the client. If the client sends data through the socket, the data will arrive as the standard input to the application.

All this functionality is very powerful, but care should be taken when invoking AIX applications that may be unaware that they are not actually interacting with a terminal. Specifically, full-screen applications such as editors should not be started through inetd.

If the client program does not care to send additional data back to the started AIX application or does not expect output from that application, it may decide to close its end of the socket. This would allow the client to continue processing other commands or even end itself. The result is that a new AIX application has been started by inetd and is executing asynchronously with the original client requestor application. When a client closes its end of the socket, an attempt to read or write to the AIX inetd-started program may result in an error in that program. The program will receive the end-of-input condition on reading and an error on writing. Either of these conditions may be unexpected to normal AIX applications. Care should be taken to redirect the outputs and inputs of such applications either to files if the output is to be saved or to the /dev/null special file, which acts as a sink for data.

For example, if the following program is started by inetd:

```
#!/bin/ksh
echo "Hello from inetd started program"
read name
echo "Goodbye, $name"
```

it will send a message down the socket to the client saying "Hello." It will then read some text from the socket and finally say "Goodbye." If the client program is connected, the client will receive the "Hello" message. The server program will now block until the client sends a response message back down the socket. The server will then receive the message and end with a "Goodbye" message.

A tight coupling exists between the client and the server. It is essential that the client and the server stay in harmony with which one is expected to send and which is expected to receive.

Figure 27.2 shows the communication flows between a client application and inetd when the client requests communication with a program.

If the client closed the socket immediately after starting the client, the AIX application may fail when attempting to write the "Hello" message. The program may not be expecting a closed standard output when writing data.

The following figures show some useful programs that can be configured to the AIX inetd. The program shown in Fig. 27.3 will execute an arbitrary AIX command. Great care should be taken with this program. Once it is defined to inetd, any user *anywhere* on the network will be able to execute commands on the machine on which it is configured. The AIX user that executes the command is the AIX user configured to inetd. With this program, never define that user as root.

The program shown in Fig. 27.4 will mail a message to the user specified in the shell script file. The first line of input will be used as the subject heading, with the following lines as the body of the message. When the mail is -delivered, it will appear to have originated from the AIX user configured to inetd.

Configuring AIX inetd to start programs.   The task of configuring inetd to listen on behalf of new programs must be accomplished by the root user. This task is composed of the following steps:

```
                                                inetd listens on socket

client requests connection    =================>
with program

                                                inetd starts the program
                                                and passes the socket
                                                connection as stdin,
                                                stdout and stderr

                                                inetd listens on socket

client communicates with     <================>  program communicates with
program                                          client
```

Figure 27.2   Communication flows of inetd.

```
#!/bin/ksh
#
# Program to execute an arbitrary command
#
# Read the command from standard input (the socket client)
#
read command

#
# Log the command and date into the log file
#
print -n "About to execute \"$command\": " >> /tmp/batch.log
date >> /tmp/batch.log

#
# Execute the command, store its output in the output file.
#
eval $command >> /tmp/batch.out < /dev/null 2> /dev/null
```

Figure 27.3 Batch command execution program.

```
#!/bin/ksh
#
# Mail the message to the user
#
# Read the message from standard input (the socket client)
#
read subject

#
# Mail the message to the user
#
mail -s "$subject" user@host
```

Figure 27.4 Batch mail program.

- Decide on the *service* name of the application.
- Decide on the *port number* on which inetd will listen on behalf of the application.
- Decide on the AIX user that will execute the program.
- Add the service/port mapping to the services configuration.
- Add the service/user/program mapping to the inetd configuration.
- Refresh the inetd demon to start listening for the new program.

The service name is a symbolic name used to refer to the program. Associated with the service name is the port number of this service. The services database allows both client and server applications to determine the port number of their partners without having to explicitly code these in the applications. For example, when a telnet client wishes to contact a telnet server, instead of having port 25 hard-coded within the client code, the mapping of the symbolic name *telnet* and the port number of 25 are stored in the services database. The client application may then access the database and key on the symbolic name. The associated port number will be returned. The services database exists as an AIX file called /etc/services that may be browsed with an editor. The file should not be modified by hand. An AIX command is supplied to allow the user to modify its contents. The command is called **inetserv** and also will be used to configure inetd.

The syntax of **inetserv** for adding a new service/port mapping is

```
inetserv -a -S -v <service> -p <port> -t tcp
```

Configuring AIX inetd requires mapping the service name (and hence the port number) to the AIX user that will execute the program as well as the program name itself. The configuration of inetd is stored as the AIX file /etc/inetd.conf and may be browsed with an editor. The contents of the file should not be modified by an editor. The syntax of **inetserv** for configuring AIX inetd is

```
inetserv -a -I -v <service> -t tcp -w nowait -U <AIX user> -r
<path/program>
```

Whenever a change is made to the inetd configuration, the inetd demon itself must be refreshed. This is accomplished by executing the following:

```
refresh -s inetd
```

Developing a CICS/6000 sockets application to start a program.   A CICS/6000 application that is to start an AIX application through inetd must be able to establish a sockets connection to the socket on which inetd is listening. This is most easily accomplished by a C language program. The program shown in Fig. 27.5 may be used as an example.

This program expects two environment variables to be set in the region environment file.

- CICS_BATCH_HOSTNAME   Hostname of the machine on which inetd is listening.
- CICS_BATCH_PORT   Port number for the service on which inetd is listening.

Complete example.   This section illustrates a complete example of using inetd to start an AIX application. The function of the example is to send a mail message to an AIX user from within CICS. The program to be executed when inetd receives the connection request is the one illustrated in Fig. 27.4. This program will be saved in the AIX file /usr/local/bin/mail.sh. The port

```c
#include <errno.h>
#include <stdio.h>
#include <sys/types.h>
#include <sys/socket.h>
#include <netinet/in.h>
#include <arpa/inet.h>
#include <netdb.h>

DFHEIBLK   *eibptr;
main()
{
    int                   s;
    int                   rc;
    struct  sockaddr_in   address;
    struct  hostent_data  data;
    struct  hostent       he;
    char                  *hostname, *port;
    char                  *commarea;

    EXEC CICS ADDRESS COMMAREA(commarea) EIB(eibptr);

    /*
     * Obtain the hostname and port address for the connection
     */
    hostname   = (char *)getenv("CICS_BATCH_HOSTNAME");
    port       = (char *)getenv("CICS_BATCH_PORT");
    if (hostname == NULL || port == NULL)
    {
        fprintf(stderr, "BATCLNT: Environment variables " \
            "CICS_BATCH_HOSTNAME and CICS_BATCH_PORT must be set\n");
        EXEC CICS RETURN;
    }

    /*
     * Get the IP address of the hostname by performing a name lookup
     */
    memset(&data, 0, sizeof(data));
    rc = gethostbyname_r(hostname, &he, &data);
    if (rc < 0)
    {
        fprintf(stderr, "BATCLNT: Error from gethostbyname_r(), " \
            "errno = %d\n", errno);
        EXEC CICS RETURN;
    }

    /*
     * Create the socket and set the address of the server
     */
    s = socket(AF_INET, SOCK_STREAM, 0);

    address.sin_family      = AF_INET;
    address.sin_addr.s_addr = *(unsigned long *)he.h_addr;
    address.sin_port        = htons(atoi(port));

    /*
     * Connect to the inetd server
     */
    rc = connect(s, (struct sockaddr *)&address, sizeof(address));
    if (rc<0)
    {
        fprintf(stderr, "BATCLNT: Error from connect(): %s\n",
            strerror(errno));
    }

    /*
     * If a commarea was supplied, send it to the batch server
     */
    if (commarea != (char *)0xFF000000)
    {
        send(s, commarea, eibptr->eibcalen, 0);
    }
    /*
     * Close the socket
     */
    close(s);
    EXEC CICS RETURN;
}
```

Figure 27.5   CICS/6000 client program.

number being used will be 4444, and the user which this program is to execute as will be *cics*.

The first task is to configure AIX inetd with this information. The following AIX commands will accomplish this:

```
# inetserv -a -S -v batchtest -p 4444 -t tcp
# inetserv -a -I -v batchtest -t tcp -w nowait -U cics \
  -r /usr/local/bin/mail.sh
# refresh -s inetd
```

Once configured, executing the command **netstat -a -f inet | grep batchtest** will result in the following line of output:

```
tcp 0 0 *.batchtest *.* LISTEN
```

The output from **netstat** displays the names of sockets being listened for.

Next, the program shown in Fig. 27.5 must be compiled and defined to CICS/6000. The program is in a file called `batclnt.ccs`.

```
cicstcl -lC -d -e batclnt.ccs
```

To define to CICS, the following command may be used:

```
cicsadd -c pd -r $CICSREGION BATCLNT PathName = $PWD/batclnt
```

The following program may be compiled and defined to CICS:

```
main()
{
   char data[1024];

   strcpy(data, "Message from CICS\n");
   strcat(data, "This is a message from CICS/6000\n");
   strcat(data, "End of message");

   EXEC CICS LINK PROGRAM("BATCLNT")
      COMMAREA(data) LENGTH(strlen(data));
   EXEC CICS RETURN;
}
```

This program is saved in a file called `caller.ccs` and is compiled and defined with the following commands:

```
cicstcl -lC -d -e caller.ccs
cicsadd -c pd -r $CICSREGION CALLER PathName = $PWD/caller
cicsadd -c td -r $CICSREGION CALL ProgName = CALLER
```

Finally, the environment variables defining the host and port must be added to the region environment file:

```
CICS_BATCH_HOSTNAME = localhost
CICS_BATCH_PORT = 4444
```

Once the region is restarted and the new CICS definitions in effect, the transaction named CALL may be executed. This will cause the CICS/6000 transaction to link to the inetd caller module, which will make a socket connection with inetd to start the `batch.sh` program. This final program will send an AIX mail message to the user specified in the `batch.sh  shell` script.

28

CICS/6000 and Databases

This chapter discusses CICS/6000 interoperation with databases. The use of databases is discussed and the X/Open XA interface introduced. The principals behind CICS/6000 XA integration are described.

Use of Databases

The database has become a powerful tool for data storage and maintenance. Most popular databases today provide the concept of a table that contains rows of records. The rows in the table may be retrieved, inserted, or updated. Powerful queries can be built and used to search the tables to obtain records that match various search criteria. Many databases provide transactional semantics when updating the contents of tables. Updates, inserts, and deletions of rows are not made permanent until the program commits the work. If the program fails or explicitly undoes the work, the tables will be left intact as though the program had never executed.

A language called *SQL* was developed to access and manipulate the tables in the database. The format of this language is similar to that of the CICS language in that each database command begins with the EXEC SQL statement and must be translated before or during compilation into the native language of the rest of the program. Database applications may be developed in many different languages including C and COBOL.

CICS applications on many environments utilize the services of a database to store and retrieve data. The EXEC SQL statements and the EXEC CICS statements are intermixed within the source of the applications. For databases that have separate precompilers for the EXEC SQL language, programs that contain both CICS and SQL statements are first precompiled by the database translator to replace the SQL statements with native code to service the database request. Once the SQL code has been removed, the programs are then passed through the CICS translator before being submitted to the compiler to build the final executable.

For CICS applications that access a database without updating the tables maintained by that database, there is no concern about the transactional integrity of the data within the database. These transactions are known as *read-only* because the database access is only searches and reads. When a CICS application wishes to update the rows in a database table, a transactional problem is introduced. A CICS transaction that updates a table also may update a CICS transactional resource such as a file or queue. Additionally, the transaction may initiate other CICS programs via a LINK CICS communication call, which may in turn update CICS recoverable resources. If the CICS program abends, backout of the database as well as the CICS resources must be ensured. If the transaction commits, both the CICS and database resources must commit. Failure of the two sets of resources to stay in synchronization will result in inconsistent data.

The solution to this problem was designed by the X/Open consortium, and an architecture describing database and transaction manager interaction was developed. This architecture is known as the *XA protocol*. Its name has no inherent meaning.

The X/Open XA Architecture

The X/Open XA architecture describes the interaction among a transaction manager, an application, and one or more resource managers. The architecture is independent of actual products. In a CICS context, the transaction manager will be CICS, and the resource managers will be databases. The XA protocol describes a series of communication flows between the resource manager and the transaction manager to ensure that updates made by an application that registers with the transaction manager stay consistent. The transaction manager takes control of the resource managers with respect to the transactional outcome of the work. The resource managers defer their commitment of work from themselves to the transaction manager.

When the application requests a commit of its work, it makes the request to the transaction manager. The transaction managers then uses the two-phase commit algorithm to first prepare and then commit the work of the various resource managers. Each resource manager is first sent a request by the transaction manager to prepare the work made by the application. The resource managers then attempt to determine if they have the ability to commit the work made by the transaction. If they do, a positive response is returned to the transaction manager. If any of the resource managers are unable to prepare their work, all the resource managers are sent a rollback request to undo the work. If all the resource managers return a positive indication during the prepare phase, they are then sent a commit request by the transaction manager, and the work made by the application is made permanent.

In the CICS/6000 environment, the CICS region acts as the transaction manager and will make prepare, rollback, and commit requests against the database. Each of the databases defers the transactional outcome to CICS/6000. Work done within the application by EXEC CICS commands is handled internally by CICS. Although CICS itself does not need to use the XA protocol to access its own resources, it too will utilize the two-phase commit protocol and may be the cause of the rollback of database work should it detect an inability to commit its own work. Figure 28.1 illustrates the XA model.

The interface between the transaction manager and the resource managers is also architected by the XA protocol specification. This is achieved in CICS/6000 by a mechanism known as the *XA switch load file*.

Integrating CICS/6000 with a Database Using XA

To integrate a database with CICS/6000 to utilize the XA protocol and hence achieve transactional integrity, the database must be XA protocol compliant. It will provide a code module that exports a series of interfaces which may be called by the transaction manager. These interfaces mask the database internal calls and mechanisms required to communicate with the database by the transaction manager. The interface names and functions are architected by the XA protocol. These interfaces include a begin transaction, an end transaction, and prepare, commit, and rollback functions.

To utilize the database through XA, a CICS-loadable program must be built that allows CICS to call the XA functions provided by the database. This program is called the *switch load file*. The commands to build a switch load file for a database are specific to the database that is being integrated. The *CICS/6000 Administration Guide* provides details for many of the most popular databases. The documentation in the /usr/lpp/cics/docs directory also should be consulted for additional information made available after the documentation was prepared. AIX Makefiles for building various database

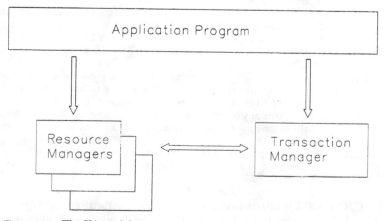

Figure 28.1   The XA model.

Switch Load Files may be found in the `/usr/lpp/cics/src/examples/xa` directory. For many database products such as Oracle and DB2/6000, an object file (loadable library) must be extracted for link editing with the XA switch load file.

How the XA interface works

Knowledge of how CICS interfaces with the database through the XA interface can provide guidance on performance and ease the understanding of the XA interface tasks. This section demystifies the CICS usage of the XA interface.

An XA-compliant database provides a code module that exports a data structure containing an array of pointers to functions within the code module itself. The names and locations of the code functions are private and hidden to the CICS system, which is able to call the functions by indexing into the table of function pointers. The offset of function pointers within the table is architected by the XA protocol. The function pointers included in the array are called with architected parameters and perform functions that are logically known to CICS. The actual implementation of the function is private to the database. The following table lists the functions provided in the array and their logical meaning:

Function	Description
xa_open	Open a connection to the database. This call is made once per application server to connect the application server process to the database. The connection to the database remains open until the application server ends and the **xa_close()** function call is made.
xa_close	Close a connection to the database. This call ends the connection to the database previously made with an **xa_open()** call.
xa_start	Start a new transaction. Whenever a new CICS logical unit of work is started, this call is made to inform the database that subsequent database calls from the application belong to this new transaction.
xa_end	This call informs the database that the transaction has come to an end.
xa_rollback	This call instructs the database to roll back or back out any changes to the database made as a result of work accomplished in this transaction. This call will be made as a result of a CICS transaction ABEND or an EXEC CICS SYNCPOINT ROLLBACK.
xa_prepare	This call is made by CICS as part of the two-phase commit processing of the transaction. The prepare phase will ask the database if it is able to subsequently commit the work performed by the transaction. If the database returns a failure indication or any of the other resource managers return a failure indication, the database changes will be subsequently backed out because the transaction will not commit.
xa_commit	Following a prepare, this call is used to commit or make permanent any work performed against the database as part of the CICS transaction.

The CICS/6000 product provides a small C language source stub for each of the popular XA-compliant databases. This C source contains a single C function whose name is known to CICS. The C function does nothing more than resolve the externally defined function or switch table and returns the address of the table back into the CICS runtime. When the C language file is compiled and linked with the database-supplied code and table, the resulting CICS executable is defined to CICS in the XA Definitions (XAD). Whenever CICS starts a new CICS application server (cicsas), the newly compiled program is loaded dynamically by CICS, and the entry points into the database code are resolved. CICS then calls the database functions indexed by the table whenever it needs to inform or request work from the database.

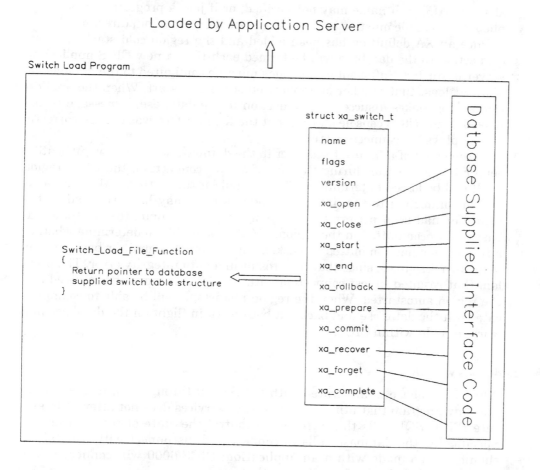

Resource Definition with XA databases

The XA Definitions (XAD) resource class allows CICS/database switch load files to be defined and used. The purpose of this CICS resource class is to define the locations in the AIX file system of switch load files and supply any necessary parameters that are to be passed to the functions exported by the database. Parameters required by some databases include the database user and password with which connections will be established and used, the name of the database with which to connect, the location of log files for debugging, and other database-specific parameters. These parameters are specified in the XA Open String resource within the definition and are passed to the **xa_open()** function within the function table. This function has responsibility for providing the initial database connection.

The switch load file itself must be located in a directory to which the CICS running system has access. Specifically, this must be a directory that is accessible either by the AIX cics user or by the AIX cics group. Permissions on the file itself also must allow read and execute by the cics user or group. An absolute AIX path name may be specified, or if just a program name is supplied, the load file must be in either the system or region bin directory.

Once an XA definition has been added and the region cold started, a new connection to the database will be formed each time a new CICS application server is started. Sufficient connections must be configured to the database to allow at least that number of application servers to start. When the application server makes a successful connection to the database, a message is displayed in the CICS console stating that the XA interface was opened correctly and displays the connection string.

In the event of a failure to connect to the database when a new application server has started or during the use of an old connection, the CICS region itself will be forced to terminate. The rational for this is that without a recoverable connection to the database, updates that may be performed in the future or had been performed previously may be uncommitted in the database and uncommitted in the region. If CICS is unable to determine whether a transaction has committed or backed out, it cannot commit or back out any of its own resources, since that may result in a data integrity error. The problem that resulted in lost connection with the database must be resolved and the region autostarted. When the region restarts, it will be able to communicate with the database and back out both work in flight on the database and work in flight within CICS.

Database restrictions with XA

When a database is integrated with CICS/6000 through XA, it is essential that any program that utilizes the database services does not attempt to execute EXEC SQL calls that attempt to control the state of the transaction. Specifically, the database calls to connect and disconnect with a database should not be made within an application; CICS/6000 will connect to the database on behalf of any application that needs it.

CICS database applications also should not attempt to issue the EXEC SQL COMMIT or EXEC SQL ROLLBACK statements because these attempt to control the outcome of the transaction that is now under CICS/6000 control.

Databases that are XA-integrated with CICS/6000 will have a connection made to them by each application server that CICS creates. Any application, whether it includes SQL statements or not, will be executed in an application server that has a database connection. CICS is unable to tell if the application made any SQL calls; as a result, it will involve itself in a prepare/commit conversation with the database. Performance of CICS applications that do not involve database will be degraded because the database interaction will be made needlessly.

Advanced Use of the XA Interface

Since the XA interface provides a point at which external code, namely, the database XA interface, may be called, alternative function code may be substituted in place of a real database switch array. This new function would allow an exit to be introduced to be called at the start of a new application server, at the end of an application server, at the start of a new transaction, and at the prepare/commit/rollback of a transaction. Although not specifically designed for user application code, as long as the code inserted is both thread-safe and compliant to the XA interface functions, no harm should result. Possible uses for such an interface include

- Advanced tracing of an XA database
- Initializing an application server–specific library or function
- Preconnection of a sockets interface
- Development of new XA interfaces to recoverable products

Any code inserted through an XA interface should be thoroughly tested. Calls made through XA should not assume that they are executed within the same thread or stack as a CICS application and may potentially cause data corruption if badly written and access storage is not allocated to them.

29

CICS/6000 Troubleshooting

When working with an environment as rich and as complex as CICS, problems will occur from time to time. These problems may manifest themselves in various forms, such as programs not executing correctly, producing incorrect output, or crashing. The CICS environment itself may fail or lock up.

Such problems may result from many causes, including a misunderstanding of CICS functions, a bug in one or more CICS-written programs, or a defect in the CICS, Encina, or DCE products themselves. Determining and correcting the cause of such problems are the focus of this chapter.

CICS-Produced Information

CICS/6000 includes a number of sources of information to allow problem determination to be performed. Some of these are available constantly, while others need to be configured explicitly to be used.

The CICS/6000 console file

As CICS/6000 starts and operates, it constantly logs system messages to an AIX file known as the *console file*. This file contains informational, warning, and error messages as the state of the CICS product changes. Messages logged to this file should be examined on a regular basis. On encountering an error, the error will probably be logged into this file first. The file is located in the CICS region directory /var/cics_regions/<region> in a file called console.msg.

The console file is emptied each time the CICS region restarts. If error messages are to be kept for later analysis, a copy of this file must be made prior to restarting the region.

The CICS/6000 master terminal file

When CICS detects an error or wishes to log other information for a CICS transaction that does not necessarily affect the operation of the CICS system as a whole, a message is logged to the CICS *master terminal file.* The file is located in the CICS data directory, which is a subdirectory of the region directory. This file is called `CSMT.out` and is found in the `/var/cics_regions/<region>/data` directory.

The CSMT file is defined as a CICS/6000 extrapartition transient data output queue. Applications also may write to this queue, which will result in additional output in the file. Applications may insert debugging or diagnostics messages into this queue.

Like the console file, the master terminal file is emptied on restart of a region, and the file should be copied prior to restarting if the messages are to be kept.

CICS/6000 symptom records

If a serious internal error is detected by CICS/6000, information about the cause and location of the error is saved in an AIX file called the `symrecs` file. This file is located in the CICS Region Directory. The file is not emptied when a region is restarted and may be removed periodically to free space. The contents of this file may be viewed, but appreciation of the data is unlikely to be meaningful to anyone other than IBM service personnel.

Understanding Messages

Each CICS/6000 message produced begins with the three characters *ERZ.* These characters designate the message as being produced by CICS/6000 as opposed to other IBM products, which would have different three-character product message prefixes. Following these characters is a message number and message sequence number. The message number is the actual identification of the message. Each different message will have a different message number. The message sequence number is provided to allow IBM service personnel to determine the actual location at which a message was issued within the internals of CICS. A specific message may be produced at separate locations within the product but will have distinct message sequence numbers.

The actual text of the message will follow these numbers and should provide a brief explanation of the message. The IBM-supplied *Messages and Codes Manual* should be consulted to determine the full meaning of the message and also some suggested resolutions to any problems that the message may imply.

When a transaction abends, an ABEND code is produced for the transaction. The ABEND code explains the reason that the transaction was abnormally terminated. Again, the *Messages and Codes Manual* provides an explanation of each of the CICS ABEND codes. The manual provides indexes to locate messages and ABEND code explanations quickly.

Encina Tracing and Debugging

This section describes tracing and debugging the Encina components used by CICS/6000. Tracing the operation of the Encina SFS or PPC Gateway servers may be beneficial in determining if they are operating correctly and in obtaining diagnostics information for solving problems or performance information for benchmarks.

Encina servers make use of common tracing functionality and have similar tracing control commands. This trace module defines a number of concepts used for controlling the trace output:

Trace class   When an Encina trace record is written, it is written as part of a trace class. Trace classes define why the trace record was written. The defined trace classes include

- **audit**   Nonerror information
- **dump**   A request to dump state
- **error**   An error or warning message
- **fatal**   A nonrecoverable, fatal error
- **trace**   Entry/exit and events
- **entry**   Function entry and exit
- **event**   Major internal events
- **param**   Parameters passed to functions

Trace classes are used to specify the destination of a trace written to those classes. Each trace class may be defined to a separate output destination.

Trace component   Within an Encina server, many different submodules are used for operation. Each of these submodules is termed a *component*. Trace for different submodules can be controlled separately to allow more or less information to be collected.

Trace masks   Each Encina trace component has its own trace mask. This is a 32-bit value defining which trace entries within the component should be collected. If the trace mask is given a zero value, no trace will be collected for that component. Setting the trace mask to all binary ones specifies that maximum trace should be collected.

Trace products   The Encina servers are composed internally of Encina products. These are collections of Encina components that together perform a discrete function. The trace commands allow control of trace masks by Encina components and Encina products.

Trace destination   Each trace class may be directed to a separate trace destination. Trace destinations include an internal memory buffer termed the *ring-buffer,* directly to an AIX file, or directly to the AIX trace collection facility.

Redirecting trace

Without redirecting Encina trace for any server, the trace classes have default destinations. The following table describes the default locations:

Trace class	Default destination
audit	stderr, ring-buffer
dump	ring-buffer
error	stderr, ring-buffer
fatal	stderr, ring-buffer
trace	ring-buffer
entry	ring-buffer
event	ring-buffer
param	ring-buffer

For the Encina servers started through CICS commands, the stderr and stdout output streams are directed to AIX files. The location of these files are /var/cics_servers/SSD/cics/<machine>/msg for the SFS and /var/cics_servers/GSD/cics/<machine>/msg for the PPC Gateway. Directing trace output to stderr or stdout will result in the trace output being appended to these files. Care should be taken to ensure that sufficient AIX file space is available to hold the trace.

Encina provides a utility command called **tkadmin** that may be used to perform many administrative commands against Encina servers. The server against which the command operates may be specified either by a **-server** flag followed by the DCE CDS name of the server or by setting the AIX environment variable ENCINA_TK_SERVER to the name of an Encina server such as an SFS or a PPC Gateway.

The Encina-provided **tkadmin** command may be used to redirect trace from the default destinations to new destinations. For trace that defaults to the ring-buffer, this is especially useful because the trace information may otherwise be lost when the server ends. To redirect trace, the following command may be used:

```
tkadmin redirect trace traceclass [-file filename]
```

The **TraceClass** parameter is the name of the trace class that is to be redirected. This may be one of either **fatal, error, audit, trace, entry, event, param,** or **dump.** The **FileName** parameter is used to specify the destination of the trace class output. It may be specified as an AIX file name, in which case trace will be directed to that file. Alternatives to specifying a file include special keywords such as stderr or stdout, which cause the trace to be sent to the server's stderr or stdout output streams (and hence to AIX files for CICS started servers). A final destination type is the AIX trace facility, which allows Encina trace to be interspersed with other product's trace output including CICS/6000. If the destination is to be the AIX trace facility, specify **aix_trace** as the destination. If the **-file** parameter to the **tkadmin** command is omitted, the default trace destination for the trace class will be reset, allowing the trace to be recollected in the ring-buffer. Since the command allows only one trace class to be specified per invocation, this command usually will be executed a number of times, once per trace class.

The following shell script may be useful to allow the trace classes to be redirected to the AIX file used to log the Encina server messages:

```
#!/bin/ksh
export ENCINA_TK_SERVER = <DCE CDS Server Name>
tkadmin redirect trace fatal -file stderr
tkadmin redirect trace error -file stderr
tkadmin redirect trace audit -file stderr
tkadmin redirect trace trace -file stderr
tkadmin redirect trace entry -file stderr
tkadmin redirect trace event -file stderr
tkadmin redirect trace param -file stderr
tkadmin redirect trace dump -file stderr
```

Setting trace components and masks

By default, only a subset of the trace mask values is enabled for components. If additional trace information is required, the masks for the various components must be modified. This may be accomplished via the **tkadmin** command. Trace masks may be set either directly by component or by product (groups of components). The **tkadmin list components** command may be used to identify the names of the components within the server and show their current trace mask settings. The **tkadmin trace component** *component mask* may be used to set the component's mask to the mask value. If a group of components are to have their masks changed, they may belong to the same set or **product.** The components comprising a product may be determined by the **tkadmin list products** command. The product name is listed immediately above the components. The masks may be changed for the product with the **tkadmin trace product** *product mask* command. A product name may contain spaces. The product name should be entered within quotes to prevent misinterpretation by the command shell.

The meanings of bits within the trace mask for a component are defined for that component with the exception of the first 5 bits. These have architected definitions and are described in the following table:

Name	Mask value	Description
event	0x01 (00001)	Events in component
entry	0x02 (00010)	Function entry and exit
param	0x04 (00100)	Function parameters
internal entry	0x08 (01000)	Internal function entry and exit
internal param	0x10 (10000)	Internal function parameters

When listing trace masks, these names may be shown in place of the numeric value for the trace bits.

Encina trace from CICS

CICS internally uses the services of Encina for functions such as SFS file access, transaction management, XA protocol, and various others. Occasionally, it is useful to obtain trace output from Encina components that are used internally by CICS. These components cannot be controlled directly by either the **tkadmin** command or by CICS trace. To obtain trace from within CICS/6000, Encina trace environment variables must be used. These variables control the content and destination of the trace.

The content of Encina trace can be specified with the ENCINA_TRACE environment variable. This variable may be set with the format **component:mask** to activate trace masks for that component.

The destination of the Encina trace can be specified with the ENCINA_TRACE_VERBOSE environment variable. This variable can have the following values:

0x1	Trace output is directed to stdout
0x2	Trace output is directed to stderr
0x80000000	Trace output is directed to the AIX trace collection facility

These variables should be set in the AIX `/var/cics_regions/ <region>/environment` file. The following example illustrates trace collection for all Encina components and has the trace directed to the AIX trace collection facility:

```
ENCINA_TRACE = all:0xffffffff
ENCINA_TRACE_VERBOSE = 0x80000000
```

When the CICS region is started, Encina trace will be directed to the AIX trace facility. These trace entries are only collected when the AIX trace program has been started. The trace program may be started with the following command:

```
trace -a -o trace.out -j 294
```

The AIX trace hookid, 294, is reserved for Encina trace.

DCE Problems

The DCE products rely heavily on two main areas; they require sufficient disk space under `/var/dce,` and they require correct TCP/IP configuration on the machines on which they operate. It is recommended that `/var/dce` should be made its own file system to prevent other applications from filling `/var` and thus not allowing sufficient space for DCE. Should `/var/dce` become 100 percent full, DCE may fail to operate and may even become corrupted to such an extent that it may become unusable.

During the configuration of DCE, the TCP/IP addresses of the interfaces on the machine on which it is configured are stored in the DCE configuration files. If the TCP/IP addresses of the machine are changed, DCE will not operate. The only recovery from this is to reconfigure the DCE cell completely, which usually requires a reconfiguration of Encina and CICS as well. A TCP/IP address change should be avoided wherever possible.

When a DCE RPC server advertises itself within CDS, it advertises its location on all the available TCP/IP interfaces that it can detect. If there are multiple interfaces such as Ethernet, Token Ring, or SLIP, each of these interfaces will be advertised. When a client queries CDS to determine the location of a DCE RPC server, CDS will randomly select an advertised interface and return this to the client. If the client is unable to use that interface, perhaps because the interface is down or it is a SLIP connection not currently dialed, the client will eventually time out on an RPC request and reask CDS for another interface. This DCE RPC timeout may be as long as a couple of minutes. This results in poor, nondeterministic performance. To determine which interfaces are installed on a machine, the AIX **netstat -i** command may be used. If more interfaces are configured than are required for DCE usage, DCE can be instructed to ignore these interfaces. This is accomplished by setting the RPC_UNSUPPORTED_NETIFS environment variable to be a colon-separated list of TCP/IP interfaces. Common interfaces that may be disabled include **en0** for Ethernet, **tr0** for Token Ring, and **sl0** for SLIP. By setting this environment variable in the /etc/environment file and rebooting the machine, all DCE processes will ignore the interfaces defined in the variable. The following example illustrates an entry in /etc/environment that disables the Token Ring and SLIP interfaces from DCE's usage:

```
RPC_UNSUPPORTED_NETIFS = tr0:sl0
```

Removing profile information after a region failure

When a CICS region becomes operational after being started, it advertises its existence and availability in a DCE CDS entry. In the event of a serious region failure or unexpected power loss, it may still be flagged as available from the list of available region menus within cicsterm and cicsteld. To remove this information, manual intervention is required using DCE commands.

When a CICS region starts, it advertises its presence in a DCE entry known as a *profile*. The name of the profile is constant and is called /.:/cics/profile/cics_profile. The current entries in such a profile can be queried by executing the DCE command:

```
rpccp show profile /.:/cics/profile/cics_profile
```

The output of this command will be a list that has the following format:

```
profile elements:

<interface id>    450bc92aafc8.02.c0.36.e2.10.00.00.00,1.0
<member_name>     /.../<cell>/cics/<region>/ts
<priority>        0
<annotation>      <region description>
```

To remove an element from this list, the following command may be used:

```
rpccp remove element /.:/cics/profile/cics_profile \
 -i <interface id> \
 -m <member_name>
```

As an example, to remove the entry listed in the preceding example output:

```
rpccp remove element /.:/cics/profile/cics_profile \
 -i 450bc92aafc8.02.c0.36.e2.10.00.00.00,1.0 \
 -m /.../<cell>/cics/<region>/ts
```

Gathering AIX Information

Problems can occur with CICS due to changes in or problems with the AIX operating system itself. Possible errors include the filling of AIX file systems, running out of swap space, permission problems on CICS files, and failures with network interfaces. This section explains some of the AIX-specific tests that should be performed and how to collect AIX data for problem diagnosis.

AIX file systems

When AIX file systems fill, CICS is no longer able to write data that it may need for operation. CICS requires free space in the /var file system, specifically in the /var/cics_regions and /var/cics_servers directories. The AIX command **df** (disk free) returns the current utilization of the AIX file systems on the machine. The output should be examined for file systems that are either 100 percent full or very close, specifically those related to /var.

Paging space

As more applications are executed under AIX, more virtual storage may be used. If the size of the paging disks is too small, applications including CICS may fail due to lack of swap space. The AIX command **lsps -a** may be used to determine the sizes and usage of the AIX paging spaces. Utilization of over 80 percent across all the disks may indicate a problem. A rule of thumb for sizing paging space is to allocate twice the amount of paging space as the amount of real memory installed.

TCP/IP problems

If TCP/IP starts to fail on the machine, CICS usually will fail as well. CICS relies heavily on TCP/IP for DCE RPC communications. The AIX command **ping** may be used to determine if connectivity is still available between the CICS machine and other TCP/IP machines that are being used.

CICS Product Defects

The CICS/6000 product consists of many millions of lines of compiled C language source contained in hundreds of source files providing hundreds of internal functions. Like the development of any sizable piece of software, testing of every possible path and state of the software is impossible. Occasionally, the CICS product will contain defects that are corrected by IBM. The correction of CICS defects is supplied as replacement files for the executables and libraries that comprise CICS. The name given to an IBM-supplied replacement module is a *program temporary fix* (PTF). The CICS product employs an incremental methodology for supplying PTFs. PTFs available for CICS will include all the PTFs previously available for CICS. This means that the latest set of PTFs supersede all previous sets. PTFs must be applied to CICS while it is shut down. Application of PTFs is through the AIX SMIT panels and menus for software installation. When a PTF is applied, it may subsequently be backed off in the event that the effect of installing the PTF causes additional unwanted functions or side effects. Once the PTF has been shown to be operating correctly, it may be commited. Once a PTF has been committed, it may no longer be removed. Space also will be freed on the AIX file system that was used to save the old versions of the files replaced by the newer PTF.

The most current list of PTFs available for CICS may be determined by calling the IBM support centers or accessing the Internet World Wide Web server at `http://www.hursley.ibm.com`.

CICS for AIX V2.1

This chapter describes the newer CICS/6000 V2.1. With this release of the product, IBM renamed the software to *CICS for AIX*. The features of the release are described, including

- Support for AIX V4
- Optional usage of DCE security and Cell Directory Services
- CICS files managed by IBM DB2/6000
- Additional programming language support
- Enhanced program debugging
- CICS ISC over TCP/IP

Support for AIX V4

CICS for AIX V2.1 fully supports the AIX V4 operating system. Previous CICS releases will not operate on this version of AIX. New features provided by AIX V4 are utilized by CICS. New features of AIX V4 include support for symmetric multiprocessing and kernel level threads.

Optional Use of DCE Security and Cell Directory Services

With CICS/6000 V1.2, DCE's security service and Cell Directory Service (CDS) were required for the operation of the product. CICS's use of DCE security and Cell Directory Services was discussed in "CICS/6000 and DCE" in Chap. 1. With V2.1, these services became optional. If security service and CDS are installed and configured, CICS for AIX V2 can utilize these services in the same manner as the previous versions. If the services are not installed, no DCE security authentication or authorization is performed. The components of CICS still utilize the DCE Remote Procedure Call (RPC) technology, but the servers must be explicitly identified to each other. This is not required when using DCE CDS because the servers can be located by querying CDS. The location of a server is specified by a DCE concept known as *string binding*. A string binding contains three attributes:

- *An RPC protocol sequence*   This attribute specifies the transport technology used to carry the RPC request. DCE architects a number of different types of communication flows. This parameter may be specified as **ncacn_ip_tcp** for TCP protocol or **ncadg_ip_udp** for UDP protocol.

- *The TCP/IP machine address of the machine on which the server is executing*   This may be specified either as an IP address or domain name services name.

- *The TCP/IP port address or endpoint on which the server is listening*   This is specified as a decimal number in the range 1024 to 65535. Port numbers less than 1024 are reserved for system use. A port number chosen for a DCE server binding must not be used by other TCP/IP applications.

When a server is started without CDS, the string binding will be used by the server to control the port number and protocol on which it will make its RPC services available. Clients of the RPC service also will use the string binding to determine the location of the server.

String bindings used by servers and clients are stored in an AIX file called /var/cics_servers/server_bindings. This file contains entries mapping server names to their associated string bindings. The server names are specified as though they were being advertised in CDS. The server names begin with /.:/. Following the server name is the binding string of the form

```
<protocol sequence>:<IP address or name>[<port number>]
```

To configure a CICS environment without DCE CDS and security, the region and server definitions must be changed. For a CICS region, the **AuthenticationService** attribute in the Region Definition (RD) must be changed to **CICS** to specify that CICS is to perform all user authentication as opposed to utilizing DCE security service. Additionally, the **NameService** attribute in the Region Definition (RD) must be changed to **none.** This specifies that the SFSs and PPC Gateways will be located by string bindings in the binding file as opposed to requesting the server's location from CDS.

Any RPC servers such as SFS or a PPC Gateway that are to be used by regions that do not use DCE CDS or security also must be configured to use string bindings. When creating an SFS, an entry on the SMIT panel asking whether DCE name services are to be used must be set to **none.** An entry must be added to the CICS binding strings file referring to the binding string for the SFS. For example, if an SFS called /.:/cics/sfs/cicsaix is to use string bindings, the SFS would be created with the **NameService** attribute of the SFS Server Definition set to **none.** A string binding also must be entered into the CICS binding file. A suitable binding might be

```
/.:/cics/sfs/cicsaix ncadg_ip_udp:cicsaix[4001]
```

If any utilities such as **cicssdt** and **sfsadmin** are to be used with DCE servers that are using string bindings, the environment variable ENCINA_BINDING_FILE should be set with the name of the file containing the string bindings. This will normally be `/var/cics_servers/ server_bindings`. Defining the environment variables in the AIX `/etc/environment` file will allow all AIX processes to use these variables.

The CICS clients such as cicsterm and cicsteld also must be able to communicate with CICS for AIX regions. If no DCE directory service is being used, the clients must use an alternative mechanism for locating the CICS regions. Any CICS client that wishes to connect to a CICS region that has not used DCE CDS to advertise its location must be explicitly informed of the AIX machines on which the region might be found. The CICS clients need only know the AIX TCP/IP address or domain name system name of the AIX host running the CICS regions. The names and port numbers of the regions can be determined once the AIX machines have been identified. The CICS clients can be informed of the AIX machines on which CICS regions may be running be specifying a space-separated list of host names with the **-h** flag on cicsterm and cicsteld. For example, if three AIX machines are running regions and the machines are called *mach1, mach2,* and *mach3,* running cicsterm with the following will list all regions on all machines.

```
cicsterm -h "mach1 mach2 mach3"
```

As an alternative to specifying the machine names explicitly, the CICS environment variable CICS_HOSTS may be set to the names of the AIX machines running CICS regions. This variable will be used by cicsterm, cicsteld, and the resource update commands to locate CICS regions.

This technique also allows CICS clients in one DCE cell access CICS servers located in another remote DCE cell, provided TCP/IP connectivity exists between the two cells.

CICS Files Managed by IBM DB2/6000

In previous releases, CICS files for user data and for internal use were managed by Encina SFSs. In V2, these files may be managed optionally by IBM's DB2/6000 database.

Additional Programming Language Support

Support for IBM's PL/1 and COBOL compilers was incorporated into this release. Continued support for MicroFocus's COBOL is provided.

Enhanced Program Debugging

A serious criticism of CICS/6000 V1.2 was the lack of support for source-level debugging for C language programs. AIX-provided symbolic debuggers such as **dbx** were not supported with CICS programs. For COBOL programs, the MicroFocus COBOL ANIMATOR provided support for symbolic debugging but required a degree of setup. CICS V2 provides a new transaction called **CDCN** that allows transactions to be debugged using the AIX **xldb** debugger. **CDCN** allows the **xldb** debugger to be invoked against a newly started program written in either the C, PL/1, or IBM COBOL languages when a terminal start, program, transaction, or request from a remote SYSID arrives. When the debugger is required, it will automatically appear as a new window on an X-Server. The **CDCN** transaction requires the name of the X-Server on which the window is to appear to be specified. X-Server names may be specified as either TCP/IP addresses or domain name system (DNS) names.

Figure 30.1 illustrates the display presented when the CDCN transaction is started. The fields on the display may be modified to achieve different debugging tasks:

```
CDCN              CICS Debugging Configuration Transaction


     DISPLAY : ■1                              DEBUG  : ON


To configure for a terminal specify the TERMID       TERMID : ■2


To configure for a system specify the SYSID          SYSID  : ■3·


To configure for a transaction specify the TRANSID   TRANSID: ■4


To configure for a program specify the PROGRAM       PROGRAM: ■5



ENTER:    COMMIT SELECTION
PF1 : HELP              PF2 : DEBUG ON/OFF      PF3 : EXIT
PF4 : MESSAGES          PF5 : UNDEFINED         PF6 : UNDEFINED
PF7 : UNDEFINED         PF8 : UNDEFINED         PF9 : UNDEFINED
PF10: UNDEFINED         PF11: UNDEFINED         PF12: UNDEFINED
```

Figure 30.1 CDCN transaction.

1. The name of the X-Server on which the **xldb** debugger is to be started must be specified in this field. The server name must be specified as either the TCP/IP address or domain name service name of the X-Server with the suffix **:0** specified, which is an X-Windows identification of the physical screen attached to the X-Server.

2. The name of a CICS terminal. Any transaction started from that terminal will cause the debugger to start and debug the first program.

3. The SYSID of a remote CICS region. Incoming requests to start a program arriving from the specified SYSID will cause the debugger to start and debug the program.

4. A transaction name may be specified in this field to start the debugger against programs associated with that transaction.

5. A program name may be specified in this field to start the debugger whenever that program is started.

To utilize the enhanced debugging features, the **AllowDebugging** attribute in the Region Definition (RD) must be set to **yes**; the default value is **no.** The purpose of this attribute is to disable symbolic debugging on a region-wide basis. The ability to examine the source of a program may possibly compromise security. Debugging also consumes large amounts of CPU and may degrade performance of a production system if CDCN is accidentally started.

Programs that are to be eligible for debugging also must be compiled with the **cicstcl** command with the **-a** flag specified. This generates executables that contain debugging information and symbol tables. These executables are much larger than those built without debugging support. The AIX command **strip** may be executed against programs built for debugging to remove the symbolic information. Once the symbolic information has been removed, the program can no longer be debugged using **xldb** until it has been recompiled to include the symbol tables. The X-Window created on the X-Server is illustrated in Fig. 30.2.

Intersystem Communications over TCP/IP

CICS/6000 V1.2 provides intersystem communications (ISC) over TCP/IP between one CICS/6000 region and another. This is implemented using the Encina PPC Executive technology, which requires that both regions be members of the same DCE cell. The full set of ISC functions is available with V1.2, including function shipping, transaction routing, distributed program link, asynchronous processing, and distributed transaction processing using SyncLevel 2.

With CICS for AIX V2.1, all the ISC techniques available in V1.2 are provided, including ISC over PPC Executive (TCP/IP), ISC using local SNA, and ISC using the Encina PPC Gateway. Additionally, ISC may now be performed

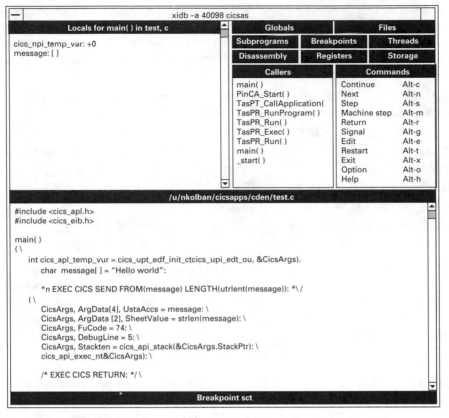

Figure 30.2   xldb debugger.

directly over TCP/IP without requiring the PPC Executive, and the connecting regions need not be members of the same DCE cells. When using direct TCP/IP for ISC, the communicating CICS regions may be either two CICS/6000 regions or a CICS/6000 region and a CICS for OS/2 region or a CICS for Windows NT region. It is expected that additional CICS products will support direct TCP/IP in the future. The direct TCP/IP ISC supports all the ISC functions with the exception of distributed transaction processing (DTP). Only SyncLevel 1 is supported with direct TCP/IP.

Configuring for direct TCP/IP ISC

The steps required to configure a CICS region for direct TCP/IP consist of

- Defining a new CICS listener in the Listener Definitions (LD) with the attribute **Protocol = TCP.** The new listener identifies which TCP/IP port on which incoming TCP/IP requests should be received.

- Defining a new Communications Definition (CD) with attribute **ConnectionType = cics_tcp.**

Multiple CICS listeners with the **Protocol** = **TCP** attribute may be defined. Each Resource Definition may specify two attributes that control the operation of the listener. The first of these is the **TCPAddress** attribute. This attribute may have a TCP/IP address or domain name system host name as its value. The attribute controls which of the local machine's network interfaces may be used for receiving incoming ISC requests for CICS processing. If all network interfaces are valid or the local machine has only one network interface, the value of the attribute may be left blank, specifying that all network interfaces available on the machine are valid. The purpose of this attribute is to restrict requests to only one interface, primarily for security purposes. If the CICS machine is connected to multiple networks via multiple network interfaces, requests from the network with the interface specified by this attribute will be serviced, while requests that may arrive from other networks via other network interfaces will be ignored.

The second attribute in the Listener Definition (LD) that is needed for ISC over TCP/IP is the **TCPService** attribute. This attribute is used to specify the TCP/IP port number on which incoming requests from other CICS regions should be directed. If the attribute is left as its default value of blank, the port used will be the CICS default port of **1435.** If an alternative port is desired, the value of this attribute should be set to a symbolic name that must be defined in the local /etc/services file. Entries in the /etc/services have the format

```
<name> <port>/tcp # <Comment>
```

The name specified in the **TCPService** attribute is used as a key in the /etc/services file to determine the port number. When the listener is started by the CICS region when the CICS region is started, it will use the port number for listening for incoming requests. Only one listener may be listening on any one port. If multiple listeners are defined or multiple regions are running on the same machine, each with a TCP/IP listener, each listener must be configured with a different port number.

When a listener is created, each listener must be defined with a resource name. In CICS/6000 V1.2, this name was not used in any other Resource Definition parameters. In CICS V2.1, the name may be referenced in Communications Definitions.

The other part of configuring a CICS region for direct TCP/IP usage is the creation of a Communications Definition (CD) defining the remote CICS region with which communication over TCP/IP is desired.

To configure a Communications Definition (CD) for direct TCP/IP, the following attributes must be specified:

ConnectionType   This attribute defines the type of underlying communication that will be used to provide ISC between the local CICS region and the remote region being defined. The value of this attribute for direct TCP/IP connection should be set to **cics_tcp.**

RemoteTCPAddress   This attribute defines the TCP/IP address or domain name system hostname of the remote machine on which the remote CICS region is executing.

RemoteTCPPort   This attribute specifies the numeric port number on which the remote CICS region is listening for incoming CICS ISC requests from the local CICS region.

ListenerName   This attribute defines the CICS listener on which incoming ISC requests from the remote CICS region will be received. The listener should be defined with the **Protocol** = **TCP** attribute. The remote CICS region should communicate with the local CICS region on the port number specified in the listener definition.

RemoteLUName   This attribute defines the remote CICS region name of the remote CICS system being defined if the remote CICS region is CICS/6000. If the remote CICS system is CICS for OS/2 or CICS for Windows NT, the name specified should be the output of executing the CICS-provided **cicstcpname** command with the TCP/IP address and port number of the remote CICS region.

Figure 30.3 shows the relationship between Resource Definitions for two CICS regions.

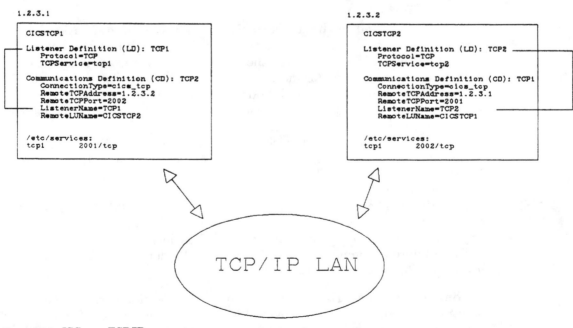

Figure 30.3   ISC over TCP/IP.

Glossary

AID Attention Identifier. 3270 terminals define a set of keys known as *attention identifiers,* which, when pressed, result in the data which changed on the display being sent back to the application.

API Application Programming Interface. A set of function calls or commands that a programmer can use to develop an application. Each call performs some specific task. Examples of APIs include the EXEC CICS commands, the ECI and EPI functions, and the DCE programming calls.

EIB (EXEC Interface Block) The EXEC Interface Block (EIB) is an area of storage that is initialized when a new transaction starts and modified by the execution of each CICS command. The storage contains fields such as the transaction name and the return code from the previous CICS command.

DCE Distributed Computing Environment. A suite of services provided to facilitate heterogeneous cooperative processing between applications. DCE includes programming interfaces to allow one program to call the services of another (RPC) and to provide security and name services.

DTP Distributed Transaction Processing. A CICS intersystem communication programming paradigm that allows two CICS applications to communicate with each other to perform work together. The DTP paradigm is similar to that of RPC. One program waits for incoming requests from the other.

Encina An OLTP toolkit product. Encina provides a series of services and functions which, when combined, provide high-availability OLTP function. CICS/6000 utilizes the services of Encina for its operation and some of its data management.

EXTFH External file handler. This is a MicroFocus COBOL interface provided to allow COBOL programs access to alternate file managers. The Encina SFS provides an EXTFH interface to allow COBOL applications executing on AIX without CICS access to SFS-maintained files.

GUI Graphic user interface. The presentation of input and output requests and data in a graphic format.

RPC Remote Procedure Call. A programming paradigm and API to allow one application to make use of the services of another. One application, called the *client,* can make a function call that is serviced by a remote application known as the *RPC server.*

SFS Structured File Server. A component of the Encina toolkit that provides record-oriented recoverable files. The SFS is a server component and expects requests from clients that wish to access the files maintained by the server.

Bibliography

The following publications contain additional CICS and CICS-related information:

- CICS/6000: *Planning and Installation Guide* (V1.2), IBM GC33-0816
- CICS/6000: *Administration Guide* (V1.2), IBM SC33-1532
- CICS/6000: *Administration Reference* (V1.2), IBM SC33-1533
- CICS/6000: *Intercommunication Guide* (V1.2), IBM SC33-0815
- CICS/6000: *Problem Determination Guide* (V1.2), IBM SC33-0818
- CICS/6000: *Messages and Codes* (V1.2), IBM SC33-0817
- CICS/6000: *Application Programming Guide* (V1.2), IBM SC33-0814
- CICS/6000: *Application Programming Reference* (V1.2), IBM SC33-0886
- *Encina for CICS* (V1.2), IBM SC33-1534
- *AIX Performance Monitoring and Tuning Guide,* IBM SC23-2365
- *IBM 3270 Information Display Programmer's Reference,* IBM GA23-0059
- *UNIX Network Programming,* W. Richard Stevens, Prentice-Hall, Englewood Cliffs, N.J.
- *CICS Clients Administration,* IBM SC33-1436
- *CICS Clients Client / Server Programming,* IBM SC33-1435

Index

About the Author

Neil Kolban has worked for IBM since 1988, and is one of the original planners and developers of the CICS/6000 product. He is currently with IBM's National Technical Support Center in Dallas, Texas, providing technical assistance to CICS/6000 customers in the United States. He holds an honors degree in computer science from the University of Glasgow, Scotland, and is a recognized AIX and DCE expert.